A Bright Light

in the

Darkness

A Modern Daoist Approach

to the

Twelve Animal Zodiac

by

Dr. Wu Baolin

and

Kevin Hil

T0376330

Three Pines Press
St Petersburg, FL
www.threepinespress.com

9 8 7 6 5 4 3 2 1

Printed in the United States of America
This edition is printed on acid-free paper that meets
the American National Standard Institute Z39. 48 Standard.
Distributed in the United States by Three Pines Press.

Cover Design by Derek Heath
Illustrations by Joshua Alvarado
Editorial assistant: Dagny Kulkarni

Library of Congress Cataloging-in-Publication Data

Names: Wu, Baolin, 1954- author. | Hill, Kevin T., 1987- author.
Title: A bright light in the darkness : a modern Daoist perspective on the
   twelve animal zodiac / by Dr. Wu Baolin and Kevin Hill.
Description: St Petersburg, FL : Three Pines Press, [2024] | Includes
   bibliographical references.
Identifiers: LCCN 2023044157 | ISBN 9781931483759
Subjects: LCSH: Astrology, Chinese. | Zodiac--Religious aspects--Taoism.
Classification: LCC BF1714.C5 W715 2024 | DDC 133.5--dc23/eng/20231127
LC record available at https://lccn.loc.gov/2023044157

Contents

Endorsements

Intriguing! I found *A Light in the Darkness* as highly provocative and entertaining as it is informative. It presents an insightful and fresh perspective on an ancient system thousands of years old. Dr. Baolin Wu's Daoist methodology is renowned for being comprehensive, concise, and always rooted in practical wisdom. In all these respects, this book does not disappoint. The authors have penned a unique guide that is filled with detailed information and yet remains understandable and easily accessible. I highly recommend this book to anyone interested in the twelve-animals zodiac or Daoist wisdom.
—Robben Ford

I was very excited to get my hands on *A Light in the Darkness*. Once I heard that Dr. Wu—senior master of taiji quan, Daoist medicine, and *qi* cultivation—was going to write about the traditional twelve-animal zodiac with Kevin T. Hill— accomplished musician and student of Eastern and Western philosophies, history, and religion—I simply couldn't wait! Anyone, even those with little knowledge of Daoism and Asian philosophies, will find the initial chapters of this book a fabulous introduction. The authors take the time to explain important basic terms, and relate Asian wisdom to familiar western concepts. The second part provides an excellent reference guide to the zodiac of the twelve animals. Each animal's function is explained, as well as their key traits, abilities, cultural and spiritual concepts, internal and external aspects, and mutual compatibility. I highly recommend it to students of the Chinese zodiac, and all those curious about the insights and knowledge that Daoism has to offer.
—Thomas Demand

Prologue

For thousands of years, our ancestors have accumulated the knowledge that they gained from interacting with the environment and by introspection. These observations have ranged from large-scale, macroscopic understandings of the stars, environment, and politics to the subtle patterns of the mind and human behavior. At first, these discoveries went unrecorded and the concepts of the greatest minds were lost quickly, never passed on to future generations. Gradually, human beings began to develop methods to record and transfer their knowledge. This led to the development of the oral traditions of many ancient cultures, which molded and shaped their unique perspectives on life. Yet even with these inventions, it remained vitally important to not only convey knowledge but to find a workable, usable, and adaptable way of utilizing these broad concepts efficiently in the world.

The tradition of storytelling can illustrate a unique situation in time and the results that it produced, but the essence of the story, the patterns and energies that lay just beneath the surface of these events, must be recognized and made familiar if the listener is to make use of the knowledge in the present moment. As more stories were gathered and more lessons were learned, various cultures developed even more advanced ways to keep track of concepts and lessons as well as various ways to compare and contrast them. They began to organize their stories into larger stories and epic tales. Writing systems and art also developed to transmit meaning and understanding to others.

All these developments allowed many of our ancestors to leverage knowledge to develop wisdom. In more modern times, the great psychologist Carl Jung described this as the process of individuation.

> We could translate individuation as "coming to selfhood" or "self-realization" . . . Once we feel more secure as individuals, more complete within ourselves, it is natural also to seek the myriad ways in which we resemble our fellow human beings. . . the essential human qualities that bind us together in the human tribe. As we individuate, we connect and identify with the entire human family.[1]

This allows us to become more cohesive and powerful as individuals and to develop purpose by recognizing that power should be used to support the larger communities and systems that we belong to. As these concepts continued

---

[1] "Individuation Process: A Step-by-Step Look at Jungian Psychology," by Scott Jeffrey (2019). www.scottjeffrey.com/individuation -process/

to develop and many new questions began to naturally arise, many people began to ask: Which part of us is natural and which part is unnatural? Which parts of our bodies and our minds are vital, necessary, and supportive of life, and which parts are accessory, fabricated, and potentially detrimental to life? Furthermore, how can we build harmony within ourselves, within our society, and within nature?

In response to these questions, our ancestors discovered that we must continue to cultivate ourselves to fully develop all of our capacities and only in this way we can discover the things in life that no one could teach us. The ancient western philosophers plainly stated their deepest philosophy as, "know thyself."

As our ancestors began to tell stories more often, it was also discovered that although the stories were invaluable, their telling context was equally important in conveying meaning. The truth remains eternal and permanent, yet each listener contextualizes the story differently every time he or she hears it. As the ancient philosopher Heraclitus said, "You never step into the same river twice." Meditating upon all of these stories, ideas and natural events eventually led to the development of the various zodiac systems that have been used all over the world for thousands of years.

As our ancestors began to understand that their unique perspectives of these stories could give them a more powerful grasp of the universe, they also began to realize that there were universal truths about our shared human nature that we were all discovering. Our ancestors intuitively grasped the existence of what we now call archetypes and what ancient philosophers called inner nature. They recognized that whenever a person felt loving, creative, or angry, he or she experienced thoughts, feelings, and behaviors common to all people. If a person from ancient Greece was passionately angry, for instance, they were said to be imbued with the spirit of Ares, the god of war. The human being would be gone or reduced to a role of observation as the spirit of the god inhabited them and directed his or her feelings and behaviors.

Ancient Chinese, Babylonians, Egyptians, Greeks, Romans, Native Americans, and many other cultures developed their own unique zodiac systems that allowed them to relate more deeply with nature. Each system had its own emphasis and preferred methods. As various cultures intermingled, their values and religious systems merged as well. The gods and stories of many different cultures combined into new gods. As new philosophies and discoveries arose, new ways of conceptualizing these ideas replaced their previous counterparts. Many ancient people understood that, even though many stories relating to specific people and events could change quite rapidly, the principles of heaven were unchanging and thus reliable. This led to the development of hierarchical systems, where the unchanging parts of the world related to changing patterns, so people could gain direction, meaning, and understanding.

Many zodiacal systems, such as western astrology, use the movements of the heavenly bodies to represent the unchanging parts of the universe, but this is only one type. The medicine wheel of many Native American tribes, for instance, is a system that is similar to the Chinese twelve-animals zodiac system. Sun Bear, a Chippewa medicine man, said:

> [The medicine wheel] seems to be similar to an astrology system, but that's really not the case. Astrology is based, mainly, on the position of the planets and the stars. The medicine wheel on the other hand, is based upon a person's relationship to the earth and to all of earth's kingdoms: the animals, plants, minerals, and humans. . . A person moves about on the medicine wheel in his own way, and knows his position on the wheel through intuition, or through his or her changing relationship with the members of the animal, the mineral, and the plant kingdoms. (1983, 181)

Similarly, the Chinese zodiac is based on the earth and the human relationship to its energies, rather than the stars or planets. By observing and learning from the various animals of the world, they enhanced personal development. John Paul Scott, the American behavioral geneticist, discovered that "if a statement is found to be true of a large proportion of all the species studied, it is correct to assume that the same statement is likely true of human beings, and that it concerns an important and basic element in human behavior" (1972, 4).

Every creature on earth developed its nature over many millennia of trial and error as it underwent evolutionary adaptations. By studying the nature of animals, we can learn the way that nature has created rather than the way we humans would create. Human beings are innovative and clever at times, but our creations are often unnatural and forced. The universe does not force things to grow in any way; it simply provides an environment where all things can grow and progress naturally. By studying animals and nature, we also develop in a natural, effortless way. Rather than forcing growth, we cultivate and maintain harmony.

> Whether we like it or not people will apply their ideas of animal behavior to human behavior. . . Animal behavior can be a yardstick for human behavior. Studying the behavior of any animal inevitably gives rise to new ideas. (Scott 1972, 2)

All of life projects itself outward onto the environment to see itself more clearly and develop wisdom. The whole universe is like a mirror, and nature speaks to us all the time. By appreciating the world around us, our sense of worth for ourselves and each other grows. This is one of the greatest tools we have to advance our consciousness and feel connected to earth as our home. It is my hope that this book will inspire the reader to grow and develop with harmony and integrity, and allow them to gain a deeper appreciation into how our ancestors learned to develop themselves as well.

Part One

Daoist Philosophy

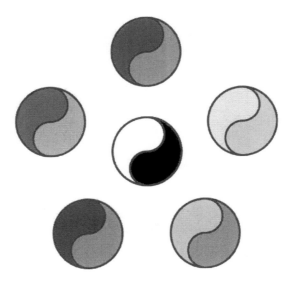

1

Daoism Today

In the modern world, religion, spirituality, and science are converging to create a holistic worldview that is all-encompassing. Daoism is modern in that it is not only a religion with a top-down perspective, but also a practical way of understanding all of nature from the bottom up. Daoism relies upon five thousand years of history and trial and error, and its philosophies form the basis of Chinese culture. It works with a complementary understanding of experience so people can create a dynamic and intelligent way of conducting themselves. Daoists often say that "there are two ways of looking at everything." Every individual part is a unique and valuable aspect of a larger whole, and every whole comprises numerous unique individual parts.

An ancient saying states that "the past is a dream and the future is a vision, only the present moment is real." We must remain focused and aware of the present moment to stay centered. If we are not centered, then orienting ourselves in the world becomes almost impossible. While it is important to go with the flow of nature and allow things to follow their own path, it is also essential to take an active role in recognizing our own unique strengths and weaknesses. In this manner, we may cultivate ourselves to become humble and strong people of integrity who take prudent action when necessary.

As the ancient Chinese got more organized, they grew from a nomadic culture into an established civilization. After social structures had developed, Laozi wrote the *Daode jing* as a guide for the increasingly complex culture. Around the same time, ca. 500 BCE, Confucius studied many aspects of philosophy, including also the *Yijing*, and went on to establish many laws, standards, and values that have been honored in China ever since. These two sages greatly contributed to the emerging culture of the east, guiding it toward progress and harmony.

In the early middle period, around the 5th century CE, Buddhism established itself in China as a reliable and virtuous practice. Daoists adopted many of its ideas and practice, just as Buddhists integrated and shared their visions and techniques. Increasingly intermingling, they further deepened and enriched the culture. People in the west tend to see Daoism as the original culture of China; however, a deeper look reveals that it is more than a national and local worldview: it is an evolving system of human knowledge. Daoists believe that the energies of heaven and humanity are ultimately one: they are divinely connected. This truth is universal, but there may be varying perspectives, interpretations, and overtones of meaning, which inevitably lead to more complex ideas. Over the centuries, Daoists have refined, cultivated, and tested their ideas, developing a solid understanding of the truth, a rich history, and an abundance of sound methods within many disciplines.

The Quanzhen School

The White Cloud Temple (Baiyun guan) in Beijing is the home of the Quanzhen school, a name that translates as All-True Authenticity, Complete Reality, or Complete Perfection. The monastery was built in the 8th century, but it blossomed greatly when it became the home of the school in 1215 after it had been founded by Wang Chongyang (1113-1170) in 1167. Wang set out to be a scholar and achieved a high rank in the written portion of the official examination. Then, as the records state, he fought consecutively for three days and nights to pass the martial-arts portion. After this, having gained fame and the respect of his peers, he politely refused the government position offered to him and instead dedicated himself to spiritual practice and used his influence to form the Quanzhen school.

Its teaching is based upon the embodiment of three ideas, whose realization and embodiment lead the disciple to a complete understanding of reality and inherent perfection. The first idea is to become "completely full of *qi* or life energy;" the second is to be "completely full of *shen* or spirit;" and the third is to be "completely full of *jing* or vital essence."

Quanzhen disciples do not marry but become monastics and dedicate themselves fully to these three. They focus their entire effort on developing a deep understanding of the *Yijing* as well as on cultivating their energy fields (*dantian*). The *Yijing* involves the study of the various phases that all energy undergoes as it progresses through the natural processes. The energy fields are developed through the practice of qigong and the taking of herbs.

In addition to this, Quanzhen students study various other subjects, such as cosmology, traditional Chinese medicine, martial arts, chemistry, mathematics, physics, astrology, and cooking. They consider anything they encounter as a worthy subject of study. The White Cloud Temple offers over two hundred courses of study plus about three hundred minor courses—this makes it a type of university.

Qiu Chuji (1148-1227) was a leading disciple of the founder and one of the Seven Perfected. He centered the school at the White Cloud Temple and served as the spiritual teacher of the Mongol leader, Genghis Khan. After hearing of his extraordinary skill and ability, the Khan sent a letter to Qiu requesting his presence at the royal court. He traveled over three years to meet the Khan near the battlefront of the Mongolian campaign and upon arrival was tested several times by the Mongol leader. Eventually he proved himself, and the Khan agreed to become a follower of Daoism under his tutelage. Soon after, he declared Quanzhen Daoism the official state-sanctioned religion of China and made the White Cloud Temple its headquarters.

While Quanzhen dominated in the north, another Daoist lineage called Zhengyi (Orthodox Unity) or Tianshi (Celestial Masters) was widespread in the south. Its followers are married householders rather than monastics; they focus on Fengshui, exorcism, purification, working with spirits, and drawing talismans. In the past, when there were droughts and the country was in desperate need of rain, Zhengyi masters would gather people together in a prayer ritual to beseech the gods for rain. Ultimately, Quanzhen and Zhengyi Daoists believe many of the same things about the universe; however, they practice different methods to cultivate themselves and exemplify those principles.

In addition to being a center for studying various academic subjects, the White Cloud Temple can also be thought of as a large zoo. Here, Daoists spend much time raising animals to cultivate natural energy and learn from the earth. When people raise animals, they grow and develop with them. Daoists have understood for a long time that animals have developed many excellent qualities through a long process of trial and error and to gain the qualities of other creatures, we must begin by observing them.

> [In Daoism] we find a diverse views of animals, but there is a recurring engagement with and reverence for their innate connection with the Dao (the Way). This includes a critique of the human tendency to distort that connection through domestication and instrumentalism. The classical and foundational Daoist worldview is more theocentric (Dao-centered) and cosmocentric and less anthropocentric. One also occasionally finds expressed a quasi-ecological and conservationist perspective. Generally speaking, Daoist views and practices tend to be more body-affirming and world-affirming than other "world religions," and this tendency includes a recognition of the cosmos, world, and all beings as manifestations of the Dao, at least in potentiality. (Komjathy 2011, 2)

Daoists worship, protect, and interact with nature reverently, and their practice benefits the whole world. Scientists now claim that we are currently in the Anthropocene age, where the behavior and actions of human beings are the single most determining factor in environmental change. Human beings have the unique capacity to resonate and harmonize with all different aspects of nature. Similarly, chaos theorists have proposed the butterfly, showing that even the smallest changes in a complex system can have profound, wide-ranging effects.

As spiritually evolving beings, it is our responsibility to listen to the world, appreciate nature, and continue to build our relationships with all of life: our actions and motivations determine the opportunities of the future. Daoism and other religions teach that, when we focus love and attention on the world around us, we all grow and benefit. When we help others, we also help ourselves.

Daoist Philosophy of Animals

All living creatures, including humans, must constantly adapt to changing conditions to live harmoniously and effectively in the environment. This is an inherently difficult task and a precarious situation that ties all living beings together. Everything in the universe is connected due to the simple fact that everything consists of energy in one state or another. In the words of the Chinese philosopher Zhuangzi: "Although the myriad things are many, their order is one" (Kemmerer 2017, 68). Managing the everyday risks of maintaining health and remaining abreast of all of the variables that can unexpectedly change can be an even more difficult situation to manage than a soldier fighting in combat.

As we attempt to manage our daily experiences, social encounters, career choices, conflicts, and relationships, we come to know ourselves more intimately. Many people today seek to express their individuality and independence to become self-dependent. While this is laudable and should be encouraged, we must also realize that, because we all share this planet and its resources, we are quite dependent on one another. The depth and manner in which you understand the value of life and peace can quickly change the way you see spiritual realities and increase your dedication toward integrity and devotion.

The *Daode jing* presents profound, simple statements that contain many-layered meanings and invite profound interpretations. It speaks of three levels of vital life energy (*qi*): heaven, human, and earth. Within the world, heavenly energy includes birds and all the creatures that fly; human energy includes people and all animals that walk the ground or live in trees; earthly energy includes the trees themselves, the plants, and anything that grows underground or that swims in the waters. Daoists use these three categories to describe how the world was created, how existence is sustained, and how all beings can return to their original nature where they feel truly at home. The twelve-animal zodiac is a system that helps us to understand the practical applications of these principles, to return to our original nature, and to benefit all of creation along the way.

To fulfill this return, we must first respect and honor the earth. As human beings, we represent and combine heaven and earth and manifest their highest achievement. Heaven is our father, and earth is our mother. As human beings, we are responsible for learning everything there is to know about heaven and earth, so that we can represent them clearly and honestly. When we do this, we can perform conscious actions with a high degree of integrity and grow as individuals. Daoists say, "If you do not know about the nature of heaven and earth, how can you call yourself human?"

Human beings and animals are part of the same category, manifesting a combination of heaven and earth. For Daoists, humans and animals have equal rights. "To return to their original connection with the Dao, humans may observe animals and other living beings for guidance" (Komjathy 2011, 2). All living creatures prefer life to death, and we must begin our spiritual journey by respecting life wherever we find it. "Nature and animals show us how to live—the preferred way to live—by revealing that which is necessary to existence, and exposing that which is superfluous" (Kemmerer 2017, 66).

The Daoist Method

For thousands of years, human beings have recognized that everything in life should be understood according to nature. All phenomena are part of a larger whole that is dynamic, responsive, and alive. Nature is the benchmark for what is real and true. Thoughts and concepts can be false or misleading, so we must always be sure to test them to see how well they describe the truth as we develop a humble, selfless, and compassionate sense of understanding.

Everything outside is also present within, and vice versa. The way a person is within himself or herself is exactly the same with others and with nature. Nature is a mirror reflecting the self. The mind extends outward toward nature, then returns as wisdom, providing us with greater understanding. Our body is nothing less than a model of the external universe as well as a tool use to interact with it. We constantly exchange energy and meaning in countless ways. The movement of this unseen energy creates our experience of the world. By developing our relationship with this wherever we find it, we develop wisdom and self-awareness.

By recognizing ourselves as similar to nature, new learning opportunities present themselves, allowing us to cultivate wisdom. An ancient example of how human beings and animals can work together is the famous story of how a hunter came to discover the healing properties of the ginseng plant.

In the early twentieth century, a man named Qu Huanzhang was in the mountains of Manchuria hunting for food. He came upon a deer in the woods, drew his bow and fired an arrow into his prey, however, he only wounded the animal and the deer quickly escaped into the forest. The hunter then began to track the deer, not knowing whether or not the animal would succumb to its wound.

After a few days, he finally found the deer again, but to his amazement the wound had already completely healed and the animal appeared to be in good health. The man was a traditional Chinese doctor by profession, and as his curiosity grew, he became determined to discover what the means by which this creature had so quickly healed itself. He devised a way to capture the deer alive and bring it to his home to learn about its knowledge of healing.

He managed to capture the animal, and after a few days of observation he decided that he would wound the deer superficially and released it into the forest to observe its behavior more closely. He followed the deer for miles paying close attention to its behavior and after a few hours the deer approached a small plant. It sniffed around the bush, ate a few leaves, and began to vigorously rub its body, especially the wounded areas, against it. After the deer had left, the hunter went to gather and study the plant that the animal was so interested in. The plant was a powerful form of ginseng, and its healing qualities have been invaluable to humanity ever since.[1]

---

[1] "Yunnan Baiyao Plaster" by ITM Editors (2020). www.itmonline.org/jintu/yunnan.htm

2

Philosophy of Life

As we mature through life, we realize that the problems we perceive within ourselves and the trials we go through are both unique to us and also part of a collective evolution we experience as living beings. Our friends, family, and neighbors all wrestle with the same key issues at one time or another. We must all learn the same lessons of existence, even though our issues may appear to have a different focus or emphasis, or show up at different times in our lives. When we understand this truth, the differences within ourselves and between each other begin to diminish. Even the animals of the world are learning many of the same lessons; because of this shared reality, we can understand and relate to one another. We always know when any living creature, human or otherwise, is hungry, lonely, afraid, or in pain, because we all know first-hand what it is like to experience these things.

> When we compare the activities of a wider variety of species, we begin to see that certain kinds of behavior occur over and over again, and that these fall into a few general kinds of behavioral adaptations which are widely found in the animal kingdom. The systems of adaptive behavior are (1) ingestive behavior, (2) shelter seeking behavior, (3) agonistic behavior, (4) sexual behavior, (5) caregiving behavior, (6) care-soliciting behavior, (7) eliminative behavior, (8) allelomimetic behavior [mutual mimickery], (9) investigative behavior. (Scott 1972, 12)

Every living being does its best to flourish and avoid dying: all of life is sacred, connected, and deserving of respect. Life is sacred because it is divine, complete, integrated, cohesive, meaningful, self-evident, and self-perpetuating. Life continues and gives freely of itself without diminishing because such is its nature. Spiritually speaking, it provides us with the opportunity to grow, develop, and discover ourselves. If we did not have the limitations of biology and physics to struggle with, we could not know ourselves and the universe at such a great depth.

> It is said that the Buddha once gave a sermon without saying a word; he merely held up a flower to his listeners. This was the famous "Flower Sermon," a sermon in the language of patterns. . . The discipline inherent in the proportions and patterns of natural phenomena, and manifest in the most ageless and harmonious works of man, are evidence of the relatedness of all things. It is

9

through the limits of discipline that we can glimpse and take part in the harmony of the cosmos— both in the physical world and in our way of life. (Doczi 1981, 1)

When we can live our lives as down-to-earth animals and at the same time internally hold on to the recognition of ourselves as divine, unique beings, just like the flower, then our behavior becomes effortless, dynamic, and ever more fulfilling. Life is vast; however, we only have control over so much, given the time we have on earth. Therefore, our motives and choices really do matter. Of all of the myriad ways we could contextualize our experience, the one we in fact choose makes a huge difference.

Ancient Teachings About Life

As human beings, we exist in a unique state. On the one hand, we are part of nature and integral to it; yet at the same time, we feel separate and apart from it. Socrates said that the "unexamined life is not worth living," and yet the paradox is that it was his own subjectivity he tried to examine objectively. The German philosopher Friedrich Schelling said that "nature is visible spirit; spirit is invisible nature. Without nature providing a background there could be no question of selfhood at all. Without nature we are unable either to come to selfhood or to knowledge of spirit."[1] Being aware of this situation is unique to humans: it is the core mechanism of conscious awareness and spiritual growth.

Confucius went to see Laozi so that he could learn about the rites and the intricacies of the *Yijing*. The *Yijing* teaches that all existence is constantly transforming: the process of transformation is most worthy of examination. Recognizing the significance of this knowledge, Confucius studied his copy of the *Yijing* until the book was in tatters. He also realized that "the present is a manifestation of the past, and the future depends on the present." Therefore, the present moment, where action takes place now, is most significant.

When Confucius passed away, he was a well-respected scholar and teacher. During his lifetime, he founded several academies that taught literature, science, philosophy, music, poetry, and other subjects. However, he also understood the great value of sage wisdom and said that Laozi should be everyone's teacher, following his instruction, "Do not force things but go with the flow: we all have different needs."

Confucianism, as well as many sections of western thought, stand in contrast to Daoism on cultural, political, and social levels. Confucius and many western thinkers tend to present a rationalistic, moralistic philosophy of social behavior, while Daoists argue for a more mystical, existential philosophy of life.

---

[1] "The Freedom of Man," by Michael Tsarion (2016). www.schellignzone.com/chapter3
.

Confucius thought that every human being was born as a pure, blank slate, and that all beings were born equal. Laozi disagreed and instead emphasized the significance of the interaction between prenatal and postnatal *qi* (yin and yang energy) within the person as the cause of individual condition and situation.

Laozi's explanation of the interaction of energies within the individual implies that we come into this world with certain energy patterns to resolve and a specific destiny to fulfill. Every decision we make and each action we take has consequences that will affect us in the future. Armed with this understanding, we can begin to cultivate ourselves in depth. Yet, even with all of this, between the time we are born and the time we die, we still have to work to survive and make a living.

Western and Eastern Thought

The ancient Greek philosophers Leucippus and Democritus stated that underneath the appearance of nature, there existed one single unit of matter constituting the basis of all things. This they called the atom, from the Greek word for "indivisible" or "that which cannot be split." Although the ancient Greeks could not prove its existence, they understood enough of the principles of nature to realize that it must exist.

from this hypothesis, all of science continued to grow and evolve throughout the centuries to prove and demonstrate the existence of this substance. Therefore, western thought focused its attention on the particle that existed as the basis of all structure. Daoism, and many other eastern philosophies, on the other hand, focused their attention on the existence of a mythical energy called *qi* that permeated all things and varied between two states, yin and yang.

The energy and frequency of these two states then determined the nature of the universe. It is said that *qi* can be defined as vibration in the same way that a wave function in western science and mathematics can be defined by its frequency. For many centuries, the scientists and philosophers have sought the energy that existed as the basis of all phenomena. Western civilization focused mainly on the particle and the individual, whereas eastern civilization focused mainly on the wave and the society. Today, we understand that the particle and the wave, subjective and objective, are the two states of the same basic energy. Physics and metaphysics do not contradict one another; some things can just be explained more simply in one system of thought than another.

> The fundamental difference between Eastern and Western views is that the West focuses on individualism, where personal ego looms in the center. In the East, especially in the Chinese Daoist tradition, the most important learning is a sense of belonging to a larger whole. It opens a wider universal vista in which the personal ego can connect and expand. While the West tries to forge ahead, the East values retreat, when necessary to create space for an extended perspective.

In the West we depend on reason and logic. Concretized, factual, and proven things become our security. We crave absolute answers, leaving little room for creative and spiritual inquiry, for "maybe" and "perhaps," and for the unknown. Whereas, it has been part of Eastern thinking to accept and celebrate the mystery that we may never understand.

But, all too often, the West gallops with giant heedless strides to break barriers, while the East stagnates in outdated traditions. As industrialized nations rely on technology, information, and accumulated knowledge, which secure an array of material conveniences, they tend to overlook the human thirst for wisdom in the deeper meaning of life.

Conversely, the East is intuitively in tune with nature and cosmic consciousness, yet feels its own kind of longing for a well-defined mechanistic model of reality, and for the excitement of free and creative expression. The ideal integration is to embrace this paradox of East and West, with open hearts and minds, to create a balanced global synthesis. (Tsu 1972, 181)

The rules of the earth are determined by the animal kingdom. In truth, this is their home, not ours. from our relationships and observations of the many species of the animal kingdom, we can deepen our relationship with the Dao, nature, and ourselves. Daoists believe that a large part of the purpose of human beings on earth is to act as diplomats and mediators between heaven and earth. To accomplish this task effectively, we must respect nature, the animal kingdom, our fellow human beings, and ourselves.

It is human beings that have decided to distinguish a delineated line between human beings and non-human animal life. We have created this separation ourselves. that does not mean that there are not differences between animals and human beings that should be examined, but that it is equally important, or perhaps more important, to understand human beings and animals as living creatures that exist on the Earth together before placing them in separate distinct categories. We must compare and contrast ourselves with the animal kingdom. We must understand what makes us unique as "rational animals," as Aristotle put it, while understanding that we cannot always make a claim that human beings are separate from animals. We must continue to develop and appreciate what we call our characteristics of "humanity" (which include compassion and higher levels of consciousness), while simultaneously refusing to classify any individual as insufficiently human or sub-human if they do not fit into our fabricated classifications of what it means to be human.[2]

Compassion and selflessness affect our karma by harmonizing our *qi* field with nature and drawing us like a magnet toward the higher, more rarefied realms

---

[2] "On the Separation of Human and Animal," by Matthew Calarco (2015). Stanford-press.typepad.com/blog/2015/09/on-the-separation-of-human-and-animal.html

of existence. The *Great Precepts* states clearly that human beings should strive to protect and harmonize themselves with the animal kingdom.

> Save all that wriggles and runs, all the multitude of living beings. Allow them all to reach fulfillment and prevent them from suffering an early death. May they all have lives in prosperity and plenty. May they never step into the multiple adversities. Always practice compassion in your heart, commiserating with all. Liberate living beings from captivity and rescue them from danger. (Kohn 2004, 175)

The Virtue of Endurance

Every virtuous action that we perform helps us in our journey. When we do things that make us feel good in a wholesome way, we reduce our stress and adjust our *qi* in a way that allows us to become healthier and achieve greater longevity. Good things lead to a greater and longer life, as long as we do not have any karmic obligations that prevent us from attaining it. This implies that endurance itself is a virtue worthy of attainment and that, to achieve longevity, we must mold ourselves into kind and virtuous people. Reaching an advanced age is a sign that we have lived in accordance with nature and learned to respect and value the world around us. The *Yijing* states that by helping others and especially saving the lives of others, we can lengthen our lives significantly.

For all of life, movement is better than stagnation. Our circulatory system is healthy when it flows freely, the lands grow green when waterways flow freely, and animals thrive when they can freely roam the earth. To maintain our health, our *qi* meridians should flow unimpeded, and they should be filled with healthy, righteous *qi*. Even the most basic life-forms, such as bacteria and protoplasm of living cells respond to healthy nutrients by moving closer to them and to poisonous materials by retracting away from them. We must take responsibility for ourselves by making the correct choices for our health and well-being. It is vitally important in life to respond appropriately to opportunities, as well as danger. John Paul Scott said, "The law of adaptation is a basic biological principle which may be stated simply thus: An organism tends to react in ways which are favorable to its existence" (1972, 8).

Qi is the life force of a living being, and it is the energy that is responsible for responding to the various conditions and qualities of our existence. An individual can cultivate their *qi* in many ways. By practicing *qigong*, eating healthy foods, and developing our abilities in various ways, we can change our luck in life. Having a wide variety of developed skills allows us to create and take advantage of opportunities to help others and when we do so, the effort returns to us as benefits, blessings, and good luck.

"[With enough skill and wisdom] an individual may be capable of transforming stimuli into something quite different from those originally received, and so in effect create new stimuli. This in turn makes possible novel solutions to problems of adaptation" (Scott 1972, 9).

There are many people and opportunities that can assist us in life, but in the end, we are responsible for ourselves. We can have great teachers, but it is up to us to learn the material and to put it into practice. When we take responsibility for our own lives, we begin to advance our self-awareness and receive the great gifts that the universe has to offer.

3

The Life Energy of *Qi*

Qi is the energy of life, which permeates all things in nature and can be found throughout the universe in various states and quantities. It is the primordial power of the universe; the energy that forms and nourishes all life and matter. In the Hindu tradition, the equivalent of *qi* is called *prana*, and this energy is the basis for the *chakra* system. The word *qi* can be translated as "breath" or "air," because it is necessary for life and shared by all of the living beings. The ancient character for *qi* shows steam air that rises from freshly cooked rice: air that is warm, circulating, and rich in nutrients.

Since *qi* represents the energy that circulates throughout the universe, it is the force that allows us to relate to the external world. *Qi* connects us to all, allowing us to relate to our body, to other people, to emotions, to concepts, and to the physical world. The interaction and exchange of *qi* between ourselves and the external world is the fundamental process of life. When a person dies, the *qi* leaves their body and they become inanimate. *Qi* exists throughout the universe; however, our bodies have designated areas within it where *qi* resides, moves, and is processed and refined.

According to the Daoist tradition, *qi* is stored within our three elixir fields (*dantian*), upper, middle, and lower. These energy fields are large reservoirs that store *qi* for later use. from them, *qi* flows throughout the rest of the body via the meridian system before returning inward toward the body's core. As *qi* is carried outward toward the edge of the body, it also forms the *qi* field (sometimes called an aura), which interacts with, and senses, the external environment. Healthy *qi* nourishes the body and aids the function of the mind similar to the rejuvenating quality of a restful sleep, and therefore gathering and developing *qi* within the body can assist every aspect of a person's life.

Everyone on earth prefers opportunity and benefits to bad luck and misfortune, and yet some people are born with good luck and opportunities while others have to strive for them. However, no matter where you find yourself in life, if you practice developing your *qi*, you can begin to change your circumstances and cultivate harmony, compassion, and happiness. We must first be strong and alert before we can help others, and when we help others, we change our destiny for the better. *Qi* can change what you are attracted to and what is attracted to you. Therefore, cultivating healthy, righteous *qi* is how we harmonize with nature and refine our lives. All forms of practice and excellence, whether it is athletic, academic, or spiritual, is a way of refining and developing our *qi* energy.

A simple way of effectively changing your *qi* field for the better is to think about your favorite person every morning when you wake up. Similar to starting your car before going to work in the morning, imagining your favorite person initiates and increases the function of the immune system. The process of imagination involves the use of the pituitary gland, which is also responsible for managing the functions of the body's glandular system. Imagining your favorite person is a method that utilizes this relationship by internally initiating the immune system. This technique motivates you internally without the use of any substances, and it provides a way of calming the emotions when things become difficult. By knowing who your favorite person of the day is, you remind yourself where you are going and why you want to get there. One of the most important factors in the success of any endeavor is to have a reason why you are striving.

Studying Matter vs Studying Qi

Modern science cannot yet explain the existence of *qi*; therefore, it is difficult to describe in definable ways. One of the main differences between western and eastern thought is the emphasis that each one puts on either atomistic or holistic ways of thinking. In the west, we are used to analyzing and conceptualizing subjects in an atomistic manner by breaking a subject into discrete individual components and studying each of these separate components in a detailed way. Once we have studied each part in detail, we add them together to visualize the whole system that they form. Academic science focuses on this method by trying to understand a subject as objectively as possible, as if it were isolated and contained in a vacuum so that subjective perceptions do not cloud the objective data.

In the east, on the other hand, the emphasis is more often placed on a holistic, clinical type of conceptualization. This is where the subject is understood to be an indivisible whole that is more than the sum of its parts. While it can still be studied in pieces, each piece must always be considered in the context of the whole system of which it is a part. Clinical science focuses are more closely related to this method because it develops its theories through the process of trial and error. Clinical researchers, however, may discover an effective method without understanding how it works in an explainable and definable manner. Neither framework is superior to the other, but one may be more effective and illuminating than another depending upon the content and context of the situation.

Often, an answer that is quite difficult to determine in one modality is much more simply explained in the other. It is important to remember that while modern science and Daoist thought often reach the same conclusion, there are still many ideas that are portrayed by the zodiac and the *Yijing* that science does not agree with. However, the eastern and western methodologies are complementary to one another and when they are both used harmoniously, progress toward deeper understanding can be made rapidly in nearly any subject.

Science and Daoism both conduct research to discover the truth of the universe. However, each of these modalities began with different axioms and proceeded with different methods. It can be argued that modern science began when Socrates stated that the universe was made from a single unit of energy called the atom. As science progressed, its goal was to discover the nature of this particle unit of energy and, after centuries of research, the atom was discovered. However, upon its discovery, quantum mechanics immediately became necessary to describe the fact that this single unit of energy seemed to exist as a both a particle and/or a wave.

Daoism, on the other hand, began with the axiom that a universal, wavelike energy permeated the entire universe. This energy was called *qi*. It was discovered that human beings could harmonize with and tap into this energy in various ways, and over time, Daoists sought the methods that could be used to condense this energy into a usable form. This was known in Daoism as the relationship between heaven and earth.

Even though the ancestors of the east and the west took different approaches to understanding the truth, both of these traditions genuinely sought an accurate method of comprehending and relating to the universe. These two modalities share a desire to understand the process of how energy, in its various forms, relates to itself. How does content relate to context? How do facts relate to motive? How does objective reality relate to subjective reality? And how do all living creatures relate to nature and the external world?

The phrase "as above, so below" has been used for centuries in the esoteric traditions of the west. In Daoism, this is described using the analogy of the microcosm and the macrocosm, which is another way of describing the relationship between heaven and earth, as well as the relationship between the human body and the universe. Daoists believe that the human being is a miniature universe with all of the processes, laws, and materials that exist in the larger external universe. Because of this relationship, anything that is discovered to exist in the human body can be applied to the external universe and vise-versa.

While it is difficult in many ways to travel to the distant stars and planets, we do not need to go anywhere to know ourselves more deeply. Every living creature can only respond to the external world in so many ways, due to the limitations of the body in which it was born, yet each of these creatures must also face the same external conditions. One of the purposes of the twelve-animal zodiac is to understand ourselves more deeply by observing how we are related to the world and how we can adapt to it. How can we continue to learn from nature? How did our ancestors learn without being directly taught? By understanding the patterns of ways in which our inner experience relates to our external one, we can come to a greater understanding of all things.

Yin and Yang

Yin and yang are the two states of *qi* energy, similar to the way in which electrons can exist as either a particle or a wave, or the way in which binary code is described as a series of ones and zeros. Traditionally, yang energy has been described as the sunny side of a mountain, while yin energy has been described as the shady side. However, the energies of yin and yang have many subtleties and implications. Yin energy is cold, inactive/passive, feminine, dark, earthly, receptive, and exists as a tangible form or substance. On the other hand, yang energy is warm or hot, active/kinetic, masculine, illuminated, heavenly, penetrating, and exists as energy without a solid shape or form, like wind or fire.

Yin energy is the result of natural processes, but yang energy must be actively ignited into being. The taiji diagram depicts these two energies and their relationship to each other. Each phase follows the other just as rest follows activity, fall and winter follow spring and summer, and maturity follows youth. Also depicted in the diagram is a single, smaller circle within each phase of energy. This shows us that yin is always contained within yang, and yang is always contained within yin; they are interdependent energies. A cigarette lighter, for instance, contains the lighter fluid, which is inactive, has a shape or form, and has the potential for combustion. This is an example of yin *qi*. The lighter also produces a flame, which is active, exists only as dynamic energy, and is the result of the combustion process. This is a form of yang *qi*. Yin and yang contain one another, follow one another, depend upon one another, and transform one another.

While it can be said that yin and yang both create one another, the yin energy is the feminine, "mother" energy, which gives birth to all things. Yin gives birth to yang, not the other way around. Every person must have both yin and yang energy (egg and sperm) to be conceived. However, the male yang energy is only present for a moment, whereas the female yin energy is required for a much longer period of time. A person may have many strong male role models in their life, but we only have one mother.

Yin and yang can be found throughout nature and, together, these two energies always form a dynamic process as they relate to one another. Strong yang energy leads to health and longevity, and strong yin energy leads to luck, destiny, and fortune. Both forms of energy work harmoniously together and are equally necessary in order for an individual to grow and develop throughout life. Through conflict, negotiation, and action, yin and yang harmonize and bring out the best in each other. Yang energy is used to create, protect, and direct processes, yet it can only fulfill its function when it is supported by yin energy. The dynamic interplay between yin and yang is the process by which the heavens gave birth to the earth. Similarly, by balancing rest and action, we have the power to shape our own destiny.

It is often difficult to differentiate between whether something should be considered yin or yang. Most things can be considered both yin and yang depending on the context in which they are being considered. For instance, water would be considered yin if it is being compared to steam because it has more form and substance. However, water could also be considered yang when being compared to ice because it is more dynamic and active.

It is always crucially important to consider the context in which energy or processes are being considered. A rose bud that is still closed is considered to be of yang energy because is tight and holds potential energy, ready to express itself at any moment. Once the flower opens, however, then it is considered to be of yin energy because it is relaxed, open, and receptive. Similarly, a young person is considered yang because his or her energy is still held within as potentiality. As they grow older and express their energy, developing into the person that they were meant to be, they transform into a yin phase of life. If you can understand this relationship, it is quite easy to understand and identify the energies of yin and yang.

Jung said that "man is both a unique individual not able to be compared with anything else and at the same time, as a member of a species, he can and must be described as a statistical unit; otherwise, nothing general could be said about him" (2006, 8). There is an interdependent relationship between human beings and nature. Our survival depends on us recognizing that we are both unique individuals and an integral part of various systems. While animals rely on human beings to be compassionate, understanding, and dedicated to caring for the environment, it is also true that the animal kingdom, as a form of yin energy, gave birth to human beings and therefore human beings rely greatly on animals as well. The animals of the world would survive easily without humans, but human beings could not survive without the presence of the animal kingdom.

The layout of the bagua diagram implies that everything in life should avoid leaning to remain balanced and follow the middle way. We must all take responsibility for our own actions and obligations. When it comes to human actions and behavior, we should avoid both excess and deficiency. We should perform actions in a way that is not too fast (yang) and not too slow (yin) and by doing this, we can maintain balance and take care of our responsibilities.

Along with the animal kingdom, human beings are also deeply connected to the plant life of our planet, especially trees. According to Daoists, trees and human beings are equally important in the eyes of the universe. They relate to each other in an equal, one-to-one ratio, inhaling and exhaling oxygen and carbon dioxide in a harmonious, symbiotic relationship. Therefore, human beings govern trees and trees govern human beings.

There should always be an equal and harmonious balance between the number of trees on the earth and the number of human beings. If this relationship is out of balance, then nature responds with various natural disasters to correct the imbalance; the greater the imbalance, the greater the disaster. Just as trees must remain flexible, adaptable, and supple to deal with extreme circumstances, so too must human beings be willing to adapt themselves to the growth and changes of the earth. When human beings avoid damaging nature and interfering with natural processes, then disasters will be mitigated and we will thrive and flourish as a species.

All living creatures must work with the fact that their physical bodies are limited. It is important to study our own limitations and use the information that we gather to cultivate and improve ourselves. When a pattern has been discovered or developed within the human body, we can then gather the rules and patterns that make this possible and organize them to discover new philosophical concepts.

The classical Confucian work *Zhongyong* (The Doctrine of the Mean), and the "golden mean" of the ancient Greeks are similar philosophies that depict the importance of the middle path. The golden mean and its various applications, such as the golden spiral and the golden rectangle, are shapes that can be found throughout nature in various naturally developing phenomena. It is a way of dividing a quantity into sections that relate to themselves proportionally, so that nothing is in excess. Aristotle's golden mean applies this same rationale to the study of morality in his work on ethics. For instance, courage, which is considered a virtue, is the "golden" middle range between cowardice, which is a vice of deficiency, and recklessness, which is a vice of excess.

The *Doctrine of the Mean* was also an elaboration of an ethical system that seeks to achieve morality by emphasizing self-awareness, self-honesty, reciprocity, and a proper understanding of relationships and virtue. This text has been a foundational work that established many of the principles of Confucianism as a guiding philosophy and religion. By understanding our behavior in this way, we can clearly see that deciding on the best course of action in any circumstance is a matter of finding the middle range between two extremes (yin and yang). In Buddhism, it is said that the middle path is achieved when the concept of moderation is applied to the subjects of the Noble Eightfold Path. These are all examples of self-correcting processes by which any individual can achieve natural harmony within themselves and within the external world.

Messages from Heaven

The theory of yin and yang is also part of the foundation for the calculations of the *Yijing*. The *Yijing* is an ancient text that describes the various ways in which all things in the universe change over time. The *Yijing* is hard to explain because it is such a vast subject and, given the average human lifespan, we only have a relatively short amount of time in which to learn it. It can take more than a century's worth of study to comprehend it entirely.

The core essence of the *Yijing* is the development of the ability to tell one's fortune and the outcome of events. Just about any phenomenon in the universe can be calculated with the knowledge of the *Yijing*. There are many things in life that are destined and inevitable, but there are also many variables that can change. Therefore, a person's destiny can change as well. Comprehending this complex process is the goal of *Yijing* studies. Everyone's life has many aspects, and each one can be used to determine a great deal about the individual.

The twelve-animal zodiac portrays the nature of the universe in a similar way to the *Yijing* text, in that both systems understand the universe as a manifestation of *qi* energy. It is beneficial to help others and to perform virtuous acts and at the same time. To do this, it is also important that we have enough energy to perform these acts well. To accomplish a task, we must apply the right energy at the right time. One person who starts a business may succeed greatly, whereas others would fail simply because they lack the proper type of energy to make the business succeed.

The five centers diagram depicts and organizes the natural expressions of the world that are visible and tangible. However, there is another invisible side of nature that, while no less valid, is seemingly abstract. Daoists believe that every person is directly linked to a star in the sky, and that this star is a literal part of the person, forming the core of the person's being. In western terms this star can be thought of as the person's higher self.

As soon as we are born, we possess the three treasures of humanity and immediately begin the practice of cultivating these three energies. The three treasures of humanity are *jing* (essence), *qi* (energy), and *shen* (spirit), and they are housed, in their pure form, in the three elixir fields of the body's *qi* system. We must become intimately familiar with these energies if we are going to create a strong foundation for our life. If we do not master the use of these energies, then they are unbalanced and we will be subject to the effects of their fluctuations.

When you are born, half of your spirit comes down from heaven to live on the earth and the other half remains in heaven, linked directly to you with a cord of energy. When we look at the night sky, the lights that twinkle and dance are stars and the lights the shine steadily are planets. The twinkle of a star means that that star is currently connected to a person that is living on the earth and communicating with them. When that person dies, then the star no longer twinkles. These are the types of concepts that the knowledge and methods of Daoism are based upon.

Each and every person lives their life according to the plan that is set out by their destiny, and their destiny has been predetermined by their past actions. The story of our destiny is written in the movements and appearance of the external universe. We are all born into different circumstances. This is not a bad thing; this simply demonstrates that our universe is dynamic and that it provides all of us with the most ideal opportunity to learn and grow in the way that we require. All human babies are born crying, which illustrates the fact that we are all here on earth to struggle with ourselves and our environment to cultivate higher and higher degrees of experience. We originally came here from the stars and when we die, we return to the stars. To be born a human being is a unique and special experience, even though it may be quite difficult at times. Though we are all trying to learn the same lessons, namely, how to manage and use the energy that we are given, everyone is learning these lessons in different orders, at different times, and in different ways.

4

Zodiac and Calendar

To understand the changes of energy within our bodies and lives that the twelve-animal zodiac system describes, we must first learn how energy changes within the external environment of the earth. As external conditions change over time, all biological life must also adapt to these changes. Therefore, the cycles of the seasons and environmental conditions determine a lot about the behaviors which will be most effective. There are multiple ways that have been developed to keep track of time and the seasons, and each of these methods has its own advantages and disadvantages. The ultimate goal of nearly every calendar system, however, is to accurately keep track of all of the changing conditions on the earth in the simplest way possible.

The Lunar and Solar Systems

A lunar calendar is a type of calendar that measures the days and months of the year by counting the number of complete lunar cycles from new moon to new moon. It takes approximately 29.53 days for the moon to complete one cycle; therefore, most lunar months are approximately 30 days in length. However, due to the fact that the seasons of the year are related to the position of the sun relative to earth (not the moon) and that the solar cycle is not evenly divisible by the lunar cycle (there are approximately 12.37 lunar cycles in a single solar year), the seasons quickly begin to drift from year to year in a purely lunar dating system. This makes it difficult to predict the occurrence of the seasonal changes with a purely lunar calendar system. The lunar calendar is important, however, because it accurately describes the growth cycles of human beings, animals, and plants. For instance, the farmers need to understand the lunar cycles to know the best time to plant and harvest their crops.

In contrast, the solar calendar is a type of dating system that measures the months and the years by synchronizing them to the position of the earth as it revolves around the sun. The earth takes approximately 365.25 days to complete one full revolution around the sun, and each of the 12 months of the solar calendar has approximately 30 days. In the Gregorian Calendar that is currently used in many western countries, a 'regular' year (as opposed to a leap year) has 4 months with 30 days, 7 months with 31 days, and 1 month with 28 days. Since the seasons of the year are also caused by the position of the earth relative to the sun, the seasons do not drift in a solar calendar, and therefore, it is much easier to predict the occurrence of the seasonal changes with this type of dating system.

The Chinese calendar system is a lunar calendar that measures the months by the cycles of the moon. However, there is also a process that is used to adjust the calendar so that the seasons do not drift from year to year. There are 12.37 complete moon cycles in single solar year (365.25 ÷ 29.53). This is a single lunar year and also the length of time between one Chinese New Year and the next. The solar year is measured by the number of days between one Vernal equinox and the next, which is 365.25 days.

In the Chinese calendar, the first day of each lunar month always occurs at midnight on the day when the new moon occurs (this is relative to the time zone of a particular location). A single lunar month is equal to the length of time between one new moon and the next, with the full moon always occurring at the midpoint of the month.

The solar months of the Chinese calendar are calculated differently than the months of the western, Gregorian calendar. In the Chinese calendar, the solar year is divided into twenty-four solar terms and twelve principal terms, both of which are used to indicate the position of the sun relative to the earth. The solar year of 365.25 days is divided into twenty-four equal parts to create the twenty-four solar terms, and the longitude of the sun across the ecliptic is divided into twelve equal parts to determine the twelve principal terms.

A single principal term is equal to thirty degrees of the ecliptic and a solar term is equal to 15.22 days, which is roughly the amount of time that it takes for the sun to travel through fifteen degrees of the ecliptic. This means that each principal term contains two solar terms. The principal terms are numbered, and the solar terms are named. The names of the solar terms describe the changes that are happening within the natural environment at that time (i.e., "awakening of the insects" and "start of summer").

Special Times

Leap years in the Gregorian solar calendar and intercalary months in the Chinese lunar calendar are used to rectify and synchronize the calendar system with the movements of the sun. In a solar calendar there are 365 days, but the earth makes a full revolution around the sun in exactly 365.25 days. Therefore, every four years, an extra day's worth of time is accrued that must be accounted for (.25 days x 4 = 1 day). Then the solar calendar must add one extra day in order for it to remain accurate. In the Gregorian calendar, an extra day is added to the end of the month of February every leap year.

Solar Term #	Solar Term Name	Principle Term #	Sun's Ecliptic Longitude	Length in Days	Gregorian Calendar Date	Season # of Solar Terms # of Principle Terms # of Days
1	Beginning of Spring	1	330°	15	Feb 4	Spring
2	Rain Water			15	Feb 19	
3	Awakening of Insects	2	0°	15	March 6	Solar Terms 1-6
4	Vernal Equinox			15	March 21	Principle Terms 1-3
5	Clear and Bright	3	30°	15	April 5	91 days total
6	Grain Rains			16	April 20	
7	Start of Summer	4	60°	15	May 6	Summer
8	Grains Fill			16	May 21	
9	Grain in Ear	5	90°	15	June 6	Solar Terms 7-12
10	Summer Solstice			16	June 21	Principle Terms 4-6
11	Minor Heat	6	120°	16	July 7	94 days total
12	Major Heat			16	July 23	
13	Start of Autumn	7	150°	15	Aug 8	Autumn
14	Limit of Heat			16	Aug 23	
15	White Dew	8	180°	15	Sept 8	Solar Terms 13-18
16	Autumnal Equinox			15	Sept 23	Principle Terms 7-9
17	Cold Dew	9	210°	15	Oct 8	91 days total
18	Frost Descends			15	Oct 23	
19	Start of Winter	10	240°	15	Nov 7	Winter
20	Light Snow			15	Nov 22	
21	Heavy Snow	11	270°	15	Dec 7	Solar Terms 19-24
22	Winter Solstice			15	Dec 22	Principle Terms 10-12
23	Minor Cold	12	300°	14	Jan 6	89 days total
24	Major Cold			15	Jan 20	

The Chinese lunar calendar, however, measures the months of the year according to the moon's cycles and it must adjust itself according to the movements of the solar cycle. This makes the rectification of this type of calendar system slightly more complex. Since there are approximately 29.53 days in a lunar cycle, a lunar month in the Chinese calendar can contain either 29 or 30 days, and therefore, a lunar year has either 353, 354, or 355 days (29.53 x 12). In a solar year of 365 days, a month has a duration of approximately 30.4 days (365 ÷ 12).

With every month that passes, a lunar calendar accrues approximately one day that must be accounted for in order for it to remain synchronized to the solar cycle (30.4 solar days— 29.53 lunar days = 0.87 days). This means that in the

Chinese lunar calendar, every two years there are approximately twenty-four extra days. To rectify this, an extra so-called intercalary month is added every two or three years. Therefore, a 'regular' year in Chinese lunar calendar has twelve months, and a leap year has thirteen.[1]

Holidays

There are quite a few Chinese holidays that are celebrated during the year. Daoists respect these holidays as special times when the *qi* of the world is changing and developing. The most significant and widely known of these holidays is the Chinese New Year, also known as the spring festival, when the events of the past year are shed and the whole world takes on a new, fresh energy. The animal that represents each year is a symbolic description of the nature of the energy that arrives during the new year holiday. The new year always occurs on the second new moon after the winter solstice. This is either in late January or the first half of February, according to the western Gregorian calendar.

Another significant holiday that is celebrated during the Chinese calendar year is the mid-autumn festival, or moon festival, which occurs on the 15th day of autumn according to the lunar calendar. This is the time when the significance of the moon is celebrated. The moon is responsible for many things on the earth. Its gravity keeps the rhythm of the tides, controls the movement of water, and protects the planet from many meteors and asteroids. Daoists consider the moon to be the mother of human beings, plants, and animals. All the creatures of the earth are children of the moon because the moon is responsible for all of the things that grow on the earth.

The moon festival (or Mid-Autumn Festival) is the time of year when the moon is the closest to the earth. At this time, the energetic connection between the moon and all of her children is the shortest, and the magnetic field of the moon is at its strongest. This causes clouds to form in the sky, joint pain and bone pain to occur in many people and animals, and the ocean life to rise closer toward the surface of the water, allowing all of life to heal and self-correct. The water on the planet, whether it is within an ocean or within the human body, ebbs and flows with the tides that are caused by our proximity to the moon. The moon has a strong effect on the earth because close to 70% of the human body and the surface of the earth is composed of water.

Many people get ill or experience difficulties during the time that precedes the moon's birthday. This is due to the fact that, as the moon gets closer to the earth, its energy begins to pull the issues and diseases to the surface to be healed. This is similar to the way in which many elderly people can sense when it is about to rain, by feeling it in their bones. During the moon festival, we should do our

---

[1] "Chinese Calendar - Chinese Zodiac," Gehrmann, Valeska (n.d.). www.nationsonline.org/oneworld/ChineseCustoms/chinese_calendar.html

best to utilize this magnified lunar energy to heal and cleanse the body of negative emotions, reduce stress, create opportunities, increase our memory, develop intelligence, rekindle love, and make up for our past mistakes.

The Stem and Branch System

The stem-and-branch system is an ancient dating method by which the years are counted within a repeating sixty-year cycle. This system is the first, original method of counting the years in the Chinese system and the classic arrangement of the zodiac. Each year within this cycle is assigned a name rather than a number, which corresponds to one of the ten heavenly stems and one of the twelve earthly branches. Each of the ten heavenly stems represents one of the five phases that is illustrated by an element (metal, water, wood, fire, and earth) in either its yin or yang aspect. The twelve earthly branches represent the twelve animals of the zodiac system. Every time either a heavenly stem or an earthly branch cycle is completed, it starts again from the beginning. Since the two cycles (one of ten and one of twelve) share a common factor of two, only half of the possible combinations actually occur, and therefore, a complete cycle of the stem and branch system has a sixty-year duration. Within this time period the twelve-year animal cycle repeats five times.

The *jia zi* year is the first year of the sixty-year cycle: it acts like a seed. As one sixty-year cycle ends, its events become the seed of the following cycle. This illustrates the truth of the saying attributed to author Mark Twain that "history doesn't always repeat itself, but it often rhymes."[2] Seeds, therefore, encompass the ideas of both the ten pillars of heaven, as well as the twelve earthly branches system. Seeds are essential to the health of the planet and the entire ecosystem. Once a seed is planted in the ground, it slowly turns underneath the soil before it breaks through the surface of the soil and begins to grow toward the sky. This turning motion is similar to the formation of rings in the trunk of a tree, or the turning of a baby within the womb. This is the circular, turning motion of taiji; the natural progression through yin and yang.

---

2 "History Doesn't Repeat Itself, but It Often Rhymes," Patterson, Richard North (2018). www.owu.edu/alumni-and-friends/owu-magazine/fall-2018/history-doesnt-repeat-itself-but-it-often-rhymes/

Heavenly Stems									
Jia	Yi	Bing	Ding	Wu	Ji	Geng	Xin	Ren	Gui
Yang Wood	Yin Wood	Yang Fire	Yin Fire	Yang Earth	Yin Earth	Yang Metal	Yin Metal	Yang Water	Yin Water

Earthly Branches											
Zi	Chou	Yin	Mao	Chen	Si	Wu	Wei	Shen	You	Xu	Hai
Rat	Ox	Tiger	Rabbit	Dragon	Snake	Horse	Sheep	Monkey	Rooster	Dog	Pig

60 Year Cycle							
Year #	Year Name	Year #	Year Name	Year #	Year Name	Year #	Year Name
1	Jia Zi	16	Ji Mao	31	Jia Wu	46	Ji You
2	Yi Chou	17	Geng Chen	32	Yi Wei	47	Geng Xu
3	Bing Yin	18	Xin Si	33	Bing Shen	48	Xin Hai
4	Ding Mao	19	Ren Wu	34	Ding You	49	Ren Zi
5	Wu Chen	20	Gui Wei	35	Wu Xu	50	Gui Chou
6	Ji Si	21	Jia Shen	36	Ji Hai	51	Jia Yin
7	Geng Wu	22	Yi You	37	Geng Zi	52	Yi Mao
8	Xin Wei	23	Bing Xu	38	Xin Chou	53	Bing Chen
9	Ren Shen	24	Ding Hai	39	Ren Yin	54	Ding Si
10	Gui You	25	Wu Zi	40	Gui Mao	55	Wu Wu
11	Jia Xu	26	Ji Chou	41	Jia Chen	56	Ji Wei
12	Yi Hai	27	Geng Yin	42	Yi Si	57	Geng Shen
13	Bing Zi	28	Xin Mao	43	Bing Wu	58	Xin You
14	Ding Chou	29	Ren Chen	44	Ding Wei	59	Ren Xu
15	Wu Yin	30	Gui Si	45	Wu Shen	60	Gui Hai

5

Years, Hours, and Phases

The seasons of the year are the energetic phases of the earth. It is vitally important to remember these phases and take advantage of the earth's changing conditions as they arise. In modern city life, the cycles of the seasons are often forgotten or neglected. In more rural areas, however, living by the cycles of the seasons is vitally important and could easily spell the difference between success and failure, or even life and death. Even though modern life may seem more removed from these environmental changes, the effects of the seasons can penetrate into our modern, urban daily lives more than we may imagine.

Daoists regard the cycle of the seasons as phases that occur as yin becomes yang and returns to yin again. Since the summer is yang and the winter is yin, and the day is yang and the night is yin, the four seasons can represent both the divisions of the yearly cycle and the daily cycle. The seasons of the year are traditionally determined by the solstices or equinoxes and the seasons of the day are determined by the rising and setting of the sun in a twenty-four-hour period. The four seasons of the day are: spring 3 am to 9 am, summer 9 am to 3 pm, autumn 3 pm to 9 pm, and winter 9 pm to 3 am.

Most of the time we divide the year into four seasons: spring, summer, fall/autumn, and winter. However, the year can also be divided into five seasons by adding the "late summer" season between the summer and autumn seasons. The late summer season is considered to be different from the normal summer season because, in late summer months, the air is usually damper and more humid, and the levels of heat reach their peak. This is an important distinction to make because many people and animals react differently to the damp, hot conditions that are present during the late summer.

Spring is when life-energy awakens from its dormant state and revitalizes itself. Throughout the world, trees blossom in the spring. It is perfect for planting crops, starting new projects, and taking advantage of opportunities. In the Daoist tradition, the spring season is represented by the color green and the element of wood. The wood element represents things that grow steadily, one step at a time. During this season, all things grow steadily because heaven and earth are coming together, and yang energy is rising and growing. In the spring, it is much easier to harvest yang energy and use it to treat the diseases that have presented themselves during the previous winter.

Spring is a time for developing health and longevity because there is plenty of fresh, healthy energy in the environment. This also makes it a perfect time for having children because the abundant energy is nourishing for a growing child or a pregnant mother. Peaches are beneficial to eat during the spring because they help the body to wake up early and spring into action. Peaches are also a symbol of health, longevity, and bliss. Peach trees are the first trees that bloom and grow new leaves as winter begins to subside.

Summer is for growth, maturity, and cultivation. During this time, it is important to continue the development initiated in spring. It is represented by the color red, and it represents a time of diligent work and a rising career. The long days of the summer allow for longer work days and extra energy. The heat of the summer, however, also often leads to irritability and aggression, so during these months it is important to maintain composure and to protect yourself. When it becomes excessive, eating a bit of watermelon can be helpful at reducing the effects of heat exhaustion and irritability. This helps the body to cool itself during the heat of the summer by nourishing yin energy.

Late summer is for the completion of projects and final touches. It is the beginning of the harvest season, represented by the color yellow or gold. Trees and plants are fully mature; most animals are busy taking advantage of the abundance of yang *qi* and flourishing plant life to make preparations for fall and winter. It is a time of scrutiny, making sure that everything is properly handled and the crops are fully ripe before the harvesting and reaping begins. The proper, small adjustments and repairs at this time can make all the difference in the future. By the middle of the late summer season, once the preparations and adjustments have been made, a sense of calm and peace arises as fall approaches.

Autumn or fall is for harvesting, money, and reaping the rewards of hard work. It is also a season for developing health by staying inside more often and beginning the process of nourishing your body's yin energy. Money is more abundant during this time, as people are beginning to harvest their crops and trade for items that they may need during the winter. Fall is represented by the color white, and it is a time when the air becomes crisp and clean because of the strong winds that begin to blow. As the winds blow, the debris that has been lodged in the trees is cleared out and the branches are thoroughly cleaned. Similarly, the crisp dry air helps the lungs and the pores of the skin to detoxify and the blood to become oxygenated more easily, cleaning the body's interior of waste materials.

The strong winds that are indicative of this season also mean that this is a time to protect the body by wearing more layers and jackets to stay warm. Strong winds have the potential to cause many illnesses within the body if proper precautions are not taken. Eating pears during the fall is beneficial for the lungs, throat, and skin, which are in the process of detoxifying themselves during autumn. Pears are also symbolic of departure and saying goodbye to the energy of the year in preparation of winter.

Winter is for storing, managing, and protecting your assets. During this time, it is important to stay inside more often and keep your valuable energy safely stored away until the spring comes again. Winter is represented by the color black, and it symbolizes being in control of your own life and circumstances. It is an ideal time for planning because you can look back upon the hard work of the past year and create new ideas for the upcoming year.

Daoism suggests that we always follow the nature of the seasons and, just as nature slows down and remains dormant during the winter, so should we. The cold weather causes the *qi* of the body to move further inwards toward the center and toward the bones. The cold weather also causes us, as individuals, to move further into our homes as well. When we protect our yin energy during the winter, we have plenty of strong energy and seeds to plant in the spring. Eating winter melon during the winter helps to strengthen your resistance to the cold weather, nourish your yin energy, and allow your body to adapt to the conditions of winter.

Fruit is a good source of energy and vitamins. The body requires a certain amount of sugar to function properly, and the glucose contained in fruit is always preferable to processed sugars found in packaged foods. Eating fruits in season helps to develop and manage healthy *qi* while eating those ripe in the opposite season can act as a form of medicine repairing any damaged *qi* energy.

The time of consuming fruits determines how their beneficial *qi* affects the body. For instance, eating watermelon during the summer helps to quell the fiery energy of the body, especially if eaten between 11 am and 1 pm when yang energy is at its peak and the sun at its highest point. Eating watermelon during the winter helps to nourish the body's yin energy, healing the kidneys and developing a strong constitution. This will also occur if watermelon is eaten between 11 pm to 1 am, when yin energy is at its peak.

Spring is when things are born, the summer is when things flourish, and the fall is when things are harvested. These are the nine months of the year when everything is growing and developing, and it is considered yang (active). The winter is when things are stored and become dormant, and it is considered yin (inactive). The winter is a time for the creation of seeds, the storing of essence, the number zero, the *jia zi*, wholeness, and self-sufficiency.

This yearly process is just like the natural life cycle of any living creature. It begins with birth (spring), grows into adulthood (summer), and continues into old age (fall). These three seasons are yang in nature because life is active during these periods, whereas winter is considered yin in nature because it is a time after death and before birth, when life becomes inactive.

This process is also the same as the daily 'seasons': 3 to 9 am (spring), 9 am to 3 pm (summer), 3 to 9 pm (fall), which are yang, and 9 pm to 3 am (winter), which is yin. Similarly, from birth to 23 years of age, we are growing (yang); from 23-45, we are maturing (½ yin, ½ yang); and from 45 onward, we are declining and becoming more yin. As we become more yin, we can cultivate our energy and combat the aging process by eating smaller portions, exercising appropriately, and drinking more water.

The winter/inactive/yin time is essential in life, and we must always take advantage of these opportunities. Yang comes from yin, not the other way around. Yin is more important than yang, and yet, yin and yang rely on each other. The sun and the moon, the left eye and the right eye, the left hand and the right hand, and the left foot and the right foot all rely on each other to accomplish their tasks. On the earth's surface, there is more ocean (yin) than land (yang), but both are important. The twelve-animal zodiac is a tool that allows us to develop our own methods for taking advantage of these changing conditions and harmonize ourselves with nature according to our own requirements.

The Hourly System

In addition to the yearly cycle of twelve years each animal is also used to represent the times of the day. In the past the day was divided into twelve sections rather than the twenty-four that we use today. Therefore, each of these twelve sections would be equivalent to a modern two-hour period. The day was originally divided into twelve sections because, according to traditional Chinese medicine, during each of these time periods a single internal organ of the body is at its most highly active state of the day and another is resting at its least active state. In addition to the myth of the twelve-animal race, this was one of the reasons that the animals were placed in their specific order. There order is as follows:

The Zang-Fu Organ Cycle			
Animal	**Time**	**Active Organ**	**Resting Organ**
Rat	11 pm -1 am	Gallbladder	Heart
Ox	1 am - 3 am	Liver	Small Intestine
Tiger	3 am - 5 am	Lungs	Urinary Bladder
Rabbit	5 am - 7 am	Large Intestine	Kidneys
Dragon	7 am - 9 am	Stomach	Pericardium
Snake	9 am - 11 am	Spleen	Triple Burner
Horse	11 am -1 pm	Heart	Gallbladder
Sheep	1 pm - 3 pm	Small Intestine	Liver
Monkey	3 pm - 5 pm	Urinary Bladder	Lungs
Rooter	5 pm - 7 pm	Kidneys	Large Intestine
Dog	7 pm - 9 pm	Pericardium	Stomach
Pig	9 pm - 11 pm	Triple Burner	Spleen

These correspondences help us to identify the strengths of each animal, as well as the proper times for various activities throughout the day. This is another way of organizing, comparing, and contrasting the animals, time periods, and phases of the zodiac to develop a deeper understanding of it. By looking at the animals and the vital organs in this way, we can see that they share similar habit patterns and daily cycles and that these habits help to contribute to the animal's qualities, behaviors, and overall energy.

The 5 Phases, the 6 Directions, and the 12 Animals

Between yin and yang, there are changes and interactions that are constantly occurring. After *qi* separates itself into yin and yang types of energy, it becomes further refined and takes on a new set of behaviors and responsibilities that allow it to be classified into the five phases. The stem and branch system combines and relates the energies of yin and yang, organizing them into the five phases and the twelve animals of the zodiac. In the stem and branch system, each of the five phases becomes a modifier for each of the twelve animals of the zodiac, giving color and contrast to each archetype.

While the stem and branch system is the primary arrangement of *qi* energy, the five phases can also be arranged and conceptualized according to many other phenomena. The five-phase system can be used to represent the seasons, the organs of the body, compass directions, days of the week, flavors, odors, climates, musical notes, grains, animals, etc. The *Yijing* even illustrates the relationship of the five phases to all of the events that occurs throughout one's life, thereby illuminating one's destiny. As we become mature individuals, these various aspects of our lives are integrated and they begin to form a network of information that can be used as a tool to guide us through life.

Another way of conceptualizing the zodiac involves combining the five phases with the internal organs of the body and the twelve animals of the zodiac. In the external world, known in Daoism as the macrocosm, the five phases refer to the occurrence of wood, fire, earth, metal, and water. Within the human body, known as the microcosm, the five phases also refer to the five primary vital organs of the body: the liver, heart, spleen, lungs, and kidneys. Traditionally, each of these primary organs is also correlated to one other corresponding organ as well, and together these pairs are known as the *zang-fu* organs. The liver is correlated with the gallbladder, the heart is correlated with the small intestine, the spleen is correlated with the stomach, the lungs are correlated with the large intestine/colon, and the kidneys are correlated with the urinary bladder.

The five phases system also relates to compass directions. The wood element represents things that grow and reach upward, and since the sun rises in the east, the wood element represents the eastern direction. The fire element represents illumination and heat, and since the sun crosses the southern sky during the course of the day, the fire element represents the southern direction. The metal element represents minerals that grow underground and remain under the earth, and since the sun sets in the west, the metal element represents the westward direction. The water element represents deep, dark oceans and coldness, and since the sun never crosses the northern sky, the water element represents the northern direction. Finally, the earth element represents the earth itself as the place around which all of these transformations take place, therefore it is placed at the center of the compass.

In Chinese, the phrase *liuhe*, literally "six harmonies," refers to everything under the sun or, more specifically, to the four compass directions, east, south, west, north, as plus above and below, or heaven and earth. This forms the three axes of the three-dimensional, physical universe. With a proper understanding of these elements, we have the ability to gain deeper insights into ourselves and the world around us. In addition to the stem and branch system and the horary system, the animals and elements of the zodiac can also be arranged according to the five phases system. In the five phases arrangement of the zodiac, the five phases (earth, metal, water, wood, and fire) and the directions of above (aka heaven) and below (aka earth) are used to classify and analyze the relationships between the various animals and the patterns that they represent.

In this system, each of the five phases is associated with two animals of the zodiac, while the above and below directions are only associated with a single animal each. The rat and the ox belong to earth, the tiger and the rabbit belong to metal, the dragon and the snake belong to water, the horse and the sheep belong to wood, the monkey and the rooster belong to fire, the dog belongs to the above, and the pig belongs to the below. This is yet another way of comparing and contrasting the animals and the energy patterns that they represent. By looking at them in this way, we can see that each of the animals and the vital organs share similar responsibilities and functions in the environment and the body respectively.

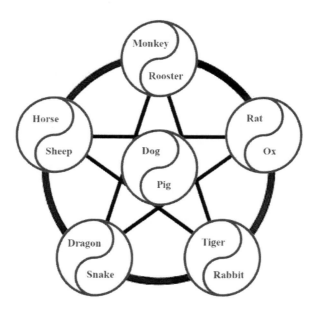

The Zodiac Perspective and the Ecological Perspective

The calendar system describes the various conditions that occur on the planet due to the movements of the heavenly bodies, and it categorizes them into five seasons that correspond to the five phases. These five phases are then used to relate these external conditions to the internal environment of energy systems. Equipped with this knowledge, we can begin to observe the behaviors and reactions of various living creatures to these external conditions and discover the methods that they use to harmonize themselves with their environment.

The animal kingdom, just like any other group or family, is comprised of many members, each of which have many different personalities, experiences, specialties, and roles. The member with the most technical or academic skill, for instance, may not be the candidate best suited to become a leader because effective leadership requires a sense of community, diplomacy, selflessness, courage, and a strong work ethic. By observing the interactions between various animals, we can begin to determine their roles within the ecosystem and the animal kingdom. This kind of approach to understanding nature is a ancient and natural method of learning. Before there were academies and universities, and long written histories, human beings learned to cultivate themselves simply by observing nature.

There is a great deal of overlap between modern science and Daoism, but the context, focus, and overtones of knowledge can vary widely between these two systems. It is important to differentiate between the zodiac perspective and the natural or ecological perspective on nature. Each system highlights different facts and areas of study as being of primary importance, setting the tone for further discoveries and applications. By seeing the discoveries of one system in the context of the other, we can discover creative ways to approach ideas and find significance in the seemingly mundane.

The twelve-animal zodiac system is a sacred tool that can teach us to manage our lives in a healthy way, to learn the best ways in which we can cultivate ourselves, and to allow us to see ourselves as an interdependent and integral part of nature. As we continue to learn from lessons that the zodiac teaches us, we begin to relinquish our illusions about reality and we place ourselves firmly on the ever-growing path of self-knowledge. The twelve-animal zodiac can help us by allowing us to recognize patterns quickly both within ourselves and in our environment so that we can achieve a harmonious balance more quickly.

6

Applying the Zodiac

Many things that can be used to measure the balance of yin and yang energies. All dualistic or dynamic energy systems embody these two states to a degree. The zodiac gives us a way to apply the phases of yin and yang to the events of our life and the events of the world. For instance, if your career is successful and prosperous, then your marriage will likely be suffering, and vice versa. This is because each of these activities must draw upon the same *qi* resources. In the west, we say that there is only so much time or resources; however, on a deeper level, it can be said that the real issue is that there is not enough *qi* energy.

If your *qi* is healthy, strong, and abundant, your efforts are efficient, successful, and prosperous, leading to both more time and more money. Yet, even with abundant and healthy *qi*, there must always be balance in all of our undertakings. If, overall, you are fortunate and blessed in your life, then the *Yijing* states that a family member may die soon, or perhaps some sort of misfortune is on its way. If you have a great abundance of wealth, then sickness and disease will likely be nearby to take your extra money and strike a balance between the yin and yang energies in your life. Life always seeks to grow and develop and thus it always requires a challenge or project to work on.

A perfectly happy life is what many people would like to achieve and then freeze in place, yet stagnation is not natural. Fortune and misfortune are brothers, they are concomitant, going hand in hand with one another. In the same way that the chicken gives birth to the egg and the egg gives birth to a chicken, yin and yang give rise to one another. Laozi said, "Being and not being, having and not having, create each other. Difficulty and ease, long and short, high and low, define each other, just as before and after follow each other" (2005, 5).

The Mechanisms of Nature

The different parts of nature work in harmony with each other, and therefore, each of these different parts exhibits its own overall balance of yin and yang energies. Plants, animals, and human beings all exist in different realms with mothers and fathers, natural habitats, natural enemies, natural friends and allies, spouses, etc. We all have situations that nourish our natural growth and also challenge us to develop our strength.

In Daoism, these are referred to as supporting and controlling cycles of the five phases diagram. While there are a wide range of variations in individual situations, in the eyes of nature, most relationships are considered to be either supporting or controlling. The relationship between a parent and child, for instance, is naturally a supporting type of relationship because in a healthy parent/child relationship, the parents do everything that they can to support and nurture their child. On the other hand, the relationship between husband and wife is a type of controlling cycle because they each place more responsibility upon one another to develop a strong relationship and a prosperous lifestyle. Therefore, due to the controlling nature of the relationship, it is normal that a married couple should fight every once in a while, as long as neither party overreacts and damages the trust and faith that they have with one another.

According to the *Yijing*, husbands and wives used to be enemies in a past life; in this life, they have come together again in a different situation to bring balance to the energy of their past. If a husband and wife never fight and always seem to get along well, then the *Yijing* states that the relationship must end in order for each of them to find other partners in which the energy of past lives can continue to be processed. Some couples argue quite a lot, and yet they still remain together. For these people, their love is stronger than their hate and their relationship becomes an intricate, dynamic part of their lives. It is important to remember that these types of relationships do not take place only in the human realm either. When we understand the dynamics of heaven and earth correctly, we can see that plants and animals can be married also. Cats and mice used to be husband and wife in a previous lifetime according to the *Yijing*, and because their differences were not resolved, they continue to fight in the present.

The Twelve Animal Race

Every animal of the zodiac has a story about its journey of self-development, along with a unique personality and skill-set. In modern science, we use the theory of evolution to describe the development of animal behavior and anatomy. However, it is also important to understand the spiritual journey that each of these creatures has gone through, both collectively and individually, to reach its current state. Human beings have also had to evolve both physically and spiritually to survive and individuate.

So much of the meaning and self-knowledge that we have discovered has not only been due to our external circumstances but also our internal, behavioral, and perceptual ones. In Daoism, there is a traditional story about a great race in heaven between all of the animals that is used to explain how each of the animals relate to one another and why they were assigned to a specific place in the twelve-year zodiac cycle. There are multiple variations to the story, and each variation has specific values and principles that it is meant to convey; each version is unique and has value. The myth is commonly told as follows:

The Jade Emperor decided to hold a race between all the animals of the world to determine which would best represent the twelve years of the zodiac. When the day of the race came and the animals lined up at the starting line, the rat quickly realized that he could not win the race with his small stature, so he asked the ox who was right next to him if he would be kind enough to let him ride on his back. In return, the rat would sing to him throughout the journey. The generous ox agreed, especially since the rat was so small and easy to carry.

The race began, and they all took off with great speed. The ox moved quickly with focus and, when he reached the river, jumped in and began swimming without hesitation. With his willful determination, the ox approached the finish line first, but just as he was about to cross it, the rat leapt off of the ox's head and crossed the finish line first. The rat was then granted first place and the ox was granted second place. Immediately after they crossed the finish line, the tiger strode in behind them. He relies on his great strength and agility to get ahead of the others, swim across the river, and take third place for himself.

After a few moments, the rabbit came hopping up. It was fast, but not being a good swimmer, it decided to carefully hop across the river on stones and drifting logs. The rabbit was awarded the fourth place and the fourth year of the zodiac. The dragon was next to cross the river and, while his ability to fly allowed him to travel quickly, he was compelled during his travels to help a group of people who were suffering from a drought by bringing them rain. He crossed the finish line and earned the fifth place in the zodiac.

The horse was spotted approaching the finish line. It was fast on smooth roads; however, it was a slow yet capable swimmer which slowed its progress. Just before the horse could cross the finish line, however, the snake appeared seemingly out of nowhere and leapt across the finish line first. Apparently, the snake had crossed the river just before the horse and waited in the tall grass to wrap itself around the horse's leg as it emerged to hitch a ride to the finish line. Thus, the snake took sixth place and the horse took seventh.

On the bank of the river, the rooster and the sheep were waiting, trying to figure out how to get across, when the monkey arrived. Together they decided to work to build a raft and float across the river by working as a team. When they reached the other side, they all made a dash for the finish and completed the race within moments of each other. The sheep took eighth place, the monkey took ninth, and the rooster took tenth. Then, the dog was spotted running up. While the dog was a fast runner and an able swimmer, he got distracted playing in a field and rolling in the grass. The dog then took eleventh place.

The pig came trotting up next with a happy smile on his face. While he was also not the slowest animal of the zodiac, he decided to take a nap along the way. The pig crossed the finish line last, earning himself a place as the representative of the twelfth animal of the zodiac. When the race was over, the Jade Emperor congratulated all of the winners and declared that each year of the zodiac would take on the qualities of the animal which represents it.

Inner and Outer Zodiac

Every animal of the zodiac is paired with another animal, forming an external and an internal aspect. The twelve animals that represent the internal aspect of each year are the twelve commonly known animals of the zodiac: the rat, ox, tiger, rabbit, dragon, snake, horse, sheep, monkey, rooster, dog, and pig. These are the animals that represent the energy of the self. The twelve animals that represent the external aspect of each year are the elephant, bees, cat, goose, tortoise, earthworms, fish, bear, eagle, deer, butterfly, and spider. These are the animals that represent the opposite energy; that of the "other".

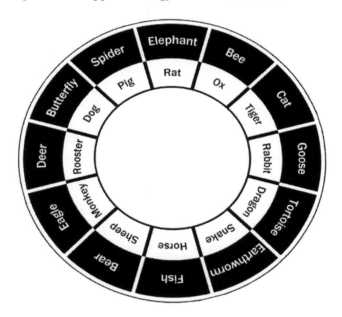

The "other", in this case, can represent something or someone that is attractive and helpful to us, or it can represent something or someone that has the ability to harm or subdue us. There is a lot of knowledge that can be gained by examining the inner and outer zodiacs and the various ways that they relate to each other.

Different people, in the same environment with the same circumstances, can produce widely different results. While a person or creature may appear one way on the surface, they may in fact be quite different once you get to know them. Sometimes, the most unsuspecting individual can be the most surprising and the most insignificant creatures can be capable of the greatest accomplishments.

The internal zodiac animals are more familiar and domesticated, while the external zodiac animals are wilder and more exotic. This illustrates the fact that our own nature is more familiar and predictable to us, whereas the energy that represents the "other" often appears dangerous, unfamiliar, exciting, and unpredictable.

In addition to the external zodiac representing the energy that opposes us in the outside world, it also reveals the nature of the hidden parts of our own psyche. In Jungian terms, the hidden parts of our psyche would include the anima/animus, the shadow, and the relationship dynamics of the archetypes. Therefore, understanding the ways that the internal and external animals relate to one another can help us to improve both our inner experience as well as our external circumstances in numerous ways.

Daoists emphasize that we must strive to use internal against external aspects to transform our liabilities into assets and our detriments into opportunities. The controlling cycle dynamic does not necessarily mean that the prey is fearful of the predator, it simply means that they do not enjoy being in the same environment together. For instance, rats and mice are not necessarily afraid of cats, they just do not enjoy being in the same environment as them. One reason for this is that cats make many high-pitched noises and rats have ears that are sensitive, especially to high pitched sounds. There are some people who cannot stand to be in the same room as a loud, energetic person, but this does not mean that they are afraid of that person. The system of controlling cycles that are found throughout nature is a useful and integral part of nature because it keeps creatures from over-populating and destroying environments.

The inner animal and the outer animal share a unique relationship where they both complement and control one another. The inner and outer aspects of every individual act in the same way. For example, the rat is both the smallest and the largest animal of the zodiac because, while it is small on the outside, its inner nature is as powerful and as noble as an elephant. This makes the rat a essential animal when it is functioning in a healthy, harmonious manner. However, an elephant can die if it enters a fight with a field mouse, and therefore, if the rat does not act in harmony with its own nature, it quickly becomes its own worst enemy. This dynamic between the inner and outer aspects of our being is true of all living creatures and all groups.

Romantic couples usually embody a complementary pair. An extremely beautiful person exists harmoniously with a plain looking person and an assertive, dominant person's strengths complement a calm, friendly person's strengths. Love at first sight cannot be scientifically studied; it is a matter of *qi* and subjective experience; however, love at first sight is a recognition of this complementary, controlling, counterpoint energy in another person.

If you want to know about the true nature of a person, you should study their friends and loved ones because these people truly represent the internal nature of that person. The phrase "birds of a feather flock together" can be applied here, because we all enjoy being around people who are similar or familiar to us. Understanding the relationships between predator and prey helps to create better relationships and find complementary pairs. This is a unique way of working with and understanding the energies of yin and yang that can help couples to overcome obstacles and create a relationship where both people can thrive.

Compatibility

Each of the animals of the zodiac have natural friends and enemies. It is important to recognize that this does not mean that these two creatures or personality types are fearful of one another or that they can never get along or tolerate the other. When two animals are raised together, they develop a deep bond even if they are natural enemies. For instance, domesticated dogs and cats can get along quite well in a home even though they are natural enemies according to the zodiac. However, there are good reasons that creatures should be considered natural friends, and therefore compatible, or natural enemies, and therefore incompatible. Rats, for example, are not necessarily afraid of cats, but there are numerous reasons why rats prefer not to inhabit the same areas as cats. The obvious reason is that cats enjoy catching and killing rats, but there are other less obvious reasons as well. For instance, a rat's hearing is sensitive to high frequencies, and a cat's meow sounds shrill and unpleasant to a rat.

The eventual outcome of the situation depends on how each of these creatures chooses to react to their instincts. To create harmony, two opposing energies must have a willingness to make things work and a knowledge of when to lead and when to follow. This means that, while there is a natural compatibility between animals and the people who embody their energies, these principles should also be understood in the context in which they occur. Some people may be natural enemies in many circumstances, and yet in other circumstances they may get along quite well with one another. happily married couples that manage to stay together for long periods may bicker and argue quite often, but underneath the turmoil they understand and trust one another. This behavior helps couples like this to communicate their feelings and air out any grievances before they grow into larger problems. On the other hand, some couples may stay together for long periods, even though they may not be communicating well and cannot meet each other's needs. Therefore, all relationships should be observed closely and understood in the context in which they occur to make sure that both partners are satisfied and thriving as individuals. The zodiac is a wonderful guide to help understand these dynamics, and it provides a way of articulating the processes that are occurring in relationships. that being said, the natural relationships between the animals of the zodiac are as follows:

The rat gets along well with the dragon and the monkey. With the help of the ox, a rat can achieve their goals with much greater ease, but they can run into problems with the horse, the rooster, and sometimes the sheep.

The ox gets along well with the snake and the rooster. The horse can be a great partner for the ox in business, and the rat can help make life their life much smoother; however, oxen can run into problems with sheep and dragons.

The tiger gets along well with the horse and the pig. The dragon can be a great partner for the tiger, particularly in marriage/romance, if both parties can learn to overcome their differences. Tigers can run into problems with the snake and the monkey, and tigers and oxen frustrate one another.

The rabbit gets along well with the pig, the sheep, and the dog. Rabbits and tigers make great business partners and rabbits and dragons can become great friends, but problems can arise when rabbits and dragons engage in closer relationships. Rabbits can run into problems with snakes and roosters.

The dragon gets along well with the rat, the monkey, and the rooster. If they can learn to overcome their many differences the tiger can help the dragon to achieve his or her goals. Rabbits make great friends for dragons, but problems can arise in closer relationships that involve commitments and shared resources. Dragons may run into problems with the dog and sometimes the ox.

The snake gets along well with the rooster, the dragon, and the ox. The monkey, the horse, and the sheep can all be great partners for the snake in business matters; however, snakes can run into problems with tigers and sometimes with the rabbit.

The horse gets along well with the dog, the sheep, and the rabbit. The horse can form prosperous business partnerships with the ox and/or the snake, but a number of differences have to be overcome. Horses can run into problems with the rat.

The sheep gets along well with the horse, the rabbit, and the pig. Sheep can run into problems with the ox, the tiger, and the dog. Miscommunication and differences in approach can sometimes lead to frustration between the sheep and the rat.

The monkey gets along well with the dragon, the snake, and the ox. The monkey can form harmonious partnerships with the rabbit, the dog, and the rooster in business matters. However, monkeys can run into problems with the tiger, and sometimes the rat.

The rooster gets along well with the ox, the snake, and sometimes with the dragon. The monkey and the ox can make great business partners for the rooster; however, the rooster can run into problems with the rat, the rabbit, and the dog.

The dog gets along well with the rabbit, the horse, and sometimes with the tiger. The dog and the monkey can make a great partner in business; however, dogs can run into problems with the dragon, the sheep, and the rooster.

The pig gets along well with the rabbit, the tiger, and sheep. The rooster, the rat, and the ox can all be great partners for the pig in business; however, the pig can run into problems with the snake and the monkey.

7

Humans and Animals

For as long as human beings have existed, we have relied upon the animals of the world. The animal kingdom has existed for a much longer period of time than the human species, and it is clear that the animal kingdom can survive without human beings, but human beings could not survive without the animals. Nature has always been our best teacher. This relationship was undeniable in the past when almost all human activity involved relating to the animals of the world and nature in some manner. In the modern era however, with so much urban development and societal issues to be addressed, this relationship is easy to forget. The laws of human beings are written down; they can be reviewed, analyzed, and debated, but the laws of nature are based on the relationships between natural things, the dynamics of the seasons, and self-evident truths. Nature's laws must be experienced firsthand, internalized, and accepted just as they are; they can neither be negotiated nor created, but discovered.

"Aristotle called human beings the rational animal. In Aristotle's schema, plants have life, animals have life and perception, and human beings have both characteristics along with rationality (the Greek word for rationality here is logos, a rich term referring to the capacity for discursive language, reason, and other similar traits)."[1] As human beings continue to rapidly develop higher levels of consciousness, our civilization follows suit, and with each development in civilization, our relationship to nature changes.

It is important for us to recognize the need to actively integrate nature and natural processes into our rapidly developing systems. We have many clear examples of cultures and civilizations that have successfully achieved a harmonious balance with nature, as well as other civilizations which collapsed because they failed to achieve such a balance.

[The early history of] Easter Island is a strong example of how over harvesting and destructive competition can cause the downfall of a civilization. Pridefulness caused the Rapa Nui who lived on the island to destroy themselves and their natural home. . .

---

[1] "On the Separation of Human and Animal," by Matthew Calarco (2015). stanfordpress. typepad.com/blog/2015/09/on-the-separation-of-human-and-animal.html

45

The people of the island of Anuta, however, have a population density rate that is higher than Bangladesh and yet they have developed a strong community and have managed to learn to live within their means.[2]

We have enormous power as human beings and we shouldn't underestimate the innate abilities that we all have. "Due to the fact that human beings have a larger brain, we have a greater ability to create our own choices in life that are not based on instinct and hereditary behavior patterns" (Scott 1972, 61). Yet, as we choose to be creative with our choices in life, we still have a responsibility to honor and respect nature because how we treat animals reveals how we are treating ourselves and the state of our civilization. We have only very recently entered the Anthropocene age and we must take responsibility for the effects that we have on other forms of life and natural processes.

Mutual Respect of Humans and Nature

Human beings came from the earth; this is our home. The earth nurtures us by providing us with everything that we need to survive and, because of this, we must respect nature and live in harmony with our environment. Human beings must give back to the earth by caring for and protecting nature. This is our responsibility on this planet; we rely on and flourish as a species because of all of the other forms of life that co-exist with us. We must stop pollution, damming, mining, drilling, and excessive construction because when we damage our natural environment, we damage ourselves and our future. Daoism states that we must live "according to nature", and we should not strive to forcibly change the world or other people. All creatures appreciate their own lives and their sense of freedom and, by nurturing these natural qualities wherever we find them, we nurture ourselves as well.

Friendship between human beings and animals benefits both parties. Every living creature on the earth plays a unique role in supporting the ecosystem that we all share. All animals help to control and support various parts of nature. Grazing animals keep many of the forests and grasslands from becoming overgrown, directing and balancing the waterways in the process, and at the same time, they provide nutrition for predatory creatures. These interdependent relationships create a network in nature that form natural enemies as well as natural friendships. Human beings have capitalized on these natural relationships by domesticating some animals and creating a frequent, ongoing relationship with them.

Each one of us resonates differently with our surroundings and we are attracted to different people, plants, areas, and creatures. When we are choosing a

---

[2] "South Pacific," by BBC Natural History Unit (2009). www.dailymotion.com/video/x6dx5oy

pet for instance, we must make sure to choose an animal that we feel a deep connection with. This is a sign that this animal can teach us a great deal and, with a bit of nurturing, we will develop a strong, mutually beneficial relationship with them. As you spend more time with animals and touch or pet them, you develop a closer bond with them and discover deeper levels of understanding. This is one method of gathering the *qi* of your pet, and whenever you gather the *qi* from plants, animals, or human beings you will notice that they become happy and actually enjoy the process. When the relationship between any two creatures becomes sufficiently deep, then each creature becomes more invested in protecting, nourishing, and supporting the other benefiting nature as a whole.

Sensory Perception

"Every animal has sense organs which determine which situations and changes in the environment it can respond to and motor organs which determine which kind of responses that they can make" (Scott 1972, 36). The senses and abilities that we possess as human beings allow us to identify and interact with the *qi* that is found throughout nature. Through these abilities we are able to grow, develop, adapt, and create relationships. These unique abilities are extremely important because they allow us to express ourselves, accomplish our goals, and flourish as living beings. When we recognize our similarities with other creatures, we begin to have more camaraderie with them and we are able to create a stable environment where we can learn from one another. As human beings, we often create many mutually beneficial relationships with animals and this helps both parties to reach their full potential.

The abundance of *qi* that can be found on the earth fuels the cells of all living beings and when this *qi* is stored, utilized, and cultivated effectively, then the cells of these beings will develop greater abilities. The energy of the moon, for instance, is especially supportive of the perceptual capacity of living organisms, and it charges the cells of the body with vital energy. There are many animals that perceive the world with sense organs that we do not possess, which only highlights the fact that we have a lot to learn from our relationships with other creatures.

The five senses that human beings possess have been very important for our evolution and they have allowed us to develop great intelligence. For instance, many animals, including human beings, have developed higher intelligence in conjunction with greater eyesight. This is due to the fact that, as they were able to see more detail, they developed the need to respond to more stimuli, including stimuli coming from further away. This led to the ability to handle ever more complex problems and situations. Each time we sense or respond to stimuli in our environment, we develop and cultivate our *qi* as well. In Daoism, the health and quality of the five senses is synonymous with the health of the body in general. In fact, one of the first signs of aging is that the five senses begin to fade and diminish.

The Five Senses

The five senses are our tools for interacting with the world around us. Three of these senses are related to the three elixir fields within the body itself. The lower elixir field, which is the center of the *jing* energy, the essence of the body, is related to the sense of hearing. This energy center of the body is closely related to the kidneys and the water element, which processes the fluids of the body. Water easily responds to resonate frequencies, as sound travels faster and further underwater because sound waves are able to conserve their energy more easily in denser substances. The work of Dr. Masaru Emoto has demonstrated that water is constantly reconfiguring its structure based upon the frequencies that are interacting with it. Water is always listening, just like the kidneys are always listening and adapting to the qualities of the energy that pass through them.

The upper elixir field is the center of the *shen*, or spirit, within the body and it is related to the sense of sight. The spirit of the individual is closely related to their consciousness and behavior. The sense of sight is closely related to the ability of an individual to think clearly, develop awareness, and remain alert. In Daoism, this is known as *ming*, or brightness. The eyes are directly related to the liver, and the liver is the organ that is responsible for our emotions and our ability to think consciously. When our emotions and mind are calm, then our liver is functioning well and our eyes will appear clear.

By observing more colors and increasing our visual acuity, we simultaneously increase our ability to focus our thoughts and think clearly. The sense of sight allows us to observe and become aware of things at a great distance, which in turn allows us to predict the outcome of events. This means that the sense of sight helps us develop the capacity to grasp complex ideas and situations. As we develop our vision, our bodies become more highly complex and developed as well in order to act upon the new information. Western science tells us that "Since sight is well developed in only three groups of animals— mollusks, arthropods, and vertebrates— we might conclude that highly developed sense organs are correlated with complex [biological] organization" (Scott 1972, 42).

The middle elixir field is the center of the *qi* of our body and it is closely related to the sense of smell. This field is related to the lungs and the respiratory function. The sense of smell allows us to identify the quality and quantity of *qi* of various objects and areas. Often times, when we are unsure of something, we will smell it first before interacting with it further. Human beings naturally have an inferior sense of smell when compared with many other animals. When human beings began to walk upright and our heads were held much further from the ground, the sense of smell became less important and the sense of sight became more important. Animals that keep their faces down toward the ground often have a highly developed sense of smell.

Along with the ability to recognize the condition of *qi*, the olfactory sense is also closely related to the body's immune system. When we breathe deeply, the blood becomes highly oxygenated and the body becomes highly energized. Oxygen is an element with a lot of potential energy within it, and when the body becomes better at utilizing oxygen, then this energy can be a great benefit to our health. The extra energy that the body obtains from oxygen flows directly to the immune system and increases the body's resistance to disease.

The somatosensory sense, or touch, is also related to the lungs and partly to the liver because the lungs are directly related to any of the sensations of the skin and the liver is related to the nerves. The sense of touch allows us to recognize, differentiate and identify objects and meaning within the world. The nerve endings can distinguish the shape of objects, texture, heat, pain, and pressure. The hands are perhaps the greatest tool of the human body, allowing us to manipulate tools and develop a much deeper relationship with the external world.

Along with differentiation, the sensation of touch is also a significant part in the function of memory and habit formation. Whenever an action is performed repeatedly, muscle memory is developed, allowing the body to be able to recognize the steps of a procedure without the need for consciously directed thought. We often say, "it's just like riding a bike", when we are referring to the way that the body remembers how to perform a repeated task even when the conscious mind may seem to have forgotten it. The lungs and the skin are the two organs that interact directly with the external world, and therefore represent the way that we receive our first impressions. By developing our sense of touch, we also develop our ability to be decisive and confident by increasing our ability to recognize things of significance and importance in the world.

The gustatory sense, or taste, is related to the heart, the circulatory process, and the spleen and stomach. The sense of taste allows us to directly experience substances at a molecular or chemical level. When our sense of taste is highly developed, we are able to experience a deep richness of flavors with a single bite of food. A highly developed sense of taste allows for a deep, rich experience of life in general. The more highly developed the sense of taste becomes, the more an individual can experience in a single moment. This allows us to be able to feel the "flavor" of a large amount of information without having to actually process it entirely. This is also the sensation that we feel when we have an intuitive feeling or a "hunch."

The tongue is also very sensitive, allowing us to become fluent in our abilities by experiencing and perceiving a great amount of detail in each experience. When we spend time examining an experience with a refined sense of detail, it is referred to as learning something "by heart." By developing a rich and detailed life, we also develop a vibrant sense of joy that supports the function of the heart and the circulatory system. This allows us to remain hopeful and positive in trying circumstances. The spleen and the stomach also play a significant role in eating and tasting by deepening the sensations of the mouth, tongue, and lips. The texture and mouthfeel of various foods and beverages play a significant role in the experience of eating that is distinct from tasting alone.

Human Beings: The Thirteenth Animal

The twelve animals of the zodiac are associated with many things, and there are many facts and relationships that can be brought to light by these various associations. In traditional Chinese medicine, for instance, there are many ways in which that twelve animals can be associated with the human body and its functions. Each of these associations can teach us a lot about human health, anatomy, and behavior.

In traditional Chinese medicine, there are twelve *qi* meridians that flow throughout the human body. These meridians allow the body to function properly by harmonizing and interconnecting all of the elements within it, as well as harmonizing the body with the external environment. When these meridians are strong, healthy, and able to flow freely, then the body will be strong and healthy as well. Each of these meridians is associated with a single internal organ of the body and any abilities that are associated with that organ.

Each of these twelve meridians is related to the one of the twelve animal energies of the zodiac system as well. In order to be able to heal a patient's meridian, the doctor must also be able to heal the animal that is associated with that meridian. To accomplish this, the doctor must be able to live harmoniously with that animal. Therefore, as a doctor or as an individual that wishes to cultivate their *qi*, it is very important to be able to live in harmony with animals and nature in general.

Each meridian contains a specific number of acupuncture points that have their own functions. There are 365 points total, matching the number of herbs in traditional Chinese medicine. Each herb is used to activate the function of one of these points. This illustrates the relationships of our body to the external environment and the vegetal kingdom. The *qi* that forms the points can be used to induce healing and allows us to function in a healthy manner. We should, therefore, make it a priority to cultivate our energy and care for these points. The twelve animals function as a guide to understand how meridians and points interact with one another and how we can support *qi* within our bodies and in the outside world. When *qi* points are nourished and healthy, they naturally develop healing qualities that emanate to the surrounding environment.

The Thirteen Ghost Points

The ghost points are used for treating psychological problems, such as depression, schizophrenia, and others. A person acquires this kind of condition by being near bad *qi*. They may have seen things that they should not have seen, or heard things that they should not have heard, etc. Sometimes, this bad *qi* could be coming from your ancestors, arising from the situations that they found themselves in or the deeds that they have done while they were alive, while at other times it could just be a matter of being in the wrong place at the wrong time. This is a large part of the Daoist understanding of moral law, and the concept of sin or error.

When these thirteen points are strong and healthy, they allow the individual to remain mentally and emotionally calm in difficult situations, and they also help to reduce inflammation throughout the body, thereby increasing longevity. By tonifying, developing, and unblocking these points, you transform them into areas that allow the negative energies of the body to escape. It is always wise to leave a route of escape and to avoid cornering your enemy; trapped energy and trapped creatures can be very dangerous.

In order to treat the diseases of the thirteen ghost points, the healer must have the proper level of cultivation and understanding. It is very tricky and potentially dangerous to treat these points because the treatment has the potential to backfire onto the healer if performed improperly. In order to treat the thirteen points successfully, the doctor must treat the patient at the proper time of day. Each of the thirteen points is related to a single animal of the twelve-animal zodiac and each animal is related to one of the twelve two-hour periods of the day that are described in traditional Chinese medicine.

Twelve of the thirteen ghost points are related to a single animal of the zodiac; the thirteenth connects to the final animal: humans. The human acupoint is appropriately called Human Center (*renzhong*, GV-26) and is located in the center of the upper lip, just below the nose. Pressing it helps to resuscitate people in emergency situations, but it only works on humans, not on animals. It is also pierced to help memory, dementia, Parkinson's disease, and insomnia. It can be quite painful to treat, but its stimulation is very effective. If you press this point in the morning (using the left hand for men, and the right hand for women) it will immediately help to make you more alert and awake.

Human beings help to balance the energies of yin and yang on the earth, and the Human Center (*renzhong*, GV-26) point helps to balance the energies of yin and yang within the human body. Human beings are omnivorous and by eating both plants (yin) and animals (yang), they keep each of these energies in proper balance. The human being is the only animal of the zodiac that is not naturally afraid of fire; instead, humans use fire as a tool. By not immediately responding to situations with fear, we are able to understand phenomenon at a deeper level and turn many situations to our advantage. As human beings, we should learn to co-exist with the bad things in life as much as possible, and to go with the flow and remain calm. If you are friendly first and living a harmonious life, then bad things can actually help you rather than harm you.

Viewing Human Beings as Animals

Every animal in nature exists in different environments and different circumstances. These differences mean that each animal must develop various behaviors, survival strategies, and defense mechanisms in order to thrive. This is an important point to recognize in both animals and human beings. While each animal has to adapt to the same universal laws of nature and the natural conditions of their environment, each animal does this in different ways and, therefore, what one creature or group regards as 'normal', another may regard as exotic or taboo.

Predatory animals, for instance, require meat in their diet in order to survive, so they must be equipped with the skills to kill, whereas a vegetarian creature must be equipped with a way of locating fresh plants and escaping or defending itself from predators. Similarly, a person with an insatiable desire to succeed in their career will often need to be assertive and less agreeable, whereas a person with a desire to start a family will need to develop understanding, patience, and a more agreeable nature (within limits).

By raising an animal and interacting with it every day, we gather their *qi* and learn from that animal's behaviors. We also learn new abilities and methods from the people we spend most time with. If the people we spend time with are different from us, it may be quite difficult at times. However, we will also develop abilities that are unique and different from the ones that are familiar to us. By spending our time with people who are perceptive, distinguished, and cultivated, we can grow very quickly as individuals.

Original Spirit

From a Daoist perspective, each person is said to have an original spirit. This spirit can take many forms, as it is a representation of what a person has been in their past lives. The original spirit often takes the form of an animal, and it can be observed in the individual's body structure, facial features, behavior, speech, gestures, and mannerisms. In Chinese, the word *xiang* means to look, or to resemble, and this is one of the main ways that are used to determine a person's original spirit.

It is important to look at a person with depth and a keen sense of observation in order to determine what creature they resemble. Sometimes, a person will strongly resemble a specific animal and at other times a person may not seem to embody an animal at all. However, with keen perception it will be noticed that most people embody one creature or another. For instance, if a person strongly resembles a parrot, then they will be quite intelligent, talkative, an expert in the use of language, quite colorful with either their expression or their personality, and good in social situations. The person's birth year animal and life experiences can modify these traits, but overall, these things will be quite natural to a person who embodies a parrot spirit.

The original animal spirit of a person may or may not be the same as the animal that represents the year in which they were born. By comparing the animal of a person's birth year with the animal spirit that they embody, you can achieve a much deeper understanding of that person's nature. A person with two very contrasting animals will have a dual nature, which can allow them to observe and approach a situation from multiple angles. However, they may also suffer from an inner conflict and/or indecision. A person with two very similar animals, however, will find luck and fortune because they will be determined, confident, and successful with their abilities. This way of understanding an individual is quite useful and practical because it allows us to grasp the complex nature of a person more easily. It is important to remember, however, that we are all human beings first and we all have the ability to grow and adapt in many ways.

Each person must be understood as a unique being with various talents and an inner nature that lends itself to certain environments, people, and situations. When circumstances are favorable to a person's inner nature, original spirit, or birth animal, then the conditions are considered auspicious and opportunities can be taken without incurring issues. When we encounter auspicious circumstances, heaven is presenting us with a blessing and we should do our best to take the opportunities that are presented with. By engaging our opportunities rather than avoiding them, we can grow as individuals, develop our skills, and gain access to new resources. Our life is punctuated by auspicious and inauspicious circumstances. We harmonize ourselves with nature by engaging life and taking opportunities or sheltering ourselves and resting at the proper times. This harmony allows us to create as much benefit as possible from all circumstances.

The Twelve-Animal Control Method

Whenever we are interacting with another individual, it is important to use the proper mannerisms and behaviors. The twelve-animal zodiac can help us greatly with this process. Whenever we engage with another person, we should do our best to create a dynamic situation that can produce benefits for both parties. To do this with the twelve-animal system, we must be able to understand which animal the other person represents and the natural predators of that animal. By imagining ourselves as a different animal, we are able to change the way that our *qi* expresses itself. This allows us to change the way that we respond to situations and vise-versa.

This method is not limited to the animals of the twelve-animal zodiac system; an open mind and creativity are required in order to use this method properly. For example, if we are in a negotiation with a person who resembles a rat, then we should imagine ourselves as a cat in order to remain in control of the negotiation. This technique is not limited to situations of conflict either; it can be used to help others as well. If a teacher wants to instruct a student, then they should imagine themselves as the natural predator of the animal that their student embodies in order to subdue their resistance to the learning process. This will greatly increase the effectiveness of their instruction. Similarly, if a male doctor wants to heal a male patient, then the doctor should imagine himself as a female during the treatment in order to control the healing process and subdue the patient's illness.

Creating a strong yin and yang dynamic in this way allows for active harmonious energy to be exchanged between two individuals. By imagining ourselves as the creature that controls the person we are interacting with, we are able to direct ourselves and the situation that we are in. If the person's birth animal is known, then this information should be considered as well. In this situation, we must imagine ourselves as an animal that is capable of subduing both the birth animal and the original spirit animal of the other person. If the person's birth animal and embodied animal are quite different from one another, then they can be rather tricky to deal with and difficult to manage. When this technique is mastered, then more luck, competency, and good fortune will result.

Part Two

The Twelve Animals

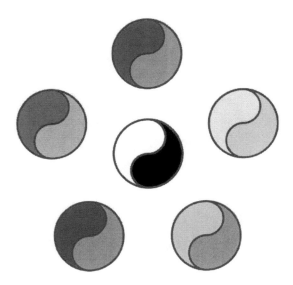

1

Rat

Wood Rat
February 5th 1924 to January 23rd 1925

Fire Rat
24th January 1936 to 10 February 1937

Earth Rat
10 February 1948 to January 28th 1949

Metal Rat
28th January 1960 to 14th February 1961

Water Rat
15th February 1972 to 2nd February 1973

Wood Rat
2nd February 1984 to 19th February 1985

Fire Rat
19th February 1996 to 6th February 1997

Earth Rat
7th February 2008 to 25th January 2009

Metal Rat
25th January 2020 to 11th February 2021

Water Rat
11th February 2032 to 30th January 2033

Wood Rat
30th January 2044 to 16th February 2045

Fire Rat
16th February 2056 to 4th February 2057

Rat

The rat category of the zodiac represents all types of rodents. Rats are industrious, intelligent, prudent, humble, timid, perceptive, and highly adaptable creatures. They spend much of their time exploring and searching for food, safe travel routes, and nesting locations. With their large, strong teeth, rats and rodents can easily gnaw through many materials. This allows them to gain access to areas, open containers, and cut down trees and plants. Rats can run, burrow, climb, and swim, which further increases the area of their search for food and shelter. Rats instinctively know how to swim, and some rodents, such as beavers, spend much of their lives in the water. Some are herbivores, while others are omnivores; however, most can survive by scavenging, consuming almost anything edible.

Rodents by and large are social, gregarious animals that travel in packs or live in colonies. Some such as prairie dogs are extremely social, congregating in organized societies, while others live in loosely organized packs. There are a few species that live solitary. Smaller rodents and rats are prolific and widespread, found in almost every environment around the world except the polar regions. They are so prolific because they reproduce rapidly, which allows them to maintain their population levels even in adverse conditions, including in human habitats and areas subject to heavy human intervention such as cities. At the same time, this also means that they form a large part of the diet of predatory animals.

At the White Cloud Temple, monastics raise many different types of rats, training each to perform different tasks and functions. They train some to alert the residents to various threats, others to detect substances and objects, yet others to bang on drums at certain times throughout the day to keep track of the hours. Rats exercise in different ways, and when they are trained to do so properly, they can greatly increase their longevity. Genetic research suggests that a rat's lifespan is between one and two years, while larger rodents such as capybaras can live as long as eight or ten; however, with proper cultivation and care, some can make it to thirty-five.

Rats always exercise in ways they enjoy to increase happiness and manage stress levels. In nature, they never suffer from heart attacks because their exercise routines make them happy as they always suit their personal situations. Rats teach us that the most effective way of increasing longevity is through higher levels of happiness. When it comes to exercise, each person's physiology is unique. They all should create their own individual plan best suited to their capabilities and the activities they enjoy. Many rats also keep a strict routine to allow their body to regulate itself efficiently. This also helps them to minimize the dangers they encounter by becoming deeply familiar with the nature of their environments at all times.

Rats are quite timid and prudent, living in harmony with their natural environment. Their burrows create living spaces for other animals, aerate the soil, and collect groundwater for surrounding plants. As rats travel through grasses, bushes, and flowers, they gather pollen on their coats and paws, then carry it on to pollinate other plants and wildflowers. They teach us that we can (and should) be industrious in the world, yet we should still act in ways that support the natural environment and our own happiness and fulfillment. Yet, even with all of the benefits that rats provide to the world, they are not capable of becoming the king or ruler of their environment because of their small size and their inherent timidity. They can increase their numbers and live harmoniously with nature by focusing on their own situations and preferring to avoid confrontation with others.

Calendar

The rat is the first animal of the zodiac. Since the astrological year begins with the winter solstice, it is associated with the 11th month of the Chinese lunar calendar that lasts from approximately December 7th to January 6th in the Gregorian calendar and with the two-hour period around midnight, between 11 pm and 1 am. Why does the rat come first? To begin, it has the highest rate of fertility and reproduction among all zodiac animals. Rats can reproduce at an extremely fast pace, a single female remaining fertile for her entire life, producing approximately 120 young in a favorable year. Rats are one of the most preyed upon animals of the animal kingdom; however, they maintain their numbers with their amazing rate of fertility. It is nearly impossible to eradicate them from anywhere because the more they are hunted the more they are encouraged to reproduce.

1948 was a rat year which saw the beginning of the baby boom in many western countries, and both governments and businesses soon catered to the growing families, leading to rapid economic growth. The trauma experienced by the veterans of World War II led many of them to seek the peace and comfort of a simple family life, leading to an increased birth rate. The experience of fear and danger motivates all creatures to reproduce.

Along with a high fertility rate, rats also have a high libido and mate year-round. They are also one of the few animals to have sex for enjoyment rather than just procreation. Because of this, Daoists consider them as the first animal to practice homosexuality, which they regard without prejudice. Rats and other animals demonstrate that all preferences in exercise, diet, and sexuality must be tailored to each person's individual needs and preferences. In the rat year of 1960, the FDA approved the first oral contraceptive pill for women, Enovid, which in the following decades radically changed the nature of sex throughout the world.[1] Rats are examples of the ways in which we can master and enjoy our sexuality as

---

[1] "Margaret Sanger and the History of the Birth Control Pill," by South Avenue Women's Services (2020). www.southavewomensservices.com/margaret-sanger-and-the-history-of-the-birth-control-pill/

living beings. They have turned sexuality into a strong tool and a major asset for themselves that benefits their health, their species, and their happiness.

Rats play an integral role in the evolution of many mammalian species, including human beings. In the 19th century, Charles Darwin hypothesized that human beings evolved from an earlier primate species, however, Daoists have taught for many centuries that even beyond that, the rat was an ancient ancestor of both human beings and primates. In fact, rats were the first mammal to make its way onto dry land and flourish.

While rats can be pests, they are not our natural enemy; on the contrary, they deserve our respect. It is important for us as human beings to recognize that rats are part of our evolutionary history and that we rely heavily on the functions they perform in nature. Rats have lived for thousands of years without human beings, but human beings cannot live without rats. Similarly, in the year of the rat, many events occur that can be seen as both progressive and controversial. These events are often inevitable or the result of actions taken in response to great pressure. A clear example is the founding of Israel, which occurred in the rat year of 1948 as a response to the rising tension between Arabs and Jews in Palestine, exacerbated by the massive number of Jewish refugees who arrived in Palestine after World War II.[2]

In the year of the rat, many big, significant changes occur, especially in the rat year that marks the beginning of the sixty-year cycle (*jiǎ zǐ*). These scale changes can be for better or worse, but they always require us to make adjustments to our lifestyle and force us to adapt to new conditions. Rat years tend to be extremely busy, often fraught with unexpected developments in projects, plans, and life direction. Often previously balanced and well-handled situations intensify and grow into larger, more complex issues.

On the other hand, rat years also tend to see new projects and ideas as well as new methods that lead to innovations. The Macintosh computer was first released by Apple just before the rat year of 1984 and soon grew wildly popular. While it sold well and many people dreamed about the possibilities of computer technology, its full implications and the way it would revolutionize the world were only understood later.[3] This shows how seeds planted during rat years can easily come to fruition and amplify in succeeding years.

Daoists often say that seeds planted in the winter sprout in the spring, and that yin must come before yang. The year of the rat is similar to the winter because it forces people to slow down and analyze things more closely due to great changes. Just like rats, we must be industrious during rat years by working hard,

---

[2] "Creation of Israel, 1948," by The U.S. Department of State (1948). www.history.state. gov/milestones/1945-1952/creation-israel

[3] "Macintosh by Apple - Complete History of Mac Computers," by History-Computer Contributors (2021). www.history-computer.com/macintosh-by-apple-complete-history-of-mac-computers/

sleeping deeply (but minimally), and storing our extra resources for the future to develop our yang energy and thrive.

Rat years often bring arguments and squabbling, but they do not usually result in full-scale fights or wars. For this reason, it is beneficial at the time to exercise to reduce stress and channel frustrations. But be careful: rats are also associated with disease, pain, and inflammation. Taking care of health and immunity is particularly important during rat years. Eating a proper diet and watching inflammation makes it possible to handle the vast changes they bring. Not just humans, but the natural environment, too, goes through vast changes during this time, so it is important to prepare for extreme weather and natural disasters. Earthquakes and flooding tend to be common.

Qi

The Chinese double-hour related to the rat is around midnight, 11 pm to 1 am, the time of the gallbladder. During this time the heart is calm, peaceful, and at rest, but the gallbladder is active, releasing bile and causing the body to create and repair blood cells. Best be asleep to rest up for the next day. The heart can rest best when we are in light sleep, while the gallbladder performs its subtle functions optimally when there is no interference from the thoughts of the conscious mind. As regards food, red dates support heart and blood: they are also a favorite food of rats who recognize their ability to calm the heart and balance the blood pressure. This also why rats tend to be attracted to the color red.

When we sleep soundly between the hours of 11 pm and 1 am, we feel rested and energized the next morning. Sleeping during these hours nourishes the gall bladder which shares responsibility for managing our nervous system and emotions with the liver. Colds, flu, and other ailments begin to take hold during this time as well. The body becomes highly sensitive to pain because the heart cannot increase blood flow to painful areas as it would at other times. The gallbladder supports the liver in detoxifying and storing blood. This reduces stress on the heart and circulatory system which then reduces pain and inflammation.

One reason why rats can to increase longevity and enhance immunity is that they can sleep extremely deeply. Their way of sleeping is known as "dead sleep" or "sleeping like the dead." Healthy and rejuvenating, this is also known as "beauty sleep," beauty and cosmetics being another area related to the rat. When we cultivate ourselves in the rat way, our face appears younger and our energy levels increase. The point Wind Pond (fengchi, GB-20) on the back of the skull, also known as the "gate of consciousness," relates to the rat. Pressing it at night reduces pain and allows the body to fall asleep quickly.

The process of giving birth also allows a female rat to increase her longevity by stimulating her body increase its immune function and produce new blood cells. Giving birth can help a female alleviate many conditions. Rats often inhabit places that are dirty, wet, and cold; reproducing helps female rats to combat any illnesses that they may encounter in these areas.

Along with the gallbladder, the rat is also related to the spleen, the intestines, and the colon. Being scavengers, rats eat many things which they can metabolize by carefully managing their digestive system. They naturally breathe deeply from their abdomen; they press and rub their bellies before they fall asleep. This massages the internal organs and keeps all materials (including food) and energies within the body flowing freely. The spleen contains extremely potent *qi* just like the rat; as an organ it decides which foods are beneficial (nutrient) and which detrimental (waste/poison). The rat is also good at using its keen senses to determine which bits of food are ripe and which are rotten; it also determine which bits of food are worth storing for the future and which must be eaten right away.

The ghost point that is associated with the rat is known as Ghost's Faith (*Guixin*); it matches the point Little Bargaining (*shaoshang*, LU-11) in the meridian system (Johnson 2014, 605). Located on the outside edge of the thumb, at the junction of the lines drawn along the radial border of the nail and its base, it is used to treat pain, inflammation, loss of consciousness, throat issues, and even cancer. Pressing this point can also provide a small boost of energy and alertness (Deadman et al. 2007, 90).

The rat in the zodiac is responsible for the spread of infectious diseases. Rats contain and generate a host of various infectious diseases including the bubonic plague, Covid-19, Lyme disease, and typhus. They are also associated with inflammation, allergies, and chronic pain conditions, and so many people feel the effects of these conditions in the year of the rat. Rats are acutely sensitive animals and so at thit time many people are extra sensitive to both physical and emotional stimuli.

Daoists see the highly potent rat energy, with its ability to bring about great change, as demonstrating the will of heaven. The rats are messengers of heaven. The Covid-19 pandemic for instance, which came about in the year of the rat, can be thought of as either a punishment for human beings mistreating the natural environment, or it can be thought of as a way for the planet to harmonize itself by naturally slowing things down and allowing nature to recover from all of the rapid economic, societal, and technological development.

One theory regarding the origin of the Covid-19 virus is that it originated in bats and was transmitted to human beings through close contact. from a Daoist perspective, this is interesting because bats are categorized as a type of flying rat. Like rats, they can carry hundreds of infectious diseases potentially devastating to other species. The fact that an infectious disease that has wide ranging societal and planetary effects originated in a rat-category animal in the year of the rat would make a lot of sense.

Throughout history there have always been many diseases and widespread outbreaks. During the last five thousand years there have been 327 pandemic events with the same magnitude as the Covid-19 virus. from 1347 to 1354, the black plague, which was caused by and spread by rats and mice, killed millions of people. Toward the end of the Roman Empire there were quite a few serious pandemics and the ancient Mayan and Native American people also suffered from devastating outbreaks of disease. In the 19th century, many people passed away after being infected with influenza or tuberculosis and it wasn't until new vaccines and treatments were discovered that these diseases finally became manageable. In the 21st century alone we have already seen SARS, MURS, H1N1, the Avian flu, and Covid-19, all of which have been serious epidemics.

Even though we may develop vaccines for Covid-19 and other viruses, new viruses always mutate and evolve. The development and evolution of these new diseases is closely related to the behavior of human beings. Global warming, the destruction of nature, and all of the rapid changes in our natural environment result in an increase in the mutation of these contagions. This is mother nature's way of communicating its displeasure with the destructive habits and behavior of human beings in regards to the environment. Yet, on the other hand, while it can be said that these diseases stem directly from human actions, we must also recognize that the rat is one that is attacking humankind by bringing these diseases about and therefore the rat is the one who is responsible and the one that should be held accountable. This recent Covid-19 outbreak may be due to the fact that nature is reprimanding human beings, however, the rat is also to blame because the rats have been acting out as well. It should not be overlooked that during the last 5000 years most of these infectious disease outbreaks have occurred in the year of the rat.

If your body is filled with righteous, healthy *qi* then evil, disease-ridden *qi* cannot invade the body. This is similar to the concept that a tire that is filled with air cannot be invaded by additional air due to the internal pressure. Righteous *qi* is gathered and cultivated when we take care of our own bodies and when we appreciate/respect nature. Daoists recognize that any disease, infection, or virus always seeks to attack our lungs first because the lungs are critical to our immune health. The lungs are categorized under the metal element of the five phases diagram and they are related to the tiger and cat categories of the twelve-animal zodiac. This relationship illustrates that strong, healthy lungs can fend off all types of infectious disease in the same way that strong, healthy cats can fend of all types of rats and rodents.

The way that cats breathe and purr strengthens their lungs and respiratory systems in a way that protects them from infection. It is rare for a cat to contract an infectious disease, such as swine flu or influenza, because their energy controls the rats which are the source of these diseases. Simply by imagining yourself as a cat, or imagining a cat at the point of pain on your body you can stimulate your body's immune system. This method works by using the mind to direct healing energy to where it is needed most.

The lungs are the body's first line of defense against infection because they are the organ of the human body that is responsible for interacting directly with the external environment. As we breathe in the air from the outside world, it comes in contact with the lungs first whereas the other organs such as the heart, stomach and the kidneys are safely housed with human organism. This is the reason why strengthening the lungs can help us prevent any external pathogens from gaining access to our bodies.

Rats are often looked down upon and even hated because of the tumultuous energy that they bring with them. Many people's first instinct is to attack a rat whenever they see one and we have spent a large amount of effort to control their populations and eradicate them when necessary. However, if we work with nature and harmonize ourselves with the natural world, we can avoid many of the painful experiences that accompany these great changes.

Special Abilities and Traits

Rats Are Intelligent

While rats are potent animals and sometimes bring unwanted energy with them, they are not our natural enemies and developing a respectful relationship with them can benefit us greatly. Rats have taught us a great deal throughout history and even the methods that we have developed to kill them have inspired many other great ideas. Rats are widely used in many scientific experiments and studies because of their acute senses and their high level of intelligence. Adult rats have an intelligence level equivalent to a three-year-old human being. Rats and rat type people can be seen rubbing their hands together which naturally relaxes the body and sharpens the mind. Rubbing the hands together opens up the body's *qi* meridians and allows thoughts to flow freely. When rats are seen rubbing their hands together, they are in the process of planning and strategizing.

Rats are skillful at counting and keeping track of a large amount of data. They can solve complex problems by practicing simple methods that are repeated many times. Rats gain access to many places that seem secured because they diligently gnaw at the most vulnerable materials until they create an entrance. Their teeth never degenerate and they continue to grow throughout their lifetime.

Rats can also create large complex underground burrows that allow them to remain healthy and safe. In nature, a rat's burrow always has an opening that faces toward the incoming wind currents so that they can determine the weather conditions and smell lurking predators without having to leave the burrow and expose themselves to danger. Beavers can redirect strong river currents by repeatedly placing trees and lumber at strategic locations within the muddy banks. Squirrels avoid hunger and starvation by repeated gathering, assessing, and storing their food. Rats are the animal of the zodiac that is the best at digging, calculating, and storing food.

Rats similarly recognize which aspects of a problem are changeable and have a chance of success versus what aspects are not changeable and will be a waste of effort. The rat's ability to reduce complex problems into simple steps is aided by natural synesthesia which allows them to classify data in intricate and complex ways. For example, if a rat hears a sound, or combination of sounds, they also experience a color that corresponds to that sound and rather than needing to memorize the entire sequence of sounds, they simply need to remember the color. If a rat wants to count a group of objects it does not need to count each object individually, but as it simply observes them it experiences a color that corresponds with their number. By utilizing their synesthesia in simple and clever ways, rats can develop a highly accurate intuitive ability. In the year of the rat, highly complex problems can be understood more clearly and large amounts of data can be reduced to simple ideas and solutions.

Rats Are Acutely Sensitive

Rats are highly acute animals, and their DNA suggests that they have a large number of natural abilities that allow them to escape from many situations. Rats can be seen massaging and rubbing their faces (where all of the sense organs are located) to increase their acute sensitivity and alertness. On the human body, the area of the temporal bone directly behind the ear relates to the energy of the rat. Massaging this area helps to increase memory and reduce insomnia.

Besides rubbing and massaging their faces, rats occasionally slap their faces to maintain their senses. According to the zodiac slapping is a technique that belongs to the rat. Slapping and clapping are both techniques that can be used to startle the senses into alertness. Rats are adept at using their hands to manipulate objects, test their environment, and to maintain their health. Nocturnal rodents and other animals that live close to the ground use their tactile senses a great deal, and this is what gives a mouse its air of constant scurrying activity. By contrast, a bird, which depends on sight, often limits its investigative behavior to simply turning its head and observing from a distance.

Rats have a highly acute sense of smell which allows them to determine whether food is beneficial or poisonous. Rats that die of poisoning only do so because they have been greedy and they disregarded their own intuitive ability. Rats always diligently taste and check their food before eating it or storing it away for the future. The olfactory senses of rats are even more acute than that of canines. At the White Cloud Temple, large breeds of rat were trained to detect contraband on anyone or anything that entered the monastery grounds. Rats can be trained to detect money, drugs, explosives, food items and even physical ailments.

The sensitivity of rats also allows them to predict many environmental threats and natural disasters. Rats, and especially squirrels, begin to store all of their food higher up in the trees whenever they predict that a flood or earthquake is likely to occur. Rats can predict floods, earthquakes, storms and strong winds.

In the past, rats were kept on board ships as they sailed across the oceans to predict the occurrence of storms and windy conditions. Sometimes rats would be kept on all four sides of a ship and by observing which of these rats was responding first the direction of a storm could be roughly calculated.

Rats can feel the weather and pressure systems in the same way that elderly and injured people can feel these events in their bones. There is a physical sensation that occurs in the body as the environmental conditions change. In the moments just before an earthquake rats become much more stressed and energetic often retreating to their burrows or up into the trees. By observing rats closely rather than simply fearing them we can learn a lot about ourselves and nature.

Cultural and Spiritual Concepts

The Spirituality of Rats

Rats are spiritual animals that recognize the relationships between the movements of the sun and the activities of the earth. Rats worship the sun and when they are observed closely, they can be seen gesturing to the sky and peacefully sunbathing. While rats and many rodents are nocturnal animals, they absolutely recognize the value of the sunlight. Many rats live in areas where there is limited sunlight and a large number of bacteria and disease and when these rats have the opportunity, they use the sunlight to heal themselves and clean themselves. Viruses and bacteria thrive in damp conditions and sunlight creates conditions where many diseases cannot survive.

Rats, especially rats that live in natural environments, are also conscious of ecology and nature. Rats are aware of the role that sunlight plays in maintaining the natural environment. Because they are so tactile and physically close to the earth and plant-life, they are acutely aware of the way that all living things rely on sunlight for growth and development. When Daoists recognized that rats were so spiritually aware, humble, and respectful they began to look at them as spiritual teachers and role models. Qiu Chuji, the famous Daoist monk who met with and taught Genghis Khan, would always keep a pet rat with him wherever he went to continue learning and advancing his spiritual practice.

Whenever rats travel along a path or road they always travel in the center. The middle of the road is always the safest part of the road to travel upon. It allows the rat to observe any incoming threats as quickly as possible and it allows them to observe the surrounding environment easily as they move. The middle path, as described by Buddha and Confucius, represents the connection between the large and the small, the male and the female. Rats also embody the middle path by creating big changes in events even though they are so small, solving complex problems by using simple means, and exhibiting both masculine and feminine behaviors when the situation calls for them.

Rats often hold small stones in the palm of their hand for long periods of time. This stimulates the Labor Palace (*laogong*, PC-8) point in the center of their hand which helps them to remain centered in their heart, meticulous, and diligent. Rats and squirrels can be seen placing their hand to the center of their chest to listen to their heart and remain spiritually centered. The symbol, or talisman, for the rat is a circle with a dot in the center. This symbol is used to represent the sun in western astrology and it represents a target. The 'target' symbol is a appropriate symbol for the rat because the rat is so diligent, careful, and precise with its actions. Rats maintain their awareness of their heart, they stay centered within themselves, they remain conscious of the sun's role on earth, and they understand the messages from heaven including the nature of their own destiny.

Rats escape from many dangerous situations and the more that they are attacked and killed the more that they proliferate. We can never rid ourselves of rats. They have existed for a long time before human beings. Rats can definitely live without us but we cannot live in a world without rats and the important role that they play in the ecosystem. This teaches us that we can never be completely rid of our enemies or people we do not like, therefore we must learn to avoid unnecessary confrontations and live in harmony with others. It is important for any country to build more churches and temples, and less prisons to create harmony between opposing groups that must co-exist together. The ratio of spiritual centers to correctional facilities in any region always says a great deal about the current events and social climate of the area.

The Twelve-Animal Race

Spiritually, the rat and the cockroach used to be husband and wife in a past lifetime. Now in their current incarnations they both occupy the same dark, tight spaces and they survive on the same food sources. Just as they bickered and fought in the past, they bicker and fight in the present, living in such close proximity to one another. They both admire and understand one another and yet they also fight and frustrate each other quite often. Wherever there is an environment where cockroaches are present, rats are always soon to follow and vice versa.

The rat and the cat also had a close relationship in past. The rat and the cat used to be brothers in a past life. They would come into contact with one another as they moved about in the fields and the darkness of the night. They knew that they were family and that they had many similarities and yet they would also pick on one another quite often; sometimes playfully and sometimes vengefully.

There are two versions of the legend regarding the twelve-animal race and the beginning of the feud between the rat and the cat. When the Jade Emperor decided to hold a race between all of the animals to determine which ones would represent each of the twelve earthly branches the rat and the cat both decided to arrive early to sign up. One version of the story says that the cat asked the rat to wake him up early so that they could sign up together. When the next morning came however, the rat woke up early and was so excited to sign up that he forgot to wake up the cat and instead went straight to Jade Emperor's gathering place. When the cat finally woke up and rushed to the gathering site, the race had already begun and the cat missed his opportunity.

The second version of the story says that the rat and the cat did show up at the gathering site on time and they both joined the race. When the race began the rat quickly encountered the ox and seeing how fast, capable and diligent he was the rat asked if he could ride on the ox's back if he sang to him along the way. The ox agreed and let the rat ride on his back for much of the race.

When the ox came to the river crossing however, the cat was already there waiting at the shore trying to figure out how to cross the river without getting wet. So, the cat asked the ox if he would help carry him to the other side of the river along with the rat. The ox, always wanting to be helpful, agreed and began ferrying the two animals across the river. However, the rat, knowing the competitive and mischievous nature of the cat recognized that the cat would try to win at any cost and that he would sabotage him at some point. So halfway across the river, before the cat could react, the rat pushed the cat into the water and continued riding the ox to the riverbank. The rat went on to finish the race, but by the time the cat got to the finish line all of the twelve winning places had been taken. In both versions of the story the cat was so upset with the rat that he hated him ever since and tried to kill him whenever he saw him.

There are also two versions of the way in which the rat ended up winning the race to become the first animal of the zodiac. The first says that the rat rode on the back of the ox all the way until the last step before the finish line, but in that moment the rat leapt off the top of the ox's head and won the race by the smallest margin. In the second version of the story, the rat rode the on the ox's back all the way to the finish line and they crossed together with the ox winning first place. After the race was finished however, the Jade Emperor threw a celebration to congratulate the participants. At the party there was a large cake with a single candle on the top, sensing danger the rat quickly leapt toward the cake and used his strong teeth to bite into the side of the candle. The candle immediately began leaking an oily substance and it was later realized that the candle was a disguised explosive device that was meant to harm the Jade Emperor.

Upon witnessing this incredible act of bravery and selflessness the Jade Emperor declared that the first year of the zodiac would commemorate the rat and the ox would take second place instead. Both versions of the story illustrate the way in which the rat is able to guide the hard-working ox and help him to direct his efforts, but only the second version of the story is able to depict the selflessness, alertness, and acute sensitivity of the rat. The rat won first place because he was able to take effective action and adapt when he saw that it was necessary.

People Who Embody the Rat

The people who embody the rat spirit often have a slim body, a long face, strong teeth, and a seemingly frantic or hurried nature. Rat people may be fidgety, tapping their feet or rubbing their hands. They usually have intense, engaging *qi*, good mental focus and a blissful personality. They always make an effort to adjust themselves so that they are in harmony with their environment and the people they are with. Rat people are good at preparing for the future by practicing delayed gratification and being attentive, focused, and diligent with their actions. Rats are mindful of themselves regarding each action as an investment in the future. The rat's motto is to "avoid conflict, be determined, and preserver."

Rat people like to collect things, store things, and invest in the future. We use the term "pack rat" to describe a person who has made a habit of storing many things just in case they may need them. The future mindedness of rat people makes them good investors in all types of businesses and ventures. Rats are skillful at managing people and meeting deadlines; they know how to organize and direct complex projects. Rats and people who embody the rat spirit are also punctual, and keep a strict schedule. Woodchucks for instance have such a strong biological clock that it is almost impossible to disturb. Their hibernation ends abruptly on February 2nd (Scott 1972, 26).

People with rat energy recognize that while money and resources are necessary to prepare for the future, reliability and hard work are the keys to achieving greatness. For all of these reasons, rats are regarded as signs of fortune and wealth. Many large companies have also used the symbolism of the rat to great benefit. The Disney corporation has always had Mickey Mouse as its mascot and Target department stores have adopted the rat talisman as their company logo.

Rat people contemplate complex issues which helps them to develop great intelligence. Eventually this also leads to the contemplation of spiritual issues and they develop a strong faith over the course of their lifetime. Their intelligence and faith also lead to the development of a strong intuition and an ability to sense the correct path or answer. Rat people are good in relationships, they are people pleasers and they are sociable, but they should be mindful of distractions. The future, complex issues, business, and enjoyment can occupy much of their attention so sometimes rat people must make a conscious effort to prioritize their close relationships. Rat people should also take time once and awhile to rest deeply, meditate and recuperate their energy because they expend so much of it in their frantic day-to-day activities.

External Zodiac
Elephant

The rat and the elephant are a unique pair because the rat is smallest animal of the zodiac and the elephant is the largest. While the rat may be the smallest animal in the zodiac it's *qi* contains the power of the elephant and cause massive changes. The elephant is also sensitive, humble, and intelligent in a way that is similar to the rat. The elephant is massive in size but it is a vegetarian creature that does not attack unless it is threatened. This also demonstrates the fact that muscle mass and body size can be developed with a vegetarian diet, for many people, meat is not a dietary requirement or it can be eaten in small amounts.

The *jia zi* year that the is represented by the rat is a year of great, massive changes in the world and the individual. What seems like a small issue in the beginning, can result in vast changes in the lifestyle of every creature. The Covid-19 virus, for instance, is a small, microscopic virus and yet it brought about a massive change on the planet in 2020. Similarly, in 1984, another rat year, the AIDS virus pandemic began, which also impacted the lives of millions. The famous taiji symbol that represents the energies of yin and yang can also be understood to illustrate a rat and the head of an elephant. These two animals go hand in hand with one another.

Elephants and rats are and inner and outer pair and this means that they are both partners and enemies depending on the context and perspective. Elephants are naturally afraid of rats. Elephants cannot be controlled by the fiercest of animals including the tiger. When a tiger approaches an elephant, the tiger becomes intimidated and confused at the elephant's massive size and when they attack, the elephant often thinks that the tiger is trying to play a game and have fun rather than be aggressive. The tiger's attacks have little to no effect on a fully grown elephant. A rat however, can have detrimental effects on a large elephant. As rats scurry across the ground elephants may step on them and slip or fall. Elephants carry seventy five percent of their total weight in the front half of their body. This makes their balance precarious which accounts for their slow and careful movements.

Elephants have developed air pockets within parts of their skull to lighten the load on the front half of their frame and it has been discovered that most of the neurons in the brain of an elephant are located in the cerebellum to help the elephant to coordinate its movements. A slip or a fall is a dangerous situation for an elephant because it is difficult for an elephant to get back up once it has fallen over and if they happen to injury themselves or land in a muddy area they may be stuck and the fall could be fatal.

Rats are also small enough to fit inside of an elephant's trunk which can be quite unpleasant and injurious for the large creature. In a severe case this can also prove fatal because the elephants rely greatly upon the use of their trunk. Elephants are also smart enough to recognize that the rat is a carrier of disease and if the rat finds its way into a sensitive area of the elephant it can cause infections and massive damage. While elephants are not afraid of the rat's attitude or intentions, it does recognize the potential damage that the rat can cause if its power is not recognized and respected.

The rat and the elephant represent the smallest and the largest animals of the zodiac and their category represents both the beginning and the end of the zodiac cycle. The time of the rat (11 pm to 1 am) represents both the end of one day and the beginning of the next. This is the turning point of the zodiac and the beginning of a new chapter in the world. Just like the ones and zeros of binary code and the yin and yang energies, the beginning and the end represent the foundation of all of the events that are to come throughout the zodiac cycle. This is part of the foundation of the *Yijing* and forms the context of the changes that unfold throughout the next twelve years.

Qi

The size and strength of the elephant is an example of the fact in some ways size truly does matter in the world. The massive size of the elephant is enough to keep predators at bay and allow them to move easily through thick jungle and forests. Elephants are even strong enough to uproot strong, healthy trees. A strong foundation is a essential asset for all creatures. The ability to remain stable in most situations is extremely useful. Elephants are unique in that they continue to grow larger throughout their life, therefore older elephants, especially the males, are significantly larger than their younger counterparts. Elephants grow both larger and wiser with age.

Elephants rely a great deal on the strength of their knees and they actively work to maintain the health of their leg joints. Strong healthy legs contribute to the strong foundation of the elephant and they help the elephant avoid dangerous missteps and falls. When elephants lay down, they begin slowly lowering themselves in the rear by bending their knees until they reach the ground. The ability to bend the knees slowly throughout its full range is a sign of great health. The knees are essential when it comes to longevity and the health of the elephant's knees contributes to their long lifespans. The knees of human beings are also essential when it comes to health and longevity.

In China, the bent human knee is sometimes referred to as the "elephant's head" partly because it resembles and elephant's head and partly because elephants are so good at maintaining the strength and function of their knees. When the aging process begins in human beings it first begins to show itself in the function of the knees. Once a person's knees begin to show signs of injury, pain, and stiffness, the aging process has begun. To combat this, it is important for people to strike their knees with the bottoms of the fists. This technique can greatly benefit health and longevity in any individual especially the elderly by helping them to move forward in their life, literally and figuratively. By striking the "elephant's head" the bones, muscles, and tendons of the knee become stronger according to the principle of Wolff's law and this in turn tightens up the muscles of both the upper and lower leg. This increases mobility, energy, blood oxygenation and allows the individual to continue living normally and protecting their longevity. Over time this technique can also treat any pain or injuries that are found in the knee area as well.

Special Abilities and Traits

Elephants are intelligent and sensitive creatures. They have excellent memories and they are emotionally intelligent. Elephants form strong emotional bonds with their family and with their herd. Just like the rat, elephants are highly social animals. Most herds are comprised of females only and are led by the matriarch, which is the eldest female. Males only joint the herd temporarily when one or more of the females is sexually receptive. Males travel in their own small groups when they are younger and become more solitary as they begin to age. Yet, all elephants join together to protect their young from predators.

Elephants also watch out for one another. They always appoint a number of lookout elephants to watch for danger as they bath and switch places when they are finished. To assist them in their duties and in their herd functions elephants have a wide variety of ways in which they can communicate with one another including vocalizations, posturing, and foot stamping. When they suffer loss elephants feel the emotions deeply. They have been known to suffer depression for extended periods of time due to the loss of a loved one and they have even been observed holding funeral ceremonies.

Elephants also have an acute sense of smell that is similar to that of a rat. Elephants cannot necessarily smell scents from a long distance the way that other animals can but they can differentiate between many different scents and they can use this to help them determine which plants are the best for them and which are unhealthy. In a metaphorical sense, elephants also have the ability to understand when something doesn't seem, or smell, right. Elephants, especially older elephants, have a strong intuitive ability to sense approaching danger and natural disasters. In Daoism, dried elephant dung has been burned as a form of incense in certain ceremonies due to its unique *qi* energy. This practice has many functions that range from boosting health to honoring the gods.

Cultural and Spiritual Concepts

For thousands of years, the elephant has been worshiped as a god of money and wealth. The Chinese depict elephants carrying a large golden weight or standing on gold coins, symbolizing the relationship between wealth and accomplishing challenging tasks. It is a symbol of protection, luck, wisdom, wealth, success, fertility, and strength. The character for "elephant," *xiang*, sounds quite like the word for "prosperity": the two ideas are closely related. Also, water is a symbol for money and wealth, and the elephant's ability to suck up vast amounts of water in its trunk is yet another sign of its ability to gather wealth and prosperity. Similar to this, people of India worship the god Ganesha as a bringer of prosperity, new beginnings, success, and wealth. The Hindu tradition even contains the idea that the spiritual vehicle or mount that carries and assists the deity is a mouse.

When God asked King Solomon what he would like in return for having strong faith and acting righteously, he requested an "understanding heart." By asking for wisdom, rather than any form of measurable wealth or gain, Solomon demonstrated his worth and was granted immense wealth and long life as well as great wisdom (1 Kings 3: 5-14). Elephants generate abundance and wealth in much the same way. By focusing their efforts on building relationships and helping each other, they develop generous and sensitive emotions. The heart-centered understanding they develop throughout is largely responsible for their long lives and their close communities.

Quotes from Famous Rats

We can only see a short distance ahead, but we can see plenty there that needs to be done.

- Alan Turing

All men dream, but not equally. Those who dream by night in the dusty recesses of their minds wake in the day to find that it was vanity, but the dreamers of the day are dangerous men for they may act upon their dreams with open eyes, to make them possible.

- T.E. Lawrence

Success isn't always about greatness. It's about consistency. Consistent hard work leads to success. Greatness will come.

- Dwayne Johnson

We live in this world to to always to learn industriously and to enlighten each other by means of discussion and to strive vigorously to promote the progress of science and the fine arts.

- Wolfgang Amadeus Mozart

The path to success is to take massive determined action.

- Tony Robbins

We can't fix all problems but we must fix the ones we can.

- Paul David Hewson (Bono)

I have learned over the years that when one's mind is made up, this diminishes fear. Knowing what must be done does away with fear.

- Rosa Parks

Privacy is not something that I'm merely entitled to, it's an absolute prere-quisite.

- Marlon Brando

There is no darkness but ignorance.

- William Shakespeare

When desire dies, fear is born.

- Baltasar Gracián

Love, having no geography, knows no boundaries.

- Truman Capote

2

Ox

Wood Ox
24th January 1925 to 12th February 1926

Fire Ox
11th February 1937 to 30th January 1938

Earth Ox
29th January 1949 to 16th February 1950

Metal Ox
15th February 1961 to 4th February 1962

Water Ox
3rd February 1973 to 22nd January 1974

Wood Ox
20th February 1985 to 8th February 1986

Fire Ox
7th February 1997 to 27th January 1998

Earth Ox
26th January 2009 to 13th February 2010

Metal Ox
12 February 2021 to 31st January 2022

Water Ox
31st January 2033 to 18th February 2034

Wood Ox
17th February 2045 to 5th February 2046

Fire Ox
4th February 2057 to 24th January 2058

Ox

The ox category includes the cow, bull, water buffalo, hippopotamus, rhinoceros, yak, and many other similar animals. Oxen are strong, loyal, generous, sincere, hard-working, diligent, determined, enduring, down-to-earth, resolute, and practical animals. However, at times, they can also be stubborn, tyrannical, micromanaging, and temperamental. They spend most of their time grazing, traveling, exercising, working hard, and resting. Oxen are usually quite calm and peaceful, although they are temperamental and can become angry quite easily.

Oxen are caring and emotionally sensitive creatures with deep and complex emotions. They form strong bonds with other cows, and they enjoy rubbing and licking each other to express their affection. They are also deeply affected by negative and traumatizing experiences, the results of which can be observed for days or even weeks after the event. Oxen gladly give what they have to others that are in need. Female cows allow calves that are not their own to suckle to nurture the herd. Their maternal, protective instinct seems to extend to the entire herd as well. Cows are quite friendly and social animals, and they socialize with a few of their close friends.

Oxen are usually healthy and strong. They have vigorous immune systems and they can maintain health even when disease is prevalent. They endure stressful and dangerous situations by remaining strong, healthy, and unshakable. Oxen mainly inhabit large, open fields, grasslands, and prairies, where they can graze slowly and easily see any approaching predators. Oxen were domesticated between approximately 5000 to 4000 BCE, and these animals have been incredibly important to human beings ever since. Oxen are wonderful providers and they have provided food, materials, and energy for human beings for many centuries.

Oxen have a wide variety of societal and mating behaviors. Most of the societal groups are not highly structured, and females prefer to mate with dominate males. Often, the herds of females with their young are led by a matriarch, and followed by smaller groups of bachelor males, who battle for dominance but not with a deadly fervor. Oxen bicker and fight quite often to establish dominance but they do not like to fight with a killer intention. Oxen have large hearts, both literally and figuratively, and they prefer a calm, loving, environment where their herds can remain safe and peaceful.

Oxen are environmentally friendly creatures. When they graze, they only eat the part of the plant that is visible above the surface, leaving the root system intact so that the grasses can easily be regrown. Oxen are ruminant animals that chew and swallow their food multiple times in order extract the highest amount of nutrients possible. This process is time consuming but it allows these animals to survive in places where there are not many sources of food, such as deserts and scrublands. The process of rumination allows these creatures to digest the cellulose of plants, which makes up a large amount of the plant energy and is indigestible by most other animals, including mammals. Oxen are therefore able to gain large amounts of mass and strength without the need to eat meat.

The creatures in the ox category are also an essential food source for large predators and human beings throughout the world. The *qi* of plants, flowers, and grasses which oxen require helps these animals to develop luck, intelligence, and acute perception. Oxen also need to eat quite a bit of salt because the plants that make up the majority of their diet are low in sodium and, therefore, they need to find external sources of this nutrient.

Calendar

The ox is the second animal of the zodiac. It is associated with the twelfth month of the Chinese lunar calendar that lasts from approximately January 6th to February 4th in the Gregorian calendar and to the two-hour period between 1 am and 3 am. The ox earned the second place in the zodiac because of its work ethic, strength, selflessness, generosity, and intelligence.

The ox is the animal that governs all types of work and production. Oxen have been helping human beings perform heavy duty and laborious tasks for thousands of years, and this in turn has allowed humanity to develop new technologies and societal advancements at a rapid pace. The strength of oxen has been utilized in agriculture, architecture, logging, hauling, and milling. In the modern era, human beings rely on engines, machines, and hydraulics to helps us transport, manipulate, process, destroy, and construct many things that are too heavy or too labor intensive for a single individual or even a group of individuals. In the past, however, these tasks were always performed by oxen with the aid of ropes, pulleys, and leverage. After agriculture first began roughly 12,000 years ago, oxen were quickly recognized as a valuable resource that could help till the soil and cultivate the land.[1]

Multiple cultures throughout the world recognized the value of the ox independently from Mesopotamia to China, the Mediterranean, and Europe. The value that oxen provided to the process of farming allowed human beings to cultivate crops, eventually leading to the development of many new varieties and breeds. This close relationship to plant-life means that, in the year of the ox, many plants and flowers flourish. The year of the ox is commonly a year with a rich harvest and strong agriculture. Oxen have also been crucial in the hauling of lumber and construction materials throughout the world, making the year of the ox a year where construction and manual labor thrive.

The year of the ox is a great year to begin any ambitious construction projects or remodeling of buildings. These types of projects will often be required, as many issues that remained hidden or manageable in buildings and structures

---

[1] "How Agriculture and Domestication Began," by The Editors of Encyclopedia Britannica (1999). www.britannica.com/topic/agriculture/How-agriculture-and-domestication-began

until this year now require attention and repairs. The year of the ox is not a year where many benefits and accolades come without effort, but nonetheless it is a year of great strides and progress. This is a year where determination and hard work are required to accomplish goals; if the right effort is made, the hard work will be highly successful. In 1961, for instance, after years of effort and research, Yuri Gagarin became the first human being to travel into space, setting a milestone in the space race and in human history.[2]

Teamwork can also be highly successful in the year of the ox, as long as the other members of the team keep up with the ox's strong work ethic. Oxen work well as part of a team, as long as their progress and momentum are not hampered by others. This means that in the year of the ox members of society must keep up with ongoing energy and extensive change. Laziness is not tolerated in any arena in the year of the ox.

This is a year when to-do lists, organization, and simple planning methods come in handy. The busy and hurried nature of the year means that many small details can be forgotten. However, this is not a good year for complex planning or over-thinking. Dee Hock, the founder and former CEO of the Visa credit card company, once said "Simple, clear purpose and principles give rise to complex and intelligent behavior. Complex rules and regulations give rise to simple and stupid behavior" (Allen 2015, 68). Similarly, oxen prefer to develop simple, straight-forward plans and quickly move into the action phase of accomplishing the tasks that they have set out for themselves.

The emphasis on effort and hard work during this year means that rest and a proper diet are also essential. While oxen like to work hard during the daylight hours, when the work of the day is finished, oxen like to eat a large meal and go to bed early. Oxen really enjoy eating and they can eat quite a lot. Oxen do not eat meat, and therefore meat, especially beef, should be consumed quite sparingly in the year of the ox unless it is being eaten as a form of medicine. This leads to better health, strength, and emotional stability. Oxen also usually sleep deeply at night as a consequence of their vast energy output during the day. Developing a schedule, especially a sleep schedule and/or a meal planning schedule, is greatly beneficial during ox years. Oxen like to accomplish their goals methodically, one step at a time, and this includes the goals of proper rest and nourishment.

The year of the ox is usually a good year for the economy, where steady progress can be made. The ox year of 1961, for instance, marked the beginning of the longest economic growth period (100 months) that the United States had experienced up until that time (Shiskin 1970, 101-12). Saving and investing in low-risk investments are strong strategies in the year of the ox. The oxen prefer safe, stable routes rather than risky shortcuts because they value the money and resources that they have had to work so hard to earn.

---

[2] "Yuri Gagarin," by The Editors of Encyclopedia Britannica (1999). www.britannica.com/topic/agriculture/How-agriculture-and-domestication-began

Markets are considered trustworthy and attract investors when they are not volatile. This is one of the main reasons why a thriving, growing economy is called a "bull market." In fact, there are quite a lot of financial institutions that have utilized the symbol of the bull in many ways. The "golden calf" or "golden bull" has been recognized and worshiped as a symbol of wealth in many cultures throughout the world for thousands of years. The golden ox represents all types of economics and market forces that form the foundation of the financial and business worlds.

The safe, stable nature of oxen also make them good providers. Oxen like to manage their own households and they are good protectors and providers for their family. They prefer to make the rules in their living situations, but because they are so loyal to their loved ones, they will always be sure to take their needs and wants into account. For instance, the Fourth Geneva Convention was agreed upon in the ox year of 1949, which detailed the rules and guidelines for the treatment of "protected persons" or persons that are not participating in hostilities during times of armed conflict.

The convention also sought to restrict the means and methods of warfare as a way of mitigating the trauma of war. It states that International Humanitarian law must be founded on the principles of humanity, impartiality, and neutrality. The convention was called in response to the atrocities that were committed against civilians during World War II, in violation of the rules established by past conventions, and it has since become recognized as international law to all nations.[3]

Personal relationships in the year of the ox usually strengthen through teamwork and the recognition of one another's accomplishments. However, the ox is also quite temperamental, so many relationships may also be fraught with arguments and bickerin. Then again, the ox's loyalty and sympathetic nature usually keep these fights from developing into serious issues. If arguments become too volatile and emotions begin to flare during this year, taking a break and separating yourself from the situation for a few moments is usually the best strategy. When a bull sees red, any further action usually only causes more frustration, but given enough time, oxen quickly calm down.

While oxen deeply value their work ethic and their career, they also like to spend their free time enjoying the fruits of their labor. In the year of the ox, it is important to make sure to rest, relax, and make the effort to spend time with your loved ones. Going on a vacation or enjoying yourself once in a while allows the mind to digest the progress that you have recently made in your life, reorient yourself, establish new goals, and visualize your meaning and purpose from your new perspective. When work is taken seriously, the time and energy that you can spend on yourself and those closest to you becomes more valuable and more enjoyable.

---

[3] "Humanity in War," by American Red Cross Contributors (2011). www.redcross.org/ihl

Qi

The Chinese double-hour related to the ox is between 1 am and 3 am, the time of the liver meridian. This is the time when the small intestine is least active and resting. At the White Cloud Temple, the monks never eat any solid food past 1 pm in the afternoon and many other nutritionists recommend avoiding eating at night. This is because, during the ox time, the small intestine should be empty so that it can rest and gather energy. When the small intestine is allowed to rest properly the immune system is regulated and tuned, the body is allowed to detoxify itself, and longevity is developed. This is also the time when the body is focusing on the liver function to detox the blood and allow the mind to process its tasks.

The liver governs our conscious mind and our emotions, so when we sleep deeply during these two hours our psyche is allowed to detoxify itself as well as our blood. The energy of strong emotions, such as anger and frustration, are stored in the liver until they can be released or until the information that they may provide can be integrated into our schema. The subconscious processing of these emotions, as well as the thoughts and events of the previous day, occurs during the ox time while we sleep. This is also known as the "ugly time" because if you were to wake up and look into the mirror at this time, your face would appear more gaunt, dark, and dull than normal. This is due to the fact that as the liver is activated, it draws the blood of the body inward from the face and extremities toward itself to be detoxified. This is also known as the winter of the day when activity should be at its minimum, energy should be recuperated, and resources should be stored away for the spring.

The ghost point that is associated with the ox is known as Ghost's Fortress (*guilei*); it matches the point called Hidden Whiteness (*yinbai*, SP-1) in the acupuncture system (Johnson 2014, 605). It is located on the dorsal aspect of the big toe at the junction of the lines drawn along the medial border of the nail and its base. Its function is to store and save *qi* for later use. Stimulating it can also help with fatigue, excessive sweating, thirst, tightness of the chest, fainting, as well as calming and clearing the mind (Deadman et al. 2007, 182).

The ox is the animal that immediately follows the rat in the zodiac, and the rat is responsible for all infectious diseases. When a pandemic strikes, it not only causes physical harm through infection, it also causes a great amount of stress because even with all of our modern knowledge and tools, vaccinations are still not able to catch up with the rapid mutations that take place with diseases and viral strains. Viruses are so small that they cannot be seen with the naked eye, which makes them difficult to contain. This means that even while we rely on our modern medical advancements, we must also be aware and responsible for the strength of our own immune systems. The *qi* of the ox helps the world recover from the detriments of pandemics and infectious diseases. Ox *qi* is strong and healthy because oxen work hard to maintain their health and support their immunity.

The smallpox virus has existed for thousands of years and it has been the source of many deadly epidemics throughout history. For a long time, there was no method of treatment for this disease. In China, during the Song dynasty (960-1279 AD), a rudimentary method of vaccination was developed where the clothes of infected individuals would be collected and given to uninfected individuals so that they could be exposed to a mild form of the virus and begin to develop immunity. This process was advanced and effective for the time, but it also carried inherent risks, including further spread of the disease.

It wasn't until the eighteenth century that a British physician named Edward Jenner developed the world's first vaccine that the disease finally became manageable. Jenner hypothesized that the cowpox virus was closely related to the smallpox virus, given their similar appearance and symptoms, even though cowpox is much less virulent. After further research, he realized that milkmaids that were exposed to the cowpox virus were also much less likely to be affected by smallpox, and thus he began developing his first vaccination.

The first vaccination was administered when Jenner scraped the pus from blisters of a cow infected with cowpox and injected it into a young boy. This eventually led to the development of the field of immunology.[4] This is just one example of the way in which oxen help and serve human beings. Oxen help human beings to carry burdens, literally and figuratively, so that both of our species can flourish. Just like oxen, "herd immunity" is an essential concept for human beings as well.

While the rat is mainly a nocturnal creature that hides in the shadows, oxen are usually awake only during daylight hours and they work in the sunshine all day long. Sunlight is essential to oxen, as it is a major contributing factor to their health and immunity. As human beings begin to come out of their homes and spend more time in the sunlight after the rat year, their immunity is increased and the prevalence of infectious diseases is reduced. Vitamin D supplements alone do not affect the brain or bone density to a great degree, but when vitamin D is obtained through sunlight, we obtain the full benefits of this nutrient. The back of the body is especially good at utilizing and storing the energy of sunlight. Oxen often graze with their backs to the sun to simultaneously gather sunlight. The thoracic vertebrae benefit greatly from exposure to sunlight, which reduces insomnia, brain atrophy, and memory loss.

While the rat makes us recognize the seriousness of disease and the consequences of our actions, oxen teach us that through responsibility, loyalty, determination, and respect we can have a direct influence on our destiny and the world around us. Daoists view pandemics as a form of punishment from heaven for the misdeeds of human beings. When we disrespect nature, pollute the

---

4 "Edward Jenner and the History of Smallpox and Vaccination," by Stefan Riedel (2005). https://www.ncbi.nlm.nih.gov/pmc/articles/PMC1200696/

environment, destroy the oceans, and interfere with nature, pandemics occur more often and with greater veracity. On the other hand, when we take responsibility for our actions, respect nature and stop polluting, then we reduce the occurrence of these devastating events and develop a harmonious way to survive with nature.

When we develop the perspective and forthright attitude of the ox, we regain normality and stability. The *qi* of the ox rises upward. This means that as the energy of disease, minutia, stress, mania, and upheaval of the year of the rat recedes, the energy of serenity, freedom, and strength arises. The economy will grow in the year of the ox as people eagerly, yet cautiously, seek to earn and spend money.

The oxen energy also encourages us to enjoy more simple pleasures like eating and resting. Oxen love to eat and gather a lot of beneficial *qi* from their diet. Grasses that are both green and yellow are quite lucky, especially financially, and plants and flowers that have large and/or round leaves contain energy that is helpful with managing and investing money. When we eat a diet that contains a lot of leafy greens, our health, energy, and quality of life benefit greatly. Leafy greens help our liver to detoxify itself and they help the tendons and sinews of the body to develop great strength and flexibility.

Oxen are known for their incredible strength, which is directly related to their diet and the superior liver function that they develop as a result. The fact that oxen have such strong muscles and tendons means that eating beef, especially beef tendon, helps to heal the muscle and tendon damage in our own bodies and develop strength in these areas as well. While eating a healthy and hefty diet helps us to restore energy and develop strength, we should also be mindful that overeating can lead to negative consequences as well. Traditional Chinese medicine, for instance, explains the occurrence of diabetes as the simple result of overeating. If a person is diabetic, reducing the amount of food that they eat is recommended.

Proper rest is also important for recovering the energy that is spent during laborious tasks. Oxen go to bed quite early and usually wake up early in the morning, eager to get outside and get moving. Oxen usually sleep with their legs bent underneath themselves, which protects their joints and maintains their mobility. It is healthy for people to sleep with their joints bent as well, preferably in the fetal position. This not only protects the joints and flexibility but it also helps the inner organs to store their energy much more efficiently during sleep.

The strength and endurance of the ox allows them to travel great distances. Oxen are intelligent creatures and they have a wonderful sense of direction. Once an ox has learned a route, they remember it easily and with great detail. Laozi famously rode backwards on an ox throughout China, trusting it to know the way without direction. Horses have been valued for their ability to travel with great speed, and although oxen are much slower, they are also careful and steady as they move, they can carry greater loads, and they swim easily across rivers and small lakes, whereas horses can only wade up to their necks. The horns of oxen were used to carry things as well on long journeys. While traveling on his ox facing backwards, Laozi would use the ox's wide, flat rump as a table to write on and he would hang his scrolls, particularly the *Dao De Jing*, on the ox's long horns. Ox *qi* is strong, practical, enduring, intelligent, and generous.

Special Abilities and Traits

Oxen are Intelligent

Oxen have a good sense of memory. As stated earlier, oxen can follow directions well and they can remember the way back to their home easily. While oxen don't like to over-think or over-plan when it comes to the practical details of various tasks, they do think about any problems that they encounter quite deeply. Just as oxen ruminate their food to digest it thoroughly, they also ruminate over ideas and concepts, usually during their down time, to fully digest information. If an ox recognizes that it is unable to figure out a logical or intellectual problem, then they think it through deeply before acting on it.

Oxen have a strong and stable mindset, and once they find a pathway or method through a difficult area they rely on their tried-and-true method until it no longer works. Oxen do not shy away from difficult tasks either, whether they require mental or physical solutions. They push through all of their obstacles with determination and patience. Oxen usually avoid trying novel methods to accomplish their goals and always search for the most practical, no-nonsense solution. Oxen live for approximately 40 years on average and as they grow older, they develop a deep sense of wisdom and serenity.

Oxen represent practice and diligence. Many people who are hard workers used to be oxen in their past lifetimes. One of the deeper reasons that Laozi rode an ox, rather than another animal, was that oxen represent successful practicing and the virtue of hard work. In ancient China, it was said that the emperor was the ox of the people due to how hard they worked for the country. The diligence and sincere attitude that oxen used to practice allows them to develop their abilities and intelligence at a steady pace. Oxen may need to ruminate on an idea for a while before they fully understand it, but once they understand a concept fluently and deeply, they incorporate it into their worldview so that it will not be easily forgotten. Through the process of patient contemplation, oxen have developed the ability to teach themselves without the aid of instructors. This is only one way in which oxen and human beings are similar to one another.

Oxen are Perceptive

Oxen have eyes that are located on the sides of their head and they can rotate them a full 360 degrees. This means that oxen can look behind themselves with little effort, only a slight head tilt is necessary. Since oxen spend most of their time in large, open fields, this extremely wide range of vision allows them to easily observe many directions and see any approaching danger from a great distance. Daoists say that you can tell the depth and intelligence of a person by the quality of the brightness in their eyes. Oxen have clear eyes that illustrate their sincerity, intelligence, sensitivity, depth, and compassion. Oxen can be seen staring at the moon during the night. By staring at the moon, oxen gather the lunar *qi* to protect and cultivate their eyes.

Oxen have tongues that can taste with great detail. Oxen have 30,000 taste buds, which is about three times as many as a human being (Bell 1959, 1071-79). The acute gustatory sense of cows is helpful in distinguishing poisonous plants from nutritious ones. According to Tradition Chinese Medicine, the rich sense of taste that cows and oxen possess also means that they are skilled with matters of the heart. In the east, it has been known for centuries that the heart, just like the brain, is an organ that perceives and thinks. In fact, these two organs are often seen as a single unit known as the heart-mind.

The tongue, according to TCM, is the organ that is the external opening of the heart, allowing the heart to express itself to the outside world. It is referred to as the "manager of the heart." The fact that oxen have so many taste buds means that they can distinguish matters of the heart with great clarity. Each bite that an ox takes provides them with a rich, vibrant experience. Oxen experience more richness and detail in each moment than humans.

Along with their acute sense of taste they also have a acute sense of smell. Usually, animals that keep their heads down near the ground develop good olfactory senses, and oxen are no different. Oxen can perceive scents from a distance of over 6km. This is a skill that contributes to their wonderful sense of direction, their perception of predators, and their ability to distinguish plants that are nutritious from ones that are harmful.

Overall, the acute senses of oxen allow them to separate that which is useful from that which is harmful physically and that which is correct from that which is incorrect mentally. In the twelve-animal zodiac, oxen are related to the liver primarily and to the stomach secondarily, both of which are organs of the body that help to separate what is necessary from what is harmful or not necessary. The liver detoxes the blood by removing latent toxins, and the stomach breaks down food material into a more readily usable material to be differentiated by the spleen and the rest of the digestive system.

Cultural and Spiritual Concepts

Generous and Selfless

Oxen are similar to human beings in their behaviors, desires, and attitudes. Oxen, like many human beings, enjoy working hard, testing their strength, and accomplishing goals. They have flourished throughout the world because they have been greatly valued by mankind. Their service to others has led them to develop wonderful prosperity. Their strong work ethic and no-nonsense approach to life is something to admire and emulate. Oxen do not only sacrifice their energy and labor, they also sacrifice their milk, their hides, and their flesh. When we develop the selfless qualities of the ox, we benefit both as a society and as individuals.

The fact that oxen spend their entire lives serving humankind allows them to work through their past karma rapidly. Oxen are so close to human beings, spiritually speaking, that Daoists consider both species to be nearly identical. In the Chinese creation myth, after the goddess Niwa plugged the great hole in the heavens, she created both men and oxen from the same mud of the earth. This alludes to the deep relationship and similar purpose that is shared by both men and oxen. Just as Adam and Eve were told that they must survive on the earth by the sweat of their brow, so too must oxen. Therefore, oxen and human beings are allies and our destinies are intertwined.

Human beings and oxen are so close to each other in the eyes of nature that after oxen die, they are often reincarnated as human beings in their next life. Oxen are loyal and repay any kindness that they are shown or debts that they may owe. When an animal is approaching the level where they can be reincarnated as a human being, they may first appear as an ox as a way of clearing up lingering karmic issues. Also, if a human being dies while having any lingering debts or minor unresolved past mistakes, they may be reincarnated as an ox their next life order to clear up these issues before they can come back again as a human being.

Oxen are symbols of wealth, prosperity, and generosity. In Eastern culture, it is known that cats are symbols of wealth, yet oxen are also known as a symbol of great wealth in a slightly different way. While cats are symbols of gathering wealth from loans, donations, or wherever it may be found, oxen are a symbol of generating wealth from your own efforts and hard work. Bulls hold their head high and they strike upward with their horns from a low position illustrating their natural tendency to rise upward toward heaven. Ox *qi*, in general, ascends past adversity and upward toward heaven. The ox, like the other animals of the zodiac, holds a heavenly position. The ox's responsibility is to regulate the effects of infectious diseases by helping human beings prosper through sincerity, endurance, hard work, and virtue.

The Empathy of the Ox

Oxen use their strength to protect society and their loved ones from harm and catastrophe. They use their physical strength to create strong safe homes for themselves and their family, and they also use their strength and compassion to defend others from danger and violence. When a predator attempts to attack a herd of cattle, the bulls confront it by standing between the predator and the cows and calves. The self-sacrificing nature of oxen gives them great courage in the face of danger.

In traditional Chinese medicine, the oxen represent both the liver and the stomach. Both of these organs are integral parts of the body's immune system, and their function is to protect the body from both internal and external pathogens. This is just like the way in which oxen protect their herd from danger, whether it is from predators, stress, or environmental conditions. The liver is responsible for managing the body's emotions and stress, and when members of the herd become stressed, other oxen do their best to soothe them. Oxen recognize the importance of friendship and they are wonderful examples of camaraderie, loyalty, and teamwork.

The liver and the stomach are both organs that make use of and control water. The liver, which represents the wood element, is nourished by water. The stomach, which represents the earth element, stores, and controls water. This means that the ox is considered a natural guardian against floods and a protector of waterways. In China, many reservoirs, dams, and waterways have a statue of an ox nearby to protect the aquatic infrastructure. Oxen sincerely enjoy and thrive on water, even more than many other land animals. This is also another explanation of why oxen are such good swimmers.

The horns of the ox are special, and they allow them to perceive a variety of phenomenon. The rhinoceros, which is also a member of the ox zodiac category, has a small canal within their horn that runs from the tip to the base and allows it to sense variations in pressure and vibrations. Most other members of the ox category can sense phenomena with their horns in a similar manner. This means that oxen often know in advance when bad weather is approaching and they can sense where their herd is located if they get separated. The horns of the ox allow them to have an intuitive ability to sense approaching danger or which pathways are fraught with difficulty.

The horns of the ox can pierce the veil of heaven, allowing the ox to understand heaven's will. For example, oxen know in advance when they are about to die, even if there are no external signs to allude to that fact. When a rancher decides that an ox is to be slaughtered, even if this decision is made a great distance away, the animal will immediately begin to cry out and crouch down on its legs to avoid its fate. Ox *qi* rises up to heaven and inspires spiritual principles wherever it appears. This allows the ox to be a helpful tool, not just for human beings, but for heavenly beings as well.

Many cultures have used the horns of oxen as instruments to blow through to create musical tones, usually for the purpose of sending signals to others either while traveling or on the battlefield. This sense of signaling and warning is similar to the spiritual intuitive ability that the oxen have developed naturally, as their horns send and receive signals across vast distances. The horns of oxen are not only used to signal danger; they are also used during holidays and ceremonies to unite people together. The *qi* of the ox inspires people, makes them feel like part of a larger society and purpose, and helps them to overcome their difficulties.

The Twelve-Animal Race

In the twelve-animal race myth, the ox was chosen by the jade emperor because of its selflessness, diligence, and all of the wonderful ways that it helped the world physically, mentally, and spiritually. The ox was so excited to be chosen that he could not sleep the night before the race began and so he set out toward the starting line early in the morning just as the sun began to rise. When the race began, the ox was the first one off the starting line and he maintained his pace with diligence, endurance, and a sincere desire to be the best. He even decided to help the rat along the way by allowing him to ride on his back. When the ox reached the river crossing, he jumped in without hesitation and began to swim steadily despite the strong current, ferrying both the rat and the cat to the other side (though the cat fell in halfway across).

In the end, just as the ox was about to cross the finish line and earn first place, the rat jumped off of his back and took the prize, leaving the ox to finish second. However, the ox with his selfless and generous nature smiled and congratulated the rat and they remain friends to this day. Other versions of the story have the ox finishing the race first and the rat being awarded the first prize afterwards for saving the life of the jade emperor. In the Chinese creation story, the goddess Niwa created the ox as the first animal of the animal kingdom immediately after creating human beings, alluding to the fact that the ox was originally meant to be the first animal of the zodiac. The ox earned his place in the zodiac because he believed that he could forge his own destiny and did not wait for difficult conditions to change or for heaven to grant him any advantages. The ox relied on diligence, perseverance, and determined effort to finish the race. Oxen teach us that virtue is achieved on earth with our actions and our decisions.

People Who Embody the Ox

The people who embody the ox spirit often have a stocky, stable body frame and a strong neck and shoulders. They are usually quite healthy and athletic and have a busy and determined nature. Ox people usually keep themselves occupied with their various projects and responsibilities. They have a stable driving type of energy while they remain active. When they are finished with their work for the day, they spend most of their free time resting, sleeping, and gathering energy for their next work project. Ox people usually sleep deeply and soundly.

In general, ox people are sincere, honest, genuine, loyal, calm, and harmonious. On the other hand, if anything inhibits an ox person in their tasks and work projects or threatens their way of life, they can quickly become salty, temperamental, agitated, angry, and even aggressive. Ox people are usually skilled with their personal finances because they recognize the value of their hard work and they are proud of the fruits of their labor. They are diligent, responsible, and good at saving money methodically at regular intervals. When it comes to investing, ox people are adept at identifying stable investments by recognizing the qualities of effective business practices. They usually show up early to many of their engagements and prefer to begin working on their projects as soon as possible. Most ox people are eager to wake up early in the morning to begin the day.

In love, ox people are loyal, sincere, generous, selfless, and kind. They are wonderful providers and protectors, stopping at nothing to create a safe and harmonious environment for their family. Ox people are open and honest about themselves, and they are also down-to-earth and unpretentious. They do not pretend to be something they are not and prefer to address issues in an open and upfront manner. However, they usually do not enjoy talking about their feelings and seek to avoid these types of conversations. Ox people are strong and stable on the outside and sensitive and heartfelt on the inside. They make loyal, forthright, and loving partners.

Ox people think long and hard about concepts and intellectual problems before expressing their opinion openly. This also means that once they have determined their position, they feel confident in their conclusions on a subject and it is difficult for them to adjust their position. Ox people are usually quite skilled at recognizing the critical components of complex systems and taking action where it is necessary. They identify and ignore extraneous information. People who embody the ox spirit can become preoccupied with other tasks but they are not easily distracted or misled by others.

Ox people usually prefer the simple pleasures in life, and they choose the familiar and comfortable, over the exotic and novel. Oxen like to be social, recreational, go on relaxing vacations, and relax when they are finished or feeling accomplished with their work. Oxen prefer to socialize with a smaller group of close trusted friends because loyalty is important to them, but they also enjoy being surrounded by others and mingling with the herd once in a while also. Ox people make wonderful friends and trustworthy associates. Though the intensity of their focus can be difficult to work with in a career setting, they are a great benefit to any team and an inspiration to others.

External Zodiac
Bees

Like oxen, bees are dedicated to their work and spend nearly all of their energy on their daily tasks. Bees are selfless and live to die for the hive, working throughout their entire life. A single bee lives for approximately six weeks, and if they are a forager bee, they gather a tenth of a teaspoon (0.8g) in their lifetime. Longevity requires rest and an effort to preserve energy, and thus bees live such short lives because they spend their lives constantly working and moving. Bees find their life's purpose in the labor that they perform to help others.

Bees produce far more honey than they can consume (2 to 3 times more) because they are so dedicated to their work. The excess honey that they produce is simply left in their abandoned hives for other creatures to find. One pound of honey requires 556 bees to gather pollen from over 2 million flowers, and a single hive with 25,000 to 10,000 bees can produce between 2 and 5 pounds of honey per day.[5] [6] [7] Bees work hard as a team to support their community, while oxen work hard as individuals to cultivate themselves. In the wild, oxen travel in herds, but they also like to maintain their own personal space.

Qi

Bee acupuncture, or bee venom acupuncture, is a treatment that has been used as an alternative form of therapy to relieve pain and inflammation for over 3000 years. The treatment involves piercing the skin at the location of various acupoints and *qi* meridians using bee venom applied to the tips of acupuncture needles, stingers that have been extracted from bees, or live bees that are held to the skin with forceps or tweezers.

> Studies have demonstrated that bee venom acupuncture contains many kinds of components which may show pharmacological actions such as anti-inflammation, anti-apoptosis, anti-fibrosis, and anti-arthrosclerosis. With these pharmaceutical characteristics, bee venom acupuncture has been used as the therapeutic method in treating osteoarthritis knee pain, Parkinson's disease, rheumatoid arthritis, etc. Moreover, studies have indicated that bee venom acupuncture with physical therapy can be more effective in improving pain and function than physical therapy alone. (Chen et al. 2020, 2)

---

[5] "How Much Honey Does a Bee Hive Produce per Year?" by Jennifer Nickson (2021). www.honestbeekeeper.com/how-much-honey-does-a-bee-hive-produce-per-year/
[6] "Bee Facts," by The Canadian Honey Council (2018). www.honeycouncil.ca/industry-overview/bee-facts/
[7] "Bee Hive Hierarchy and Activities," by Philip Grad (2010). www.bigislandbees.com/blogs/bee-blog/14137353-bee-hive-hierarchy-and-activities

Bees and bee products have been known for their healing qualities for many centuries. The selflessness of bees is invaluable to human beings and to nature as a whole. Bees teach us that by doing your best and pouring your heart into everything that you do, not a single bit of effort is ever wasted. Without the harmonious and healing qualities of bees, both the plant and animal kingdoms would be in great peril.

Like oxen, bees work in the light of the sun and they also have a deep respect for yin energy. Bees are activated by the warmth of sunlight, and seek out the morning light to warm their bodies and gain enough energy to move and fly. When the sun goes down, the energy of bees quickly fades as well. Bees also understand the importance of the female yin energy. In a hive, the drone bees are the only male bees, with their only purpose being to mate with the queen, while all of the other bees in the hive are female. Bees understand the importance of the nurturing female energy and their entire social structure depends on it. The hive would not survive without the continuous work of all the female worker and forager bees or the continuous reproduction of the queen.

Special Abilities and Traits

Bees follow a strict hierarchy of organization within the hive, which contributes to their incredible efficiency. The queen of the hive is the only bee that reproduces and this is her sole purpose. The queen is not chosen, she is simply a female that is raised in a larger brood cell and fed "royal jelly" that contains more nutritional value than the regular honey that the drones and worker bees eat. All the drones of the hive are male, and their only purpose is to mate with the queen. The drones need to be fed by the workers and they have no stinger, so without the help of the hive they are helpless. The rest of the bees are worker bees that perform all of the tasks of the hive, including foraging. There are one hundred worker bees to every drone.

The amount of work that worker bees accomplish is incredible. The hive workers care for the queen, produce honey, nurse the larvae, clean the hive, clean other bees, remove dead bees that could otherwise attract predators, build honeycomb cells, cap honeycomb cells, store pollen, ripen the nectar, and repair the hive. The forager bees work just as hard by scouting for nectar, guarding the hive, gathering nectar and pollen, gathering propolis from tree sap, which is used for repairing the hive, and gathering water to regulate the humidity in the hive. Each of the bees is capable of performing a number of these specific tasks and they may be responsible for accomplishing several of these tasks at any one time. Each bee continues to work diligently throughout life while remaining in constant communication with the other members of the hive. Their incredible organization and division of labor allows their society to thrive for numerous generations.

Bees are an essential part of the ecosystem and their behavior is harmonious with nature. While bees are not the only creature in nature that can pollinate plants and flowers, they are certainly efficient pollinators. Butterflies, ants, beetles, wasps, moths, and other insects all contribute to the process of pollination as they travel from flower to flower and from tree to tree.

[In order for pollination to occur,] the pollen must be transported from plant to plant so that each kind of flower receives its own kind of pollen. It must be placed precisely on the female parts of the flower, and this must be done swiftly, for many blossoms remain open for only a short time. . . Worker honey bees possess dense body hairs that catch pollen, which is removed by comb-like structures on the legs and transferred to pollen baskets on the hind legs. (Farb 1962, 125)

Just like many forms of agriculture would not have been able to develop and thrive without the help of oxen, many lush areas and types of plant-life would not have been able to thrive without the pollination of the bees and the insect kingdom. Honeybees communicate with one another through a few different types of dances that they perform. When a forager bee returns to the hive after discovering a source of nectar, it will immediately move onto the vertical face of the honeycomb and regurgitate a single drop of nectar to announce its discovery. It begins to dance to indicate the location of the nectar in relation to the hive. Each species of bee has slightly different variations on these dances, but the basics are described below.

If the source of nectar is located within 100 yards of the hive the bee will dance in a circular motion moving both clockwise and counterclockwise. The scent of the flower will be identified by other members of the hive and they will immediately go out in search of the source. If the source of the nectar is further than 100 yards from the hive than a different dance will be used to indicate both its distance and direction. The bee will dance in a figure eight formation on the face of the honeycomb waging its tail the whole way.

The speed at which the bee moves around the "eight" and the speed of the tail wagging indicates the distance of the nectar from the hive, faster meaning nearer and slower meaning further. The direction of the nectar is communicated by the direction of the center lines in the middle of the figure eight. With the top of the honeycomb representing the direction of the sun at the current moment the direction that the bee moves as it travels through the center of the eight indicates the nectar source in relation to the direction of the sun. For instance, if the bee travels straight upward as it moves through the center line of the figure eight, then the nectar source is located directly in the direction of the sun, if it travels downward then the nectar is located in the direction opposite the sun, and any variations left or right indicate corresponding course adjustments. (Farb 1962, 131)

These dances are also used to locate new hive locations as well. Bees communicate a surprisingly large amount of detailed information in simple efficient ways and this allows them to work effectively as a unit and achieve so much more than they would achieve on their own.

Cultural and Spiritual Concepts

The spirit of the bee is one that represents fertility, creativity, and giving life. Many ancient civilizations have recognized the role that bees play in the continuation of life on earth. Bees pollinate so many of the plants and flowers of the world, giving life not only to them but to all of the animals, as well as through their assistance in the production of fruits, flowers, and seeds. Bees also create life, giving honey with all of its nutritional value, healing properties, and exquisitely sweet flavor. For many centuries, the only way to sweeten foods and beverages was through the use of honey because sugar was so difficult to grow in many regions and trade was geographically limited. Even the bees themselves are extremely fertile, with a queen bee producing thousands of larvae per day. Bees teach us that while hard work is necessary in life, the journey can be quite enjoyable, it is well worth the effort, and the fruits of labor are sweet.

Bees are clear demonstrations that seemingly impossible tasks are within reach when we work together in harmony with others. By disregarding their individual needs, bees recognize that they are part of a larger whole and are constantly inspired to accomplish anything that is necessary for their hive to thrive. Community and connection are integral parts of our lives on earth, creating a dynamic of give and take as needs arise. To create a healthy society, the members must not only be connected with one another but each member must be integrated within themselves as well. Heaven, Human, and Earth, and Mental, Emotional, and Physical must all be connected and communicate with one another to fulfill their part in the function of the whole. Life, community, expression, health, integration, and purpose are the ingredients that create the sweet experiences of life.

Quotes from Famous Oxen

You may have to fight a battle more than once to win it.

        - Margaret Thatcher

Thought gives birth to a creative force and creates a new heaven, a new firmament, a new source of energy from which new arts flow... such is the immensity of man that he is greater than heaven and earth.

        - Paracelsus

Impossible is a word only to be found in the dictionary of fools.

        - Napoleon Bonaparte

I was obliged to be industrious. Whoever is equally industrious will succeed equally well.

        - Johann Sebastian Bach

We keep moving forward, opening new doors, and doing new things because we're curious, and curiosity keeps leading us down new paths.

        - Walt Disney

The fishermen know that the sea is dangerous and the storm terrible, but they have never found these dangers sufficient reason for remaining ashore.

        - Vincent van Gogh

The way of heaven can be known and experienced through the heart.

        - Manly P. Hall

I say I am stronger than fear.

        - Malala Yousafzai

One chance is all you need.

        - Jesse Owens

You can't put a limit on anything. The more you dream, the further you get.

        - Michael Phelps

The only way to deal with an unfree world is to become so absolutely free that your very existence is an act of rebellion.

        - Albert Camus

Get mad, then get over it.

        - Colin Powell

3

Tiger

Fire Tiger
13th February 1926 to 1st February 1927

Earth Tiger
31st January 1938 to 18th February 1939

Metal Tiger
17th February 1950 to 5 February 1951

Water Tiger
5 February 1962 to 24th February 1963

Wood Tiger
23rd January 1974 to 10th February 1975

Fire Tiger
9th February 1986 to 28th January 1987

Earth Tiger
28th January 1998 to 15th February 1999

Metal Tiger
14th February 2010 to 2 February 2011

Water Tiger
1 February 2022 to 21st January 2023

Wood Tiger
19th February 2034 to 7 February 2035

Fire Tiger
6th February 2046 to 26th January 2047

Earth Tiger
24th January 2058 to 12th February 2059

Tiger

The tiger category of the zodiac represents all types of feline creatures. Felines, large and small, share similar traits, body structures, and behavioral patterns. Tigers are powerful, courageous, honorable, impressive, attractive, independent, optimistic, ambitious, enthusiastic, and adventurous. They are quite curious and they spend a lot of their time exploring new places. They require a large territory partly because they love to roam, setting up multiple dens along the way, and also because they hunt large animals which migrate. Tigers run, crawl, swim, and jump; and, their ability to move silently and stalk their prey with stealth is unmatched in the animal kingdom.

Tigers are ambitious and courageous because they are built for hunting animals that are far larger than themselves. They are equipped with lithe, muscular bodies, acute senses, highly evolved teeth and claws, lightning-fast reflexes, and camouflage coloration (Burnie and Wilson 2001, 208). Tigers have extremely strong, dense, and flexible tendons. Tigers and other felines can be seen stretching their limbs to keep these massive tendons supple and healthy. Tendons are not only powerful and durable, but they do not require nearly as much oxygen and blood flow as muscle tissue. Tigers have incredible eyesight that allow them to see clearly in darkness. Their pupils greatly expand and contract to adjust to the amount of light in the environment, and their eyes are located on the front of their head which allows them to have accurate depth perception for stalking, jumping, and pouncing.

Felines can also have acute olfactory senses aided by a special organ, called the "Jacobson's organ," located on the roof of their mouths which can "taste" the scents in the air. Some large cats rely on their running speed to chase down their prey while others prefer to stalk and pounce. Felines have an amazing jumping/pouncing ability. "Some big cats, such as the serval, are able to pounce upon prey from a distance of 13ft (4m) away while others like the caracal can spring vertically 10ft (3m) to swat birds from the air" (Burnie and Wilson 2001, 210). Lions hunt in groups to take down large prey such as giraffes and zebra. Being carnivores, tigers need to consume meat to survive and maintain their health. The larger cats survive mainly on the red meat of larger creatures such as zebra, buffalo, pigs/boar, deer, and cattle and the smaller cats survive mainly on rabbits, rodents, reptiles, birds, and fish.

Along with meat they also require the dense cover of the forest and trees and ready access to water to thrive. The habitat of tigers used to extend across Asia, to parts of the middle east, and even eastern Europe. However, today, due to hunting and poaching, all five remaining species of tiger are endangered and they only exist in pockets of southern and eastern Asia.

"Tigers do travel in groups and males will often partner up with females while feeding or resting but in general they prefer to remain solitary" (Burnie and

Wilson 2001, 213). Lions are one of the only types of felines that forms close, long-term social bonds in the prides that they form, which usually number approximately four to six adults and their cubs (Burnie and Wilson 2001, 215). When tigers gather in groups, they are playful and they enjoy interacting with each other. Most of their play consists of mock fighting which allows them to develop their hunting skills and discover their strengths. Preferring to rest for most of the day, the only time that big cats attack one another is if a dominant male is challenged, either for status within the pride or for mating privileges.

Tigers generally live to about the age of eight to ten years. Their explosive strength and speed allow them to be formidable and effective in combat, but longevity is sacrificed as a result. Young tiger cubs completely rely on their mother for food until about the age of two until their bodies develop strength, coordination, and experience. Tiger mothers are protective and nurturing with their young. They set firm boundaries to keep their cubs safe and they actively teach them to hunt, fight, move silently, and hide their food from scavengers. Once they can fend for themselves, they leave their mother and become solitary hunters. They continue exploring territory, developing their hunting skills, and gaining experience as they approach the age of four or five, when they begin breeding.

Calendar

The tiger is the third animal of the zodiac. It is associated with the first month of the Chinese lunar calendar that lasts from approximately February 4th to March 6th in the Gregorian calendar and to the two-hour period between 3 am and 5 am. Tigers are the most ferocious and courageous animals of the zodiac. In the east, tigers are known as the king of the jungle, and in the west lions are given the same title. Tigers are assertive, aggressive, and extremely brave when necessary. In China, if a military leader has proven themselves and performed exceptionally well in battle they are often referred to as a "tiger general" or "tiger commander."

Tigers prefer to hunt in the dark of night so that they can make the best use of their incredibly stealthy stalking ability. They live their lives according to their own rules, conducting themselves as leaders and not followers. They strategically assess the situations that they find themselves in, and adjust their approach accordingly. Tigers are amazingly self-sufficient and resourceful. Their ability to think on their feet, and accomplish so much on their own earned them the third place in the zodiac. While tigers can be team players, they do not like to rely on others, or upon variables that they cannot control.

Tigers are risk-takers, and this leads them both to great successes and to great failures. When a tiger has set their sights on their prey or on a task, they quickly decide whether to make an attempt, and once they've decided, they cannot be deterred. Their extreme level of focus and determination makes tigers somewhat stubborn at times but they have the skills to take advantage of rare opportunities and risky endeavors. World War I began in 1914, the year of the tiger, as tensions continued to grow between many European countries after the assassination of the Austrian Archduke Franz Ferdinand, which sparked conflict between Austria-Hungary and Serbia.[1] During this time, many people and groups began positioning themselves and taking strategic advantage of any opportunities that presented themselves.

Tigers are curious creatures that like to explore and expand their vast territories. For instance, in the tiger year of 1938, Adolf Hitler pressured other European powers to allow Germany to annex the Sudetenland, an area that was home to nearly three million people, by supporting the rise of the Nazi party in Czechoslovakia.[2] The Tiger's curiosity leads them to engage in a wide variety of activities and create multiple dens for themselves. Tigers do not get attached to any specific task, and instead they try something out until they become bored or frustrated with it, then move on. If they are unsuccessful hunting large game, they often change strategies and perhaps go fishing for a while instead. Similarly, fighting tigers circle around their opponent looking for an opening or weakness to exploit and they test many approaches before fully committing themselves to an attack. This helps the tiger to be adaptable and resourceful. Tiger years are times when it is good to implement new strategies to the problems that we face and avoid becoming too attached to any one method.

Tigers are attractive, impressive, and confident. While tigers are incredibly stealthy and enjoy the darkness, they also enjoy the limelight and showing off their prowess. Tigers are champions that strive to be the best in any arena, and during tiger years many people show interest in this kind of energy. In 1938, the first Superman comic was released by Action Comics marking the beginning of a decades long interest in super heroes and champions.[3] Tigers are wonderful at drawing in a crowd, and despite their ferociousness, they are also quite friendly with many different creatures. Tigers are flamboyant, creative, and they love to play. Tigers play in the water, with sticks, with other creatures, and by leaping skillfully in precarious areas.

Tiger years are filled with many new ideas and ambitious projects. These are years when many people can be extremely ambitious, and quick to anger. Therefore, it is advisable to make an effort to be humble, gentle, and patient when necessary to avoid unnecessary conflict. Tigers present themselves in a direct and straight-forward manner, and while this can be effective in many situations it can also create many enemies. It is wise to be clear in advance about morals and principles during tiger years; both to demonstrate competence and

---

[1] "World War I," by Dennis E. Showalter (2000). www.britannica.com/event/World-War-I

[2] "Sudetenland," by The Editors of Encyclopedia Britannica (1998). www.britannica.com/place/Sudetenland

[3] "Superman," by Michael Eury (1998). www.britannica.com/topic/Superman-fictional-character

integrity, as well as to stand your ground and push forward with what you know to be correct, regardless of the opinions of others.

Tiger years also require discipline and a strong focus. Many of the tasks during this year require a great amount of effort and skill to accomplish, and often times many people watch closely. On the other hand, many projects during this year are carried out in secrecy; however, it is important to keep in mind that even they will eventually be made public. A good example was the Chernobyl nuclear disaster of 1986, when a Soviet nuclear reactor experienced a meltdown that resulted in a devastating explosion. The Soviet government tried to keep the details secret for a number of weeks; however, it was one of the worst environmental disasters of the century with obvious and far-reaching effects. Eventually, the Soviet Union was forced to acknowledge the disaster, and in the decades since, the Chernobyl site has received help from around the world in order contain the radioactive remnants of the destroyed reactor.[4]

People, problems, and situations can be quite stubborn and immovable during tiger years, so a varied and adaptable approach is highly recommended. During tiger years their will, be many times when a situation either requires a flexible, adaptable approach or a determined, immovable focus. There will be little to no room for a halfhearted or "middle of the road" approach when the tiger energy is present and engaged.

Qi

The Chinese double-hour related to the tiger is between 3 am and 5 am, the time of the lung meridian. During this time, the lungs are detoxifying themselves and the body naturally enters its deepest levels of sleep. The lungs are related to the skin and the *wei qi*, or defensive *qi*, both of which exist on the exterior of the body. These are the body's first defense against attack and external pathogens, and therefore they are closely related to the body's immune system. As we breath in the air from the outside world, it comes into direct contact with the lungs, whereas other organs such as the heart, stomach and the kidneys are safely housed with human organism.

The hours between 3 am and 5 am are a time when we have a significant number of dreams and the memories of the previous day being processed by the subconscious mind. At night, the *wei qi* that resides on the body's exterior travels inwards toward the heart and the body's center carrying the memories of the day with it. If there are any issues or challenges that were experienced during the day that still require resolution, we often experience symbolic representations of these experiences in our dreams. This entire process is fueled by the lungs and reaches its peak during the time of the tiger.

---

4 "Chernobyl Disaster," by The Editors of Encyclopedia Britannica (1998). www.britannica.com/event/Chernobyl-disaster

This is a time when both the lungs and the *wei qi* are detoxifying themselves. This also means that during this time our breathing, pulse, and blood pressure will all be at their weakest point. This is not a good time for practicing meditation, or relaxation practices, because deep breathing further slows the heart rate and lowers blood pressure. It is recommended that we remain asleep during this time to allow the lungs and defensive qi to fully detox. This is also when the bladder is at its most inactive state allowing any liquids that have been consumed before falling asleep to remain in the body. Food and beverages that are consumed before falling asleep are slowly absorbed by the body's tissues rather than being quickly processed out as waste.

Tigers are related to the lungs because felines have extremely powerful lungs which accounts for their ability to roar with ferocious strength. The lungs are one of the most important vital organs of the body. We can live for days without food or water, but it only takes moments to pass away if we cannot breathe. However, when we have strong lungs and develop our breathing ability, the extra oxygen within the body can allow us to develop the explosive power and strength of the tiger. When the blood and tissues of the body are properly oxygenated, the immune system is boosted, digestion improves, the nervous system is calmed, the mind becomes focused, and the anxiety is reduced.

When the lungs are healthy, then the body's immune system is able to function efficiently as well. The cat and the tiger are the natural enemy of the rat, and the rat represents all types of infectious disease and viruses. Therefore, the feline energy can protect us from these types of illness. Tigers and cats exhale more deeply than they inhale. This increases their lung volume, increases their blood circulation and it detoxifies their body, especially their lymphatic system. The nutrients that we get from our food eventually enter our blood stream and our lymphatic system and therefore it is essential to detoxify these two systems. When the lungs become ill, infected, or damaged, a lot of phlegm is produced and begins to fill the lungs making breathing more difficult. The energy of the tiger helps to detoxify and regulate the lymph system in our body to protect the lungs and allow for deep breathing.

Cats rarely become infected by disease because of the strong lung *qi* that they develop throughout their life. There are many infectious disease treatments that have been developed from studying cats because of their enhanced immunity. Cats are even able to produce a substance within their body that is highly effective in combating infectious disease. In traditional Chinese medicine, the lungs are paired with the large intestine and the colon, and these two organs form a dynamic relationship. When breathing becomes difficult, constipation often results, which can exacerbate the condition. Similarly, constipation can be relieved by deep breathing and stimulating the lungs. By developing our breathing ability in the same way as the tiger, we can develop the strength, protection, and health to handle many of the difficult situations in our life.

The ghost point that is associated with the tiger is known as Ghost's Heart (Guixin); it matches the point Great Mound (*daling*, PC-7) in the acupuncture system (Johnson 2014, 605). It is located at the wrist joint, between the tendons of palmaris longus and flexor carpi radialis. This point is used to increase strength and immunity, aid digestion, relieve tightness in the chest, as well as calm and clear the mind (Deadman et al. 2007, 378).

All felines spend a lot of time exercising their wrists. They walk on this area of their paws, they scratch and claw at various things both to strengthen and stretch their wrists as well as maintain the sharpness of their claws, and they can be seen flexing their wrists and paws in the air while they lay on their back. Developing their wrists increases the tiger's immunity and aids in their blood circulation. By exercising our wrists in similar ways, we can also increase our immunity as well. By doing push-ups every day we can develop strength and immune functions similar to that of the tiger. It is recommended that people soak their hands in warm water every morning for five to ten minutes to increase the body's immunity and detoxify the blood. This is largely related to the functions of the Great Mound (*daling*, PC-7) point and the large amount of blood that is circulated through the hands and wrists. When the blood circulation is naturally increased in these ways, it helps to clear out cholesterol and maintains the supple flexibility of the arteries.

Unfortunately, tigers have been hunted to near extinction and they are often killed for the health benefits of their bones and tendons. The bones as well as the penis of tigers contain *qi* and nutrients that are extremely beneficial for a person's health and they are appropriately called the "treasures of the tiger." These health benefits have been studied by both western medical, as well as Chinese medical, researchers and many new drugs and treatments have been developed from this research. This is one of the many reasons that these creatures must be protected and allowed to flourish.

It is also not only the physical body of the tiger that is healing, but the function that they perform in nature. Tigers are extremely important because they are the 'king of the jungle', and they control the other animals of the animal kingdom. The Covid-19 virus, for example, originated with bats and other similar rodents. The energy of the tiger, with its physical prowess and the signals that it sends through the wilderness (chemical, biological, behavioral, etc.) provides a control mechanism on the spread of diseases such as this; keeping animals and humans separated when necessary. The function of tigers in nature cannot be over-stated, and as human beings, we must make sure that these creatures are protected, supported, and reproducing at a healthy rate to keep them around for centuries to come.

Special Abilities and Traits

The Ferocity of Tigers

Tigers do not have many thoughts, instead they respond to situations quickly and instinctively. When it comes to fighting, tigers have three main abilities, they can pounce, attack the throat with their fangs and teeth, and they can rip and shred flesh with their claws. Lions on the other hand only have two fighting abilities, they can pounce and they can attack the throat. While lions can swipe and claw at their enemies, they cannot rip and shred flesh with their claws in the same way that tigers can. This is mainly due to the fact that lions rely heavily on their muscle strength for power, whereas tigers rely on their tendon strength.

Tendon strength is closely tied to the health of the lungs. The powerful lung strength allowed the tiger to develop such large, strong, and flexible tendons. Strong lungs are also a major contributing factor to the explosiveness of the tiger. Tigers can act with incredible speed and strength, and while this does allow them to handle difficult situations, such as hunting and fighting other large creatures, it also reduces their longevity. Sprinters, fighters, and other people who practice their explosiveness and quick reflexes, often exhaust their life-force to achieve these abilities.

Tigers and cats are closely related, yet it is always the larger of the two that is the most ferocious. Cats and tigers belong to the same category, but it is the tiger that was chosen to represent the third year of the zodiac due to its ferocity and strength. Size truly does matter in this world, especially during combat. This is demonstrated by the fact that tigers, even with all of their ferociousness, are helpless against elephants, which are much larger than them. Tigers become confused and intimidated when they are confronted by elephants. A tiger may jump on an elephant's back to attack the neck, but the elephant's hide is too thick for them to penetrate, and the elephant can easily grab the tiger with their trunk to throw them off. Elephants are so heavily protected that they think that the tigers are trying to play with them, rather than attack them. A strong foundation is an essential component of protection and longevity for all things in nature.

Cultural and Spiritual Concepts

The King of the Jungle

In Asia, the tiger rather than the lion is considered the king of the jungle. In fact, the stripes that appear on the forehead of a tiger form the Chinese character *wang*, which means "king." Tigers do not fear any creature, and they consider the jungle to be a territory that belongs to them. Tigers, represent the energy that must be fierce and responsive to be effective, therefore tigers represent the 'active king' of the jungle. Lions, on the other hand, represent the energy that must lie in wait and be patient to be effective, therefore lions are the 'passive kings' of the jungle.

Tigers can be likened to business leaders that must actively work to improve their company, while lions can be likened to investors that must be patient and pay attention to circumstances to get ahead. To differentiate further, bulls are often used as the symbols or mascots of large companies on wall street looking to take advantage of a bull market; however, tigers are used as the symbols of large casinos and gambling institutions because both the casinos, as well as the gamblers, are looking to compete for their share of the winnings.

Large felines can be found in three different colors yellow/orange, white, and black. Yellow tigers represent soldiers and the military. In China, when a general is brave and has proven himself in battle he may be called a "tiger general;" similarly, a brave soldier is a "tiger soldier." The yellow tiger is considered to be the tiger that rules over the earth and is the king of all tigers. In the past, after training for many years, Daoist martial artists would test their skills by fighting a trained tiger in hand-to-hand combat. Similarly, the military is designed to consist of the most effective and ferocious fighters in the country. Soldiers wear light-colored camouflage uniforms that are designed to blend in with the tall grass and natural environments just like the stripes of a tiger.

The black felines, such as the black panther, represents the police officers and law enforcers. In the same way that these creatures are found in the densest parts of the jungle, most law enforcement officers are found in the densest parts of the city. Police officers also wear black or dark colored uniforms which is a color that represents physical safety. Tigers are creatures that protect good people and ward off evil spirits. At the White Cloud Temple, the tigers are known as the animal that can ward of the "three disasters" of fire, thieves, and ghosts. In China, young children can be seen wearing colorful shoes that have the face of a tiger embroidered on them to protect the children. Tigers are also depicted quite frequently on tombs and headstones, so that they may protect the dead and allow them to have peace in the afterlife.

The white tiger is special in Chinese culture, representing spiritual courage, enlightenment, and progress. White tigers are actually the same species as Bengal tigers, except that are born with a different coloration and features. Only one out of ten thousand Bengal tigers is born as a white tiger, and they are typically larger than other tigers as well, measuring approximately 10-13ft (3-4m) in length and weighing approximately 600 lbs. (272kg).

The bodhisattva Guanyin is often depicted riding a white tiger, symbolizing both the fact that this spiritual being has learned how to tame the tiger's ferocious energy, and that the tiger is the protector of the buddha. The white tiger has beautiful green and yellow eyes that demonstrate the unique and special *qi* that this creature has. The white tiger is the rarest and most magnificent of the tigers. In the five phases theory, the lungs are represented by the color white, and therefore, the white tiger reinforces and exemplifies the strength of all tigers. The tiger is considered to the king of the jungle, and of all animal life. They are responsible for policing and judging human beings and the animal kingdom when they are not fulfilling their responsibilities by disregarding the laws of nature.

The white tiger also represents women, femininity, and sensuality. Tigers are naturally attracted to the color pink which is traditionally considered a color that represents females and femininity. Tigers, like cats, enjoy things that are luxurious and soft. When tigers are not hunting, they quickly relax and become playful. The powerful energy of tigers is also expressed through their passion and sensuality, in addition to their ferocity. Tigers are often calm and patient, but they are also passionate and they can quickly become savage and ruthless when they are angered, especially when tiger mothers are protecting their young. Angry or scornful women are referred to as "ferocious tigers" in China. The Daoist practice known as the "white tiger, green dragon" refers to the practice of dual cultivation, or sexual alchemy. This is the practice of cultivating energy through the combining and refining of the *qi* of two people in the act of sex. In this practice, the white tiger refers to the feminine, yin energy and the mastery of the female reproductive system.

People Who Embody the Tiger

People who embody the spirit of the tiger are strong, slender, have a square jaw, and move in a relaxed, confident manner. In Daoism, people born in the year of the tiger are classified into two categories, uphill tigers and downhill tigers. An uphill tiger is a person that is born during the daytime hours. Tigers hunt at night, usually during the early morning hours, so during the daylight hours, tigers have usually already eaten, and they travel uphill to rest and recuperate during the heat of the day. Uphill tiger people generally have a natural talent that allows them to be fruitful in their careers and achieve success with less effort, however, their love life is often difficult. Uphill tigers live longer lives due to the fact that they rest more often and do not have to exert themselves as much as others, relying instead upon their reputation and talent.

Downhill tigers are tiger people who are born at night. Tigers travel downhill toward rivers and water sources during the night to drink and find prey. Downhill tiger people are generally ambitious, but they often have to work a lot to succeed in their careers; however, their love life is often fruitful. Downhill tigers live shorter lives due to the fact that they have to work so hard and often have to defend their position in their career. According to Daoism, fortune and misfortune are like brothers; they are concomitant. When either fortune or misfortune appears, the other is soon to follow. Tiger people can become so successful in either their work life or their love life that they then have to work harder to maintain themselves and their lifestyle. Similarly, when tiger people experience misfortune, it only provides them with more energy and determination to apply to their efforts in new ways.

Tiger people are often direct, courageous, and confident which is a double-edged sword, it can be quite intimidating to their rivals, but it can also earn them a reputation for being harsh and uncaring. Tiger people would benefit greatly by developing the awareness of the way that their words are received, and the ability to be flexible. Yet, even though tigers may be intimidating and self-sufficient, they are also sensitive and caring. People born in the year of the tiger are often wonderful teachers and protectors of the young and vulnerable. Tiger people are honorable and have a strong sense of compassion, along with the will and determination to fight against injustice.

Tiger people are often curious, adventurous, and open-minded, exploring various pathways before committing to a single approach. Their courage, assertiveness, and willingness to take risks allows tigers to be great leaders and reach success in many challenging arenas. Tigers enjoy travelling as every new experience allows them to imagine more ways to approach their own life. While tiger people enjoy their solitude, they also appreciate the company of others. Tiger people often have a large and diverse social circle that provides a great resource for them in difficult situations. People born in the year of the tiger are magnificent and impressive, usually taking great care in their appearance. They especially enjoy hosting parties and events which allows them to impress their guests and exercise their leadership abilities.

Tigers are often blessed with either the ability to make money easily or attract partners easily. This is a wonderful blessing and should be appreciated, however, the tiger's exploratory and risk-taking nature can lead them to continue changing their goals. Tigers can increase their effectiveness, power, and happiness by committing to their undertakings and developing strong roots in their relationships. Tigers have good reason to be confident in their prowess and creativity. They are spontaneous, determined, and enthusiastic and their talents create many unique and exciting opportunities in their life.

External Zodiac
Cat

Tigers and cats are perhaps the inner/outer zodiac pair that have the most in common with one another. All felines are remarkably similar to one another, and share much of the same DNA. In China, it is even said that "if you look at a cat, then you can draw a picture of a tiger" because their physical features are so similar. Even though there are differences between these two animals, in general, tigers often behave in much the same way as domestic house cats except that tigers rely heavily on their impressive strength. While the tiger is considered to be the king of the jungle and is ambitious, the cat displays its royalty with its elegant movements and its love of a luxurious lifestyle. Cats always appreciate clean luxurious environments and rich flavors. Like all felines, cats are independent creatures that live life according to their own rules. If a cat is determined to avoid being trained, it is nearly impossible to teach them, but if they are willing to learn, then they can understand and master many tasks.

The Teacher of the Tiger

Daoism contains many stories of the interactions between the cat and the tiger. The cat is known as the tiger's teacher. The cat taught the tiger how to pounce, stalk, swipe, fight, breath, roar, sense, walk, and sleep. In the beginning of their relationship, the tiger was a sincere and appreciative student, and after many lessons, the cat said "I have taught you everything." Soon the tiger became pretentious and arrogant, thinking that he had surpassed his teacher, and one day he decided that he would attack the cat and eat it. When he made his move, the cat quickly fled up a nearby tree where the tiger could not follow. The tiger then exclaimed, "you said that you taught me everything. Why did you not teach me how to climb trees?" The cat replied "if I had taught you everything that I know, then I would be dead by now."

Along with tigers, cats are teachers of human beings as well. Cats are perceptive and sensitive creatures, and they can sense the inner nature of a person. They never hesitate to punish a person for ill-treatment or injustice. If a person has an evil nature or bad intentions, a cat will recognize this at a glance and either leave or attack. If a person is good-natured, a cat will behave in a friendly manner and treat them with respect. However, if a person successfully befriends a cat, it will soon begin to teach by example, demonstrating many useful skills and techniques to achieve success.

Being a brilliant teacher, the cat understood that some things must be left unsaid. This allows the student to discover the truth on their own and develop their own unique understandings. Skilled educators understand that the totality of the teaching should not be given all at once. Things must be taught slowly so that the information can be properly digested. The cat never taught the tiger how to climb trees, or how to eat fish without choking on the bones. Cats hunt both fish and land animals; however, they prefer fish over other types of meat. Fish have many bones, and they need to be eaten with patience and care to avoid choking on the bones. It is similar to the way that information and concepts must be digested; carefully and meticulously. The tiger, on the other hand, does not have this type of patience, and it often chokes on the bones of the fish.

Cats are extremely skillful when it comes to climbing up steep surfaces, and they love to perch themselves in high places so that they can observe a large area. From a high vantage point, cats can also prowl, sneak, and pounce more effectively. Tigers enjoy high vantage points as well, but they are not adept at climbing trees, so they utilize hillsides and small ledges instead. When stalking prey, tigers prefer to maintain their stealth by staying in low places like bushes and tall grasses, rather than climbing up into the canopy.

Cats have the ability to eat fish without choking on the bones, which can be numerous, small, and sharp. Cats are able to do this partly because they eat meticulously and carefully, and also because they have a special enzyme in their saliva which helps to breakdown and soften the bones, allowing them to be easily swallowed and digested. Tigers, on the other hand, do not eat slowly and they lack this digestive enzyme; instead, they eat their food in large bites, relying on the crushing power of their jaws to make their food easier to swallow.

Saliva is an essential healing substance in Daoist medicine. Swallowing your saliva, especially in the morning as soon as you wake up, can help to soothe a sore throat, and treat pain in the chest and lungs. Many animals lick each other to treat pain and illness. Licking is not only a medical treatment either; it is also an expression of love. Exemplifying the tiger qualities of enhanced immunity, and sensual passion. Whomever you lick, even yourself, demonstrates your love for that person. Many animals understand the healing power of saliva; however, the saliva of cats is unique and is particularly therapeutic.

In Daoism, licking is considered to be the highest form of healing massage. Licking a wound is often the first instinct that an animal has after being injured. Many animals use licking to maintain their health, groom each other, and express their affection. Many times, when a child gets hurt, a mother will offer to kiss the child's wound to make it feel better. This is not only to ease the child's mind as a kind gesture, it does in fact have special healing effects that water, medicine, or medicinal herbs cannot replicate. Since the rat is the animal that represents pain in the zodiac, the cat, being the rat's natural enemy, has healing properties and methods that can reduce pain. The application of saliva is one of these methods.

The cat's saliva in particular is an effective medicine for pain and open wounds. Daoists would extract the cat's saliva by holding the cat upside down over a plate of fish, and as the cat becomes excited to eat and begins salivating, the saliva would be captured with a small glass or a cloth. Drinking the saliva of a cat allows a person to eat fish bones and other items without choking just like a cat. It is also an effective treatment for acid reflux, heartburn, esophageal tumors, inflammation of the digestive tract, and similar conditions.

Topically applying the saliva of a cat to an open wound helps to reduce the pain and assist the healing process. If you combine the saliva of a cat with the bones of a fish and cook them together, this substance helps to cure pain, joint issues, bone spurs, arthritis, Tuberculosis, lymphatic issues, and blood related diseases when consumed. There is even a special type of vinegar that is produced in China which is designed to replicate many of the medicinal qualities of cat saliva, however, it is not as effective. While they should be used sparingly, the animal "herbs" of TCM are more effective than plant herbs.

Cats demonstrate one of the most effective ways to sleep. Cats sleep peacefully and soundly even if they have had a difficult, stressful day. This is because before falling asleep, cats consciously calm the activity, energy, and emotions in their heart allowing them to rest and restore their energy. This is a natural practice and it is therapeutic for all living beings to calm the heart before falling asleep for the night.

Qi

As mentioned above, the *qi* of the cat is healing and therapeutic. In the zodiac system, this is explained by the fact that the cat is the natural enemy of the rat, which symbolizes all types of infectious disease and pain related conditions. The *qi* of cats can reduce pain, reduce inflammation, heal the esophagus, lungs and respiratory issues, and treat many skin conditions. There is also a substance that is only produced in the body of a cat that can help to greatly increase the cat's immune system and cure a number of infectious diseases. In fact, there are hundreds of diseases that can be treated with this substance, that has yet to be identified by western science; however, this substance can only be found in cats that have interacted with carp fish.

The abdominal breathing techniques of cats also helps them to increase their immune function and benefit overall health. Human beings have many pores and sweat glands that allow their skin to breathe and oxygenate their blood. However, cats do not have this ability, and to oxygenate their blood they must regularly practice deep abdominal breathing. Cats exhale more deeply than they inhale, which increases their lung volume, cleans the lymphatic system, and assists with blood circulation. The nutrients that we get from our food eventually enter our blood stream and lymphatic system, which can eventually lead to blockages over time. Therefore, it is essential to detoxify these two systems and keep them clear in order to develop longevity. Abdominal breathing also helps to massage and tonify the inner organs, which allows the body to better manage its *qi* energy.

In traditional Chinese medicine, the phrase "cat condition" refers to a person who is lethargic, fidgety, and sometimes anxious. Today, this condition is often the result of having spent too must time at a computer or on a cell phone. Cats develop these symptoms when they spend most of their time lazing about the house; however, they combat this by regularly stretching their limbs and clawing on various objects. This demonstrates the importance of carefully stretching and pulling on the limbs to maintain health. Cats and tigers do not practice vigorous exercise to develop strength; instead, they slowly stretch their limbs and tendons while patiently walking throughout their territory. Similarly, regular stretching and walks around the neighborhood can greatly increase health, immunity, and strength.

Cats have unique, powerful, and effective *qi* energy. If a cat approaches you in a friendly way, do not turn it away. They are trying to help you by assisting your *qi* and teaching you how to live better. Cats can be strict teachers, but their ultimate intention is to assist humankind and protect the good energy in the world.

Special Abilities and Traits

Cats are swift and agile, and they can gracefully travel vertically whether they are jumping, climbing, or falling. Cats are not easily injured when they fall from a significant height. Cats have the ability to right themselves as they fall so that they always land upright given enough height. This means that even when cats fall, they almost always land on their feet. Also, due to the fact that cats jump and stretch so often, they have strong and limber spines which allow them to absorb impacts more easily without injury.

Cats are skilled at recognizing tonal differences. Cats mimic many of the tones that human beings use to communicate and because of this many pet cats have learned to communicate their needs to humans vocally. The meowing sound of a cat contains powerful *qi*, and it assists them in catching their prey. Cats often give out a loud shrill in the moment just before pouncing. Rats have acute hearing and they are especially sensitive to high pitched noises. The cat's meow is so shrill that it disorients the rat causing it to freeze in place for a moment while the cat attacks. This same shrill sound reduces pain and supports the lungs in humans by harmonizing and tonifying the *qi*.

Cats are Highly Intelligent

There is a Daoist story in which the gods of wisdom decided to host an examination for all of the animals to determine which one was the most wise and intelligent. In the end, it was the cat that scored the highest on this exam. Cats are extremely intelligent animals; they understand the intricacies of intelligence and psychology. It is near impossible for a human being to comprehend the thoughts of a cat. Many Daoists keep three hairs from the top of a cat's head with them while they take exams to help them focus and achieve their best score.

Cats have strong skulls due to the strong *qi* that is centered in their heads. This contributes to their extraordinary eyesight and their incredible wisdom. The psychologist Fritz Kunkel said "the best way to learn psychology is to watch and observe" (Johnson 2008, 3). It is through patience and observation that the behavior of others can be understood. Cats can differentiate, identify, and navigate the outside world effectively with their observation skills and eyesight, which is exceptional in dark conditions. Cats have 20/4 (5.0) vision which is five times more acute than the average human being. Cats use their eyes to identify danger and differentiate between people with good intentions and bad intentions. To find partners in life, whether in business, romance, mentorship, or anything else, we must differentiate between people who are good or bad for us. Each animal does this in different ways. Daoism has thousands of years of history and cultivation that allows its followers to effectively differentiate patterns and navigate the world.

Cats are even more ferocious than tigers. When a cat and a tiger fight, the cat is usually the victor. This is the effect of the cat's gaze. An individual's gaze is essential and it cannot be disguised; it represents their heartfelt intentions. Cats are able to embody the energy of lunacy and madness in order to subdue their opponents. Many animals freeze or shake when they catch the gaze of a predator. Cat's have a particularly strong gaze that demonstrates their determination, focus, and courage. Police officers, soldiers, and martial artists all practice the strength of their gaze in order to subdue criminals or their opponents.

A gaze can become so powerful that an enemy will begin to tremble the moment that they make eye contact. A cat's gaze scares off all diseases carried by rats. Therefore, developing a strong gaze is one way of developing righteous *qi* energy. When you have righteous *qi*, then the demonic *qi* of infectious diseases cannot enter your body. All human beings use this energy when they negotiate with others to determine how genuine they are. Many people do not say what they mean, and to determine how genuine or truthful they are, we must pay attention to the strength and quality of their gaze.

Cultural and Spiritual Concepts

Cats Represent Wealth

Rats are collectors, and therefore they acquire wealth by gathering it piece by piece, like business owners. Cats are the creatures that manage and control the energy of the rats, which means that cats are more akin to bankers. Cats help us to manage money, create good financial habits, and protect our valuables from loss. The yin nature of cats is similar to the yin nature of money. Both cats and money can appear to be dormant and inactive, while simultaneously developing increased energy. Cats enjoy clean, extravagant, and luxurious environments to cultivate themselves in, just like the interiors of banks and financial institutions.

Cats are also used in feng shui, mainly due to their association with the energy of money. The famous money cat, or welcoming cat, statues can be seen in many businesses around the world because they are believed to attract wealth. Daoists recognize that for this method to be completely effective there should be three of these statues next to one another; one large, one medium, and one small. This creates a strong *qi* field in the environment which will welcome business, wealth, and luxury.

The yin nature of cats makes them magnets for wealth, as well as protectors and nurturers of their loved ones. There is a story in Daoism which describes the respectful nature of cats, their spirituality, and their relationship to money.

> There was once a wealthy man who deeply loved cats. He was married, had a wonderful career, and a large luxurious house. Every day the cats from all around would come to his house because they knew that he would feed them

well and allow them to come and go freely. Soon the man was feeding and housing so many cats that it began to irritate his wife and cause problems in their relationship. Before long, his wife left him, yet he continued to feed all of the cats that came to him, and enjoyed their company. This continued until the man was spending so much money on feeding the cats that he was in danger of going broke. When he finally ran out of money, the man was distraught and not long after, he lost his house too.

Homeless and depressed, the man began praying to heaven every night for money so that he could get back on his feet. One night, one of his cats came to visit him on the street and to the man's surprise the cat was carrying a gold coin in its mouth which it placed at his feet as a gift. The man was overjoyed and thanked the gods and the cat deeply. Recognizing that his prayers had been answered the man continued to pray for more money and the next night the cat showed up again with another gold coin. This continued for seven days, each night with more prayers and more coins, until the man began to notice that the cat seemed to be getting weak and ill.

On the eighth night, the man prayed again, and again the cat brought the man a gold coin, however, this time the man decided to follow the cat to see where the cat was getting all of this gold. He followed the cat as it traveled out of the town and deep into the forest. The cat slept, awoke the next day and continued its journey until it came to a small hole in a hillside deeply secluded in the forest.

The man approached and peered into the small cave and observed the cat kneeling before a statue of buddha. The cat began to pray to the statue, and said aloud "Lord Buddha, the man that has been so kind to me for so many years is still poor and desperate. Please allow me to trade my ninth life for a gold coin so that I may repay him for his kindness." And in that moment, the man watched as the cat disappeared before his eyes, and gold coin appeared from out of the earth where the cat had once been.

There are also many stories about how the relationship between the rat and the cat in Chinese mythology as well. It has been said that the spirits of the rat and the cat used to be husband and wife in a previous lifetime and so in this life they were born as natural enemies as a function of their karma. It has also been said that the rat and the cat are actually brothers that used to get along with one another until they had a falling out and they have been enemies ever since. This is illustrated in the story of the twelve-animal race.

The cat and the rat were good friends, and they supported each other in everything that they did. One day, they heard about the twelve-animal race that was to be held by the Jade Emperor to determine the rulers of the years of the zodiac, and they both excitedly entered. They arrived together and wished each other luck. When the race started, the cat took off rapidly, and was soon out of sight. The rat on the other hand knew that he could not win the race with his short legs, so he decided to ask the ox if he could ride on his back. The ox, with his caring and generous nature, quickly accepted and the rat rode on his back the entire way, singing songs as they traveled.

When the ox and the rat came to the river crossing, the cat was waiting on the shore trying to figure out how to cross the river without getting wet. The cat saw that the rat was riding on the ox's back and asked if the ox would also give him a ride across the river. Again, the generous and hard-working ox agreed and the three of them began to cross the river. Halfway across the river however, the cat began thinking to himself that he could easily push the rat into the water and have one less competitor to worry about.

The rat, sensing the ill-will of the cat, decided that he would strike first, before the cat could take action. So as the cat began to gather his energy for a quick swipe, the rat leapt into the air and knocked the cat off of the ox's back and into the water. The cat began frantically swimming for the shore and when he arrived, soaking wet and exhausted, he was too far behind to earn a place in the winner's circle. Ever since that day, the cat was so angry that he vowed to be the eternal enemy of the rat.

The cat has a deep and passionate sense of revenge. Cats are even more fierce than wolves in their attitude and vengeful spirit. Finally, there is another story of the origin of cats and the way that they came to be the natural enemies of rats.

During the Song dynasty, the famous judge and criminal investigator Bao Gong, was assigned the task of discovering the cause of the many rampant diseases that had been greatly afflicting mankind. He quickly discovered that the rat was causing the spread of disease, and realizing that controlling the rats was a seemingly impossible task, he sent a request to heaven for help.

To control the rats, heaven sent cats to the earth from the moon temporarily, until the situation was under control. After the situation was under control however, human beings felt that the cats were so extraordinary at controlling disease that they refused to return the cats to heaven. Ever since this time, cats have remained on the earth without a specific goal or purpose. This is why cats are can be indifferent, and they often seem to be simply waiting. This story is also the reason that cats are seen as the messengers of the moon.

Cats Have Nine Lives

In folklore, cats are known to have nine lives. Each of these lives has a specific meaning and serves a specific purpose. Daoists believe that cats are not from the mortal realm, they come from another place altogether. Cats were sent to earth from heaven, and therefore, they have an inner nature that is unlike any other creature on the planet. The nature of the nine lives is as follows:

The first life of the cat is its heavenly life: it is protected from heavenly disasters. Lightning will strike trees, buildings, human beings, elephants, birds, and even tigers, but never a cat. The anatomy of a cat allows them to naturally conduct electricity from their head to their tail. This creates an energy field around the cat that repels lightning and electricity. Even the homes and buildings where cats live are almost never struck by lightning.

The second life relates to the fact that the cat has the ability to live in cold and wet environments that many other animals would quickly perish in. The snow leopards of the arctic and the jaguars of the rain-forest are examples of this. The second life of cats is also related to the phenomenon that cats often leave or hide before they are about to pass away. They do not like to be seen when they die. Cats have their own way of leaving this world.

The third life represents the ability of felines to live in both extremely hot and extremely cold environments. Cheetahs and lions live in the heat of the savanna. Siberian tigers live in the freezing tundra.

The fourth life of the cat connects to its ability to adapt well to all kinds of environments. All cats, big and small, attack their prey with amazing skill and strength; they all have the ability to hide and pounce and most also can easily climb trees. They also all have powerful lung strength which allows their immune system to function well in nearly any environment.

The fifth life relates to good fortune and longevity. Because cats put their heart and concentration into each of their tasks, they are often successful. Most cats live for about twenty years; and given their explosive power and willingness to engage in combat, this is quite an advanced age.

The sixth life occurs because felines can survive many natural disasters, from floods to forest fires. Cats are able to use their agility and strength to escape from many precarious situations. When earthly disasters occur cats naturally climb as high as possible to avoid the chaos. But rather than remain there, they will quickly look for additional escape routes and take them as soon as they appear.

The seventh life relates to the ability to adapt their diet to environmental conditions. Cats will eat fish if there is no red meat, and they will occasionally eat a vegetarian diet if there are no prey animals available.

The eight life illustrates the cat's ability to sleep efficiently. Cats move a lot while they sleep. They toss and turn quite often. Cats use this movement during sleep as a form of exercise, carefully choosing the postures that they lay in. This allows them to exercise and rest simultaneously.

The ninth life has to do with the ability to jump, leap, and pounce with grace and skill. This ability allows cats to be effective hunters and survivalists in a variety of situations and environments. Being fast and accurate is often enough to be effective.

Quotes from Famous Tigers

This is the mark of a really admirable man: steadfastness in the face of trouble.

-Ludwig von Beethoven

Nothing great in the world has ever been accomplished without passion.

-Georg Wilhelm Friedrich Hegel

I restore myself when I'm alone.

-Marilyn Monroe

Life has meaning only in the struggle. Triumph or defeat in the hands of the Gods. So let us celebrate the struggle.

-Stevie Wonder

A person doing his or her best becomes a natural leader, just by example.

-Joe DiMaggio

The quality of a leader is reflected in the standards they set for themselves.

-Ray Kroc

Power does not corrupt. Fear corrupts. . . perhaps the fear of a loss of power.

-John Steinbeck

Freedom is not given to us by anyone, we have to cultivate it ourselves. It is a daily practice. . . No one can prevent you from being aware of each step you take, or each breath in and breath out.

-Thich Nhat Hanh

The more relaxed you are, the better you are at everything: the better you are with your loved ones, the better you are with your enemies, the better you are at your job, the better you are with yourself.

-Bill Murray

You don't learn to walk by following the rules. You learn by doing, and by falling over.

-Richard Branson

Power is competence.

-Jordan Peterson

4

Rabbit

Fire Rabbit
2nd February 1927 to 22nd January 1928

Earth Rabbit
19th February 1939 to 7th February 1940

Metal Rabbit
6th February 1951 to 26th January 1952

Water Rabbit
25th January 1963 to 12th February 1964

Wood Rabbit
11th February 1975 to 30th January 1976

Fire Rabbit
29th January 1987 to 16th February 1988

Earth Rabbit
16th February 1999 to 4th February 2000

Metal Rabbit
3rd February 2011 to 22nd January 2012

Water Rabbit
22nd January 2023 to 9th February 2024

Wood Rabbit
8th February 2035 to 27th January 2036

Fire Rabbit
26th January 2047 to 14th February 2048

Earth Rabbit
12th February 2059 to 2nd February 2060

Rabbit

All types of rabbits and hares, or lagomorphs, are classified together in the rabbit category of the zodiac. These creatures are often stable, calm, intelligent, selfless, and peaceful, yet, they are also courageous, alert, quick, and agile. They move by leaping and hopping with their strong hind legs, which are placed beneath their body rather than out to the sides to increase their forward speed. Rabbits are friendly, and family oriented. They are skilled at digging burrows which allows them to stay safe and hidden from most predators. However, in open environments rabbits use their intelligence, speed, and agility to evade attack.

Rabbits are found almost everywhere in the world, with the exception of a few islands, Antarctica and the southern parts of South America (Burnie and Wilson 2001, 141). Their diet consists mainly of grasses, leafy greens and vegetables. The *qi* of healthy grass represents luck, good fortune, and money. At the White Cloud Temple, the Daoists cultivate various types of grass including some that have special healing qualities. The rabbits of the temple are used to process and manage all of the grasses that are grown there. Rabbits are environmentally friendly and their presence in an area helps to increase the growth of plant life. The burrows of the rabbit help to aerate the soil, as well as hold moisture and manure that are later absorbed by the growing roots of nearby plants. Rabbits will also refrain from eating the grasses that are nearest to its burrow, preferring to eat grasses that are further away. This process allows rabbits to remain nourished during times when food is scarce or when it is unsafe for them to exit their dens or warrens.

Mountains are governed by the rabbit, which take advantage of the readily available hollows within the moving rocks and earth. The rabbit's elongated spine causes their body to resemble the shape of a mountain when they are at rest. The unique landscape of mountains along with the rabbit's agile speed means that this landscape is ideal for the rabbits to avoid predators and remain safe. Species such as the volcano rabbit found in Mexico and the endangered Ili pika of China are especially suited to mountainous regions (Burnie and Wilson 2001, 141-43).

Calendar

The rabbit is the fourth animal of the zodiac. It is associated with the second month of the Chinese lunar calendar, called *mao*, and it lasts from approximately March 6th to April 5th in the Gregorian calendar and the two-hour period between 5 am to 7 am. This is the time of the year when the world is getting warmer and the yang energy is rising. This is also the peak breeding season for many animals, including lagomorphs, which causes them to be excitable and unpredictable. "It is during the breeding season that hares display the 'mad' behavior that gave us the phrase 'as mad as a March hare'. It is not unusual [at this time] to see an excited male hare jumping vertically around a field."[1]

Rabbit years are usually busy times that see a lot of projects and ideas in rapid development; however, there may also be a lot of red tape and procedural delays. Rabbits prefer everything to be done meticulously, fairly, and 'by the book'. For instance, The Manhattan Project, which produced the first atomic bomb, began taking form in the rabbit year of 1939, when Albert Einstein and Enrico Fermi took it upon themselves to inform the US president of the dangers of atomic energy. This project employed a large group of people who worked tirelessly for years and carried out their work with the utmost secrecy and exactitude.[2]

Rabbit years are usually good for socializing, communication, mutual respect, and romance due to the rabbit's highly diplomatic nature. In nature, rabbits often feed and tend to the young of their neighbors if necessary, and with the exception of breeding season, rabbits usually get along quite well with one another. This diplomatic energy can also lead to negotiations and clearer understandings, or on the other hand, revolutions or restructuring in the name of fairness and equal rights. For instance, in the year of the rabbit 1963 Martin Luther King Jr. delivered his iconic "I Have a Dream" speech during the *March on Washington* which would be known as one of the most defining moments of the civil rights movement.[3]

Rabbits are attracted to dazzling visual displays and movement, sometimes to their detriment. "Many well-known stories describe stoats killing rabbits and other large birds by "dancing" to distract attention from imminent attack, or stoats mesmerizing rabbits by their behavior or odor" (King and Powell 2007, 120). Similarly, rabbit years often see the development of new technologies and great works of art that dazzle the senses, especially in visual media. In 1927, for instance, the film *The Jazz Singer* was released, which marked the end of the silent film era and the introduction of the "talkies."[4]

In general, rabbit years are calm and routine times interspersed with events that occur rapidly and without warning. The rabbit's association with mountains is also partly inspired by the fact that large earthquakes are quite common during rabbit years. We must take the proper precautions at this time regarding earthquakes and other types of events that may, literally or figuratively, shift our foundation. This requires mindfulness, intuition, and forethought. In the rabbit year of 1927, the Xining earthquake struck mainland China with a magnitude of 7.9

---

[1] "Mad March Hares - Boxing Clever," by Sophie Leszczynska (2021). www.heartofengland forest.org/news/mad-march-hares-boxing-clever

[2] "The Manhattan Project," by Ushistory.org Editors (n.d.). www.ushistory.org/us/51f.asp

[3] "I Have a Dream, " by Amy Tikkanen (2017). www.britannica.com/topic/I-have-a-dream

[4] "The Jazz Singer," by Lee Pfeiffer (2011). www.britannica.com/topic/The-Jazz-Singer-film-1927

on the Richter scale. Some estimates suggest that this earthquake killed over 200,000 people.[5]

There can also be brief episodes of confrontation, opportunistic violence, or attacks as the more predatory people of the world seek to consolidate their power during this year. Shifting circumstances, excited energy, and the need to follow the rules more closely in the name of fairness or compliance can lead to frustration, deception, and anger in many people. When confronted in this way, or taken by surprise, instinctive reactions, skill, and alertness are the best strategies to employ. Afterwards, when the dust settles and the environment becomes safe enough, a more organized plan can be developed. For instance, Germany attacked Poland in the rabbit year of 1939, when their troops were fresh and their military was at full strength. This attack was in direct defiance to the *Agreement of Mutual Existence* in which England pledged military support to Poland if attacked. There was not much that the country of Poland could do about this invasion when it occurred because they did not have a military that was adequately strong enough to repel the attack, therefore, situational alertness and quick, instinctive reactions were the only recourse for the Polish people.[6]

Qi

The Chinese double-hour related to the rabbit is between 5 am and 7 am, the time of the large intestine meridian. This is the time when the large intestines are most active, and when many people wake up with the urge to use the bathroom. During this time, the kidneys are inactive and the mind is naturally still and peaceful. If you wake up at this time, you will have a strong and productive amount of energy throughout the day; however, if you fall back asleep quickly, then a lasting, sluggish energy may result.

The ghost point that is associated with the rabbit is known as Ghost's Path (guilu); it matches the point Extending Vessel (*shenmai*, UB-62) in the acupuncture system (Johnson 2014, 605). It is located on the lateral side of the foot, approximately 0.5 cun inferior to the inferior border of the lateral malleolus, in a depression posterior to the peroneal tendons. This point is used to calm the Spirit, quiet the mind, and treat conditions of the head and eyes.

The rabbit is also associated with the Crouching Rabbit (*futu*, ST-32) point, and the Support the Prominence (*futu*, LI-18) point. The crouching rabbit point is located on the upper thigh in the center of the quadriceps; it is used to treat the lower back, as well as leg and knee issues. When an acupuncture needle is inserted into this point, the thigh muscles, and the needle itself, will often jump

---

[5] "1927 Xining, China Earthquake," by Caitlyn B. (2010). thegeosphere.pbworks.com/w/page/24743188/1927%20Xining%2C%20China%20Earthquake

[6] "The War in Europe, 1939–41," by Thomas Hughes and John Royde-Smith (1998). www.britannica.com/event/World-War-II/The-war-in-Europe-1939-41

and twitch with the speed of a rabbit. Maintaining strong and healthy quadricep muscles helps to hold both the hips and the knees in their proper alignment which avoids damage to these areas.

In Chinese, the Support the Prominence point is a homophone of the Crouching Rabbit point, both pronounced *futu*. The former point is located on the side of the neck at the level of the Adam's apple, between the sternal head and clavicular head of the mastoid complex. It is used to treat throat issues, especially hoarseness and loss of the voice, sore throat, swelling of the neck, cough, hiccups, and pain or stiffness in the neck, cervical spine, shoulders, and arms (Deadman et al. 2007, 118-19). Rabbits have flexible necks that allow them to turn their head in excess of 180 degrees. They turn their heads often to remain aware of their surroundings, and groom themselves thoroughly. Having a strong, healthy, flexible neck allows their *qi* to flow more easily. The narrowness of the neck area forces the *qi* to pass through a tight space, which often leads to blockages, stiffness, and stress around the cervical vertebrae. By maintaining the health of their neck, rabbits manage their stress and develop awareness simultaneously.

Rabbit energy is associated with the large intestine meridian and the gastrointestinal tract. Rabbits feel most comfortable when they can run along straight, familiar, pathways that are free from obstructions. Similarly, the large intestine is a long, straight pathway in the body, that is most healthy when it is clean and free from blockages. Rabbits spend time maintaining their pathways so that they can move along them with great speed when the moment requires. Similarly, it is wise to keep the large intestine empty much of the time, so that qi and food waste can easily pass through it.

Rabbits can often be seen shivering and shaking their bodies. Many observers tend to think that the rabbit is shaking due to fear; however, this shaking is actually a method of unblocking the acupuncture meridians, focusing awareness, and gathering *qi*. This technique allows the rabbits to reduce their stress and gather courage to achieve their goals by intuitively responding to situations with explosive speed.

Special Abilities and Traits

Rabbits are Fast and Agile

Rabbits, especially hares, are swift, agile creatures. There are many breeds of lagomorph. Some of the fastest can run up to 35-45 mph, while others can leap 10ft in a single hop. "When pursued the hare runs fast, and close to the ground."[7] The hare's speed is due to the strength and anatomy of its hindlegs and feet. They can cover long distances quickly by pushing off the ground with both feet simultaneously, and gliding through the air for as long as possible. Rabbits are

---

[7] "Speed of a Rabbit or Hare," by Glenn Elert (2001). www.hypertextbook.com/facts/2001/RobertCohen.shtml

alert, and when they sense danger, they can move into swift action without a second thought. Due to the fact that they move at such high speeds, rabbits and hares often move along pathways that are straight. This allows them to continue moving quickly without the need to change direction, or lose momentum.

Rabbits Reproduce Quickly

Rabbits have some of the highest libidos of the zodiac and they live harmoniously in groups that vary in size depending on their species. In general, rabbits and hares get along with one another, and often their groups, called warrens, are governed by loose hierarchies. Some types of rabbits even exhibit "flocking" behavior, where a group moves together as a single unit. Due to these close bonds, lagomorphs easily understand the intentions of others, especially those within their family group and neighboring families within their warren. Rabbits even share their winter stores of grasses and mosses with other rabbits that may need nourishment. Daoists say that rabbits have three homes and three families in order to remain safe in the event of disaster or misfortune.

> Although lagomorphs are hunted intensely by many predators, they are able to maintain healthy population levels through a high reproductive rate. Because ovulation is not cyclical but is instead triggered in response to copulation, females can become pregnant directly after giving birth. Some species may even conceive a second litter before giving birth to the first. Rabbits, the most prolific breeders of all the lagomorphs, can produce litters of up to 12 young 6 times annually. Furthermore, rabbits are sexually mature at a young age (the European rabbit is able to conceive when only 3 months old), and the gestation period may be very short (the Florida cottontail rabbit gestates for as little as 26 days) . . . Newborn [rabbits] are helpless with eyes closed, and for warmth the mother lines the nursery chamber with dry grass, moss, and fur plucked from her own belly. She visits to suckle them for only a few minutes daily (Burnie and Wilson 2001, 143).

The mother rabbit understands the importance of taking care of herself and maintaining her own health. This allows her to have the strength to care for her young, produce milk, and to lure predators away from her nest. Rabbit mothers often parent from a distance, leaving their young alone in the nest for long periods of time to avoid attracting the attention of predators. Rabbit mothers only return to the nest if they are sure that they not bring any unwanted attention to their young. They are also diligent when it comes to maintaining their nests by cleaning out any waste or debris. They are able to skillfully maintain their own health, as well as the tidiness of the burrow, and still have the energy to manage protect and care for their young.

Rabbits are Skilled Escape Artists

Rabbits, which are not quite as fast as hares, are skilled at burrowing underground. Their burrows keep them safe from predators and harsh weather. Their burrows are also designed to be good homes for their leverets. When they create their burrows, they always create many entrances and exits so that they can avoid getting trapped inside. Rabbits always make sure to maintain a number options in any situation as a precaution. People who are born in the year of the rabbit also think in this way, and they always have alternative, diversified plans that can be put into action if their initial efforts run into difficulty.

Rabbits are hunted by many predators. Human beings, eagles, snakes, dogs and many other creatures all see the rabbit as a healthy meal. Rabbits are among the most preyed upon of all the animals, and because of this, rabbits have become skilled at escaping predators. Rabbit people are also adept at escaping, and they have good instincts when it comes to sensing approaching danger. This alertness and sensitivity to approaching pitfalls allows people born in the year of the rabbit to remain diligent and steadfast in difficult circumstances. Rabbits are often easygoing, but they are also keenly aware of the seriousness of life. The Greek storyteller Aesop illustrated the rabbit's sense of danger quite well when he recounted the ancient fable *The Hare and the Hound*.

> A hound started a hare from her form, and pursued her for some distance; but as she gradually gained upon him, he gave up the chase. A rustic who had seen the race met the hound as he was returning, and taunted him with his defeat. "The little one was too much for you," said he. "Ah, well," said the hound, "don't forget it's one thing to be running for your dinner, but quite another to be running for your life" (2003, 131).

Sunzi stated clearly that many strategies of war are based on the behavior of rabbits. When being pursued by a determined predator such as a hound, rabbits utilize their burrows in the same way that soldiers utilize their trenches and underground bunkers. The many exit points that are built into these structures allow the rabbit to maintain the element of surprise by forcing the enemy to predict which of the passageways it will use. Even when the predator chooses to observe a single exit, the rabbit can sense which exits are safe by listening to the ground and tasting the air. Being such a highly valued prey animal has caused the rabbit to develop highly acute senses.

Being in danger so often has also contributed to the rabbit's appreciation of peace and calm. Yet, while they can be patient and tolerant, their patience does have its limits. In the past, Daoists would place a rabbit in a room with a group of cats and observe their interactions over a prolonged period. In this experiment, the rabbit often remains calm and peaceful while the cats grow ever more curious. In a short time, the cats become curious enough to approach the rabbit, and test its boundaries by pawing and swiping at it. The cats never attack the rabbit with a determined effort, but simply bully the rabbit and test its boundaries. The rabbit often remains tolerant and passive for a long period, however, after being poked, hit, and scratched numerous times, the rabbit would eventually fight back furiously. When the rabbit finally retaliates, it doesn't do so in a cautious or playful manner, but tries to bite the cat's throat area to cause a fatal blow. When a rabbit is backed into a corner, or its patience is pushed past its limit, it will attack in a wild, ferocious, determined manner. Rabbits are not afraid to fight or take risks, and they often demonstrate great courage.

Cultural and Spiritual Concepts

The Jade Rabbit

All myths have many interpretations and complex layers of meaning that are used to describe various experiences and archetypal relationships. One of the most famous of ancient Chinese legends is *The Tale of Chang'e, the Moon Palace, and the Jade Rabbit,* which illustrates the intimate relationship between rabbits, divinity, and feminine yin energy. This tale is also understood as the origin of the Mid-Autumn festival, commonly called the moon festival, that is celebrated on August 15th of the lunar calendar in China and many countries throughout the world.

> A long time ago in ancient China, there was a god named Wu Gong. Wu Gong's job in heaven was to create various divine medicines by grinding and mixing herbs. During a trip to earth, Wu Gong gave away a few pills of immortality, infuriating the ruler of heaven, the Jade Emperor. As part of his punishment for this transgression, Wu Gong was banned from making divine medicines. The Jade Emperor then needed to find someone to take Wu Gong's place as the divine medicine maker. Feeling that human beings were too corruptible, he immediately sent three divine beings to the earth to find an animal worthy of this heavenly responsibility.
>
> The three divine beings arrived on earth in the form of three feeble, elderly men. Weak and desperate, they called out to the forest, begging for food. Many animals heard the cry of these three men, but only four felt sympathetic enough to assist them; a monkey, an otter, a jackal, and a rabbit. The monkey returned to the men with some fruit from high in the trees; the otter brought them some fish from deep in the river; and the jackal brought them a lizard, and a bowl of milk curds that it had stolen; however, the rabbit could not find any food to give the men. Feeling extreme guilt for not being able to help the men, the rabbit quickly jumped into the fire the men had made to offer itself as their meal.
>
> The three men saved the rabbit from its fate and brought it before the Jade Emperor as their choice. After hearing of the great sacrifice of the rabbit, the emperor knew that he had found the proper animal to be the next maker of

divine medicine. After learning the craft, the Jade Emperor was so pleased with the rabbit's dedication and skill, that he turned its fur a brilliant white color and made it extremely luxuriously soft, like white jade. From then on, the heavenly rabbit became appropriately known as the Jade Rabbit.

The Jade Rabbit represents the virtue striving for higher ideals to better provide for others. To sacrifice, work hard, and remain determined to help others without a guarantee of success requires a courageous and humble heart. The Jade Rabbit represents the sense of responsibility and commitment that we have to our fellow human beings and to the animal kingdom. Though responsibility, community, and love demand the best of us, they are the practices that produce effective, reliable results as well. The Jade Rabbit is located on the moon to watch over us, and remind us that, even in the darkness, the light of hope, comradery, generosity, and kindness can guide us to a feeling of home.

One day the Queen Mother of the West came to the Jade Rabbit and asked for a few extra pills of immortality, fully knowing that she was only allowed one. The rabbit refused at first, but fearing the wrath of the goddess he reluctantly conceded.

Soon thereafter, on earth, the hero Hou Yi, a man who was once an immortal, but had been condemned to live a mortal life, sought out the Queen Mother of the West to ask for help. He wished to live forever as an immortal with his wife Chang'e. Feeling sympathetic toward the couple, she gave them one pill of immortality to share. "Eating half will cause you to live forever on earth," she said, "but eating the entire pill will make you ascend to heaven."

When Hou Yi returned home, Chang'e was thrilled with his success, but exhausted from his long journey, Hou Yi decided to rest before sharing the medicine. However, he was resting his wife's curiosity got the better of her, and she was compelled to try it immediately, consuming it all. She quickly began float up into the sky against her will, and with earth now beyond her grasp, Chang'e decided to drift toward the lonely moon palace where at least she could be as close as possible to her husband, who was now left to live out the rest of his life on earth as a mortal man.

When the Jade Emperor discovered this situation, he furiously confronted the rabbit about his actions. The Jade Rabbit immediately fell to its knees and confessed that it had given the queen mother the extra pills out of fear, and that it would gladly accept any punishment that the emperor deemed suitable. Seeing his genuine remorse, the Jade Emperor allowed the rabbit to determine its own punishment.

After some thought, the rabbit realized that it was responsible for Chang'e being confined to the moon palace, and decided that it would also stay there to keep Chang'e company. The rabbit would also continue to make medicine, isolated on the moon free from distraction and temptation. The Jade Emperor accepted, and to this day Chang'e and the Jade Rabbit reside on the moon to-gether.[8]

This part of the story illustrates that the strength of the rabbit can also be its downfall. The generosity and selfless nature of the rabbit means that it is will-ing to go to great lengths to prevent the suffering of others. When the selfness of the rabbit is misguided, it can quickly become gullibility. The jade rabbit re-minds us that being generous and selfless is a virtue, but that lacking boundaries or a greater understanding of the implications of our decisions, is a fault. The heart perfects wisdom, and wisdom perfects the heart; both aspects are necessary for achieving self-realization and wholeness.

Rabbits Represent Motherhood

The legend states that even today, in the moon palace, there resides a woman, a rabbit, a man, and a tree. The fable of Chang'e, the moon palace, and the Jade Rabbit represents the feminine, yin energy of nature as well as the unconscious mind within us all. The moon's energy is responsible for managing and nurturing all of life on the earth.

[People who embody rabbit energy] will begin to see a cycle of 28 days begin-ning to manifest in their lives. . . They see movement occur in their lives in varying degrees of leaps and hops, starts and stops. It won't be a steady step by step movement. The "leaps and hops" do not usually take more than the cycle of the moon (28 days) to occur (Andrews 2007, 304).

The cycles of the moon and the tides have regulated and nourished life on Earth for billions of years. All human beings (especially women), all plant-life, and all animal life on Earth are deeply connected to the movements of the moon. This nourishing relationship that we have with the moon is extremely similar to the relationship that we share with our unconscious mind; therefore, the moon is also a representative of the unconscious forces within us all.

The moon represents the great mother archetype in all of its aspects. This is a powerful archetype, shrouded in mystery, and therefore, understanding of all of the nuances of this archetype in particular, can be difficult. The Jungian analyst Sibylle Birkhäuser-Oeri describes the difficulty that many people have in under-standing the archetype of the mother as follows:

The mother archetype is especially concerned with that part of the psyche which is still wholly nature (natural), which is why we often speak of Mother Nature. . . One difficulty in understanding the mother image arises from the

---

[8] "Story of the Jade Rabbit of the Moon," by Off the Great Wall (2014). www.youtube.com/watch?v=KbxwiIZQIMw

fact that it is simultaneously one of a number of [individual] contents of the unconscious and also a symbol for the whole collective unconscious. But the unconscious, as the original unity, contains all opposites. . . The mother is thus an inconceivably powerful force that can all too easily overwhelm a human being. At the same time, she is the source of everything new (1988, 14-15).

The jade rabbit represents the instinctive and intuitive nature of life on earth and it is regarded as a sign of selflessness, piety, righteousness and sacrifice. These are the same virtues ascribed to the divine mother in cultures around the world. The jade rabbit represents the instinctual animal aspect of the mother archetype, which is passionate, caring, sensual, authentic.

An animal lives with its environment; not in isolation, but bound up with the whole. . . The mother as an animal can allow us to switch off our consciousness to such an extent that we can follow our instincts and so become whole, sacrificing a merely egocentric use of our powers. Thus, animals are particularly appropriate symbols for the mother archetype" (Birkhäuser-Oeri 1988, 41).

In Daoism, this wholeness is achieved through the practice of meditation and through a deep reverence for nature. Daoist's respect for nature has led them to a deeper understanding of it than that of most people. It is this instinctual knowledge of balance and reciprocity, yin and yang, that animals embody. By connecting with mother nature, we simultaneously progress toward states of divine ecstasy and greater knowledge. The jade rabbit is a reminder of the innocence of the animal mind, which is bound to the experience of life on the earth and has unconscious needs that must be fulfilled.

The particular mark of the animals is the fact that they live out their drives and instincts without the restraints of conscious, rational considerations which inhibit human beings. They are still entirely contained in their unconscious nature. Their desires and wills are the desires and wills of nature, in other words, the law of the collective unconscious of their species. Animals still live entirely within this knowledge. Whoever returns to the Great Mother, to the alpha and omega of all life, returns to this absolute knowledge, of which animals are especially suitable symbols. They thus become symbols of wholeness (Birkhäuser-Oeri 1988, 41).

Rabbits Represent Good Luck and Fortune

In the story of the moon palace, the jade rabbit sacrifices itself for the good of others, and is thereby rewarded by being taken up to heaven by divine beings. In Daoism, the various gods of fortune are often depicted as being surrounded by rabbits. Many Asian cultures are familiar with the worship of the "money cat" that is believed to attract money and good fortune. The jade rabbit is often worshiped in much the same way. There are many depictions of the rabbit holding coins and dressed in fine robes. Where the cat attracts wealth, the rabbit itself represents money. In the past, many cultures raised rabbits to the point that rabbits were being used as an early form of currency. Their value in meat and fur, and their small size made rabbits a natural choice for this purpose.

In the zodiac, rabbits are thought of as diplomats with a noble character, good manners, and a peaceful demeanor. This diplomatic sensibility often earns them rapport, luck, and good fortune. For instance, the way that rabbits hold their hands up loosely in front of their body, bent at the elbows, is a gesture that suggests good fortune and successful ventures. They have dexterous hands that allow them to manipulate objects, and this has led to the development of reasoning and intelligence. Rabbits keep their hands to themselves, close to their body, leaving them poised and ready to take advantage of any opportunities that may present themselves. Therefore, while rabbits may be hesitant, they are also ready to adapt themselves to changing situations.

Rabbits represent wealth because their intelligence lends itself to understanding the strategies that are used to invest in the stock market. Investing requires maintaining many diverse options and exit strategies, and this is similar to the ways that rabbits think as they construct their burrows. Even the way that the rabbit moves up and down, in leaps and bounds, yet always continues moving forward is similar to the way in which the stock market fluctuates. People who have a talent for investing think and strategize in a way that is similar to rabbits; they prepare for difficult future scenarios.

Rabbits can maintain a calm demeanor and mental clarity even when situations become stressful. This is another quality that readily lends itself to accumulating wealth, and it accounts for the rabbit's reputation for being lucky as well. They have long flexible necks that allow them to remain both alert and relaxed. Their cervical health contributes to the rabbit's longevity, their low stress levels, and their acute awareness. This unimpeded flow of *qi* greatly helps to contribute to the rabbit's fortune and good luck.

The rabbit and the deer are both considered symbols of fortune, good luck, and abundance. "In China, the deer is a sign of good luck, happiness, longevity, and fortune. In fact, the Chinese word for deer, *lu*, is a homonym of the Chinese word for abundance and also synonymous with the word for income."[9] Both are highly valued prey animals, they are noble, and they each have a unique connection with heaven. In Daoism, there is fable that explains how the rabbit and the deer both became the representatives of good luck and fortune.

> Many years ago, the Jade Emperor was walking through the forest in search of an animal that would represent fortune, love, and good luck in heaven. It occurred to him that only a creature of a noble, dignified quality and understood the value of life could undertake the great responsibility that this position

---

[9] "Deer Symbolism & Meaning" by Garth C. Clifford (2021). www.worldbirds.org/deer-symbolism/

would require. After observing the creatures of the forest for three days, he decided that the deer and the rabbit were the two best nominees for the position, so he took them both up to heaven to make the final decision. They were both beautiful, honest, and righteous creatures with a noble heart and a self-sacrificing love for others, making the decision inherently difficult.

The Jade Emperor decided that he would have them race across the heavens as a test to see which one of them was more determined and suitable as a luck deity. The race began and both animals took off with great speed. Before long the beautiful spots of the deer's coat began to glow with such intensity that they lit up the dark night sky, forming the stars. His large antlers, which had connected him with the heavens for so long, allowed him to rise above any obstacle that blocked his path. As the deer proudly continued to light up the sky with its grace, it was unaware of the fact that early in the race the rabbit had swiftly hitched a ride on its head, perched between its antlers.

As they traveled, the rabbit's white fur began to glow as well, and reflecting the light of the heavens, forming the moon. Together they created a beautiful sight, illuminating the entire sky. Eventually, as the deer approached the finish line, the rabbit leapt from the head of the deer and won the race by a small margin. Impressed by the singular focus, humility and ingenuity of both animals the jade emperor declared the rabbit to be the primary representative of luck and fortune in the heavens, associated with the moon, and he declared the deer to be the representative of luck and fortune on the earth, associated with the stars.

As a reminder of humility and the fragility of life, being one of the most preyed upon animals in nature, the rabbit also represents the abundance of new life and rebirth with its extraordinary fertility. The high reproduction rate of rabbits generates strong energy in their lower abdomen which contributes to their longevity. All mothers cultivate a strong lower elixir field which stores and purifies the yin energy of the body. In the process of giving birth, the mother will inevitably lose blood. This greatly boosts the immune system, relieving many previously chronic conditions, and it stimulates the body to begins creating fresh healthy blood cells. This strong abdominal energy allows women in general to have a strong sense of intuition and to know when to trust their gut feeling.

Daoists and many modern health experts have often referred to the abdomen as the "second brain." This implies that intelligence in the head, and intuition in the gut, are both distinct, essential skills to develop throughout life. The brain and the gut work in conjunction with one another to help process all of the information coming to the body from the external environment. A mother's intuition is a powerful and acute form of awareness which is often described as a combination of a series of mental images and a strong 'gut feeling.' Mothers also know instinctively when it is time to let their young be free and independent. "Within one month, 28 days, the young [rabbits] are able to be out on their own. They can stay in the nest, but they can survive on their own. If a new litter arrives, the mother will kick the old litter out. This 28-day period again reinforces the lunar connection with the rabbit" (Andrews 2007, 303-4). The jade rabbit is an appropriate symbol for the innate innocence of animal nature, and for the significant function that animals serve in earth's ecosystem. Rabbits help nature run smoothly by nourishing and maintaining the environment and its inhabitants.

The rabbit also symbolizes the cultural and technological development that people crave and naturally produce. Like the stock market, cultural development is sporadic, yet always oriented upward toward greater growth and development. This is the way in which rabbits move. The greatest example of the this is the timeless tale of *The Hare and the Tortoise*. This story, that was made so famous by Greek folklorists and others is, a fable that describes the ongoing battle (or marriage) between cultural/technological evolution and biological evolution.

The rabbit tries to speed ahead of the tortoise in the same way that human beings try to develop their culture, technologies and intellect faster than the methods of adaptation that drive biological evolution. "Cultural evolution is independent of changes in genetic makeup, whereas every individual is the product of its biological evolution" (Barash 1987, 36). These two methods of evolution are working simultaneously to form the reality that we have today. Over time, as we begin to grow in intelligence, wisdom and integrity these two modalities of culture and biology work more harmoniously together. While culture and novelty are necessary, it is also true that "slow and steady wins the race" because integrous growth and adaptation takes time. Yin energy, which is slow, instinctual, and cyclical is the foundation for our cultural drives, our destiny, and our desire for uniqueness.

People Who Embody the Rabbit

People born in the year of the rabbit are clever, intelligent, skillful, agile, determined, kind, and compassionate, though they can sometimes be over-cautious, timid, gullible, rigid and indecisive. Rabbits are patient; they can remain still and calm for long periods of time, and this makes them good listeners, friends, and companions. Rabbits are friendly and sociable, and they can be great company in small or large groups. They can listen well to others, providing a safe environment free from judgment for others to vent their frustrations and feel heard and appreciated.

Rabbits are often caring, fair, and compassionate people. In China, the terms "rabbit grandma" and "rabbit grandpa" are sometimes used to refer to gentleness, kindness, and wisdom of elderly people. Rabbit people often develop a healthy respect for their elders due to their similarities. Through sharing experiences and communicating with our elders we are able to develop a much greater understanding of life and avoid many common mistakes.

Even though rabbits are often courteous and have good manners, they are also alert to unusual behaviors, unfairness, and predatory people. They are not easily fooled by others and they always trust their instincts when it comes meeting new people. "The physical features of rabbits and hares reflect their need to perceive danger and elude predators. Large ears provide excellent hearing, eyes positioned high on each side of the head give almost 360-degree vision" (Burnie and Wilson 2001, 141). People who embody the rabbit energy are able to skillfully communicate and navigate relationships. They are always paying attention to the cues of others, even when they seem to be minding their own affairs. By intuitively recognizing where others are most vulnerable, rabbit people are able to know how best to help them, and how to protect themselves if necessary.

In general, rabbit people often maintain good physical health, though they can be depleted and fragile at times. They can suffer from anxiety, depression, fear and other emotional issues if they do not take care of their health. Rabbit people especially benefit from moderate exercise and a diet that includes leafy greens. Walking or running are often favorite types of exercise for rabbits because it helps them to relax their mind and solve problems. Rabbit people sometimes over-complicate situations because being able to easily see things from the perspective of another makes it difficult to be decisive or to establish healthy boundaries.

Rabbit people are often modest, attractive and hygienic. Females born during the rabbit year often have a pure heart and a beautiful, demure appearance. Their hair and nails usually grow quite fast. Grooming and an orderly environment, are essential to rabbit people because to function optimally, they need a clean working space. This is similar to the way in which rabbits compulsively need to clean their fur, burrows and pathways from debris. Yet, even though they make sure to groom and clean themselves, many rabbits, and rabbit people, can also appear wild or even crazy.

Rabbits prefer low risk endeavors and a calm approach to reaching their goals. Though they make steady progress over time, it will often occur in varying starts and stops. Rabbits are often thorough and can sometimes be perfectionists. They often do their best to get all the value that they can out of every opportunity, partly because their indecisiveness causes them to miss opportunities at times. Rabbit people know when to work hard, and when it is time to rest. They are usually strict with themselves, but tolerant of others. Rabbits regularly wear a sincere, peaceful smile and they are not deterred by the negativity of others; but, are driven forward by their own persistence and inner confidence.

External Zodiac
Goose

Rabbits and geese are both animals that are graceful and caring, while maintaining strength and integrity. Both rabbits and geese are nurturing parents and focused on their family life, however, they do so in different ways. Rabbits are not monogamous, and while they definitely provide for their young, they also leave their young unattended for long periods of time to avoid drawing unnecessary attention to the burrow from predators. Geese, on the other hand, rarely leave their young unattended, with the mother and father taking turns caring for them at all times until they have reached an age where they can fend for themselves. Rabbits rely heavily on the strength of their lower limbs for speed and agility on land, and geese have powerful legs for swimming and for taking off. Rabbits also have dexterous shoulders and arms which they use in nearly all of their behaviors, and similarly, geese rely heavily on their upper limbs for speed and endurance while flying, with some species able to fly up to 60mph (100kph) (Burnie and Wilson 2001, 282).

Qi

The goose category of the zodiac includes geese, swans, cranes, and ducks. They like to eat fish, shrimps, other small animals and aquatic plants. Swans are the largest members of the goose category, and they live in lakes and marshes, forming their nests on the water's edge often on small islands. They feed on snails, mollusks, and aquatic plants. Swans are models of grace and elegance, and even their long take offs and landings on the water's surface seem to be executed with smooth precision (Burnie and Wilson 2001, 282-84).

All waterfowl have similar features such as a semi-waterproof layer of feathers, a long flexible neck, and a layer of fat beneath their skin to keep them warm, however, each species is also anatomically unique in many ways. Cranes, for instance, are large wading birds that are usually white with red crests on their head which make them easy to distinguish. They often travel in small groups, inhabiting the shallow waters of lakes, rivers, swamps, and oceans and they are often active at night.

Geese are not afraid of addressing potential threats and they are the natural enemy of snakes. Geese have feathers that are strong and packed tightly together which protect them against snake bites, and their long, flexible necks allow them to attack from indirect angles just like a serpent. When threatened by predators, a rabbit's first instinct is to run and find the cover of a burrow as quickly as possible. When geese feel threatened, they directly address the aggressor as a group, often while honking and making large displays.

Geese have a natural ability to sense the quality and intentions of other creatures, and they have little tolerance for and ill will. In the past, at the White Cloud Temple, geese were trained as guards to patrol the grounds to keep snakes, predators, and other undesirables from gaining entry. A full-sized goose or swan can weight up to 25lbs (12kgs) and with their flexible and powerful necks they have the strength to bring an adult human being to the ground (Burnie and Wilson 2001, 283). Geese have been known to chase down people they find threatening or intrusive with determination and fervor.

Eating the meat of geese or ducks is beneficial for overall health because it helps to reduce inflammation and body temperature. The ability to lower the temperature of the body can help to protect its yin energy, avoid heat stroke, and reduce the severity of high fevers. By protecting the body's yin energy, duck and goose meat also allows the body to stay warm in cold conditions, while simultaneously preventing over-heating in warm conditions.

Special Abilities and Traits

Geese spend most of their time paddling on the surface of lakes and small bodies of water. They have short yet powerful webbed feet, which give them a great amount of traction in water, and their fourth toe faces backwards without being webbed, giving them stability when walking on land. They preen their coats regularly to keep their feathers packed tightly, which makes them water resistant. Furthermore, they have a gland that produces oil on their rump, which they then spread over their feathers using their beak, making them even more waterproof and buoyant.

Geese are also quite skilled at "upending," where they use their long necks to dive beneath the water's surface to pluck aquatic plants and small animals from the lake-bed while their body remains buoyant on the surface. Cranes have developed long legs that can enter and exit the water without causing much disturbance and a long beak that they can use to quickly snatch up anything edible from the lake or riverbed (Burnie and Wilson 2001, 282-301).

While they are some of the largest and heaviest flying creatures on earth today, geese travel great distances during their migratory season. Some geese take off straight out of the water with their powerful wings; while other, heavier birds, such as swans, must gather momentum by 'running' on the surface of the water with their webbed feet before they can become airborne. Once in the air, geese fly in a distinctive V-formation, which creates an area of reduced wind resistance for all but the lead bird. The position of leader, being the most strenuous position of the formation, is shared by all of the birds and is changed quite often to avoid exhaustion. Geese have great endurance and can fly at swift speeds once their direction and altitude are established (Burnie and Wilson 2001, 282-84).

Cultural and Spiritual Concepts

Geese Represent Devotion

All geese mate for life, and they raise their young together, taking turns at the nest to care for their young. Swans, however, are particularly devoted to their partner and demonstrate their romantic affection often. Swans and their partners can be seen swimming side-by-side with one another, nuzzling, and synchronizing their movements as they swim in unison. The "dance of the swans" is symbolic of the virtues of romance and devotion. Swans demonstrate grace, intuition, and the power of feminine elegance as they move together in affectionate, meaningful synchronicity.

The phrase "dance of the swans" is also used to describe the act of making love. Daoists refer to the act of opening and closing the legs, for any reason, as "swan movement." In the Daoist manuals on sacred sexual techniques, many movements and positions are based upon the graceful actions and behaviors of the swan, as well as the behaviors of the rabbit.

Goose down feathers are a common and popular form of bedding material due to their softness and ability to retain heat, but the *qi* of the goose feathers also helps to promote restful sleep by warding off evil *qi* and nightmares. The goose's connection to the rabbit means that goose down feathers are also able to support a healthy libido as well. This only highlights the relationship between geese and romance. Geese dive beneath the surface in life, both literally and figuratively, to appreciate the value of what is concealed. By looking deeper at life, ourselves, and our loved ones, we can develop closer relationships, graceful excellence, and a deeper appreciation for life's hidden treasures.

Geese instinctively know when peaceful conditions are becoming disturbed, and they quickly fly off into the distance before conditions become dangerous. When the weather begins to change, geese instinctively know that it is time to fly toward warmer climates. Geese are sensitive to the dynamics of yin and yang energy. When cranes sense even subtle amounts of disturbing energy, for instance, they calmly fly off without hesitation. When the abundant yin energy of winter begins to approach, geese fly south, and when the abundant yang energy of summer begins to approach, geese fly north; remaining in a balanced energy environment all year round. By staying alert and aware, geese are always able to find themselves in favorable conditions. The primary concern of geese is to live in a harmonious environment that is conducive to health, happiness, and peace.

Geese protect their environment when slight disturbances such as predators attempt to enter, but when things become untenable, they quickly leave in search of a new, peaceful home. Geese are adventurers that enjoy travelling long distances; discovering new places and having fresh experiences. Geese teach us to reach for a higher perspective, and then follow our own sense of direction until we find a peaceful, comfortable place that we can call home.

Fairies

Daoist mythology says that geese are not originally from this world, instead it is believed that they came from the moon palace; the home of the fairies, the jade rabbit, and Chang'e. In the Vietnamese version of the story of the Jade Rabbit, when the rabbit achieves its heavenly status, it is carried to the moon palace by geese. These geese are the fairy daughters of the jade emperor that can travel between the moon palace and the earth. They assist in all of the duties and tasks that the moon seeks to fulfill on earth, including supporting all forms of life. The moon is considered the mother of all living beings on earth, and geese, or more specifically the swan, is considered to be a symbol of a nurturing, mother. The only two animals that are said to reside in the moon are the swan, and the jade rabbit.

Geese, like our imagination, often bring us messages from heaven and other far away, legendary places in the form of fables, myths, and fairy tales. For many centuries the principle writing utensil was a quill made from large, hollow goose feathers. Geese and rabbits represent the wisdom that is conveyed through writing, symbolism, conceptualization. The relationship between geese, the lunar quality of motherhood, and fables has been recognized in Europe for centuries as the famous tales of "Mother Goose." Mother Goose was a literary device used by many early authors to illustrate morals and wisdom for children. Geese and swans are examples of responsible parents and devoted partners. These creatures are focused on caring for their young and teaching them the ways of the world in a way that is safe and understandable. For this reason, geese represent storytelling, the responsibilities and freedom of adulthood, and the magic of curiosity, imagination, and joy.

Quotes from Famous Rabbits

One makes a gift of one's life and endeavors by sanctifying it with love, and devotion, and selfless service. When seeking to uplift others, we are uplifted in the process. Every kind thought or smile therefore benefits oneself, as well as all the world.

-Dr. David Hawkins

The only source of knowledge is experience.

-Albert Einstein

On the whole, human beings want to be good, but not too good, and not quite all the time.

-George Orwell

The end of all knowledge should be service to others.

-Caesar Chavez

Let us put our minds together and see what life we can make for our children.

-Sitting Bull

The best revenge is massive success.

-Frank Sinatra

No matter what people tell you, words and ideas can change the world.

-Robin Williams

If you cannot find peace within yourself, you will never find it anywhere else.

-Marvin Gaye

I believe you have to be willing to be misunderstood if you're going to innovate.

-Jeff Bezos

I believe the world is one big family, and we need to help each other.

-Jet Li

Eternal life can mean utter reverence for life itself.

-Seamus Heaney

5

Dragon

Earth Dragon
23rd January 1928 to 9th February 1929

Metal Dragon
8th February 1940 to 26th January 1941

Water Dragon
27th January 1952 to 13th February 1953

Wood Dragon
13th February 1964 to 1st February 1965

Fire Dragon
31st January 1976 to 17th February 1977

Earth Dragon
17th February 1988 to 5th February 1989

Metal Dragon
5th February 2000 to 23rd January 2001

Water Dragon
23rd January 2012 to 9th February 2013

Wood Dragon
10th February 2024 to 28th January 2025

Fire Dragon
28th January 2036 to 14th February 2037

Earth Dragon
14th February 2048 to 2nd February 2049

Metal Dragon
2nd February 2060 to 21st January 2061

Dragon

Dragons are the only mythological creature that are represented in the twelve-animal zodiac, as no one has actually ever seen a dragon as they have been depicted. The dragon category of the zodiac represents all types of lizards, crocodiles, and many of the world's reptiles. Dragons have been depicted as integral parts of numerous cultures ad mythological systems throughout the world, each of which is described in a unique manner. The Chinese culture, for instance, depicts dragons as an honorable and helpful beings, while other groups depict it as an evil monster. The Aztec Quetzalcoatl, Egyptian Apep, Aboriginal Rainbow Serpent, Viking Fafnir, the Greek Hydra, and the Hebrew Tanninim are all variations on the idea of the dragon.[1] While the dragon category represents lizards, and reptiles, especially the gecko, they are also partly inspired by the fossils of dinosaurs. In China, the fossils of dinosaurs are often referred to as "dragon bones."

Dragons are often difficult to describe because they represent such a wide variety of concepts, being an amalgamation of many different ideas and qualities. The fact that dragons in many cultures are related to rainbows, illustrates the fact that dragons are elusive, ethereal, and composed of a variety of qualities. The dragon is the highest and most powerful creature of the twelve-animal zodiac because of its strength, wisdom, and numerous talents.

Dragons are depicted in many ways throughout the world; with the dragons of western Europe and the Mediterranean differing greatly from the dragons of China and east Asia. In western Europe, dragons are fire breathing creatures with wings, scales, and claws that are often destructive and malevolent. In China, dragons are related to water and the heavens, they fly without wings, and while they have reptilian scales and claws, they are considered wise, protective creatures that bring good luck.

Dragons are associated with water, rain, rivers, lakes, and oceans. Crocodiles, iguanas, geckos, and many other lizards are attracted to bodies of water and feel comfortable in humid, damp environments. Geckos are the lizard that are most similar to the dragons that are described in Chinese folklore. Geckos are usually found in tropical climates, islands, and oceanic environments where water and humidity are plentiful. Geckos climb and move in a unique and elegant manner, they have unique smooth scales that can either be brightly colored or camouflaged, and most species can see quite well in darkness. Just like the dragons of folklore, many lizard species are capable of developing unique talents such as the ability to walk on water, fly with their feet, change the color of their skin and scales, and hold their breath for long periods of time. Lizards and dragons have adapted remarkably well to aquatic environments, caves, and darkness.

---

[1] "Snake Gods and Goddesses: 19 Serpent Deities from Around the World" by Cierra Tolentino (2022). www.historycooperative.org/snake-gods-and-goddesses/

Dragons require the *qi* of the mountains, the snow, the ocean, water, and the clouds. So along with aquatic environments, many stories of Chinese dragons describe them residing in caves, mountains, rocks, and stones. In Chinese mythology dragons can travel up to the heavens and down into the earth with equal ease. Dragons easily move through stone, water and physical matter. These descriptions further illustrate the connection between the dragon and hydrologic cycle of the earth.

Dragons are most often described flying elegantly through the open sky and bringing rain with its magical movements. The way a Chinese dragon flies is described as distinctly different from that of a European dragon. Rather than flying in a manner that is similar to that of birds, using wings, Chinese dragons fly through the air in the same way as a silk ribbon or scarf. The Chinese ribbon dance demonstrates this principle as ribbons, pulled from the front, remain in constant motion while appearing to remain still periodically. Traditional myths describe dragons as being composed of nine anatomical aspects that resemble other animals. They are said to have the antlers of a stag, the head of a camel, the eyes of a demon, the neck of a snake, the belly of a clam, the scales of a carp, the claws of an eagle, the paws of a tiger, and the ears of a cow.

Calendar

The dragon is the fifth animal of the zodiac. It is associated with the third month of the Chinese lunar calendar, that lasts from approximately April 5th to May 6th in the Gregorian calendar, and to the two-hour period between 7 am and 9 am. This is the height of the daily spring season and the rising of yang energy, which lasts from 3 am to 9 am. This is a time when the plants and animals are flourishing, transforming, and establishing themselves to take advantage of the abundant, fresh energy. This is a time of awakening, development, progress, and change. Similarly, dragon years are times of hard work and accelerated progress. The many colors and talents of the dragon express themselves during this year with an abundance of opportunities to grow, learn, and develop. This is a time when work and personal projects come into greater focus, and applying effort is especially fulfilling.

During dragon years, many social events and friendly occasions will encourage you to display your vibrant colors and your many talents. These events naturally lead to new friends and acquaintances that can benefit you in a multitude of ways. The energy of this year is one of synergy, progress, cooperation, and accomplishment. While dragon years are full of social gatherings and events, there are also times during the year that require rest, recuperation, and solitude. Just as the mythological dragons would often inhabit caves and the bottom of the oceans, during the dragon year, people find it necessary to escape from the pressure and chaos of society when their energy is low or when they need to process complex thoughts and emotions.

Dragon years are all about talent, strength, and personal development. In the year of the dragon, many creative solutions appear as well as the power to act on them and form practical solutions. Being the most powerful animal of the zodiac, dragons are focused on accomplishing their goals and creating solutions to the problems that they encounter. Dragons are broad-minded, self-determined, and authoritative; assisting people by leading and discovering new methods. Many new, large-scale ideas are implemented during this year and while not all of them can be successful, the power of the dragon will see that many of them are. The fierce determination of the dragon leads to success at nearly every turn, to the point where success itself can become overwhelming.

Imagination and creative thinking soar this year as the energy of the environment inspires people to take action. This is a year when big dreams have the possibility of taking root and becoming a reality. On the other hand, to achieve their great determination and success, dragons have to face many great challenges and learn from past failures, which can be significant. The fearless nature of dragons means that they march forward in the face of insurmountable odds, and rely on their inner drive to see them through difficult circumstances. In the dragon year of 1940, for instance, the battle of Dunkirk between German and British forces occurred which threatened to completely eliminate the British Expeditionary Force. The British Expeditionary Force made up a large portion of British ground troops at the time, and the loss of this unit would have been disastrous for the country. The battle ended when hundreds of British civilians boarded their own personal vessels and took to the sea to rescue their countrymen from certain disaster on the shores of France.[2]

Conscientiousness and patience increase during dragon years, as the dragon is seen as a generous and helpful creature in eastern culture. Resilient integrity and honor are the proper methods for handling the intense power and vision that dragon years bring about. Dragons represent the duty, honor, talent, humility, and the strength of mature masculinity. In the dragon year of 1928, Alexander Fleming discovered penicillin as a form of treatment for many of the world's diseases, and introduced the use of antibiotics, which greatly reduced the number of deaths from infection.[3]

The Chinese royal family is often associated with dragons and dragon mythology is a symbol of their responsibility to honor, serve, and protect their people. In dragon years, the energy of serving the greater good becomes accentuated. Many of the changes and ideas that are implemented during these years have the goal of benefiting society as a whole and uniting people. Policy changes and new leadership are common in dragon years, as are large trials and the theme of

---

[2] "Dunkirk Evacuation," by The Editors of Encyclopedia (2009). www.britannica.com/event/Dunkirk-evacuation/

[3] "Discovery and Development of Penicillin," by American Chemical Society International Historic Chemical Landmarks (n.d.). www.acs.org/content/acs/en/education/whatischemistry/landmarks/flemingpenicillin.html

serving of justice. In 1964, for instance, the civil rights act would be passed into law in the United States officially ending policies of racial segregation.[4] There are many myths in Chinese culture of magnificent dragons bringing rain to the people so that they can grow their crops, and nature can thrive. Similarly, royal authority, originates with the elite, top levels of society, yet its duty is in service to the common people, to make their lives more prosperous.

The progress of society and civilization accelerate during dragon years. This rapid progress can be uncomfortable and overwhelming for some; however, the dragon's sense of honor and protection directs progress toward positive outcomes. By 1940, the progress of World War II was well underway, and the operations of all involved parties were increasing dramatically in quantity and scope. Twenty-four years later, in 1964, the same type of increased military action would be taking place in Vietnam after the sinking of the U.S. Destroyer Maddox in the Gulf of Tonkin.[5]

Dragons are also the rulers of water and any of the ways that water is controlled or utilized. During dragon years there are many floods and significant rainfall. Water seems to find its way into many arid areas as well during this time and droughts often come to an end or be mitigated. In the dragon year of 1928, the Boulder Canyon Project Act was passed authorizing the construction of the Boulder Dam, later to be renamed the Hoover Dam, at the Colorado River Basin in Nevada. Upon its completion the dam produced four billion kilowatt-hours of electricity per year and delivered reliable water supplies to vast areas of surrounding land.[6] [7]

Many fears and perceived catastrophes are often averted, unmasked, or dispelled when dragon energy is applied. This allows people to continue to progress in a clear, straight-forward manner without undue worry or stress. Dragon energy produces a no-nonsense approach to problems and a fearless confrontation of one's limitations. Overall, dragon years produce a solid, assertive, determined, and practical energy that remains open-minded and adaptable.

Qi

The time of the day that relates to the dragon is between 7 am and 9 am; the time of the stomach meridian. During this two-hour period, the body becomes fully awake and alert, yet remains relaxed. This is a wonderful time to eat breakfast

---

[4] "Civil Rights Act (1964)," by The National Archives and Records Administration (1964). www.archives.gov/milestone-documents/civil-rights-act

[5] "Gulf of Tonkin Incident," by Patricia Bauer (2017). www.britannica.com/event/Gulf-of-Tonkin-incident

[6] "Boulder Canyon Project Act (1928)," by The National Archives and Records Administration (1928). www.archives.gov/milestone-documents/boulder-canyon-project-act

[7] "Hoover Dam," by The Bureau of Reclamation (2018). www.usbr.gov/lc/hooverdam/faqs/powerfaq.html

because the stomach has extra energy to digest and process food. This is also a time when the mind is able to concentrate easily, and mild exercise or *qigong* meditation can further enhance this mental state.

The stomach is one of the most powerful organs of the body because it houses and manages the body's post-heaven *qi*. The stomach nourishes this *qi*, which is gathered from the foods that we eat and the air we breathe. The energy of the stomach is the primary energy that helps us complete the tasks of the day. This powerful energy is also the powerhouse of the body's immune system, and maintaining a healthy diet and GI tract greatly increase the body's ability to fend off pathogens and disease. The stomach can be likened to a large hydro-electric dam that holds water and resources, and the processing of these resources provides an abundance of energy.

Also, between the hours of 7 am and 9 am, the pericardium, which is a membrane that surrounds and protects the heart, is at its least active, and seeking rest. The pericardium acts like a protecting wall around the heart and protects it from negative influences. This means that during these hours emotional issues and matters of the heart should be set aside while the practical tasks of the day are attended to. By avoiding conflict and negative emotions which attack the heart, the pericardium is able to rest and repair itself.

The low energy of the pericardium is also partly responsible for the calm, relaxed energy that many people experience at this time. When the pericardium is able to rest and function properly, the mental and emotional state of the individual is more stable and clearer throughout the day. When negative thoughts and emotions are engaged during this time then the person often keeps a negative mood throughout the day. The saying "someone woke up on the wrong side of the bed" is a response to this phenomenon of addressing negative emotions too early in the day.

Along with the stomach, dragons are associated with the kidneys. The kidneys are a powerful organ in the body, and together with the stomach they provide the raw power that is necessary for the body to function, in this case, pre-heaven *qi*. Pre-heaven *qi* is present before birth, and remains until the moment of death; it represents our genetic predispositions, our DNA, our memory, and our karma. The pre-heaven *qi* manifests as the yin and yang energies of the body, which the kidneys manage and regulate by separating and recombining them.

Just like the mythological dragons that control the water systems of the external world, the kidneys are the organs that control the water metabolism and the fluids of the body. The fluids of the body provide nourishment for all of its systems, tissues, and organs. The energy that is generated by the kidneys protects and strengthens these same systems by filtering and mobilizing these fluids. The kidney *qi* provides the body with a healthy, strong constitution, so that it can withstand harsh environments, danger, and physical labor. Energetically, the kidneys provide strength to both the body and the mind, so that they can focus and coordinate their efforts more skillfully.

The kidneys are considered to be the organ that is primary in men. They generate the *mingmen* fire, in the center of the lumbar area, which houses the body's life-force, and is responsible for the qualities associated with healthy masculinity. The *mingmen* fire provides the vitality that allows for unwavering determination, and long periods of work. Similarly, the kidneys work hard, in a straight-forward, practical manner; constantly balancing the body's energy. This keeps the qi and various body fluids clear and healthy, and to make sure that they flow smoothly.

The kidneys are also the organ where fear is originates, linking these organs and the body's survival mechanisms. When the individual senses fear, the *qi* moves downward into the kidneys and the lower energy centers to increase strength, vitality, and mental acuity. The kidneys 'open to' the ears according to Chinese medicine, which means that the functions of these two organs are deeply connected. If either the ears, or the kidneys, are damaged, the other will be affected as well. When the body enters survival mode, and fear is activated, the energy that enters the kidneys increases hearing sensitivity and mental acuity to respond to approaching danger.

The kidneys are the place where the body's original essence, or life-force, is stored and managed. This is the known as *jing qi* in Chinese and it represents the original energy that each person is born with and which guides and nourishes them throughout life. It is closely related to the prenatal qi which is also housed in the kidneys. The amount of this energy that one has access to throughout life is limited and determined before birth. Though it can be protected and nourished, the exhaustion of this energy is synonymous with the exhaustion of life. This energy represents the limitations that we may experience as human beings, and the parameters that we must work within to grow and develop throughout life. The original essence nourishes the entire landscape of the body, it provides protection all of its physical structures, and it generates both strength and intelligence.

The dragon is also associated with the health and function of the male reproductive system. The 'green dragon' is a term that represents men, masculinity, strength, and sexual potency. Dragons, like honorable men, are kind, loyal, and caring, however, they are also capable of ferocity, great strength, and passion. The Daoist practice known as the "white tiger, green dragon" refers to the practice of dual cultivation, or sexual alchemy. This is the practice of cultivating energy through the combining and refining of the *qi* of two people in the act of sex. In this practice, the green dragon refers to the masculine, yang energy and the mastery of the male reproductive system. This includes the practice of protecting the *jing* essence, and refining it to supplement spiritual growth.

The ghost point that is associated with the dragon is known as Ghost's Pillow (*Guizhen*); it matches the point Wind Palace (*fengfu*, GV-16) in the acupuncture system (Johnson 2014, 605). It is located on the back of the neck between the C1 and C2 vertebrae, in the depression just below the external occipital protuberance. This acupoint is essential for the health of our life force and longevity and treating this area can clear the brain of negative *qi* increasing mental acuity (Deadman et al. 2007, 548).

This area between the cervical vertebrae allows *qi* to flow up into the skull, providing a connection between the energy centers of the torso, and the sense organs of the head. This point also functions as a center of the body's memory; recording events in a way that is similar to the way in which a tree records the past within the rings of its trunk. This helps the individual to develop strategies and methods that can withstand the test of time, determined through trial and error. This point relates specifically to long-term memory and our more entrenched habit patterns, which is one of the reasons that dragons are said to be wise creatures that possess ancient knowledge.

In the human body, the dragon itself is represented by the spinal column which provides strength and constitution for its structures, as well as a direct link from the kidneys to the *fengfu* point. The dragons of mythology can travel throughout the world and have their home in the water, and similarly, the spinal column provides communication, protection, and nourishment to the entire body while remaining rooted in the kidneys. The spinal column is also surrounded by the bladder acupuncture meridian which is another illustration of the dragon's connection to water and abundant yang energy.

Special Abilities and Traits

Just like water in the hydrologic cycle, from ocean to cloud, dragons are said to travel up to the heavens, and down to the earth with equal ease. In China, the clouds and rain have long been associated with dragons. When droughts occur, people often gather together to say prayers, asking the dragons for rain. After rainstorms, rainbows appear as symbols of the dragon's many talents; illustrating how dragons are composed of the aspects of many different animals, including: the body of a serpent, the antlers of a deer, and the whiskers of a carp. By helping the earth and humanity in general, dragons develop unique opportunities which help them to further understand others.

Dragons are sometimes depicted with an orb or pearl in their claw which represents the lightning and thunder that sometimes accompany the rain. Daoists believe that all seeming misfortunes contain the seeds of future success, just as dark clouds contain the necessary conditions for lightning and thunder. The dragon's orb is said to possess magical powers, such as the ability to cure diseases and grant wisdom. The powerful energy of the kidneys has the strength to see us through difficult circumstances; inspiring deep insights and renewed tenacity. The orb of the dragon represents the ability to go beyond our perceived limits through sheer willpower.

In feng shui, dragons represent mountain ranges which are like the bones (or spinal column) of the land. Many mountain ranges resemble the ancient illustrations of Chinese dragons, and just like these mythological creatures, they also provide strength, protection, and nourishment to the land. The rain run-off of mountains provides the water that is necessary for the large rivers that form at their foothills. Mountain ranges span the distance between heaven and earth, creating a moisture barrier, and forming the clouds that provide rain to the lands below.

In Chinese mythology, dragons often assist in regulating the climate and controlling floods. This is also closely related to the association between dragons, mountains, and stones. The ancient Chinese Emperor Yu, known as Yu the Great, was believed to be assisted by a great yellow dragon and the legendary tortoise dragon, Bixi, while he helped the people deal with extreme flooding. For nearly two generations, numerous floods continued to destroy town, villages, crops, and livestock, leaving the people in desperate poverty. Rather than creating dams and dikes to hold the water back, like his predecessors, Yu deepened and widened the channels so that the water could flow more efficiently toward the sea. This allowed the land to be nourished by the new channels and flood plains, while the people remained protected from flooding.

Cultural and Spiritual Concepts

In Asia, many people believe in the existence of dragons. The most of these traditions state that human beings are the descendants of dragons, though there are no credible reports of their existence. Some people believe that the dragon myth came about when ancient people observed dinosaur fossils, and imagined how they appeared and behaved in life. However, the ancient people were specific about their descriptions of dragons, and many of them mention qualities that do not appear in dinosaurs, such as creating rain. The dragons which the ancients' myths describe were beings that never existed physically; their existence is validated only through faith, trust, memory and self-knowledge. Still, the qualities that dragons represent were embodied by our ancient ancestors, and as evolution progressed, they became fundamental aspects of human nature.

Every skill and career has its own deity, according to Daoists. These are the legendary people who greatly excelled in these fields during their lifetime. To reach our fullest potential in life, we must believe in the achievements of these people, admire them, and believe that we are, or can become, them. They act as examples that are worth striving for; demonstrating the proper use of one's faculties. Myth and symbolism is both imaginary and practical, and dragons exist as guides that are able to provide insight, strength, and mastery through achievement. In order for human beings to have reached their fullest potential throughout our history we must have believed that we are descended from dragons, the creature that combines the qualities of all creatures.

Daoists believe that any moving body of water such as rivers, large lakes, and oceans are said to have dragons that live within them. Therefore, dragons represent water currents and the immense power of moving water. Even today, when rivers are either overflowing, or when there is a severe drought, the Chinese people will often pray and make offerings to the dragons, asking them to adjust the amount of rainfall. Some dragons are believed to live on the tops of mountains, where the headwaters of the rivers are located. These dragons were often considered extremely powerful because they were the source of all of the waters below. The waterfalls that are often found in mountainous areas are representations of this powerful energy. In China, water faucets on sinks are often referred to as the "dragon's head", as a reference of dragon's association with waterfalls.

The four famous 'dragon kings' have also been said to live in the four oceans that surround China. The eastern dragon king is Ao Guang; the blue-green dragon who rules over the East China Sea. The southern dragon is Ao Qin, the red dragon who rules over the South China Sea. The western dragon is Ao Run, the white dragon who rules over the modern Indian Ocean and Qinghai Lake. Finally, the northern dragon is Ao Ming, the black dragon who rules over Lake Baikal. These dragon kings are all said to live at the bottom of the sea that they rule over in magnificent palaces made of coral, crystals, and rare metals.

Dragons are celestial beings that bring good luck and prosperity to the people of the world. While dragons are known to have short tempers and ferocious anger, they are most often depicted as patient helpers, heavenly messengers, and teachers. Dragons are worshiped in many parts of China, and there are many temples that are dedicated solely to dragons. Some temples are dedicated to the dragon kings of the four oceans, some are dedicated to the ancient yellow dragon, and there are many smaller shrines dedicated to the local dragons of various lakes, rivers, and villages.

While no one has been known to have ever seen a physical dragon, Daoists believe that these creatures exist nonetheless, in one form or another. The messages they send, and the results they produce are practical and tangible. When droughts have plagued the lands, and the crops could not grow, Chinese people would gather together to pray, and make offerings to the dragon deities, in the hopes that they would bring rainfall. The famous dragon dance that is performed during the Chinese New Year festival is a way of worshiping the dragon spirit and welcoming in the vibrant energy of the new year. The dragon year of the zodiac is a popular and auspicious year in China. The birthrate spikes in the country at this time because children born in dragon years are thought to be naturally talented, powerful, and successful.

The Strength of the Dragon

The dragon's skill and enthusiasm for helping people, along with nourishing the land and crops lends itself well to the concept of leadership, authority, and the royal family of China. The royal family aligned itself with the symbolism of the dragon for centuries and during the Yuan and Ming dynasties. It was even forbidden for anyone other than members of the royal family to create or wear certain depictions of the dragon. The dragons were embroidered on the robes of the emperor, and various members of his court, as a reminder that it was the duty of these individuals to serve as protectors and heavenly guides for the people of the country. Just like mythological dragons, the royal family had to be capable of ferocity and great strength, as well as the capacity to listen patiently to the prayers and wishes of others.

The royal family acted as the life-blood of the country in the same way that the rivers, lakes, and oceans acted as the life-blood of the land. When the emperor values and listens to the people, then the country prospers and society becomes healthy. Some legends speak of the ancient beings, part dragon, creating the people of the earth, and the ancient Chinese considered themselves to be descends of these "dragons." The emperor, was especially thought to embody the spirit of the dragon, represented by the throne, elaborately decorated with dragon carvings.

The Daoist Scholar Wang Jia wrote many stories that included ancient legends and dragons. In his work, the *Shi Yi Ji*, or the *Forgotten Tales*, he tells a story about a carp that became a dragon.

> One day while a carp was swimming in a riverbed, he looked up as saw the peak of a tall mountain. Fascinated by the sight, the carp imagined what could reside at the top, and quickly decided to swim upstream to find out for himself. The brave fish began to swim upstream, through the strong currents and waterfalls. The constant swimming exhausted the fish, but still him swam. As it traveled the carp began to grow larger and stronger; it developed more skills, and eventually, changed its shape.
>
> Just before the summit, the fish discovered that the water was flowing over a tall, precarious Dragon Gate, built many years before. Climbing this gate was the most challenging task of all, but the determined carp pushed ahead undeterred. When it finally passed the gateway and reached the top of the mountain, the determined fish discovered a sacred lake. Upon entering the sacred waters, the carp's transformation was magically completed, as he turned into a great celestial dragon and flew into the sky.[8]

This story illustrates many of the qualities and strengths of the dragon. A clear vision, talent, and hard work can transform any individual into a powerful being. The dragon is a creature that remains resilient in the face of obstacles, and works long and hard to achieve its dreams. With such strong determination, the dragon is able to develop its many talents and its powerful strength. It also admires other individuals who are dedicated and understanding, and seeks to assist them whenever possible. Dragons understand the strength, commitment, and

---

[8] "Eastern Dragons: The Majestic Creatures of Oriental Culture," by See U in History Contributors (2020). www.youtube.com/watch?v=LkDVIC1xsCY

willpower that is required to accomplish great deeds, and they respect others who willingly accept this responsibility.

People Who Embody the Dragon

People who embody the dragon spirit display a confident and tenacious attitude, and carry themselves in a powerful, elegant manner. Dragon people are often extremely talented individuals, that can rely on the variety of effective tools in their arsenal. Dragons are adaptable; constantly seek to improve themselves and transform their abilities. Along with having many talents, dragons are also able to display them masterfully, along with many emotions and perspectives. This charisma seems to give them an almost magical way of navigating through situations. Just as the mythological dragon has the ability to travel through rock and stone, the people who embody the dragon have the ability to easily navigate themselves through difficult circumstances.

The dragon person does not develop his or her many talents arbitrarily or superficially, on the contrary, they actively seek out difficult situations that force them to develop their talents. Dragons are the types of people who burn the bridge behind themselves, forcing themselves to forge ahead. Dragons are risk-takers. They hold high standards for themselves and for the people around them. Depending on the context, this can mean that they are eager, tenacious, and in-spiring, or it can mean that they are pushy, high-strung, and critical.

In general, dragons are outgoing, colorful, helpful, congenial, and pleasant to be around. Their energy is both stabilizing and illuminating. The dragon's many interests and abundant enthusiasm makes them wonderful friends, advis-ers, mentors, and socialites. They rely on their perceptions, and feelings, of oth-ers; and while realistic, they are often encouraging and supportive. Dragons often have many friends and associates, but their determined focus on their goals and their need for solitude sometimes leaves them aloof and hard to get a hold of. Dragons require a certain amount of isolation to restore their energy, organize their plans, and realign themselves.

Dragons are born leaders and risk-takers. Many dragon people have the power and capacity to lead nations, fight injustices, and use their creativity to change the world. Dragons are not only imbued with many talents; they are also diligent and responsible workers that remain focused accomplishing goals. Drag-ons are disciplined workers that are ambitious and goal oriented.

Dragons have the ability and drive to accomplish the greatest goals that they set for themselves. They are also excellent team leaders, and their confidence is greatly inspiring to those around them. The strength and confidence of dragon people can ease the fears and worries of others, giving their team the freedom to be creative and develop new methods. However, dragon people would benefit greatly from investing a bit of energy into scrutiny and fact checking, because they have the tendency to assume that the people around them are as talented and determined as they are.

Dragons can be wonderful, loyal partners in relationships, but they still need to live have a busy, rich, and ambitious lifestyle to feel fulfilled and happy. Dragons need to exert their great strength in order to remain healthy, happy, and confident. Dragons are strong, inspiring, encouraging, and protective as both romantic partners and as parents. In a family situation it would be wise for a dragon to focus on being encouraging and listening deeply to their loved ones. Dragons hold high standards and demand a lot from themselves, this energy can make others feel intimidated or pressured to keep up, but it can also make them feel protected and cared for.

External Zodiac
Tortoise

While the dragon represents celestial beings that are capable of magnificent accomplishments, the tortoise represents the common people, and everything that is mundane and earthly in the world. Just like dragons, tortoises are creatures that can live and travel in both the earth and the oceans. Tortoises represent everything that supports heaven, and the virtues that lead to opportunities for growth and development. Just like the dragon, tortoises also support the environment by nourishing the earth and allowing it to flourish.

If a tortoise is introduced into a desert or savanna, they immediately begin to transform the land into a lush oasis. This process takes many years, but over time a tortoise will dig extensive burrows that are capable of holding rainwater, protecting it from evaporation. Simultaneously, the tortoise grazes daily on any vegetation that manages to grow in its harsh environment, including dry grasses and weeds. Tortoises often defecate and urinate in their burrows, and after many years, the combination of collected rainwater and waste provides an ideal environment for plant growth, eventually forming an oasis. Therefore, tortoises are one of the first creatures that must be introduced into an environment to transform it into a more fertile landscape. In these environments, the removal of the tortoises quickly results in the disappearance of the oasis. Tortoises represent the entire animal kingdom as they help to provide the energy that supports mother nature. Tortoises naturally cultivate and protect the natural environment, supporting all forms of life on earth.

All tortoises, male or female, represent yin energy, and by extension water, the earth, and femininity. Tortoises are naturally attracted to colorful items, and therefore, they are the natural partners of the vibrant and talented dragons. Tortoises are relaxed, passive, and gentle creatures, but they are also resilient and capable of great strength when necessary.

Dragons represent masculinity and active movement, while tortoises represent femininity and passivity, yet both animals are closely associated with water, the life-giving energy of the world. While dragons mold the world in their image, tortoises adapt themselves to their environment, making the most of what is available. Dragons represent the currents that form in water, and the tortoise represents the water itself, which takes the shape of the vessel it is poured into. The tortoise represents the gentle aspect of masculinity that is protective and strong, but also calm, and mindful. They are supportive creatures that help other living beings with their behaviors. Tortoises have no natural enemies; they have a neutral relationship with all other creatures. Even large creatures, such as tigers and bears, which could kill and eat a tortoise, avoid doing so because they don't represent a threat, and the carapace can cause internal damage when consumed.

In China, there are many tortoise statues that are carved with a stele or tablet on their back. This is an ancient symbol that is meant to support and protect the inscription with the tortoise's energy. The birth place of the Yellow Emperor in Shou Qiu contains many scriptures inscribed on these tortoise tablets. In Chinese, the word *ling* means sensitive, spiritual, or therapeutic; however, in a different context, this word can also refer to the energy of the tortoise. There are many tombstones in China that are carved in this way, with a tortoise at the base to protect and support the sensitive and spiritual nature of the grave-site. Similarly, there are many tombs and crypts in China which contain living tortoises in the hope that their energy will protect the deceased in the afterlife. Sometimes live tortoises are also buried beneath large buildings as well, as a way of supporting and protecting the energy of the landscape and the integrity of the structure.

Qi

Tortoises are famous for their longevity, and they have the longest lifespan of any animal within the zodiac. Tortoises are capable of living for a thousand years if they manage their *qi* properly. For all living beings, movement is better than stagnation, but to achieve extraordinary longevity, tortoises move in slow, subtle ways. Quick, explosive movements expend large amounts of *qi*, reducing longevity. Tortoises avoid explosive movement as much as possible. Today, some of the best professions for developing longevity are postal carrier, college professor, or classical composer/conductor. The lifestyle of these professions is well suited to the development of longevity because they remain active, but tranquil. Each one requires slow, steady movement, and a strong routine. Just like the movements of *taiji, yoga* or *qigong*, which are crucial to the development of longevity in human beings, tortoises move slowly, smoothly, and consistently.

Tortoises increase their lifespan by practicing moderation in both their movements, and their lifestyle. Tortoises hibernate for many months to conserve their energy, which allows their body to preserve its yin energy, and use its yang energy efficiently. Tortoises also practice moderation in their diet. Tortoises eat opportunistically. They are known to eat quite a lot when they find an abundance of food, however they don't overeat, because this would have an adverse effect on their life energy. Daoists have calculated that a human being is capable of eating approximately sixty-five tons of food throughout their life. Once this amount of food is consumed, the body will quickly expire. Based on this information, a simple, effective way of increasing longevity, is to eat proper proportions at every meal. While eating less is a good guideline in general, it is vitally important to eat at least one meal per day to protect the stomach *qi*, and keep the body's metabolism normalized.

Raising a tortoise increases a person's longevity by developing their *qi* energy. Pon Zhu was an ancient Daoist *Yijing* master who helped to build the imperial palace in China. He is most well-known for the extraordinary longevity that he achieved. The legends state that Pon Zhu lived approximately to the age of 800. While this is a legend, living past the age of 200 is definitely possible with *qi* cultivation. Pon Zhu spent a great amount of time cultivating the *qi* of tortoises. The average human lifespan is 120 years of age. With *qigong* cultivation, this can be increased beyond 200 years, yet the study of human DNA suggests that human beings have the capacity to live for up to 1000.

Due to the fact that tortoises are related to the oceans and all things feminine, if a man cares for a tortoise, this becomes a balanced relationship of yin and yang. Similarly, masculinity relates to the mountains. Therefore, if a woman cares for mountainous creatures such as deer, squirrels, dogs, and cats, then this also represents a balanced relationship between yin and yang. Both of these scenarios will manifest blessings and long life as the harmonious energies flourish.

At the White Cloud Temple, small turtles and tortoises are used to diagnose patients in need of healing. First, the patient must lay face up, then a small tortoise is placed on their torso. The tortoise then immediately walks to the point on the body where the injury or disease is located, and sit down for a moment, indicating the source of the illness. Tortoises are always immediately attracted to the area of an environment which requires the most support and protection.

The spine is directly related to both dragons and tortoises, and the health of the spine is essential for the development of longevity. While it is beneficial to stretch the chest muscles and the sternum occasionally, tortoises rarely stretch out their chest area. Instead, tortoises spend their energy developing a rounded back. Any creature with a rounded back, including human beings, has enhanced longevity. Tortoises can be seen to stretch and exercise their necks often. The cervical spine is where a lot of life force energy is located, and by stretching their neck, tortoises greatly increase their longevity.

The area of the spine from the T7 to L1 vertebrae relates to the tortoise, the kidneys, and the *mingmen* point, which houses most of the body's life force. These vertebrae are known as the dragon horse. At the end of the spine is the sacrum, with its eight foramens, which is closely associated with the tortoise energy. The eight foramens are similar to the Chinese good luck symbol of the

Yijing coins tied together in two strands, which represents treasure, fortune, money, fertility and children. The tortoise is familiar with everything beneath the ground; therefore, it has developed a reputation for guarding buried treasure. Similarly, within the body, the tortoise energy guards the treasure that is located at the bottom of the spine, in the form of *jing* energy and spinal fluid.

Just like tortoises, by practicing the cultivation and development of our *qi* and breathing techniques, we can achieve longevity, harmony, compassion and happiness. The lungs are the organ that allows us to make direct contact with the external world by internalizing the outside air. The skin is an extension of the lungs, and they share similar functions. The lungs can be trained to use the skin and pores to respirate, in addition to the nose and mouth. By learning to breathe with the pores, we can change the body's magnetic field, allowing us to interact and harmonize with nature.

The tortoise and the rat are the two animals of the zodiac that practice proper abdominal breathing to develop their longevity. Tortoises breathe by inhaling and pulling the abdomen inwards simultaneously, followed by exhaling and pushing/relaxing the abdomen outward simultaneously. If a human being learns to breathe properly in this way at all times, they may greatly increase their lifespan.

Special Abilities and Traits

Intelligence and wisdom have a lot to do with age and longevity. Human beings are smarter than dogs because they live much longer, and therefore, they must adjust their habits and lifestyle in a way that allows them to remain healthy and prosperous over a longer period of time. Similarly, tortoises live much longer than human beings, and they too must develop habits that are compatible with their advanced longevity.

Tortoises are also able to perceive subtle differences in the *qi* of an environment or an individual. Tortoises have senses that are quite acute, and they recognize patterns of energy at a young age. For this reason, tortoises have been used in *feng shui*, *qigong*, and TCM practices for centuries. Even subtle changes are registered by tortoises, and they always respond accordingly by adjusting their position, their posture, or their *qi* field.

Tortoises do not often look upward, toward the sky. They often keep their head up, but they keep their eyes on the ground. Tortoises sunbathe during the day with their backs toward the sun, and their limbs extended outward. This allows them to capture as much sunlight and heat as possible, as it exposes the most surface area of its body to the light. The tortoise also keeps its head up high to stretch its cervical spine, and to get a better view of the ground directly in front if itself. If a predator attacks the tortoise from behind, the tortoise will see the shadow on the ground in front of itself, and still have enough time to retract quickly into its carapace. This method allows the tortoise to remain aware of all directions, and sense anything that approaches.

In Daoism, the type of strength that is cultivated by tortoises is called 'cold strength', which refers to a powerful form of prying, compression, and leverage. The development of this type of strength allows tortoises to become powerful, and as the grow, they move objects that are many times heavier than themselves. While practicing and developing their strength, tortoises also keep their limbs bent at almost all times. This protects their joints and their *qi,* while also keeping them in a relaxed state of readiness so they can respond quickly to danger.

Tortoises often find themselves flipped over onto their backs, either from attempting to walk or climb through difficult terrain, or from a curious animal flipping them over. On its back, a tortoise is in a vulnerable and uncomfortable position. In this situation, the tortoise often retracts into its shell initially to protect itself, however, it quickly recognizes that it is necessary for it to flip over as soon as possible. When a tortoise is flipped over and needs to right itself, it rests for a moment, and then quickly extends its head and limbs downward, flipping and pivoting itself into an upright position. This is a complex, swift, and powerful movement, especially for a creature that normally moves so slowly. This is one of the movements that is unique to the tortoise, and it is considered powerfully significant by Daoists.

This movement utilizes the five energy centers (the limbs and the head) to create power, leverage and strength. It completely engages the core muscles of the body and the cervical spine, simultaneously. By correcting misalignment and alleviating tension in the cervical spine, the whole-body benefits, ensuring that any other issues of the body begin to heal more quickly as well. Without a strong neck and head, the tortoise would not accomplish this movement, and it would be completely helpless when on its back. Tortoises rarely attempt to use their limbs to push upward, or flex any of their limbs behind them due to their large shell. When they are flipping themselves over, they are also flexing their body in new ways and stretching hard-to-reach tissues. This helps them keep their muscles and ligaments soft within their carapace, increasing their longevity and immunity, and decreasing stress.

Tortoises are focused on the Earth, and they consider themselves to be inhabits of the Earth. It is beneficial for a tortoise to be on its back once and awhile to help them develop strength. When tortoise is alive, the shell of the tortoise is oriented with the convex side facing upward forming a shield that protects it from attack. When a tortoise has died, its carapace is often oriented with the convex side facing downward. With the concave side of the shell facing upward, toward the heavens, it forms a bowl shape which captures the heavenly *qi,* creating a field of positive energy.

When a living tortoise is flipped over for a short period, it captures the heavenly *qi* in the same manner; bringing blessings, harmony, and luck. Tortoises don't look at the sky often, yet when they do, they develop quickly. When a tortoise looks at the sky, its relationship to the birds and to heaven is accentuated. There is a strong connection between birds and tortoises. "Scientifically, US scientists have recently used a newly developed genetic sequencing technique called Ultra Conserved Elements to determine the truth about the evolutionary history of tortoises. The results of this technique have revealed that turtles and tortoises belong to a large group of creatures called 'Archelosauria', along with their relatives, birds, crocodiles, and dinosaurs."[9] Birds often gather around tortoises, and they will often observe it closely, recognizing the relationship between them.

Daoists perform the tortoise flipping movement themselves as an effective form of cervical strength training. The arching motion of the neck is naturally self-correcting, and when this exercise is performed properly, the weight of the body engages all of the core muscles. These muscles do not often get the opportunity to move in this direction because gravity is constantly pulling the mass of the body downward. When the body is arched backwards, the mass of the body is allowed to naturally relax in a different position then it is accustomed to, correcting many joint issues caused by misalignment. The temporary and controlled compression of the spine also decreases stress, and maintains the health of the spinal discs.

Cultural and Spiritual Concepts

The dragon king is a celestial deity that is the ruler of dragons, rain, and all of the creatures of the sea. Legend states that the celestial dragon king, took the form of the dragon kings of the four seas while on earth. The dragon king is worshiped in many areas throughout China, and he is considered great, powerful being. The legend of the dragon king states that he had nine sons, the last of which was the tortoise, whose special gift was longevity. Given that tortoises and turtles are members of the dragon family, they have the ability to travel freely between heaven and earth. Tortoises prefer to remain down to earth and stable, unlike the dragons that prefer to fly through the sky and take risks.

Like its dragon relatives, tortoises are hardworking, headstrong, and determined creatures, and they are skilled at overcoming any obstacles that stand in their way. Since the main goal of tortoises is advanced longevity, they develop patience and peacefulness. To enhance longevity, destiny and luck are as important as diet and exercise habits. Helping other living beings, especially saving a life, will benefit a person's destiny. Practicing *qigong* and longevity exercises also increases luck, and the ability to make the best of any situation. Tortoises are cautious creatures that avoid confrontation and dangerous situations; however,

---

[9] "Turtles Are Related to Birds: 'Tree of Life' Genetic Sequencing Reveals Reptiles' Distant and Unexpected Relatives," by Ellie Zolfagharifard (2014). www.dailymail.co.uk/science-tech/article-2851774/Turtles-related-BIRDS-Tree-life-genetic-sequencing-reveals-reptiles-distant-unexpected-relatives.html

they rarely fear other creatures. Tortoises have no natural enemies, and they do not bother other creatures; they simply work on their own development in solitude.

Legend states that the *Yijing*, the sacred book of Daoism and ancient China, was written by the god-king of China, Fuxi, also known as the "original human" and one of the Three Sovereigns that founded civilization. Fuxi was said to have created the *Yijing* text after observing the markings on the back of a sacred tortoise after emerged from the Lou River. Because of this legend, tortoises have always had a close association with the *Yijing* and Chinese divination.

In ancient past, the carapace of a tortoise was one of the original ways, diviners used to ask questions of heaven. A question would be written on a flat part of the shell with a special ink, and a hot metal poker would be pressed into the area next to the inscription. The resulting cracks and splits in the shell would then be interpreted to ascertain the answer. This also led to the development of "oracle bone script," one of the first written languages of Asia.

The markings and shapes of the tortoise's shell have many significant meanings, because they reflect the will of heaven. Each of the "pyramids" on the back of the tortoise lay upon areas of its body that need to be tonified and strengthened. Each of the five points of the pyramid represent the five centers of the human body, and the connection between human beings, and lunar energy. Carl Jung expressed this connection in his theory of individuation as follows:

> Individuation is the process of achieving such command of all four functions (intuition, feeling, thinking, and sensation), that even while bound to the "cross" of this limiting earth, one might open one's eyes at the center, to see, think, feel, and intuit transcendence, and to act out of such knowledge (2006, xxviii).

Similarly, the thirteen scutes in center of the tortoise's back (three surrounded by ten) represent the thirteen new moons, and full moons, of the lunar calendar. The tortoises' shell is an organized pattern of yin and yang aspects, and with understanding, these patterns can help us to elucidate the timing and nature of numerous phenomena.

The tortoise is closely related to the number four because the base of each pyramid on its carapace forms multiple square shapes. This number relates to the moon, to mothers, the physical world, and to all of the lessons that mothers wish to teach their children including survival, nurturing, self-care, patience, grace, compassion, and the difference between good and evil. The relationship between the tortoise and the identification of good and evil, illustrates why tortoises are considered to be holy animals in Daoism, that shield against evil influences. In feng shui, a tortoise carapace placed on a wall will make the *qi* round and repel evil, making the environment more peaceful and comfortable.

Quotes from Famous Dragons

It is better to create than to learn. Creating is the essence of life.
- Julius Caesar

The history of science shows that theories are perishable. With every new truth that is revealed, we get a better understanding of Nature, and our conceptions and views are modified.
- Nikola Tesla

Love and work are the cornerstones of our humanness.
- Sigmund Freud

There is nothing invincible for the courageous, and nothing secure for the cowardly.
- Alexander the Great

Both the man of science, and the man of action, live always at the edge of mystery, surrounded by it.
- J. R. Oppenheimer

The ultimate measure of a man is not where he stands in moments of comfort and convenience, but where he stands at times of challenges and controversy.
- Martin Luther King Jr.

He who would learn to fly one day, must first learn to stand, and walk, and run, and climb, and dance; one cannot fly into flying.
- Friedrich Nietzsche

Opportunities to find deeper powers within ourselves come when life seems most challenging.
- Joseph Campbell

Intelligence without ambition is a bird without wings.
- Salvador Dali

Morality is not the doctrine of how we make ourselves happy, but how we may make ourselves worthy of happiness.
- Immanuel Kant

We may encounter many defeats, but we must not be defeated.
- Maya Angelou

6

Snake

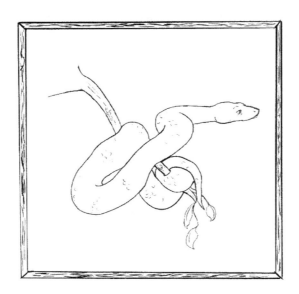

Earth Snake
10th February 1929 to 29th January 1930

Metal Snake
27th January 1941 to 14th February 1942

Water Snake
14th February 1953 to 2nd February 1954

Wood Snake
2nd February 1965 to 20th January 1966

Fire Snake
18th February 1977 to 6th February 1978

Earth Snake
6th February 1989 to 26th January 1990

Metal Snake
24th January 2001 to 11th February 2002

Water Snake
10th February 2013 to 30th January 2014

Wood Snake
29th January 2025 to 16th February 2026

Fire Snake
15th February 2037 to 3rd February 2038

Earth Snake
2nd February 2049 to 23rd January 2050

Metal Snake
21st January 2061 to 9th February 2062

Snake

The snake category represents all types of serpents. All snakes are calm, patient, cautious, alert, caring, thoughtful, gentle, perceptive, intelligent, wise, explosive, and formidable. Snakes are versatile and adaptive creatures that have developed a variety of unique skills which allow them to survive in most of the world's environments. Snakes are found on every continent, with the exception of Antarctica, and many remote islands as well. Tree snakes and climbing snakes are usually long and thin to help them climb, burrowing snakes are short and stout with blunt snouts to aid in digging, and sea snakes usually have flattened, paddle-shaped tails that they use for swimming.

All snakes have a single row of wide ventral scales on their underside and numerous smaller scales on their upward facing surfaces. Even their eyes are covered with a single, transparent scale that is replaced when they shed their skin. Under normal conditions, their skin is smooth, cold, and slippery, with only a few species developing rough skin in order grip tree limbs and/or prey. Their internal organs have also evolved to fit within their elongated bodies. The paired organs are staggered within the body cavity, and in some species only one lung is functional, with the other being reduced in size, creating more space for the other organs. Sea snakes have developed an enlarged lung, part of which forms a buoyancy chamber allowing them to swim more easily on the water's surface (Burnie and Wilson 2001, 376).

Snakes spend much of their time maintaining their body temperature, digesting their food, and searching for prey. Snakes are strictly carnivorous. While some consume a wide variety of prey, others are specialized feeders. Small snakes may feed on insects, lizards, and small rodents while large snakes may feed on small antelope, caimans, or apes. Egg snakes, on the other hand, are specialized feeders that only consume eggs. They have a specialized "saw" protruding from their spine, inside the throat, which cuts through the egg's outer shell, that is later regurgitated (Burnie and Wilson 2001, 376).

Snakes have a few different methods of subduing their prey including simple striking, venom, and constriction. The two latter methods are used to subdue prey that is strong or has the ability to defend itself. The venom of snakes is a fast-acting form of digestive fluid that attacks the prey's nervous system. After striking, constricting snakes wrap themselves around their prey multiple times and begin to tighten their grip with each exhale. Constrictors often prefer to attack warm-blooded mammals because their high metabolism makes it necessary for them to breath more often, and therefore, they are more easily subdued.

As a cold-blooded (ectothermic) reptile, a snake's body must be heated externally for normal cellular activity, metabolism, and other essential biological functions. In cold environments, snakes and other reptiles become sluggish and inactive. In deserts, snakes must burrow underground or rest in the shade during the hottest part of the day to avoid becoming overheated. This could potentially cause them to develop a fever; inhibiting their mobility and their ability to cool themselves.

Being creatures that spend most of their lives close to the ground or under-water, snakes often have poor eyesight, with tree snakes having only slightly im-proved vision. Snakes don't have external ears, making it difficult for them to hear high pitched sounds; however, their underbellies are sensitive, and most snakes have developed the ability to sense low frequencies as they travel through the earth and other surfaces. With their sensitivity to low frequencies, snakes are able to sense when earthquakes are imminent, quickly hiding in the swallow opening of its burrow.

Some snakes sense minute changes in air temperature with organs located between their eyes and nostrils, called heat pits. Snakes rely on their highly de-veloped ability to smell or "taste" odors in the air using their forked tongue and Jacobson's organ. The Jacobson's organ is an area of odor sensing cells located in an animal's palette just behind the upper front teeth. Other reptiles and mam-mals, also have this organ, however, snakes have evolved particularly sensitive olfactory organs, and they rely on them quite heavily. Snakes use their forked tongues to capture moisture and air particles from the surrounding environment and press them against the Jacobson's organ, allowing them to smell with great acuity (Burnie and Wilson 2001, 376).

Snakes have developed a variety of locomotive methods to compensate for their lack of limbs. They have learned to slither and undulate their long bodies in different ways according to their needs. These methods help them account for their weight, increase stealth, increase speed, and aid in travelling over different surfaces and environments. Lateral undulation, which is an s-shaped slithering, is the most common method that snakes use for travel over land and through water. Concertina movement, when a snake bunches and expands one end of its body while thrusting the other end forward, is mainly used for traveling through borrows and tight areas. This is also similar to the motion that a snake uses to strike at prey. Linear progression, a wave-like sequence of the underbelly, is used to move slowly and silently. Finally, side-winding, in which the snake throws its weight forward over the surface, rather than remaining in contact with it, is used by desert snakes to keep their bodies as cool as possible over hot, loose sand (Burnie and Wilson 2001, 377).

All snakes shed their skin as they grow larger in a process called ecdysis which can last for up to two weeks. During this time, they become much less active, and prefer to remain hidden in their burrows, away from harm. Over the course of a few days, the snake begins to display a cloudy, dull color as the outer-most layer of skin becomes dry and begins to separate from the layers below. The scales over the eyes become cloudy as well, making it difficult for snakes to see clearly. Eventually, when the outer layer of skin is ready to be shed, the snake will begin by rubbing its face against a hard object such as a tree or a rock to begin the process. Once the first part of the skin has been scraped away, the snake will slither and wriggle its way out of the remaining skin revealing a bright, new, healthy layer of scales beneath.

Snakes are unique in that some species reproduce by laying eggs while others reproduce by giving birth to live young. Snakes in temperate regions, are forced to hibernate because of the cold temperatures of winter, they mate in early spring and lay their eggs in the summer. Snakes in more tropical regions where the weather stays warm all year round usually mate in response to rain; and consequently, they may produce multiple clutches of eggs throughout the year. Some snakes may only produce eight to ten eggs per year, whereas other species can give birth to up to fifty young in a single litter. Many snakes do not parent their young, leaving them to fend for themselves from birth; however, a few species wrap themselves around their eggs until they hatch to regulate their temperature (Burnie and Wilson 2001, 377).

Calendar

The snake is the sixth animal of the zodiac. It is associated with the fourth month of the Chinese lunar calendar that lasts from approximately May 6th to June 6th in the Gregorian calendar, and to the two-hour period between 9am and 11 am. Snakes are similar to dragons in many ways, perhaps the most obvious being that they are intelligent, passionate, talented and creative. In China, snakes are often referred to as "little dragons" due to their similarity. Due to the fact that snakes are often so close to ground, which limits their vision, and that they lack endurance over long distances (on land), they must rely on their intelligence and their senses to capture any prey that may be lurking nearby.

Snakes rely on their explosive speed and masterful techniques to quickly seize any opportunity that comes their way. During snake years, opportunities seem to emerge and pass by quickly; and therefore, this is a year when decisive action must be taken to seize opportunities when they arise. Snakes also do not move or expend effort unnecessarily, but they always remain alert to their surroundings. Snakes must spend a great deal of time managing their energy levels by absorbing sunlight and conserving their strength. Similarly, in the year of the snake, energy management becomes increasingly important and energy stores must be protected from unexpected losses. If this is not done properly then the loss of energy will be difficult if not impossible to recover. For instance, the Exxon Valdez oil spill off the coast of Alaska in the snake year of 1989 was a loss of 11 million gallons of crude oil that caused terrible damage to the ecosystem and cost billions of dollars in cleanup and economic loss.[1]

---

[1] "Exxon Valdez Oil Spill," by The Editors of Encyclopedia Britannica (2009). www.britannica.com/event/Exxon-Valdez-oil-spill

Many clever and intelligent solutions to problems are implemented in the year of the snake. Its wisdom allows the snake to succeed where nearly all other creatures would fail, and similarly, these years bring a mood of revision, organization, and diligence. These years see systems, projects, and inventions significantly benefit from the added intellectual power that the snake energy brings to bear. While snake years don't always bring about completely novel ideas and new inventions, they always greatly enhance the ideas of the past. For instance, while computers had been in development for many years, 1977 saw the introduction of the first commercially available personal computers. The "1977 trinity" is a group of three revolutionary personal computers that hit the market during this revolutionary year. The Apple II, Commodore PET 2001, and the TRS-80 all contributed to the microcomputer revolution and led the way for the development of further advanced electronics.[2]

While snake years are times when resources can be lost due to carelessness, a conscientious attitude can bring about stability and security for the future. Snakes are skilled at gathering and conserving their energy, and similarly, snake years require a mindful approach to finances. With the diligent energy of the snake year, financial resources can be moved into stable investments and savings can grow quickly.

Snakes enjoy the energy of sunlight and the therapeutic effects of a warm, cozy environment. They are sensitive to stress and over-excitement, and prefer tranquility. During the year of the snake, this energy of timidity causes people to be more conservative with their finances, and investors to prefer safer stocks. The growth of the economy during these years is usually slow, but steady; however, the opportunistic energy of snake years also means that even seemingly safe and established investments could experience significant difficulty.

Snakes are ambitious creatures, and they often attack prey that are much larger than themselves. They have also learned to attack the most vital areas of their enemies and their prey. For example, most snakes naturally aim for the eyes of an opponent, and attempt to strike at their face when confronted. During snake years, many ambitious attacks and revolutionary changes are attempted; therefore, this is a time when many people and organizations should stay alert and defensive against small vulnerabilities that can be exploited. In the snake year 2013, Edward Snowden publicly revealed information regarding the digital information gathering programs of the NSA in the United States. And, in 1941, the

---

[2] "History of Personal Computers - 1977 and the Emergence of the 'Trinity,'" by Liquisearch Editors (2020). www.liquisearch.com/history_of_personal_computers/1977_and_the_emergence_of_the_trinity

Japanese attacked pearl harbor in an attempt to cripple the United States naval presence in the Pacific before they could enter World War II.[3] [4]

During snake years, the management of resources is essential and while luxury can be enjoyed at times during this year. The snakes use their tongue often, and similarly, snake years are good for communicating with others or promotional activities. On the other hand, snake energy is peaceful, honest, and calm, so flamboyance and boasting should be always avoided. Major opportunities appear during these years, and significant gains can be made. Snakes prepare themselves in advance, and when they see an opportunity, they strike at it immediately. This is the mindset that will lead to success during snake years.

While snakes are capable of digesting prey that is much larger than themselves, they can easily underestimate the size of their prey as well. Snakes may kill prey that is too large for them to digest. During snake years, people's eyes are often bigger than their stomachs, and idealistic plans can quickly become unbalanced and overwhelming when practical realities are taken into account. In the snake year of 1929, many investors prospered greatly on Wall Street, but by October, the stock market crashed and the economy had to spend many years regaining the value that it lost.[5] Despite the difficulties of the Great Depression, many smart and scrutinizing businessmen managed their resources well during this time, and actually grew their wealth a great deal. For instance, Howard Hughes, himself an intelligent and successful snake man, used his money to develop new companies and projects during the late twenties and early thirties with great success.[6]

Qi

The time of the day that relates to the snake is between 9 am and 11 am, which is also when the spleen meridian is most active, and the triple burner meridian is at rest. This is the beginning of the summer in the daily cycle, when the sun and the yang energy of the earth is approaching its highest point in the sky. The spleen is an essential organ in Chinese medicine because it is responsible for distributing the energy that is gathered from food to the rest of the body. Snakes have unique and highly developed spleens that are sometimes attached to their pancreas. The spleen of a snake must work hard to distribute blood and *qi* throughout its elongated body. The metabolism of the snake is efficient in that

---

[3] "Edward Snowden," by Michael Ray (2013). www.britannica.com/biography/edward-snowden

[4] "Pearl Harbor Attack," by The Editors of Encyclopedia Britannica (1998). www.britannica.com/event/Pearl-Harbor-attack

[5] "Stock Market Crash of 1929," by Gary Richardson (2013). www.federalreservehistory.org/essays/stock-market-crash-of-1929

[6] "Howard Hughes," by The Editors of Encyclopedia Britannica (1998). www.britannica.com/biography/howard-hughes

it conserves its energy until the snake's body is warmed externally and activity becomes easier.

In human beings, the function of the spleen is also responsible for transporting the abundant *qi* of the stomach to the limbs, supplying the muscles with energy. While snakes do not have limbs, the function of their spleen is nonetheless important because they rely heavily on the strength of their muscles for locomotion and digestion. The period of time between 9 am and 11 am is essential for snakes because it is when they charge their spleen, digest their food, and gather yang energy from their environment. As the spleen circulates blood throughout the body, it is also responsible for regulating heat within the body. In snakes, this is extremely important because while it is necessary for snakes to absorb heat, it is also essential that they do not allow their bodies to overheat.

The spleen's energy flows, or 'opens', to the mouth. According to Chinese medicine, each of the internal organs is said to open to the external environment via one of the body's orifices. The spleen energy is responsible for giving the individual the capacity to taste, and differentiate between the five flavors. In snakes, this is vital because they rely so heavily on their Jacobson's organ to taste/smell the air while tracking prey and potential threats. The highly developed spleen in a snake's body enhances the function of their Jacobson's organ allowing them to taste the air with sensitivity and accuracy.

The ghost point that is associated with the snake is known as Ghost's Bed (*gui chuang*); it matches the point Jaw Vehicle (*jiache*, ST-6) in the acupuncture system (Johnson 2014, 605). This point is located approximately one fingerbreadth anterior and superior to the angle of the jaw, at the prominence of the masseter muscle. It is often used to treat toothaches, facial pain, and lockjaw (Deadman et al. 2007, 134). Snakes have unique mandibles that are not firmly connected to the skull. They are held in place mainly by a strong, stretchy ligament so that the snake can consume prey that is larger than the diameter of their mouth. With its enlarged, gaping jaw, and the elastic skin of the snake's mouth and torso, it can stretch itself around its prey. This point is also related to geese, and it is able to increase energy, ambition, concentration, and good fortune.

Along with the spleen, snakes are also related to the urinary bladder. The urinary bladder is responsible for gathering the waste fluid that has been filtered out of the lungs and intestines by the kidneys. Snakes are closely related to the water element, and they are creatures that direct the flow of water. Snakes and rivers move in similar ways, slithering across the landscape, creating channels that direct the flow of water. Snakes are uniquely equipped to travel in water. Some snakes, are able to remain buoyant by holding their breath, seeming to slither across the surface of water just as easily as they would across land.

The urinary bladder is also the organ that houses the "common people's fire," which is the energy that heats fluids in the body, transforming *jing* into *qi* (Johnson 2014, 518). This fire is located near the perineum, and it provides the energy that fuels the triple burner, as well as spiritual progress in the individual.

As this fire heats the *jing* and body fluids, it refines them and creates new materials that are necessary for the development of the vital organs housed above the umbilicus. Categorized in this way, the snake, along with the dragon, represent the yin and yang aspects of the water element in the zodiac system.

The urinary bladder meridian travels from the feet, up the back, and over the top of the head. It is the longest meridian in the body, and the one that contains the highest number of acupoints, which gives testament to its power. Snakes have developed strong urinary bladders because they rely on the bladder meridian to convey coordinated energy patterns across the entire length of their body. As snakes slither, they must learn to direct their energy to the entire length of the spine and engage the muscles of the back in unison.

With their acute sense of smell and taste, snakes are living examples of the healing potential of saliva. Swallowing saliva is a beneficial treatment for the throat, esophagus, stomach, and the digestive tract. This can be used to treat a sore throat, and to prevent infection of the esophagus. Snakes swallow their saliva regularly throughout the day to heal themselves and to assist in their digestion. Daoists practice swallowing their saliva immediately upon waking in the morning while they imagine their "three favorites." Thinking of your favorite person, your favorite sound or instrument, and your favorite color as soon as you wake up activates the mind and jump starts the body's energy systems making qi flow more smoothly. Snakes practice this method of activating the mind before the body as well because they have to manually engage their energetic systems when they wake up. Snakes do not sleep in exposed places where the morning sun will reach them; therefore, they always wake up in the darkness, and must make their way to warmth while their blood is still cold and their energy is low.

Special Abilities and Traits

The Patient Hunter

As mentioned above, snakes have ability to eat prey that is much larger than themselves. Their unhinged jaws and elastic skin allow them to swallow large prey. Daoists say that snakes have the ambition to swallow an elephant. Larger snakes like boas and anacondas are even able to swallow average-sized deer and antelope; digesting them over the course of multiple weeks or months. This allows snakes to conserve their energy, and survive off of opportunistic hunting techniques. While other creatures, especially warm-blooded mammals, must hunt regularly to maintain their metabolism, snakes go long periods without a kill as each meal provides such an abundant amount of energy.

Snakes are skilled at martial arts and combat because they naturally understand the principles of movement and struggle. Snakes can subdue creatures much larger than themselves, and they are the only animal of the zodiac that is able to subdue the bear. Snakes strike with lightning-fast speed at a creature's most vital areas; always aiming for the eyes, head, and throat of their opponent. Once they have made contact, they immediately begin to rotate to wrap themselves around their enemy. Snakes use rotation to generate strength, tighten their grip, and further subdue their prey.

The practice of taiji was partially inspired by the way that snakes are able to generate so much strength through rotation. Snakes wrap around their opponents in the same way that ropes and handcuffs are used to bind people. When limbs are immobilized, they are unable to increase their momentum or use leverage to generate power, leaving the individual defenseless. Snakes are only truly fearful of geese and the goose's "brothers," the duck, the swan, and the rooster because they are the snake's natural enemy.

The Protector of Children

Most people are surprised to discover that snakes, especially pythons, are actually quite good family pets, and they make wonderful babysitters. Snakes are naturally highly protective of babies and children, and with their high level of intelligence they are able to recognize danger early and protect the child from it. For instance, if babies or small children begin to climb too high, then the snake will gently wrap itself around them, and slowly pull them back to safety. Snakes also protect the children from predators and approaching danger, fearlessly fending off anyone that intends harm.

In the ancient past, many Chinese farmers would have to spend the entire day out in the fields, working the land. If no one was left to watch over the children during the day, the snakes would be trusted with this task. In the rural areas of modern-day Asia, snakes can still be found babysitting children. A number of snake species naturally protect their eggs until they are hatched, and this instinct is easily transferred to the children of other species as well. Most human beings naturally have an acute fear of snakes, and they would never imagine that their children would be safe with these creatures. However, if this fear can be overcome, then the protective and nurturing side of snakes can be recognized and nourished. Just like other animals, when snakes are well-fed and cared for, they can become benign and caring companions.

The Healing Quality of Snakes

While tortoises are extremely skilled at diagnosing illnesses in patients, snakes are equally skilled in treating those illnesses. For thousands of years, in both eastern and western cultures, the snake has been revered as a symbol of medicine and healing. In the Old Testament, God told Moses to "Make a fiery serpent of brass, and set it upon a pole; and it shall come to pass that everyone who is bitten by a serpent, when he looks upon it, shall live" (Numbers 21:8-9). Many ancient religions depicted the snake being crucified on a cross, the staff of Moses was transformed into a snake, and in ancient Greece the rod of Asclepius, a staff surrounded by a single snake, was used to represent people and places that are related to medicine.

There are many theories and explanations as to the reasoning behind the symbolism of the serpent and the staff, but the essence lies in the serpent's ability to correct illnesses and issues with their energy; creating upright and healthy people. Many temples that practice the ancient healing methods, including the White Cloud Temple, often allow snakes to roam freely and interact with the patients to provide healing. The staff represents the fire energy within the spinal column that allows the individual to develop spiritually, and the snake represents the master of that fire within ourselves which tempts us to "know thy self" (Hall 2011, 90). Snakes represent the principles of rebirth, and of conquering the energies of death, illness, and ignorance.

Snakes wrap themselves around a patient, squeezing and twisting areas of the body in various ways to correct issues. At the White Cloud Temple, the monks that are skilled in this form of treatment have trained their snakes to respond to various types of sounds, calls, and whistles. First, the patient's issue would be diagnosed by the doctor, then the snake would be placed over the affected area and commanded to squeeze in the proper way. If the patient is injured and suffering from a dislocation that requires a manual adjustment, then the snake will be told to squeeze, massage, and twist the affected area until the adjustment has been made.

The snake's ability to undulate and coordinate its movements across its entire body length allows them to squeeze out toxins and stagnate blood in the tissues while engaging the joints in a gentle, but firm manner. If the patient is suffering from a *qi* blockage or reduced blood flow, then the snake would be placed above the affected area, closer to the heart, and told to squeeze and hold, acting like a tourniquet. After a time, the snake will release its grip allowing a large amount of fresh blood to flood the area, clearing out toxins, plaque in the arteries, and bringing nutrients to areas that were previously blocked.

Apart from their ability to squeeze and adjust patients, snake venom has also been used to create many forms of medicine. In ancient times, snake venom was used by many forms of traditional folk medicine to treat inflammation, joint pain, arthritis, immune deficiencies, high blood pressure, cardiovascular diseases, osteoporosis, impotence, various skin conditions, and even opium addiction.

In many Native American traditions, an individual must experience being bitten by venomous snakes, and incorporating their energy into their own, to become a snake medicine healer. This "allows them to transmute all poisons, be they mental, physical, spiritual, or emotional" (Sams et al. 1999, 61). The energy of snakes grants the knowledge that "those things which might be considered as poison can be eaten, ingested, integrated, and transmuted if one has the proper state of mind" (Sams et al. 1999, 61). In modern times, snake venom is used to create antivenom serums to combat snake poisoning, and well as to develop many forms of medicine, combating everything from strokes to cancer. The toxins in snake venom have been shown to stimulate the body's immune system, increasing its production of antibodies (Grunbaum 2013, 16).

Cultural and Spiritual Concepts

Swordsmanship

To become a skilled swordsman, you must learn from, and practice the techniques of snakes. Daoist swordsmanship has utilized the energy of snakes for thousands of years. Serpent *qi* is considered essential to both the swordsman, and the sword itself. At the White Cloud Temple, after a sword is forged it is cast into a well that contains a large number of snakes and left there for many years. Over the years, the snakes wrap themselves around the sword, squeezing it and scraping their body against it many times. The snakes use the edges of the sword mainly to help them remove their old, damaged scales and also to remove any parasites. This behavior inevitably infuses the sword with the energy of the snakes, granting it a life of its own. A sword that has been treated in this way becomes more flexible, responsive, and it gains abilities that other, similar weapons lack. Swords that are made in this way call down the energy of heaven, similar to the way that an antenna can utilize the surrounding radio frequencies to convey information.

The practice of acupuncture is also closely related to snakes, and just like swordsman, aspiring Daoist acupuncturists must practice a great deal with snakes to develop the proper skills and cultivate their energy. The twisting and rotating motion of snakes is vital in the practice of acupuncture, as well as massage. The way in which a snake is able to be both strong and supple simultaneously is a skill that is absolutely essential for an acupuncturist to develop.

The courage, bearing, and mental fortitude of a snake are also essential to develop in acupuncture because some areas of the body are dangerous to pierce and require confidence, stillness, and concentration to treat properly. If a patient jumps or screams in pain, then the acupuncturist must be prepared for this, and remain undeterred and undistracted. Like swordsmen, doctors must develop trust and predictability in themselves so that their righteousness and honor can be relied upon by others.

Snakes represent dualism. They represent both life and death, light and dark, strength and softness. Snakes are used to represent life-taking with swords and venom, as well as life-giving with acupuncture needles and various medicines. Just like the dualism of the taiji diagram, which illustrates the yin and yang energies following one another, the ouroboros of the ancient Egyptian and Greek traditions represents the cyclical nature of the universe's dual energies.

The ouroboros is the symbol of a snake swallowing its own tail. This shows that while the energies of life and death exist, these two states follow one another in the process of reincarnation. Snakes represent this process by shedding their skin; symbolically throwing off their previous body, and reappearing in new corporeal form. The wisdom of snakes is deep and profound. Snakes understand that life should be protected and appreciated, and yet, it is also wise to avoid clinging to life unnecessarily when the time has come to let it go. The spirit simply moves through the cycles, gaining wisdom and maturity with each revolution.

The Legend of the Immortal White Snake

In China, snakes are highly regarded as protectors, healers, and omens of potential good luck. Traditionally, the famous legend of the immortal white snake, who transforms herself into a beautiful woman, illustrates many of the wonderful qualities of the snake energy. Over the centuries this legend has become quite popular, and it is now considered to be one of the four great folktales of China.

Many years ago in China, during the spring Qingming festival, two immortal snake sisters transformed themselves into two beautiful young women to enjoy the celebration. The white snake called herself Bai Suzhen, and the green snake called herself Xiaoqing. Not long into the day, it began to rain and a young boy named Xu Xian, offered the two women his umbrella. Unbeknownst to Xu Xian and Bai Suzhen, their destinies were intertwined, and they quickly fell in love. Soon they were married, and they moved to Zhenjiang where they opened a medicine shop.

Meanwhile, a tortoise spirit that harbored envy over Bai Suzhen's immortality had accumulated enough energy to transform himself into a Buddhist monk named Fahai. Fahai planned to break up the marriage between Bai Suzhen and Xu Xian out of spite and jealousy.

Soon after, during the dragon boat festival, Fahai approached Xu Xian and revealed that his wife was actually demonic serpent. The monk continued, saying that if he wished to discover this for himself, all Xian had to do was get his wife to drink some realgar wine; a special alcoholic drink.

When he got home, Xu Xian offered the wine to his wife. As soon as the wine touched Bai Suzhen's lips, she became terribly ill and ran into the adjacent room. In an attempt to help his wife, Xian prepared medicine for her, yet when he entered the room, instead of finding his wife, he found a great white snake. The sight sent Xu Xian into shock; he had a heart attack, and died immediately.

When Bai Suzhen gathered enough strength to transform herself back into a woman, she quickly realized what had happened. Desperately trying to figure out how to save her husband, the only thing that she could think of was a legendary magical herb that was said to grant longevity and revive the dead. Bai Suzhen had to travel all the way to Mount Emei, and past numerous dangers to retrieve the herb, but in the end she succeeded. After returning and applying the herb to her husband, Bai Suzhen watched as he awoke. The look of shock that was frozen on his face melted away, and it was replaced with an expression of joy and love at their reunion, despite knowing his wife's true nature.

Snakes represent the tender care and devotion that devoted partners and loved ones share with one another. Snakes are easy-going and determined over long periods of time; waiting patiently for their dreams to manifest themselves, in the form of prey. This kind of patience and dedication always produces numerous benefits in the long-run. Snakes are excellent at being able to recognize special opportunities and seizing them without hesitation. They take the time to be patient and work step-by-step toward their goals. Snakes understand that the wishes of our heart will arrive just as surely as a sprout that is well cared for will grow into a tree. In addition to the tenderness and care that snakes are capable of, they are also courageous and selfless, readily protecting the innocent from harm without a second thought. As the legend of Bai Suzhen continues, it further illustrates the compassion and tenderness of serpents.

Years later, Bai Suzhen gave birth to a son, and Xu Xian became a proud, happy father. When the child was a month old, Fahai appeared at their door, repentant and remorseful about his past behavior, and he eventually offered Xu Xian his magical alms bowl to protect his family. Xu Xian was reluctant, but not wanting to refuse the gift of a monk, he accepted. Immediately upon entering the house, the bowl flew into the air, captured Bai Suzhen, and returned to Fahai who quickly fled, and buried the bowl underneath the Lei Feng Pagoda.

While on her way to visit her friend, Xiaoxing witnessed this act of treachery, but unable to defeat the monk, she vowed vengeance. When Xu Xian begged Fahai to release his wife, he refused and said "I will release her when the iron tree blooms." Xu Xian then left his son in the care of Xiaoxing, and went to go pray for his family's forgiveness and reunion. However, no one had realized that Xu Meng Jiao, the son of Bai Suzhen and Xu Xian, was actually the reincarnation of the god of wisdom, born to the couple as a reward for their devotion.

Twenty years later, Xu Meng Jiao had grown up to become a wise man, and after taking the imperial examinations, he earned the position of top scholar in China. He was then given a luxurious hat, decorated with jewel encrusted flowers as a symbol of his accomplishment. Overjoyed, he decided to return home to visit his long-lost parents and share the good news with them. When he arrived however, he learned of the fate of his mother. He immediately went in search of his father, and they both decided to return to Lei Feng pagoda together, to pay respects to Bai Suzhen.

Meanwhile, Xiaoxing, who had been training and gathering her strength for nearly twenty years, travelled to Jinshan temple to finally confront Fahai. Overwhelmed by her immense strength, Fahai quickly fled and hid. Meanwhile, upon reaching the pagoda, Xu Meng Jiao knelt, and placed his flowery cap on a nearby iron sculpture as an offering to his mother. Magically, with a blossom on the iron tree, and her sins absolved by the tribute of a god, Bai Suzhen was released and reunited with her family.[7][8]

Snakes represent the virtues of patience and faith. Snakes will wait for hours or longer for an opportunity to catch prey. Similarly, people with snake energy are able to wait things out and see how they go before reacting. Being cold-blooded, snakes are temperature sensitive, making them cautious about entering extremely cold or hot environments for extended periods. Snake people are often picky about their living environment, but with patience their home becomes a great source of comfort. Bai Suzhen had to wait for her son, and Xu Xian prayed for years for his wife's freedom, illustrating the importance of hope, patience, faith, and devotion.

The Twelve-Animal Race

In the story of the twelve-animal race, the snake began well, and moved quickly through the rough terrain that the other, larger animals could not traverse. When the serpent got to the river, he began to swim across, but quickly realized that he was exhausting himself. He needed to conserve his energy if he was going to finish the race. At this point a number of other animals, more skilled at swimming, were approaching fast, and he was beginning to fall behind.

As soon as he reached the other side of the river, the snake hid in the tall grass near the shore and waited. Within seconds the horse emerged from the water, and the snake stealthily slithered around the horse's leg without him noticing. The snake held onto the horse as it ran full-speed through the rest of the course, saving its energy for an opportune time. When the finish line was approaching, the snake leapt off of the horse's leg, startling the horse and causing it to rear and whinny. In the chaos the snake crossed the finish line earning it sixth place in the race, and the position of ruler of the sixth year of the zodiac.

People Who Embody the Snake

The people who embody the snake spirit are usually flexible and strong, literally and figuratively. They have particularly flexible necks, and they often hold their head high. They can be sociable, but they often wait for others to speak first, preferring to respond rather than initiate. When snake people are happy, they usually have an animated and unique energy which can light up a room. Their faces are expressive, and they communicate most of their intentions and feelings clearly through body language. Snake people are elegant and move grace, holding

---

[7] "The Chinese Myth of the Immortal White Snake," by Shunan Teng (2019). www.youtube.com/watch?v=eEeeClBoqK0

[8] "The Chinese Myth of the Meddling Monk," by Shunan Teng (2019). www.youtube.com/watch?v=mO6eMTKalRE

themselves in a dignified, serene and conscientious manner. While they are not as extroverted and demonstrative as some of the other animal types, they are nonetheless gentle, kind, and have a wonderful depth of character. Snakes often dress in colorful unique ways that express the depth of their personality.

Snake people are wise and knowledgeable, and they make wonderful teachers, mentors, and advisers. Snakes can accomplish great things with their patience and ability to plan and recognize opportunities. Snake people have limited stamina. It's necessary for them to rest when they notice that they are low on energy because over exhaustion can quicky lead to qi deficiencies and health issues. When they are applying effort however, they are incredibly strong, determined, and effective. Snake people would benefit greatly by keeping their energy levels in mind when making dietary choices. Snake people require some meat to function at their best, and they lack energy if they don't consume enough protein. Eggs are especially good for people born in the year of the snake because it is a form of protein that is easy for the body to digest.

Snake people do not enjoy chaotic situations or being pressured. Instead, they prefer to proceed at their own pace and in their own way. The stillness and patience of snakes should not be confused with laziness. They are thorough and diligent people, and they prepare in advance for nearly every scenario that they may come across. By preparing in advance, snakes enhance their ability to respond to opportunities with lightning speed.

Snakes do not care about being outsiders; preferring the benefits of being unique and developing rare gifts, as opposed to being popular and following the crowd. This attitude, combined with the snake's ability to think deeply and perceive important details, has allowed many snake people to develop creative and unique solutions to otherwise common problems. Snakes refine their ideas until they near perfection, and appear vastly different then when they were first imagined. With the necessity to conserve energy, snake people usually prefer to choose careers and tasks that are more intellectual and cerebral. Due to the association between snakes and healing, careers in the medical field are a natural fit for many snake people. They may take a while to establish themselves in their chosen field because of their preference for planning and their need to understand things thoroughly, but once established, snakes are skillful, formidable, and intelligent.

The careful planning and depth of study that snakes bring to their finances allows them to make intelligent and enlightened decisions regarding money. When snakes focus their attention on their personal finances, they develop wealth at a swift pace. However, snakes also have eyes that are bigger than their stomach, and they enjoy the warmth of a cozy and luxurious environment, so they must be careful not to indulge and overspend when the temptation arises. Snakes have a dualistic nature, and while they enjoy luxury and gratification, they are also wise and prudent.

Snakes prefer to take their time with relationships, preferring to understand their partners and friends thoroughly before opening up or settling down. Snakes are gentle, caring, and compassionate; however, they reserve these qualities for opportune moments, when they are certain that they will have the desired impact. They enjoy the excitement and passion of love, and when they choose to love they do so from the heart without reservations. When they do decide to settle down and create a home for themselves, they always create it in a way that is unique, and nourishes the desires of their heart.

Snakes do not have "cookie-cutter" homes, and if they buy a place that seems ordinary, it will not remain that way for long. Snakes are protective, compassionate, and gentle with their loved ones, and they often develop strong bonds with the people closest to them. A snake's home is a place where they can let their guard down and allow their inner warmth to be expressed. Their unique imagination and colorful personality allow them to create genuine connections with others, and help them think creatively. Snakes prefer to cut their own path through life rather than walk one that has already been traveled, and their relationship with themselves is cultivated as a result of this solitude. Snake people embody the ancient maxim "know thyself."

External Zodiac
Earthworm

While snakes are considered small dragons, earthworms are small snakes. Like snakes, earthworms are humble, gentle, shy, intelligent, and sensitive. Earthworms have neither eyes nor ears, relying on other senses to navigate the world. While snakes can only hear low frequencies, earthworms cannot hear at all, however, both of these creatures are highly sensitive to vibrations. Snakes have eyes, though their acuity is low, but earthworms have no eyes at all. Instead, they have the ability to sense even subtle changes in light with their skin. While snakes usually rely only on a single or enlarged lung, earthworms have no lungs at all and respirate directly through the skin. They spend most of their lives in the darkness, and they are self-reliant; navigating the world through touch, and trust in their own instincts.

While snakes understand that everything that is observed through the senses must be properly interpreted within to be fully understood, earthworms rely on their senses and do not question themselves. Both creatures are self-reliant, but while snakes are decisive, earthworms are instinctual. Earthworms have adapted to living the majority of their lives underground because above ground they are preyed upon by birds, rodents, and reptiles. Snakes have to come out of their burrows during the day to absorb sunlight and find food, however, earthworms rarely leave their underground habitat.

Qi

Earthworms are hardworking and diligent creatures that spend their entire lives searching through the soil for nutrients. However, while they spend their whole lives eating, they thrive off the work, growing quickly. As earthworms continue their work, they create rich, live-giving soil by digesting small plant debris, fungi, manure, and small creatures. Furthermore, the tunnels that worms carve in the earth, till the soil; aerating it, and allowing water to penetrate.

While slithering through the soil they also leave behind their waste, called vermicast. Earthworm castings are rich forms of fertilizer that improve soil aeration as well as water retention and drainage.[9] Aristotle called earthworms the "intestines of the earth," recognizing that they are incomparable master builders of soil.[10] Earthworms are experts at recycling waste, and transforming it into something more potent and supportive of life.

Like snakes, earthworms enhance the things that others find mundane, transforming them into unique and valuable materials. Because of their connection with earthworms, people born in the year of the snake would benefit a great deal by gardening, digging, and working with the earth. Having a strong connection to the earth can help snake people refresh themselves, protect their health, relieve stress, and develop understanding.

Special Abilities and Traits

Earthworms are an extremely important part of the ecosystem. They are hermaphroditic; and therefore, contain all of the power to reproduce within themselves. Earthworms, like snakes, are experts at combining yin and yang energies within themselves, balancing of energy wherever they go, and increasing fertility. Each worm has the power to give live to the earth, to predators, and to other earthworms.

Earthworms continue to work at a slow and steady pace for as long as their energy will sustain them. Without the need for light, earthworms can continue to work and grow unimpeded until they reach their next larval stage. Earthworms are humble creatures that transform the world with a slow and steady pace. Earthworms are at home in the soil, and they rarely venture to the surface; therefore, they recognize the value of working locally where they can be happy, protected, and of the greatest benefit.

---

[9] "Using Organic Worm Castings: How to Harvest Worm Castings for Your Garden," by Nikki Tilley (2021). www.gardeningknowhow.com/composting/vermicomposting/worm-castings.htm

[10] "Nature's Best Recyclers: The Earthworms," by Joan Lee Faust (2000). www.ny-times.com/2000/01/30/nyregion/in-the-garden-nature-s-best-recyclers-the-earth-worms.html

Earthworms accomplish so much because they pay attention to the subtle details, such as moisture levels, and they work without thinking about themselves. Similarly, people born in the year of the snake find the fine details to be essential to success because of the way that they approach problems. Snake people recognize that deep feelings are rarely apparent; therefore, they make an effort to appreciate others for their efforts in small ways, cultivating deeper appreciation, and assuaging their unspoken feelings.

Cultural and Spiritual Concepts

Earthworms rarely expose themselves by coming to the surface, preferring to remain in the safety of their underground burrows. However, when it rains the soil becomes saturated and it becomes difficult for worms to breathe, so they climb up to the surface for air. Earthworms demonstrate that when situations become difficult it is necessary to leave the comfort zone, face the light of truth, and transform our understanding.

Humble earthworms are soft and vulnerable, and they remind us that the humble parts of ourselves are soft as well. Being vulnerable with people we trust helps us to breathe easily, like the earthworm, resolving emotional imbalances and processing memories. When we find that completing our lifestyle has become overly difficult and stifling, then we must allow ourselves to be vulnerable while remaining compassionate toward ourselves.

Quotes from Famous Snakes

All labor that uplifts humanity has dignity and importance, and it should be undertaken with painstaking excellence.

- Martin Luther King Jr.

When we are no longer able to change a situation, we are challenged to change ourselves.

- Victor Frankl

The true genius shudders at incompleteness, and usually prefers silence to saying something which is not everything it should be.

- Edgar Allan Poe

The man who has sufficient power over himself to wait until his nature has recovered it's even balance is the truly wise man.

- Giacomo Casanova

He who is not courageous enough to take risks will accomplish nothing in life.

- Muhammad Ali

There is no subject so old that something new cannot be said about it.

- Fyodor Dostoevsky

I've always wanted people to know who they are from the inside. Then they can create the life they desire and deserve. I've always believed that my job was to facilitate the evolution of the human consciousness.

- Iyanla Van Zant

If a man coaches himself, then he has only himself to blame when he is beaten.

- Roger Bannister

To know that we know what we know, and to know that we do not know what we do not know, that is true knowledge.

- Nicolaus Copernicus

Make haste, cautiously.

- Augustus Caesar

The best way to find yourself is to lose yourself in the service of others.

- Mahatma Gandhi

7

Horse

Metal Horse
30th January 1930 to 16th February 1931

Water Horse
15th February 1942 to 4th February 1943

Wood Horse
3rd February 1954 to 23rd January 1955

Fire Horse
21st January 1966 to 8th February 1967

Earth Horse
7th February 1978 to 27th January 1979

Metal Horse
27th January 1990 to 14th February 1991

Water Horse
12th February 2002 to 31st January 2003

Wood Horse
31st January 2014 to 18th February 2015

Fire Horse
17th February 2026 to 5th February 2027

Earth Horse
4th February 2038 to 23rd January 2039

Metal Horse
23rd January 2050 to 11th February 2051

Water Horse
9th February 2062 to 29th January 2063

Horse

The horse category of the zodiac represents all types of equine animals, including zebras, asses, and wildebeest. Horses are passionate, gentle, sensitive, popular, animated, graceful, skillful, friendly, successful, powerful, determined, and enduring. Equine animals spend the majority of their day grazing on grasses and shrubbery. Though there are nearly no truly wild horses left in the world, feral horses are found in many of the world's deserts, prairies, arid plains, grasslands, and steppe areas. Horses enjoy the natural, wide-open pastures of the world. Horses spend most of their time in wide open areas where they can run freely and graze, however, they also require trees, forests, or rocky outcrops to act as shelter from the elements at times (Burnie and Wilson 2001, 226).

Human beings began domesticating horses between 5000 and 3000 B.C. and since this time horses have traveled around the world. With the assistance of human beings, horses are capable of living in most of the world's environments. Some horses are suited for warm environments, such as the Arabian horse, and others, like the Icelandic horse, are suited for cold climates. The long history of interaction between human beings and horses has led to the development of a vast and unique equestrian culture.[1]

Horses have a deep chest area, a semi-elongated neck with a mane of hair, a long-haired or tuft tail, and a single toe on each foot encased within a hoof. Horses often travel in small loose herds of females, guided by an elder matriarch. Usually, a small number of males follow this herd, but remain on the outskirts, grazing on their own. The males fight to defend their harem of mares from predators as well as competing stallions.

Like snakes, horses make use of their Jacobson's organ to smell/taste the air, however, they only use this organ to assess the fertility and receptivity of mares in a behavior called the "Flehmen response." For the most part, horses are highly social animals, preferring to gather in herds and graze together for increased protection. To reinforce their bonds, horses often groom one another by facing in opposite directions and nibbling. However, occasionally horses and wild asses spend large amounts of time roaming alone across large territories.

Horses are herbivores, and while their diet consists mainly of grasses, they also eat leafy plants, buds, bark, and fruits. Unlike oxen, horses do not ruminate their food. Instead, they use a hindgut fermentation system where the food is only chewed and swallowed once, but fermenting bacteria that are contained in the cecum aid digestion. This type of digestive system moves food through the body more quickly, which means that animals employing this method specialize in eating a diet of grasses that are low in nutrients, but grow in plentiful amounts (Burnie and Wilson 2001, 224).

---

[1] "Horse," by Alois Podhajsky (1998). www.britannica.com/animal/horse/origin-of-horse-domestication

Horses have excellent eyesight, acute hearing, and a heightened fight-or-flight response that allows them to quickly respond to predators. Horses graze in open environments and in herds, so that they can maintain awareness of their surroundings in all directions. If a single horse responds to the presence of a threat, then the entire group is signaled to escape.

Horses are known for their incredible speed and endurance. Zhuangzi writes "To munch grass, drink from the stream, lift up their feet and gallop, this is the true nature of horses" (Kemmerer 2017, 71). Their swiftness is their primary defense against predators, as they can outrun most other animals. Their long, muscular limbs are housed deeply in the body-wall of their cylindrical torso, leveraging the muscles of the shoulder joint during forward motion. The metapodial bones, which are the bones of the palms and feet in human beings, are greatly elongated in horses, providing additional length to their lower limbs, giving them a longer stride and increased speed. Finally, having only one toe means that horses have less muscle tissue and more tendon in the extremities, reducing energy expenditure and increasing endurance (Burnie and Wilson 2001, 224). Horses on average can run between 30 and 40 miles per hour for approximately two miles. With regular breaks and energy management, some endurance horses can travel up to 50 miles in a single day, and 100 miles in a 24-hour period.[2]

Horses also have a wide variety of coloration. Many horses have a coat that contains a single, solid color; however, mustangs can be spotted, zebras have black and white stripes, and wild asses often have a dark mane, a solid coat, and striped legs. The variety of coloration in horses helps them to differentiate themselves for recognition in the herd, regulate their temperature, and in the case of zebras, potentially confuse and mesmerize predators with optical "dazzling" effects.

Calendar

The horse is the seventh animal of the zodiac. It is associated with the fifth month of the Chinese lunar calendar that lasts from approximately June 6th to July 7th in the Gregorian calendar, and to the two-hour period between 11 am and 1 pm. This is time of year when the summer is at its height and nature is flourishing. Due to the fact that yang energy in the environment is at its most abundant during this time, it is also an optimal time to gather resources, develop health, and increase productivity.

During horse years, the emotions of many people are highlighted, and a sense of social harmony and comradery arises. Horses enjoy the feeling of freedom, and the bonds that are formed when individuals act together toward the same goal(s). Horse years are times that are forward looking and driven toward

---

[2] "How Far Can a Horse Travel? Horse Running Endurance Explained," by Henrietta Szathmary (2022). www.horseyhooves.com/how-far-long-can-a-horse-run/

ideals. The world's resources, both material and intellectual, are dedicated toward progress and advancement during horse years.

The strength and speed of horses makes vast distances seem small, and similarly, the technologies that are developed during horse years also seem to bring people closer together, and erase previously insurmountable boundaries. The Hubble telescope, for example, was launched in 1990 allowing us to perceive objects with crystal clarity across the vast distances of our universe.[3] The images that have been captured by this telescope have led to numerous discoveries and advancements in science. These results evoke a feeling of humility in the face of nature and develop a genuine sense of unity and hope among many people.

During horse years, many companies seek to streamline their operations and increase productivity, while many employees become more dedicated as they strive for more freedom in their careers and personal lives. This means that there is often many career and business changes that happen during these years. Some companies downsize to streamline their efforts, while others grow rapidly to keep up with demand, but dedication to success is universal at this time. The time of the horse relates to the point in any cycle when yang energy reaches its peak. Therefore, horse years are often related to the point when economies and the job market reaches a fever pitch. If these moments are prepared for in advance and navigated with skill, then significant career opportunities and investments can be taken advantage of.

Personal finances are often a focus of horse years, and many people become more fluent in money management, savings, and budgets. These are years when productivity and success require a majority of our time and effort, and the proper application of these resources. Horses are associated with travel, and during its year, the desire for security, and the familiar is replaced by the love of adventure. While travelling, a conscientious attitude should be taken with regards to the security and management of all types of personal resources. This is a mindset that leads to success in horse years as well.

Horse years are times when people gather together to socialize, share ideas, and develop various relationships. The social barriers that usually keep people separate seem to dissolve at this time. In these years, what seemed to previously be insurmountable barriers are softened and discussed openly, creating a sense of transformation, cooperation, and hope for a brighter future. The first analog cellular mobile phone network was tested during the horse year of 1978 by Bell Labs in Chicago, and twelve years later, the first web server and browser of the world wide web was running at CERN laboratories in Switzerland; both of which brought people around the world into instant communication with one another.

---

[3] "Telescope Quick Facts," by Space Telescope Science Institute (2021). www.hubblesite.org/quick-facts/telescope-quick-facts

This ability to communicate easily and cheaply to almost anyone, anywhere has changed the dynamics and social fabric of the world in innumerable ways.[4] [5]

The dissolving of social barriers means that human rights and the freedom of both individuals and nations are a significant theme during horse years. Horses are naturally peaceful creatures; however, their sense of freedom and camaraderie often challenges many previously established boundaries and traditions. In 1954, the court case of *Brown v. Board of Education* ruled in a unanimous decision that racial segregation in public schools is unconstitutional.[6] This was a major step forward for the civil rights of African Americans, and Americans as a whole, however, many people's previously held beliefs were disturbed by this decision, and it was clear that a lot of work was still required before their hearts and minds were unified. Horse years are times of great progress and change; however, they are also a time for staying alert, and protecting yourself from mismanagement and the people who wish to remain in familiar, outworn habits.

Many countries and groups, have either achieved freedom or formed friendly alliances during horse years. Horses are creatures that rely heavily on their nervous systems to control their powerful muscles. On one hand, this makes them jumpy creatures that can be frightened easily. They are quite averse to chaos and disharmony, and they are also hyper-aware of nearby danger. On the other hand, horses are capable of great emotional strength, and rely on their powerful nerves to carry them through the most chaotic situations when necessary.

For thousands of years, horses have fearlessly carried soldiers into combat risking their lives time and time again. Even with the invention of firearms, horses have learned to ignore the sound of explosions, and continue moving forward with determination. In the year of the horse, military conflict is avoided if possible because horse energy is not naturally aggressive; however, if conflict is necessary, then massive power can be brought to bear. In 1918, for instance, the arrival of American troops and resources to the western front in Europe tipped the balance of power in the Allies' favor. And, in November of the same year, Germany surrendered, officially ending World War I.[7]

---

[4] "Bell Labs and Motorola Develop the AMPS Analog Mobile Phone System," by Jeremy M. Norman (2004). www.historyofinformation.com/detail.php?entryid=1172

[5] "The History of CERN," by CERN Editors (n.d.). www.home.cern/about/who-we-are/our-history

[6] "Brown v. Board of Education Re-Enactment," by United States Courts (1955). www.uscourts.gov/educational-resources/educational-activities/history-brown-v-board-education-re-enactment

[7] "Armistice Day: World War I Ends," by History.com Editors (2010). www.history.com/this-day-in-history/world-war-i-ends

Qi

The time of the day that relates to the horse is between 11 am and 1 pm. This is the time of the heart meridian, the most active period of the day for the heart. This time is the height of the day, when the yang energy reaches its peak, and the sun reaches its apex. During this time, the pulse is strong and rhythmic, which causes all of the body's functions to operate more harmoniously. This reduces stress, suppresses the symptoms of illness, and increases overall health. This is also a time when the gallbladder is at its most dormant period of the day; resting while the heart mobilizes the blood.

In Chinese medicine, the heart is the responsible for managing both the flow and creation of blood within the body, as well as the body's psycho-emotional functions. The heart is said to be the house of the body's spirit which is responsible for the thoughts, feelings, behaviors, and values of the individual. The brain is seen more as an information processing center, presenting various options, while the heart is more stable and decisive. Just like the horse, the heart is sensitive to stress, chaos, or shock, and requires regularity, continuous movement, peace, and freedom to function naturally. The heart transforms the *jing* energy and the *qi* that is acquired through digestion (*gu qi*), into blood that can be used to nourish the body's tissues and connect the energies of the vital organs.

The heart is also said to open via the tongue, and because of this connection the tongue is often referred to as the "manager of the heart." When the heart's energy is troubled or disturbed, it creates a strong desire for the individual to speak their mind in order to reconcile their feelings. The appearance of the tongue illustrates the condition of the heart and its energy. Color, texture, moisture, structure, and coating are all factors that can be used to assess the quality of qi in the body.

In Chinese medicine, the heart's function is paired with the small intestine which acts as a guide or advisor to the heart. The small intestine is responsible for separating the clean usable *qi* from the food essence that has passed through the stomach and the digestive system. The veins and blood vessels that are connected to the small intestine carry the pure, clean energy into the blood stream, and eventually to the spleen where they can be distributed to the rest of the body's tissues.

The small intestine also guides the thoughts and emotions of the heart by assisting the heart's ability to focus on specific, relevant issues. The small intestine allows the heart-mind to separate the pure thoughts from the turbid ones in order to distinguish the difference between right and wrong. The heart is generous, responsible, and works hard to provide the necessary nutrients for all of the body's organs, tissues, and functions to thrive. It does this by remaining free from the constraints of limitation, maintaining constant motion, and being sensitive to the changes in the environment, both internal and external. Like horses, the heart is strong, enduring, intelligent, and sensitive (Johnson 2014, 495-99).

The ghost point that is associated with the horse is known as Ghost's Market (*gui shi*); it matches the point Container of Fluids (*chengjiang*, CV-24) in the acupuncture system (Johnson 2014, 605). This point is located above the chin, in the depression in the center of the mentolabial groove. It is used to treat mental/emotional issues, especially mental disorders; to dispel wind and cold *qi*; clear hot *qi*; and to transform dampness, mucus, and phlegm. It is also used to treat facial pain, facial paralysis, dental pain, speech issues, and difficulty swallowing (Deadman et al. 2007, 524). When this point is deep and pronounced, it signifies a skillful person that has great potential in life.

Along with the heart, horses are also associated with the liver. The liver harbors and filters the blood of the body, renewing it so that it can continue to nourish the body's tissues. Horses require a circulatory system that is functioning at its optimal level so that its massive, hard-working muscles can be adequately supplied with blood. The liver stores blood so that it can be released at a moment's notice when physical activity requires it. Together, the heart and the liver keep the circulatory system healthy and strong. The liver is also the organ that is most intimately connected to the body's nervous system. Therefore, having a healthy liver allows the body to respond quickly to subtle signals. When the fight or flight response is triggered, the nervous system has to react immediately, to implement the appropriate defense measures as soon as possible. The strong livers that horses have developed to supply their large muscles, also greatly contribute to their quick reaction time.

The liver is largely responsible for the management of emotions in general, but it directly governs anger and frustration. When an abundance of neurotransmitters enters the blood stream, flooding the person with emotion, the liver is responsible for managing the situation by filtering out toxins from the blood, thereby soothing the individual's mental-emotional state. On the other hand, the liver also responds to a person's libido and sexual attraction by supplying blood to the reproductive organs and the brain when aroused. If the liver's function is impaired, then rash, hasty, emotional decisions are likely, and anger and depression become more resistant to change. Horses demonstrate that happiness, health, and longevity is largely the result of a calm heart and a healthy liver.

The liver is also responsible for the health and strength of the body's tendons, which are essential to the development of physical strength. Horses rely heavily on their massive tendons which allow them to run with such great speed. If a horse damages its tendons, it is greatly debilitating for the animal. Unlike muscle tissue, tendons only require minimal blood flow, reducing stress on the heart and increasing endurance.

The liver is associated with the wood element in Chinese medicine, which represents all things that grow and develop. It is also the only organ of the human body that has the ability to regenerate itself. If, up to two-thirds of the liver is removed, then over time it can completely regenerate and regain its full capacity. If other animals spend a great deal of time with a horse, then its will begin to heal physically, as well as mentally and emotionally. The energy of horses stimulates recovery, rejuvenation, and restoration.

Just as the heart opens to the tongue, the liver opens up through the eyes. The quality of the gaze demonstrates the quality of their mind, soul, and spirit. The ability of the spirit to illuminate the eyes means that the energy of the heart is also able to observed here. In Daoism, the quality of a person's gaze is known as their "life degree," and this is one aspect of a person's appearance that cannot be faked or altered. When a person has achieved a great deal, experienced many difficulties, or significantly developed themselves, the quality of their gaze will become clearer, deeper, and more mature. Horses have acute vision, and their eyes are almost always clear, bright, and healthy; demonstrating their friendly spirit, and depth of character.

In Chinese medicine, the liver is also understood to be the home of the soul, known as the *Hun*. The soul of an individual is experienced as energy patterns, such as Jungian archetypes, that represent universal values, behaviors, and lifestyles that form the foundation of an individual's personality. Therefore, with their association to both the heart and the liver, horses are also associated with both the soul, and the freedom of the spirit. Riding a horse has often been described as being akin to flying through the sky. A horses' love freedom, peace, and liberation is a result of its powerfully vibrant spirit.

With their long, muscular necks, horses rarely suffer from any type of cervical spine issues. When horses walk or run, their large heads bob up and down gently massaging and exercising the muscles of their neck. Also, as they graze, they pivot from their neck until their mouth can reach the ground, exercising their neck's full range of motion. This allows blood and *qi* to move smoothly from their torso, to their head, and back again; reducing stress on the heart, clearing the lymphatic system, and increasing circulation. This also contributes to improved memory and brain function because blood flow to the brain is increased. Furthermore, the cervical neurons also function well because the vertebrae do not compress. When a horse is emotional and its brain releases neurotransmitters, these chemicals flood its blood stream, and are quickly carried to the rest of the body. This is another contributing factor to their extraordinary emotional strength and sensitivity.

Special Abilities and Traits

The most unique aspect of the horse is their amazing running ability. Horses love to run, always seeking the excitement of running over the next hilltop. Horses enjoy land that is smooth, and free from obstructions, so that they can run at full speed without concern. Rather than settling down or planting roots, horses prefer the enjoyment of exercising their abilities and experiencing new things. Horses do not spend their resources on developing attack or defense techniques.

Instead, they prefer to live their lives on their own terms and focus their energy on reducing stress, increasing health, and doing the things that they enjoy.

Horses greatly rely on the strength of their legs, and when their legs are damaged, it is often a fatal injury. In the past, at the White Cloud Temple, within days of a horse being born its leg would be intentionally broken. The bones would be immediately reset, packed with healing herbs, and bound with a sturdy splint. The foal would then be fed a special diet of grasses and herbs which would fully heal the leg quickly. After this procedure, the bones of the young horse's leg would be significantly stronger for the rest of its life.

The Five Beans

Horses develop great strength and speed without eating meat, and because they are vegetarian, they are also not naturally aggressive creatures. At the White Cloud Temple, the monks would often eat five types of beans as a way of developing strength and energy, and they would also be fed to the horses for the same reason. The five types of beans each have a different color that represents the different types of *qi* that they contain. Yellow soy beans, white navy beans, black beans, green mung beans, and red adzuki or kidney beans are all rich sources of fiber and healthy *qi*. Beans contain an abundance of proteins, fats, vitamins, and lipids, all of which are necessary for proper health and developing strength.

These beans can also be categorized according to the five phases theory. Red beans and adzuki beans belong to the heart and the fire element; yellow beans, such as soy beans and mayocoba beans, belong to the spleen and the earth element; white beans and navy beans belong to the lungs and the metal element; black beans belong to the kidneys and the water element; and mung beans belong to the liver and the wood element. Beans contain the essence of the earth, as well as the rich yin qi of the moon. Therefore, the *qi* of these beans can nurture our own essence, supporting us physically and spiritually. Even though the beans may be small, they contain the essence of the sun and the moon. Daoists often say, "the universe is contained in a single grain of rice." The same could be said of a single bean.

During the spring, our yang energy blossoms and comes out of our bodies from within, while during autumn, our *qi* is being harvested and returning within to prepare for the approaching winter. During the harvest season, it is beneficial to eat beans because it protects the body against the cold and the wind. Daoists eat boiled beans often for their numerous benefits. The Daoist diet includes many fruits and vegetables; however, beans and grains are also essential for the carbohydrates and essential nutrients they provide.

Black beans help to build strength and immunity, reducing the risk of cancer. They can support a poorly functioning immune system, and the overall constitution of the body. Daoists explain that black beans are so nourishing to the body and the immune system because their energy treats the body as a whole.

The color black is a combination of all other colors; and therefore, the black color of the beans illustrates the holistic nature of their energy. Black is also a natural color, and natural things have the ability to support health and increase immunity. If you want an ox to plow the earth efficiently, then you need to feed it a diet that includes black beans. As a human being, yellow beans are the most beneficial for our energy and our constitution, because yellow beans support proper digestion and a clear mind. Digestion fuels the entire body and healthy grains, such as beans, support healthy digestion. Identifying the beans according to the five phases theory is a simple, practical way to work with *qi* and improve health.

In nature, colors are significant, and each elicits various qualities in observers. When all five types of beans are arranged according to their positions in the five phases diagram for a significant amount of time, then they begin to regulate the *qi* of the surrounding environment. This harmonizes our thoughts and feelings, and allows us to perceive color in new ways, literally and figuratively. The soothing effect that this energy field generates can greatly aid in the development of happiness and longevity. Five small bowls filled with a single type of bean is preferable, but if space is limited, then one bean of each color, placed inside or underneath the pillow while you sleep produces similarly powerful effects. The beans can even be placed underneath the length of the bed so that the whole body will be near the beans during the night.

The Mongolians have been skilled horsemen for a long time. They have trained horses for many purposes, including fighting in wars, and they rely heavily on them in daily life. Mongolian warhorses run fast and travel long distances. A fully trained Mongolian warhorse is often referred to as a "thousand-mile horse" because of the great distances that they can cover in a short period. Historically, many Chinese and Mongolian generals have fed beans, especially black beans, to their horses to give them plenty of energy and develop their strength. Black beans are far more effective at developing strength than meat, mainly because it develops the strength of the kidneys, which are considered the roots of the body in Daoist medicine.

In the past, beans have often been used quite for counting. In ancient Greece beans were often used to tally the results of elections. Similarly, the past generals of Mongolia and China would meticulously keep track of the amount of beans that they fed to their horses in order to determine the distance that they would be able to travel the following day.

One day Qiu Chuji, the famous Daoist monk, was talking with Genghis Khan, and he expressed his concern for the fact that the Mongolians had constantly engaged in war for many years. He said that the heavenly spirits would not approve of this, and that it could lead to negative repercussions for the Mongolian people themselves. Genghis said "During war, it is strategically important not to lose momentum, and so I must continue moving forward, or risk retaliation. As long as my armies could keep marching, the war must continue."

Qiu Chuji then explained, "The day that the lead horse of your herd does not eat all of his beans, then this would be a sign that the Mongolians were beginning to lose their momentum, and that the front lines of the army would quickly cease to advance further. This behavior would be a sign that the horses were being affected by emotions, exhaustion, illness, and/or bad energy." It is believed that this comment was one of the determining factors in Genghis Khan's decision to stop advancing toward Europe.

Cultural and Spiritual Concepts

Horses Represent Spirit

The inner spirit of human beings wants to overcome all boundaries and limitations so that it can achieve freedom, liberation, and salvation. The horse also abhors restriction and prefers to run free in the fields and pastures. While horses are sociable and intelligent creatures that can understand the intentions of others, if it is not in the mood to follow orders, it will jump, buck, and run away. Horses are self-determining creatures, and it requires a special type of qi to tame and work with them. Mountainous regions are the only type of environment where horses are not capable of running; and therefore, they use these areas to rest. Horses enter mountainous areas from time to time for safety and to recuperate their energy. Since horses travel so often, rest and stillness greatly benefit their nervous system and overall health.

The power of spirit in a living being is closely related to, but not limited to, their level of intelligence. Horses have an intelligence level that is roughly equivalent to an eight-year-old child, and their aptitude is supported by an exceptional memory. At the beginning of the twentieth century, a horse named Jim Key was taken on tour with his trainer Dr. William Key. Jim Key was famous throughout the United States for being an incredibly intelligent horse. He could read, write, and calculate math problems. He was declared the winner in a spelling contest against a class of sixth grade students, and was even believed to solve simple trigonometry problems.

Jim Key's trainer William Key always emphasized the fact that only gentle, patient, and kind treatment was used in teaching his horse, never violence. Eventually, the pair became major advocates of the American humane society, espousing the kind treatment of all animals. The spirit and behavior that was observed in both Jim Key, and his trainer William, was unique and inspiring.[8]

Often times, reduced thinking ability, awareness, and spirit are accompanied by decreased visual acuity and liver function. In Daoism, the left eye of an individual represents the sun, and the right eye represents the moon. When the

---

[8] "Beautiful Jim Key," by Mim Eichler Rivas (2007). www.beautifuljimkey.com

Chinese characters for the sun and the moon are combined, they form the character for the word "brightness." Therefore, the Hall of Impression (*yintang*, M-HN-3) point in human beings, commonly known as the third eye, is the place where the 'brightness' of an individual can be observed. This point is associated with a person's level of intelligence and by observing this point, the quality of a person's spirit can be assessed.

By observing various colors and beautiful sights in nature, the energy of this point can be trained, thereby increasing brain function and brightening the spirit. In the past, the Mongolian people would train their horses by using various colors, and color-coding patterns. By utilizing color, they were able to communicate with their horses more effectively, increase their intelligence, and simultaneously helping them become happier and more vibrant.

Horses are dignified creatures that represent posterity, honor, and nobility. While it can be difficult to tame a wild horse, and a horse's inner spirit is unconquerable, they are also loyal and devoted when that type of respect has been earned. When a horse master has proven themselves worthy of respect, then their horse will carry them fearlessly into the chaos of battle. While horses enjoy peace and the tranquility of nature, they also understand the value of camaraderie, and the necessity to have a fearless and compassionate heart.

Horses are intelligent enough to understand the complexities of social interaction, including emotional reactions, sentiment, and honor. Horses recognize that sometimes difficulty and hardship are meaningful and worth enduring. While horses greatly appreciate their freedom, they gladly commit themselves to a worthy cause. Horses do not only desire freedom for themselves, they desire it for all living beings. Horses demonstrate the value of both obedience and disobedience; the freedom to direct one's own life, and the freedom to commit one's life to others.

Horses represents success through teamwork, determination and endurance. The vibrant spirit of the horse lends itself to success and commitment to worthy pursuits. Horses are often depicted in mythology travelling between heaven and earth, and transporting others. Endurance, commitment, and teamwork inspires the same value in others, and given time, these energies help us find our way to heaven.

While horses can thrive on their own, they are also wonderful companions and they truly enjoy working together with others. The virtues of teamwork, passion, and endurance have also associated horses with sexuality since ancient times. Horses themselves represent the combination of both masculinity and femininity being both muscular, virile, and active as well as elegant, gentle, and compassionate. Through the practice of sacred sexuality, the heights of heaven can be reached as the heart opens and the spirit is liberated.

People Who Embody the Horse

Horse people are often friendly, engaging, passionate, and colorful. They love having conversations with others and discussing topics they find interesting and important. Most horse people are often quite extroverted and social, and rarely turn down an offer to spend time with others, yet they're careful to maintain their independence. Horses also love projects, sports, and extracurricular actives, as a way of channeling their abundant energy and indulging their many interests. Because they enjoy social interaction so much, they often find themselves with a fully booked schedule. While horse people are known for their endurance, they can also push themselves too far as well, causing burnout. It would be wise for people born in the year of the horse to schedule a break occasionally, to process recent experiences and recharge their batteries.

While horses naturally have a friendly disposition, they are also willful and headstrong, preferring to do things their own way. Horses would rather create their own path to their goals, rather than following the well-worn paths of others. Left to handle things in their own manner, horse people are capable of achieving great things and becoming exceptionally productive; however, horse people can sometimes have difficulty slowing down and listening to the advice of others.

Horse people are often deeply emotional and sentimental, and while most wear their heart on their sleeve, some prefer to deal with their emotions in private. This quality often only enhances the horse's colorful, passionate nature, and their resilience allows them to be patient with others. When the energy becomes overwhelming however, they often unleash a burst of unbridled anger, and perhaps say things that they would later regret. Like a pressure valve, these outbursts are usually short lived, and horses prefer to return to a peaceful state as soon as possible. People born during horse years would benefit greatly from learning to recognize when frustrations and negative energy is becoming too much to handle. Taking a bit of time to themselves, or going for a walk, can prevent emotions from boiling over and causing irreparable damage to our relationships.

Horses are skillful, dexterous, and diligent which allows them to develop a wide variety of talents. Due to their strong will and skillset, people born during horse years often have numerous interests. While their need for variety can cause them to quickly lose interest in a subject, they often return to them later, when they feel prepared, and develop quickly.

With an enduring spirit and a wide variety of talents, horses make valuable employees for nearly any business, and they usually succeed in any career that they choose. Horse people are natural athletic, and they enjoy the outdoors. Careers that allow them to exert themselves, travel, or socialize are usually the one's that they find most satisfying. People who embody the horse spirit make fantastic athletes because the love the sense of friendly competition, teamwork, self-development, and freedom that sports involve. Horses often do quite well in the entertainment industry as well, because they love to entertain others, host parties, and they thrive in festive environments. Many horses often become leaders of business with their sense of drive and teamwork. With their determination and grace, horses can achieve great success in any field.

Career success and the ability to easily build rapport with people often leads horses to significant financial success. People born during horse years can become quite wealthy in a short period of time when they put their mind to it, and they usually manage their resources well. Horse people always make sure to pay their bills and repay their debts as quickly as possible because mismanaged resources weigh heavily on their minds, causing them to feel unsettled. After their responsibilities are met, horses vary between investing for the future and splurging on a more lavish lifestyle. If a person born during a horse year dedicates themselves to a savings plan and a budget, they can build wealth swiftly, and avoid overspending when their freedom loving spirit emerges.

Horses are passionate, gentle, and caring partners and they truly shine in relationships. Horses enjoy the 'dance' of romance, and all of the subtly and nuance that goes into developing attraction, and maintaining partnerships. Horses love companionship, but they also love their independence. As long as they are given the freedom to be themselves and pursue their own interests, they will remain happy, supportive partners. Horses love to develop their homes and create peaceful, welcoming environments, for relaxing and entertaining. Yet, most horses avoid spending too much time at home because their desire to continue moving is insatiable. Horses can make great parents as they are naturally supportive, gentle, and understanding. Their strong drive will inspire their children to work hard and explore the world around them. As parents, horses are stern and have high expectations of their children; however, they are understanding, and they have an abundance of wisdom and compassion to offer.

External Zodiac
Fish

Just like horses, fish are related to abundance, prosperity, emotions, knowledge, freedom, human beings, and drive to continually move forward in life. Fish represent our ancestral past, our subconscious, and our vital *qi*. Fish have been a major source of sustenance for human beings for tens of thousands of years, linking them with prosperity, good luck, and fertility. In China, the koi and carp fishes are especially revered. Koi fish are considered to be signs of peace, fertility, devotion, wealth, longevity, and happiness; while carp are considered to be signs of endurance, aspiration, determination, freedom, and achievement.

Fish represent yin and yang, and they are often used as an analogy for these energies, especially when describing the taiji symbol. While water is passive, nurturing, and nearly imperceptible (yin), fish are active, determined, and colorful (yang). Fish represent powerful strength and endurance, as well as the capacity for emotional consideration. Fish are strong and skillful in nearly all of their activities. They can move with great precision and speed, which can be observed when they travel in large schools and when they catch prey. Fish can eat algae from rocks and other sea creatures with great delicacy, and they can leap out of the water with incredible speed.

Fish are also compassionate creatures, that are often deeply devoted to their young, and highly sensitive to stimuli. Fish can be found in nearly every color imaginable, and their brilliance can be astonishing. Fish display lavish colors for many reasons. Some use coloration for camouflage, while others use it for communication, or as a warning to others. The beautiful colors that fish display associates them with the heart, and with emotions in general. While many fish are preyed upon by predatory creatures, they maintain their happiness and emotional stability by humbly focusing on migration, finding food, being with others, and reproduction.

Qi

In Daoism, fish are revered because of their close association with human beings. Western science now recognizes evolution as a natural process of growth and development. When discussing human evolution, many scientists often state that we are descended from primates, while still recognizing the full, modern understanding of our evolutionary history, because we share so much DNA, and behavioral traits, with them. Primates represent the step in our evolution when our brains, and intelligence, began to develop rapidly, contributing greatly to our success as a species. However, Daoists have long emphasized the fact that human beings have descended from fish because they consider the movement of life from sea to land to be our most significant evolutionary adaptation.

The human genome is closely related to that of a fish, and because of this we share many anatomical similarities. The texture and pigmentation of a fish's flesh, for instance, is quite similar to that of a human being. Also, the way in which the ribs of the fish extend from the spine, to form the fish's torso and flanks, as well as the way in which their nerves follow their bones and tissues, are both similar to human anatomy. It has even been recognized that "the ear of higher vertebrates was apparently developed first by fishes as a balancing organ" (Scott 1972, 40). Daoists and numerous ancient texts speak of a creature that lives in the deep ocean, with a head and torso that greatly resembles a human being, and the tail and fins of a fish. Mermaids, or the "missing link," have been the subject of legend for thousands of years, and a number of accounts are quite specific. The White Cloud Temple contained many accounts of these creatures and interactions with them. The discovery of these creatures by science in the future would greatly enhance our understanding of human evolution.

Fish are also the ancestors of birds, as well as human beings. As fish began to evolve in ways that allowed them to breach the surface of the water, they eventually learned how to glide for longer and longer periods, eventually resulting in the development of wings and flight. Birds inherited their stamina and endurance, as well as their general anatomy, from their fish ancestors. While birds can fly incredible distances, there is truly no limit to the distance that a fish can travel. The taiji diagram can be interpreted as the image of a crane and a fish, illustrating the close relationship between birds and fish.

The Healing Qualities of Fish

As described earlier, water is considered yin energy, while fish are yang. The yang energy that fishes contain is beneficial for health, strength, and immune function in human beings. Fish contain vitamins C, D, and E, which all benefit the body's immune system in various ways. In general, it is better to eat more fish and less meat, such as beef, pork, or chicken, though meat is necessary at times. Eating fish creates energy within the body, which nourish its functions, whereas eating meat mostly creates phlegm and mucus. There are an abundant variety of fish in the world, and each one of them has special qualities that can benefit the body when consumed.

When cooked thoroughly, fish bones become crunchy and edible. Eating fish bones provides wonderful support for the kidneys and the skeletal system. The healing of bone spurs, osteoporosis, and other skeletal conditions can be greatly assisted by the consumption of fish bones. Fish bones are also known to have been used as the earliest form of acupuncture needles. Ancient fishing communities developed many uses for all parts of the fishes they caught, helping human beings to thrive, and develop healing methods to treat a variety of conditions.

Special Abilities and Traits

The fish represents steadfast forward-movement, and endurance. The taiji diagram is most often interpreted as depicting two fish following one another, continually swimming after their counterpart. Fish can swim indefinitely, and over their lifetime they travel an incredible distance. Just like horses, fish represent endurance, stamina, and freedom because of their love of exploration, self-development, and fully expressing their energy.

Fish are adaptable creatures that have developed numerous unique skills and survival methods. Fish have an amazing ability to adapt and transform themselves to new environments, and each of their adaptations can teach us new lessons. For instance, immediately after birth, salmon naturally separate themselves into two groups, each consisting of a single gender. This voluntary segregation helps them to harness their energies, and transform themselves throughout their lives.

Salmon are not only able to transform their understanding and behavior, but they transform their physical bodies as well. As Male salmon grow older and prepare to meet their female counterparts once again to mate, they drastically transform their bodies. Similarly, advanced spiritual students take advantage of powerful biological energy to cultivate themselves. By remaining segregated, monks and nuns enhance and transform themselves for the benefit of future generations.

Sharks are unique in that they almost never develop cancer. Sharks must continually move because they have to keep fresh salt water moving through their gills to breathe. This continual activity prevents the development of cancer. Similarly, the human heart is also continually in motion, and because of this, heart cancer is extremely rare.

Being yang in nature, and inhabiting the ocean, fish are deeply in touch with yin energy. Fish depend upon the quality, and regularity, of yin energy, and there-fore, they are familiar with the cycles of the moon. The moon's cycles are re-sponsible for the tides of the ocean, and they regulate the dynamics of yin and yang energy on earth. When the sun is out, the oceans begin to warm, and the fish rise toward the surface to feed on the growing algae. Many types of fish wait until the presence of a full moon, when the yin energy is at its maximum, to gather together and spawn. Needless to say, fish are perceptive and intelligent creatures, which can be observed in their insistence on living their lives according to the cycles of nature and the moon.

Cultural and Spiritual Concepts

Fish are naturally associated with the water and they demonstrate various meth-ods of moving skillfully through complex and dynamic environments. By under-standing the tides of the oceans and the flow of the rivers, fish know where they are and what is necessary to achieve their goals. Water has long been associated with the darkness and mystery of the unconscious mind, and fish represent the deep insights and revelations that arise through introspection and contemplation. By exploring the unexplored parts of ourselves, we can develop character, and ignite the spirit within us. Just like horses, fish teach us to make the best out of every opportunity that we come across, and to appreciate the personal growth that we experience as a result.

In many religious traditions, the symbol of the fish has been a sign of sal-vation, freedom, and happiness. In Christianity, the fish represented the spirit of the Christ, and the achievement of salvation. It also is a reminder of the miracle of feeding the thousands of people with only two fish and five loaves of bread performed by Jesus of Nazareth. In Buddhism, the image of two golden fish is among the eight auspicious symbols, used to describe the state of enlightenment. In India, two fish represent the two sacred rivers of Hinduism, the Yamuna and the Ganges, as well as the masculine and feminine energies. In general, the two fish symbol represents good fortune, fertility, harmony, prosperity, and happiness.

The famous conversation between the Daoist master Zhuangzi and his friend Huizi, uses fish as an analogy for human beings, emphasizing their close association. This story is used as a way of illustrating the innate relationship between all living creatures, and the verifiable understanding that it provides.

Zhuangzi and Huizi were strolling along the dam of the Hao River when Zhuangzi said, "See how the minnows come out and dart around where they please! that's what the fish really enjoy!"

Huizi said, "You're not a fish— how do you know what fish enjoy?"

Zhuangzi said, "You're not I, so how do you know I don't know what fish enjoy?"

Huizi said, "I'm not you, so I certainly don't know what you know. On the other hand, you're certainly not a fish— so that still proves that you don't know what fish enjoy!"

Zhuangzi said, "Let's go back to your original question, please. You asked me how I know what fish enjoy— so you already knew I knew it when you asked the question. I know it by standing here beside the Hao" (Zhuangzi 1968, 188-9).

Quotes from Famous Horses

There is no good in anything until it is finished.
- Genghis Khan

Respect your efforts, respect yourself. Self-respect leads to self-discipline. When you have both firmly under your belt, that's real power.
- Clint Eastwood

To be free is not merely to cast off one's chains, but to live in a way that respects and enhances the freedom of others.
- Nelson Mandela

I have become so great as I am because I have won men's hearts by gentleness and kindliness.
- Saladin

It is surmounting difficulties that makes heroes.
- Louis Pasteur

Own only what you can always carry with you: know languages, know countries, know people. Let your memory be your travel bag.
- Aleksandr Solzhenitsyn

Without passion, you don't have energy. Without energy, you have nothing.
- Warren Buffett

The real value in setting goals is not in their achievement. The acquisition of the things you want is strictly secondary. The major reason for setting goals is to compel you to become the person it takes to achieve them.
- Jim Rohn

Patient endurance is a sign of progress.
- Hazrat Inayat Khan

There's always a new challenge to keep you motivated.
- Sean Connery

Forgiveness enables actors to become freed from vengeance.
- Hannah Arendt

Let your tongue speak what your heart thinks
- Davy Crockett

8

Sheep

Metal Sheep
17th February 1931 to 5th February 1932

Water Sheep
5th February 1943 to 24th January 1944

Wood Sheep
24th January 1955 to 11th February 1956

Fire Sheep
9th February 1967 to 29th January 1968

Earth Sheep
28th January 1979 to 15th February 1980

Metal Sheep
15th February 1991 to 3rd February 1992

Water Sheep
1st February 2003 to 21st January 2004

Wood Sheep
19th February 2015 to 7th February 2016

Fire Sheep
6th February 2027 to 25th January 2028

Earth Sheep
24th January 2039 to 11th February 2040

Metal Sheep
11th February 2051 to 1st February 2052

Water Sheep
29th January 2063 to 17th February 2064

Sheep

The sheep category of the zodiac represents all types of sheep, goats, rams, and even antelope. Sheep are peaceful, calm, careful, reliable, gentle, considerate, gracious, agile, adaptable, practical, courageous, defensive, timid and formidable. Goats spend most of their time grazing, ruminating, climbing, playing, fighting, and migrating. During spring and summer, goats and sheep climb to higher altitudes to graze on wild, nutrient rich grasses, and during colder months, they descend to lower altitudes to feed on mosses, shrubs, weeds, and twigs. Goats, like oxen, are ruminant animals that repeatedly chew and swallow their food to extract as many nutrients as possible. This allows goats and sheep to survive in areas where food may scarcer, like the rocky cliffs and hillsides of mountainous regions. Their four stomachs hold previously digested food until they find the proper opportunity to ruminate (Burnie and Wilson 2001, 255).

Most goats and sheep travel in groups that are segregated by gender. Females form harems of between two and twenty-five, and they live in relative harmony with one another. Males gather in bachelor herds of approximately the same size, and regularly battle for both dominance and mating rights. During their mating, or rutting, season, which usually lasts from August to January, male bucks become more aggressive, protective and territorial. They often charge and make loud vocalizations at any creature that travels too close during rutting season. Females give birth to 1-3 young at a time, after a gestation period of roughly five to six months. The females give birth during the spring, and the young remain with the females. When they reach adolescence, the males join the bachelor herds (Burnie and Wilson 2001, 256).

Goats and rams exhibit a number of variations in horn shape and size. Some species have small horns, while others have horns that are so large, their weight accounts for half of their total body weight. Some goats have horns that are relatively straight, some have horns that form spirals, and others have horns that form a complete 360° spiral. The horns of rams and goats are made of the same material as the bones of the body, and they are encased in a sheath made of keratin, the material that forms human fingernails. During rutting season, bucks use their horns for establishing dominance and fighting for mating rights. Bucks head butt each other until one of them surrenders, and they lock horns while thrashing their heads, to throw their opponent off balance. Sheep and goats have powerful legs, and their skeletal system is robust, allowing them to deliver a great amount of force with their head strikes. Many goats also increase their power by rearing up on their hind legs, and crashing their heads downward with explosive force (Burnie and Wilson 2001, 244-56).

When they are threatened, or when they are in need of essential nutrients, goats and sheep climb upward onto steep cliffs and hillsides. These are areas that few creatures can reach, and they provide protection as well as untouched food sources. The hooves of goats have hard outer rims and soft inner pads that allow them to grip even small ledges and slippery slopes. With hooves that are specially adapted for climbing, and thick wool coats, most species of goat are ideally suited for life at high altitudes. The ibex, for instance, can thrive at altitudes as high as 22,000 feet. On the other hand, impalas and gazelles are suited to life on flat grasslands. With legs that are designed for sprinting, these animals are capable of reaching speeds of nearly 60 miles per hour (Burnie and Wilson 2001, 250-56).

Calendar

The sheep is the eighth animal of the zodiac. It is associated with the sixth month of the Chinese lunar calendar that lasts from approximately July 7th to August 8th in the Gregorian calendar, and to the two-hour period between 1 pm and 3 pm. This is the end of summer, and the approach of the late summer, when the trees and plants are fully mature. Most animals are busy at this time taking advantage of the abundance of yang *qi*, and the flourishing plant life. Goat years are times when settling down and creating peaceful harmony are emphasized. In the year of the sheep, there will be many opportunities to mingle and meet other people, both professionally and personally. This is also a time for calm appreciation, gathering resources, and creating a comfortable, stable environment.

Goats are creatures that pay close attention to detail. When goats climb steep cliffs, they always look closely at where they are about to step next, adjusting their footing by using their cloven hooves to grip the rock. Similarly, in the year of the goat, many scientific and technological issues are reviewed, scrutinized, and finalized. This is a year when details and nuances matter, and many professionals will be focusing on fine tuning their work. Albert Einstein's theory of relativity was tested and confirmed in the sheep year of 1919 with the Eddington experiment.[1] The news of this discovery had a huge impact around the world and for the future of science, as it completely revolutionized the way the that universe and its laws were understood. Furthermore, in 2003, the Human Genome Project completed and presented its work on the mapping of the human genome. This laid the groundwork for extensive development in medicine, genetics, history, anthropology, and numerous other fields of study.[2]

In the year of the sheep, economies often see steady growth and progress; however, goat years also see many taxes, price adjustments, and regulations being put in place as a way of stabilizing this progress. Throughout 1931, economies in the United States and around the world were implementing many measures to mitigate the effects of the Great Depression. The economic collapse had begun two years earlier, but its wide-ranging effects were only beginning to be fully

[1] "Einstein, Eddington and the 1919 Eclipse," by Peter Coles (2019). www.nature.com/articles/d41586-019-01172-z

[2] "Advances Based on the HGP," by Judith L Fridovich-Keil (1998). www.britannica.com/event/Human-Genome-Project/Advances-based-on-the-HGP

understood. In the following goat year, 1943, the Great Depression was officially declared to be at an end, and the industrial demands of World War II provided rapid, steady economic growth.

Thriving economies go hand in hand with lavish spending, and this means that during sheep years, sales increase, and most products become more widely available. On the other hand, this also means that people who have in-demand resources will begin taking measures to protect their assets, including raising prices and restricting access. With discipline, the year of the goat can produce great financial growth and stability; however, with a lack of conscientiousness and attention to detail, accidents and difficult situations become more likely. In the sheep year of 1979, immediately following the overthrowing of the Shah of Iran, the world began quickly purchasing oil for fear of shortages. This dramatically increased demand for oil in many parts of the world, and caused its price to rise rapidly.[3]

Mountain goats enjoy discovering new places and climbing to extreme heights, despite the risks involved. Similarly, recent goat years have seen quite a lot of advances in aerospace technology, including numerous attempts to reach greater distances and make new discoveries. As we become capable of reaching further into space, it will be crucial that the people of the world learn to cooperate, share their discoveries, and develop mutual trust. In 1967, the Outer Space Treaty, between the United States, the United Kingdom, and the Russian Federation, became the first treaty that addressed the "Principles governing the activities of states in the exploration and use of outer space, including the moon, and other celestial bodies".[4] This treaty laid the foundation for the laws and boundaries that would guide us during the decades of rapid development that followed.

During goat years, in general, people get along quite well with one another, and there are often many social events and entertaining parties to attend. However, while these years carry an atmosphere of cheerfulness, they are also times when territorial sentiments are inflamed, and strong boundaries are formed. Goats enjoy open spaces and being surrounded by their loved ones, and while they don't dislike other creatures, they prefer to keep most at a safe distance. Valuing healthy boundaries leads to a strong sense of self-worth in individuals, and it also gives rise to many larger discussions regarding rights, policies, and the governance of nations. During 1955, for instance, Rosa Parks refused to give up her seat on the bus to a white passenger in Alabama; sparking the beginning of the Montgomery Bus Boycott, and striking a crucial blow for the advancement of Civil Rights in America. In the same year, the Soviet Union and several other

---

[3] "Oil Shock of 1978–79," by Laurel Graefe (2013). www.federalreservehistory.org/essays/oil-shock-of-1978-79

[4] "Treaty on Principles Governing the Activities of States in the Exploration and Use of Outer Space, Including the Moon and Other Celestial Bodies," by The United Nations Office for Outer Space Affairs (1967). www.unoosa.org/oosa/en/ourwork/spacelaw/treaties/introouterspacetreaty.html

eastern bloc nations, signed the Warsaw Pact in response to the recent formation of NATO, and its decision to admit West Germany as a member state. The alliance further solidified the boundaries between the east and the west, and set the stage for the Cold War that followed.[5] [6]

The focus on defense and protection that is seen during goat years, means that militaries will be active, and the enforcement of border security will be a priority. While military operations and incursions can be quite intense during these years, most of the time they do not lead to ongoing conflicts or extended wars. Goats do not like to fight, they prefer peace; however, they are quite willing to defend themselves, their homes, and their resources. In the goat year 1967, the Six-Day War took place between Israel and a number of its Arab neighbors. It occurred when Egypt refused to allow Israeli shipping to pass through the straits of Tiran, which Israel viewed as an act of war, during a time of high tension between the two countries. The war ended in six days, after Israel made significant gains and all parties agreed to a cease-fire.[7]

The defensive posture that many people assume during goat years also leads to labor strikes, and negotiations regarding compensation in the workplace. When productivity increases and defensive measures must be taken to protect profits, the people who have worked hard to make these things happen, quickly and acutely feel the need to be properly compensated for their efforts. When the sense of comradery and responsibility is strong within a group, the need for personal freedoms, privacy, and a safe place to call home become strong as well. In order for a society to succeed, a harmonious balance between generosity and healthy boundaries is required.

During World War II, for example, many industries converted to full-time war production in the United States; as war-time inflation began to rise, work became increasingly demanding, while purchasing power decreased. This led to numerous strikes in many key industries, and threatened the ability of the United States to produce the necessary materials for its military. Therefore, in 1943, the War Labor Disputes Act was passed into law, allowing the government to seize control of certain industries that were under strike, and allow them to continue with the production of war materials.[8]

During Goat years, art and entertainment is abundant and vibrant. All goat years produce an abundance of art and vibrant self-expression no matter which medium is used. New music, paintings, movies, video games and television all

[5] "Rosa Parks," by Academy of Achievement Editors (n.d.). www.achievement.org/achiever/rosa-parks/

[6] "Warsaw Pact," by The Editors of Encyclopedia Britannica (1998). www.britannica.com/event/Warsaw-Pact

[7] "Six-Day War," by The Editors of Encyclopedia Britannica (2009). www.britannica.com/event/Six-Day-War

[8] "War Labor Disputes Act," by Thomas Carson (1999). www.encyclopedia.com/history/encyclopedias-almanacs-transcripts-and-maps/war-labor-disputes-act

become popular and innovative in the year of the goat. Goat energy is especially conducive to art because it allows people to share ideas and feelings, while maintaining comfortable boundaries. In the modern age, this is truer than it was in the past, because numerous forms of art can now be enjoyed easily at any time.

Qi

The time of the day that relates to the sheep is between 1 pm and 3 pm, the time of the small intestine meridian. This is the time when the yin energy of the day slowly begins to rise, and the yang energy of the day begins to recede after reaching its peak. During this time, the small intestine has an abundance of energy, and any illnesses that originate in the small intestine can be more easily treated and dispersed. In China, sheep trails in nature are often referred to as "small intestine paths" because their great length and numerous turns resemble the organ. This is also the time when the liver is at its least active point of the day, resting and detoxifying in preparation for the next twenty-four hours.

The small intestine is responsible for extracting the usable nutrients from the food material that has been processed by the stomach, called chyme. It then transports the chyme to the spleen via the blood stream, so that it can be distributed to the rest of the body. In this way, the small intestine separates the "clear" *qi* from the "turbid" *qi*. The unusable food material and liquid, are passed on to the large intestine and urinary bladder respectively, and excreted from the body. The duodenum of the small intestine is also the location where the bile and other enzymes are introduced to the chyme to break it down further. This allows it to be absorbed into the blood stream. Before reaching the end of the duodenum, glands excrete alkaline liquids into the chyme, neutralizing the acids that were introduced in the stomach.

In the *zang fu* organs system of classification, the small intestine is paired with the heart. Physically, the small intestine separates the "clear" nutrients (*gu qi*) from the "turbid" waste. Psychologically and emotionally, however, the small intestine assists the mind, or "spirit", that is housed in the heart, to separate clear, true thoughts and feelings, from turbid, false ones. In this way, the small intestine acts like a lens through which the heart can more closely analyze its own thoughts and feelings. If the small intestine is ill or unable to function properly, then confusion and indecision will result. When the small intestine is strong and flows smoothly, it decisively claims and protects usable resources to distribute to the rest of the body (Johnson 2014, 510-16).

The ghost point that is associated with the sheep is known as Ghost's Cave (*guicu*); it matches the point Labor Palace (*laogong*, PC-8) in the acupuncture system (Johnson 2014, 605). This point is located in the center of the palm, between the second and third metacarpal bones. It is used to calm the mind, clear the head of blockages, revives consciousness and treat all types of mental disorders (Deadman et al. 2007, 380).

The *laogong* point is an essential point for both physical and spiritual health. It is part of the Five Centers system that represents a vast, significant spiritual practice. Important parts of the human soul are located at each of the five centers; the bottoms of the feet, the centers of the palms, and the heart. Just like the roots of a tree, when these five points are nourished and cared for, the organism thrives, and overall health is improved. Therefore, protecting these points is essential for proper physical, mental, and emotional health. When its cold outside, wearing socks and gloves helps to protect the warmth of these energy centers, maintain immune function, and increase longevity.

By soaking the hands in warm water every morning, and soaking the feet in warm water every evening, the roots of the body are nourished, and the qi meridians are mobilized, protecting the body against many illnesses. The hands and feet contain many acupuncture points and an abundance of qi. Soaking the hands is particularly effective at improving overall health because the heart meridian travels down the arm to the hand. The heart meridian closely follows the path of the brachial artery as it moves further down the arm, therefore, heating the hands reduces stress on the circulatory system. Similarly, exposing the hands to sunlight for a few minutes every day, or holding the hands near a warm fire at night are also quite beneficial practices. Daoists consider the hands to be similar to solar panels, that can soak up the rays of the sun to nourish the heart, stimulate the mind, and produce clear thinking.

Sheep and goats are also associated with the function of the gallbladder according to the five phases system. In sheep, the gallbladder does not concentrate bile as much as in other creatures, including human beings, and the bile is released into the small intestine more regularly. This type of gall bladder function is generally found in ruminant animals. With rumination, food material is mostly digested before it reaches the duodenum, and therefore, less bile is required to continue digestion. This also means that the bile produced by the liver can be released into the GI tract more regularly, thereby maintaining its health.

When the liver and gallbladder are functioning properly, then the mind becomes calm and emotions are more easily regulated. Sheep are naturally quite cheerful and gentle creatures, which has a lot to do with the robust health of their digestive system. Creatures that are vegetarian are naturally less aggressive, but no less formidable, than creatures that are carnivorous. Oxen and horses are both vegetarian animals, and while they can both be quite ornery and irritable, they are rarely aggressive. Rams and goats, which are large and powerful, will often rear-up, buck, jump, and behave wildly when threatened, but they rarely attack another creature with the intention to kill. Gall is naturally vitriolic, acidic, and volatile; rams and goats can display such explosive strength and emotion, however, with their strong small intestine they are also able to effectively neutralize the volatile nature of this liquid, and its psychological manifestations.

Lamb meat and mutton are both healthy forms of dietary medicine that should be consumed occasionally. Eating lamb helps to heat the body from within, which boosts the immune system and protects against external cold. For this reason, lamb is especially beneficial during the winter, when the cold can be quite extreme and penetrating. If cold temperatures are allowed to penetrate the body, then the body's yin energy can be damaged resulting in illness and chronic pain. By eating lamb, the yin energy of the body is protected, and body remains full of vitality, and free of disease. The powerful yang energy that mutton contains is also helpful in relieving numerous sexual issues and maintaining a healthy libido.

The liver of a sheep is especially potent and healthy because of their strict diet of grasses. Eating a bit of sheep's liver regulates the emotions and protects eyesight. The hair and fingernails are also nourished and supported by the energy of the liver. Women rely heavily on the function of their liver, and the strength of this organ determines the health and appearance of their hair, nails, and gaze. The fact that sheep's wool grows so quickly, and in such abundance, is a sign that these animals have strong liver *qi*.

Special Abilities and Traits

Sheep are Highly Intuitive

Sheep are able to interpret the will of the heavens, and to follow the energies of the earth. Along with cattle, sheep can intuit when the end of their life is near. When a rancher decides that a particular sheep is to be slaughtered, the animal immediately knows that the decision has been made, often before the rancher has made the final decision. When the sheep senses its death approaching, there is a distinct change in its mood and demeanor, and it will often kneel down on its front legs to avoid being led away. Sometimes the sheep will also bleat and cry out in remorse when it knows its fate.

Sheep are able to intuit these events because of their powerful horns. The horns of any creature are able to connect that creature's mind and spirit to the will of the heavens; however, the way in which a ram's horn curls into a circular, spiral shape allows them to decipher both the messages of heaven, and the processes of the earth in great detail. Sheep know when earthquakes and natural disasters are approaching, when their life is nearly over, and when danger is lurking nearby because they are so closely associated with the will of heaven.

Sheep migrate together in herds, and they move in accordance with the direction of the wind. With their strong intuitive ability, sheep can anticipate which direction the wind will blow, and they quickly migrate to a position downwind. This keeps the wind at their backs, allowing them smell any danger that may be approaching them from behind. By literally going where the wind blows, sheep are able to follow the natural energies of the earth, helping them to managing the excessive growth of grasslands as they graze.

The sheep, the ox, and the rabbit are the three animals of the zodiac that are most responsible for managing the overgrowth of grasslands. Goats are known for being one of the least picky eaters of the animal kingdom, consuming plants that are not easily digested by most animals. Goats and sheep can survive in dry, rocky areas by eating small grasses and weeds that manage to gain a foot-hold. The close connection to the earth allows them to predict many natural events such as earthquakes, drought, and widespread disease.

Unlike cattle, as sheep graze, they also eat the roots of the grass, preventing future growth. As sheep consume the foliage in an environment, predators are able to observe them and hunt them more easily. Some types of brambles and other thorny plants that grow in dry, harsh environments have even evolved in a way that allows them to easily snare and entangle the wool of sheep. The de-ceased sheep then fertilizes the surrounding plants and nourishes the soil. Sheep can easily understand when they are vulnerable, and they intuitively seek higher ground.

Sheep Represent Unity

The *qi* of the sheep, and their naturally insulating wool coats, make them quite safe form lightning strikes and electricity. While nearly all animals become spooked by approaching thunder and lightning storms, sheep are less fearful of these conditions. However, erratic wind conditions pose a potential problem for sheep because it confuses them, and cold, wet weather can easily lead to illness.

Shorn sheep are quite sensitive and vulnerable to the elements, and when windy, cold, and/or wet conditions arise individuals call out to their herd for help. Newly shorn sheep will also display this type of behavior. The herd will naturally gather around the vulnerable sheep to keep them warm and protected. Similarly, when a person has a bald head, it creates an energy field that is similar to that of a shorn sheep, and the lunar *qi* of the moon descends upon the person's head to protect him from negative energies and influences. When we are at our most vulnerable, the nourishing yin energy arrives to restore our strength.

Along with severe weather, sheep are also not overly afraid of tigers, be-cause tigers are weary of the horns and defensive power of goats and rams. Sheep are normally calm and peaceful, but they are courageous in the face of danger. When sheep are threatened, they gather closely together and the male rams move toward the outer rim of the herd to fend off any danger. Sheep are not necessarily powerful when they are caught alone, but when they gather into groups, they are quite formidable. Sheep and goats are agile on grassland and rocky cliffs, and they intelligently use the lay of the land to defend themselves. Tigers and other predators can't easily penetrate these defenses, and they could be easily gored or brutalized by the horns of the rams.

While sheep are quite courageous against most opponents, they are fearful of wolves. Wolves use their cunning and planning abilities to separate individual sheep from the herd and attack them when they are vulnerable. Working as a pack, the wolves drive the sheep into different directions, separating the herd into smaller groups. Even a lone wolf can easily hunt a sheep when it not protected by its herd.

Reaching Great Heights

Sheep are hard-working, determined, and courageous which allows them to climb treacherous, near vertical rock faces. Sheep are related to the function of the gallbladder, and while the kidneys are responsible for the individual's willpower and drive, the gallbladder provides the courage and confidence to act on this drive and make it practical. In the English language, the word "gall" refers to both the bile produced by the liver, as well as boldness, bravery, and imprudence. Sheep and goats climb to great heights to take advantage of the hard-to-reach plant-life that flourish in these areas during the spring and summer months. They also use their incredible climbing ability to reach areas where salt can be found to satisfy the salt hunger that all ruminant animals possess. The ability to traverse extremely treacherous areas also provides a means of escape for goats when they are pursued by predators. Few predators can follow mountain goats onto the rocky cliffs.

Sheep reproduce quickly for being moderately large creatures. Sheep normally have one to three lambs per birth in the spring, and some types of sheep can give birth twice a year, producing a second liter in the early summer months. In addition, sheep are not monogamous, and both male and female sheep often have multiple partners, producing a large number of lambs. Often, this type of behavior is often found in four-legged animals that jump often, including sheep, horses, deer, and rabbits. Due to the sheep's high sex drive, the qi contained in lamb meat is beneficial for sexual issues, such as erectile dysfunction, as well as stress and anxiety.

Cultural and Spiritual Concepts

The Cheerful Sheep

Sheep are naturally happy, cheerful creatures that love to play and enjoy life. Sheep, especially young lambs, can be seen jumping, playing, wrestling, bleating, and rolling around in the grass. In general, sheep are friendly, gentle, and obedient creatures, especially the females who do not compete with each other during the rutting season.

Sheep often look shy and timid; however, they are quite powerful and they understand the principle of strength in numbers. In the *Yijing*, sheep represent the mindset of the common people. This is a sentiment that is also expressed in the west. The common phrase "don't be a sheep" means to be an individual, and avoid following the crowd. The sheep energy represents the opinions of the masses, and while it's important to think for yourself, it is also important to remember the strength of unity and comradery. The sheep, just like the common people of the world, are hard-working, forthright, and live simply.

The cheerful, harmonious, and adaptable nature of sheep also allows them to be wonderful leaders that can accomplish great things. Mountain goats, like leaders of the people, can conquer great obstacles that seem impossible, and they do it with skill and cheerfulness. While similar creatures, such as horses and oxen, are headstrong and stubborn, sheep are adaptable, courteous, and receptive to change. Sheep are great communicators, and they patiently listen to the thoughts of others. George Washington, a courageous, skillful leader who embodied the spirit of the sheep, once said, in his *Rules of Civility,* "[It is polite to] be not forward, but friendly and courteous; be the first to salute, hear, or answer; and be not pensive when it is time to converse" (1988, 22).

The Sacrifice of the Sheep

In the Chinese creation myth, the goddess Nuwa created sheep and oxen to help serve humankind, by helping them to manage the land, and by providing meat and valuable materials. Every part of the sheep is useful to human beings. Wool, for instance, is able to protect against the penetrating qualities of the wind, trapping warm air and creating a barrier against the cold. Sheep horns have been used as communication devices, cups, vessels, and ceremonial items for thousands of years. The meat, organs, and flesh of the lamb provide sustenance and medicine, while the bones have been carved into numerous tools, items, and building materials.

The skin and leather of the sheep has also been used for many centuries as clothing items, horse saddles, construction materials, and as the skin of drums. Sheep's leather is considered ideal for drum skins because it contains an abundance of heavenly yang energy, and therefore it creates a more heavenly sound. The word for sheep in Chinese is "yang", which also refers to sunlight, warmth, cheerfulness, and heaven. When a drum made of sheep's skin is beaten, the sound is able to induce heavenly and cheerful feelings in the heart of the listener, and healing their *qi*.

In many Asian temples, a sheep's front legs would be suspended, while their back legs would be placed on a large drum, beating it with each step. The heavenly energy of both the drum and the sheep creates a special energy that brings cheerfulness and happiness to the surrounding environment. The heavenly sound of these drums also helps to protect mental health and allow individuals to recognize their own true nature more easily. Sheep skin drums have been considered sacred for a long time because of these special heavenly qualities.

Similarly, the bleating of a sheep is special as well. In order for a sheep to yell or bleat, it must project its voice from the abdomen by practicing proper abdominal breathing. This is a great form of exercise and it keeps the sheep in good health, maintaining their longevity. This sound brings the mind to attention and focuses it on the energies of heaven and earth, allowing us to connect with the surrounding environment more easily. By hearing or even mimicking the sound of a sheep, human beings become simultaneously relaxed and alert.

Sheep Represent Prosperity

There is a saying in China that says "three sheep can open the doors of your business." Daoists believe that by having the energy of three sheep in your business, prosperity and good luck are bound to arrive. This is because sheep represent yang energy, and when three forms of yang energy are combined, they invite the energies of heaven to enter the space. This could mean that the image of three sheep should be placed in the business, or it could mean that three sheep people become business partners together. The sheep's ability to be extremely adaptive and to adjust well to new information lends itself well to business success, fitness, and any project that requires active, conscious engagement.

In feng shui theory, water is closely associated with money, and sheep always follow sources of water. Similarly, the color white is also associated with both money and sheep. By keeping a small water fountain in, or near, the home, or by frequenting a nearby body of water, the spirit of the sheep can be attracted, as well as wealth and prosperity. Sheep also love bamboo, and the sheep spirit can also be attracted by keeping a small bamboo plant near the home during sheep years. Both cows and sheep require the *qi* of flowers and grass to survive. The *qi* of flowers, especially ones with large, thick leaves, or round leaves, helps the cultivator to manage and invest their resources well. The *qi* of grass, especially grass that is both green and yellow, helps to develop luck and prosperity.

People Who Embody the Sheep

People born in the year of the goat are naturally kind, gentle, cheerful, and considerate. Goats and sheep love to gather, and their desire for interaction has led them to develop sociable and considerate personalities. Sheep people love to attend gatherings and be part of the crowd. They always have a large social circle, and they make friends wherever they go. Having the support of others is essential for them, and if they feel ostracized, or that other people are disapproving, it can affect them deeply. On the other hand, they also enjoy developing themselves as individuals, and deepening their character, if only to develop their self-confidence. Self-worth, recognition, and appreciation are essential to sheep people, and with a little encouragement they become confident and determined.

Sheep are emotionally sensitive, and they can easily see situations from another's perspective. With experience, goats can learn to manage their emotional sensitivity skillfully, by being sensitive to the needs of others, and strong in the face of overwhelming emotion. Many goat people are extremely valuable in emergency situations because of their ability to handle intense feelings as they arise. Goats are courageous and bold, especially when it comes to protecting their loved ones.

The sensitive and emotional nature of sheep also causes them to become deep thinkers. Just as sheep and goats ruminate their food, chewing it over and over again to get the most out of it, sheep people often ruminate over their thoughts. They continue to think a subject through until they are satisfied that they fully understand the subject. This can also lead many of them to be worrisome, skittish, and defeatist. Sheep people can alleviate this rampant mental energy, and calm their nerves by being given the opportunity to discuss their thoughts with others, or externalize them in writing.

Sheep are supremely creative, and they are great lovers of art. No matter what they apply themselves to, they always add their creativity and style to it. They are often dexterous, skillful with their hands, and they have an eye for detail. When sheep people apply themselves to a creative project, they always do so with a sense of perfection. They enjoy taking their time and being meticulous in their work. Art and creativity are greatly therapeutic for sheep people, and by developing their talents, they can center themselves and stabilize their abundant mental energy. Their talents in art also allow goats to have opportunities to interact with others and share interesting experiences. Goats can often be found frequenting local art museums, galleries, theaters, or musical performances.

People born during sheep years excel at any career that requires interaction with others, especially when it involves creative ideas. They make wonderful real estate agents, designers, party planners, hosts, performing artists, and teachers. They are also great at any profession that requires deep thinking and critical analysis. Many great scientists, researchers, and leaders of industry embodied the sheep spirit. Goats enjoy professions that allow them to reach as high as they can climb, and they abhor strict structures, limitations, and dull activities.

Financially speaking, goat people often do quite well for themselves. Their creative and personable nature, helps them find the resources that they need to provide for themselves and accomplish their goals. Sheep people are wonderful at creating teams, and bringing together people of various talents to accomplish a goal. Andrew Carnegie, a powerful sheep person, clearly stated, "it marks a big step in your development when you come to realize that other people can help you do a better job than you could do alone." Yet, even though sheep people can often earn quite a bit throughout their lives, they can also be fond of spending their money lavishly, and engaging in risky investments. With discipline and mindfulness, sheep can manage their personal finances successfully and quickly develop wealth.

In relationships, sheep people are kind, gentle, and adaptable. They enjoy discovering all the small ways that they can make their partner happy and comfortable. Sheep recognize the value of having a partner in life, and the wealth of love and support that is only developed over time. Being highly social beings, they may be indecisive in choosing a mate, but their burning desire for companionship and playfulness often leads them to develop loving, caring relationships.

While goat people are social and outgoing, they are also fond of domestic life and when they find a loving partner, they often discover that they enjoy the peace and harmony that comes from settling down. Goats make wonderful parents that listen to, and intuit, the needs of their loved ones, however, this can also lead to a lack of boundaries, and entitled children. Goats find it difficult to discipline their loved ones, and they may need to develop a firm, yet gentle, manner in order to set healthy boundaries.

External Zodiac
Bear

The bear is the outer animal of the sheep category, and people born under the sign of the sheep contain the spirit of the bear within. Like sheep, bears are naturally peaceful, harmonious animals that would rather spend their days eating, playing, and foraging, rather than fighting and being territorial. When human beings encounter a bear in the wilderness, giving it a wide berth is often enough to avoid a confrontation. However, if they feel threatened, bears fight with strength, courage, and ferocity. A mother bear with cubs is especially territorial and ferocious, and great caution should be shown in her presence.

According to the zodiac, the only animal that can truly defeat a bear is a snake. When a bear encounters a tiger (the most ferocious animal of the zodiac) the tiger is often the victor, however, the bear is rarely decisively defeated. Its interest in fighting diminishes more quickly than a tiger, and they escape to fight another day. Bears are formidable and ferocious, when necessary, but once they feel that a threat no longer remains, their violence quickly dissipates. It is commonly known that in the event of a bear attack, often the best strategy is to play dead and avoid posing a threat so the bear will lose interest.

A significant difference between sheep and bears is their social preferences. While sheep, usually prefer the company of others, gathering into herds, bears enjoy their solitude, and often remain reclusive. People born during sheep years often display both of these qualities, enjoying the friendship of many people, as well as the solitude and comfort of domestic life.

Both bears and goats inhabit mountainous habitats and high altitudes. They love to climb, and to view the world from a higher perspective; however, while sheep prefer to climb rocky cliffs and hillsides, bears enjoy climbing trees. Both animals rely heavily on the strength of their hind legs while climbing. By climbing regularly, sheep and bears develop both their physical strength, and their bold courage.

While both sheep and bears have highly developed sense organs, they rely primarily on their sense of smell to guide them. Bears are omnivores, whereas sheep and goats are strictly herbivores. Their highly developed sense of smell helps bears to forage for plants and berries, as well as recognize the trails and markings of other animals. Bears and sheep have similarly shaped faces, with elongated snouts for focusing their olfactory senses. A strong sense of smell is a sign of strong lungs, a strong immune system, and the ability to easily calm the nerves and the mind. Both sheep and bears practice abdominal breathing, which aids in their digestion and their fortitude.

Qi

There are many types of bears, and unfortunately many of them are endangered due to poaching, climate change, and the encroachment of human civilization. Bears can thrive in many climates, but they greatly value solitude, and they will only enter human civilizations when they cannot find other sources of food. Most bears are omnivorous, but polar bears are carnivores, and panda bears are mostly herbivores. Like goats, bears are not especially picky about what they eat; instead, they are more concerned with how much they eat. Bears must consume a large number of calories to support their large bodies, and in the months before winter, they must significantly increase their body fat to survive and care for their newborn cubs.

Bears have powerful *qi* in their inner organs, and this leads to the development of great strength and power. Bears have a strong and well-developed stomach and spleen, due to the large number of calories that they consume daily. When the spleen is strong and healthy, then digestion flows smoothly, and the body develops large, strong muscles overall. Bears also have extraordinary kidney function. When they enter hibernation, their kidneys shut down entirely, which allows them to rest and heal. This unique ability also preserves the bear's abundant yang energy, contributing to their longevity. Bears have strong lungs that produce extraordinary olfactory senses, allowing them to follow the scents and trails of other animals. Their strong livers allow them to develop enhanced tendon strength, fortifying the strength of their muscles. Finally, the bear's strong gallbladder allows them to quickly and efficiently digest the large amount of food that they consume, and it is responsible for their boldness, and courage.

In traditional Chinese medicine, the tendons of bears are considered a delicacy that have many curative and healing properties. By consuming bear tendons, the spleen, liver, and muscles of the body are nourished and strengthened. The gall bladder of the bear is highly valued for its medicinal properties as well. When used properly it can treat high fever, blurred vision, dizziness, lightheadedness, confusion, low blood pressure and fainting.

Special Abilities and Traits

Most bears are wonderful climbers. Their large, non-retractable claws, and strong grip are ideal for grasping tree bark, and their powerful limbs are easily able to carry their weight. Bears often scratch the bark of a tree to mark important locations on the trails that they use. In general, they climb trees to find food or as a form of play. The berries, honey, fruit, nuts, and bird eggs that are found in trees are important sources of calories for bears, especially the more agile species, like black bears.

Bears can often be found rubbing and striking themselves against tree trunks. While other animals like horses, dogs, and cats can been seen exhibiting this behavior, bears strike trees the most. In Daoism, the practice of striking trees is considered a powerful method for exchanging *qi* with nature. By exchanging *qi* with a tree, both the individual, and the tree benefit.

It is well known that proper exercise is a crucial component of a healthy lifestyle, and in Daoism, emphasis is placed on the degree to which a person enjoys their exercise routine. Every person should find the forms of exercise that are suited to their abilities, and that they truly enjoy. When exercise creates happiness, its benefits are multiplied, and a routine is more easily formed. Bears demonstrate this principle with the obvious enjoyment that they experience while rubbing and striking themselves against trees. Bears have large spines and back muscles, and their arms are always oriented toward the front, preventing them from reaching their back. Therefore, to scratch and rub their back muscles, which support so much of their weight, they must find a large, strong tree. Some of the body's most powerful *qi* meridians are located on the back, as well as some of the largest nerves. Bears rely on these meridians, and when they are able to adjust these areas, their whole-body benefits.

By striking the body against a tree, unblocks and straightens the meridians of both the practitioner and the tree, allowing them to flow more easily, and produce a healthier state. This is a treatment that is used to cure numerous conditions and illnesses in Daoist medicine. It is also a way of developing the spirit, and cleansing the soul. By striking the body against a tree, stagnant emotions are released, and the liver function is normalized. This practices both oxygenates and cleanses the blood, which then nourishes all of the body's vital organs. After striking a tree, a feeling of euphoria and happiness is produced. This practice produces more powerful healing results than taiji, yoga, acupressure, *guasha*, or foot massage. Like other types of physical fitness, the results of tree striking are reciprocal; the greater effort, the more significant the rewards.

Cultural and Spiritual Concepts

Bears spend much of their time in solitude, happily foraging and exploring. They are comfortable in their own skin, and they have high self-esteem. Bears are rarely timid, anxious, or self-conscious; instead, they know themselves deeply, which gives them self-confidence. Along with spending much of their active lives in relative solitude, they also hibernate for long periods of time during the winter, often without interacting with any other creatures. This ability to intuitively go deep within leads to self-reliance, innate happiness, and inner strength.

Bears teach us to get in touch with our wild side that is natural and spontaneous. The primal, untamed nature of the psyche can be quite intimidating, but the bear's strength, and its slow, peaceful nature is a demonstration of how to properly handle this energy. Bears recognize the need to leave the outside world occasionally, and enter the darkness of the den to develop inner strength. With their deep connection to the earth, bears are associated with the yang energies of nature including courage, bravery, and determination; and by demonstrating strength, they set healthy boundaries to keep threats at a distance.

Bears appreciate the sweetness of life, literally and figuratively. The drama of the crowd, and the opinions of others can cause chronic anxiety, timidity, and depression; to mitigate this stress, bears make it a regular habit to play and enjoy themselves. By facing the harsh reality of nature and the depths of one's psyche, simple pleasures, like honey and berries, become experiences of pure bliss. Bears remind us to enjoy the journey of life, and to keep our inner child alive and well.

Bears represent honorable, upright people and divine energy. Just like sheep, bears recognize that there is a time and place peace, as well as strength and fortitude. Bears climb up into the trees, and down into their dens, relying on their intuition and inner strength to orient themselves through the changing seasons. Bears teach us to adapt to nature, rather than try to fight against it. By taking advantage of the abundance of summer, bears prepare themselves for the coming winter; and during the winter months, they protect their health and physical energy. By living in accordance with nature, bears are closely associated with the feminine yin energies of the earth. They demonstrate nurturing, motherly, and protective behaviors both with their young, and with themselves.

Quotes from Famous Sheep

Never let your sense of morals get in the way of doing what's right.
- Isaac Asimov

What you are will show in what you do.
- Thomas Edison

There is a wisdom of the head, and a wisdom of the heart.
- Charles Dickens

If I have ever made any valuable discoveries, it has been due more to patient attention, than to any other talent.
- Isaac Newton

The only way to do great work is to love what you do. If you haven't found it yet, keep looking. Don't settle. As with all matters of the heart, you'll know when you find it.
- Steve Jobs

If you feel lost, disappointing, hesitant, or weak, return to yourself, to who you are here and now, and when you get there, you will discover yourself, like a lotus flower in full bloom, even in a muddy pond, beautiful and strong.
- Masaru Emoto

Teamwork is the ability to work together toward a common vision. The ability to direct the individual accomplishments toward organizational objectives. It is the fuel that allows common people to attain uncommon results.
- Andrew Carnegie

We can't command our love, but we can command our actions.
- Arthur Conan Doyle

It's fine to celebrate success, but it is more important to heed the lessons of failure.
- Bill Gates

People do not decide to become extraordinary. They decide to accomplish extraordinary things.
- Edmund Hillary

9

Monkey

Water Monkey
6th February 1932 to 25th January 1933

Wood Monkey
25th January 1944 to 12th February 1945

Fire Monkey
12th February 1956 to 30th January 1957

Earth Monkey
30th January 1968 to 16th February 1969

Metal Monkey
16th February 1980 to 4th February 1981

Water Monkey
4th February 1992 to 22nd January 1993

Wood Monkey
22nd January 2004 to 8th February 2005

Fire Monkey
8th February 2016 to 27th January 2017

Earth Monkey
26th January 2028 to 12th February 2029

Metal Monkey
12th February 2040 to 31st January 2041

Water Monkey
1st February 2052 to 19th February 2053

Wood Monkey
17th February 2064 to 5th February 2065

Monkey

The monkey category of the zodiac represents most primates in nature including monkeys, apes, lemurs, and gorillas. Monkeys are curious, animated, boisterous, expressive, wise, intelligent, clever, confident, optimistic, adaptable, spontaneous, observant, arrogant, impatient, and opportunistic. There are roughly 200 species of primate in the world, and each one is uniquely adapted to their specific environment. Unfortunately, many species are endangered due to the destruction of their natural habitats. Most primates spend a great deal of time in the tree canopy, while the rest is spent exploring the forest floor. Monkeys spend their days engaging in a variety of tasks and activities, including feeding, socializing, grooming, exploring, and playing (Burnie and Wilson 2001, 116).

Primates can be found in a variety of sizes and each species is unique. Some primates only weight a few ounces, whereas gorillas can weight nearly five hundred pounds. All primates have five fingers and toes. Most species have thumbs that are at least partially opposable, and some have feet that are similar to hands, which allow them to easily grasp tree branches. Primates have large skulls that house large brains. They have one of the highest brain-to-body-size ratios of all mammals, which is largely responsible for their high level of intelligence. Their cerebral hemispheres are highly developed, allowing them to masterfully coordinate their movements and devise creative solutions to problems (Burnie and Wilson 2001, 116).

Many primates, especially monkeys, have long, prehensile tails that can easily grasp branches while climbing. Furthermore, the shoulders of all primates are situated outside their body-wall, allowing for increased flexibility and range of motion, which also aids in climbing. In animals, such as horses, where the limbs are situated within the body-wall, have more restricted movement, but their large hip and shoulder muscles power their forward movement, which accounts for their high running speeds (Burnie and Wilson 2001, 117-22).

While nearly all primates are social creatures, each species live in groups of different sizes, with varying rules and ways of organizing themselves. Some species travel in groups of up to one hundred individuals, while others travel in small families of only four or five. Some travel in harems of females where only one male is present, and others form groups of mixed gender. Still others travel in large groups that occasionally separate into smaller, task-oriented groups, such as foraging parties. Playing and grooming are activities that help primates facilitate the formation of social bonds, and develop skills that they carry into adulthood. Grooming is especially important in developing social bonds in primate societies, with lower ranking members grooming higher ranking members to gain favor and support (Burnie and Wilson 2001, 116).

Many primates communicate with others through the use of various vocalizations. Some species such as the Siamang, have large areas of elastic skin on their throats, which can be inflated to amplify their loud vocalizations. Chimpanzees have over thirty distinct calls that they use to communicate various types of information to other members of their community. Gorillas issue a series of barks, "yawns," and chest beating sounds when they feel threatened, or when feel the need to declare their dominance in a territory (Burnie and Wilson 2001, 133-34).

Primates practice a variety of coupling and mating behaviors. Some types of monkeys form monogamous pairs that mate for life, while others form large, mixed-sex groups that mate opportunistically. Gorillas often form harems of many females. Each harem is led by a single male, who fiercely defends his status from other competing males. In childbirth, females often give birth to one to three young, and they care for them until they are ready to fend for themselves, which is usually two to four years old. The mothers of some species, such as chimpanzees, care for their young for nearly five years before giving birth again (Burnie and Wilson 2001, 133-35).

Nearly all primates are omnivores, but their diet consists mainly of fruits and other plant materials. Only western tarsiers are fully carnivorous, surviving on a strict diet of insects. Primates have learned to survive on many types of food including leaves, fruits, seeds, nuts, insects, eggs, and small animals. Their highly developed memory allows them to remember where and when food sources can be found, and their creative intelligence helps them develop various tools to reach food sources that would otherwise be inaccessible (Burnie and Wilson 2001, 122).

Calendar

The monkey is the ninth animal of the zodiac. It is associated with the seventh month of the Chinese lunar calendar that lasts from approximately August 8th to September 8th in the Gregorian calendar, and to the two-hour period between 3 pm and 5 pm. This is the beginning of the autumn season, when the yin energy continues to rise before the harvest. This is a time when crops reach their ripest stage, and when the final details of work projects are completed. This is also a time of year when health and relationship issues become emphasized, and rise to the surface of the body to be healed. Monkey years brings about numerous and dramatic changes, but by being highly adaptable and flexible these changes can be successfully navigated.

Monkey years are one of the most powerful times for change in the zodiac. While all zodiac years provide opportunities for changing luck, the year of the monkey is especially suited to bringing about dramatic change and developing versatility. The United States of America was founded in the year of the monkey, 1776, and its presence has continued to bring about countless, drastic changes throughout the world ever since.

Monkey years often see new innovations, revolutionary inventions, and out of the box concepts being introduced. There have been many monkey years when great change was brought about by the introduction of new technology. These revolutionary ideas and inventions often create entirely new fields of study. The first electric battery was invented in 1800 by Alessandro Volta, and with the steady current that it produced, the field of electrical engineering was poised to grow rapidly in the future.[1]

Over a century later, physics and electrical engineering were combined to create a generator that was used to split the first atom in 1932 (another monkey year) in Great Britain by John Cockcroft and Ernest Walton. Their experiment confirmed the existence of Einstein's theory of relativity, brought about the beginning of the atomic age, and led to the development of nuclear physics.[2] Monkey years allow for the achievement of goals and advancement by bending the rules and producing options that were previously unavailable. The ancient writer Vitruvius wrote that the Greek mathematician and inventor Archimedes coined the term "Eureka", meaning "I found it", when he finally discovered the principle of liquid displacement.[3] The sentiment that this story evokes precisely describes the feeling of monkey years. With enough interest, effort, and engagement, elegant solutions can appear in simple, effortless ways.

Economies usually becomes less volatile and grows steadily during monkey years. The reduced economic growth of previous years reverses, and productivity stabilizes before rising again. For example, in the monkey year of 1932, the Great Depression had become a worldwide phenomenon, and unemployment levels reached between twenty and thirty percent in many countries. However, by the beginning of 1933, economies started to stabilize and recover. It wasn't until years later, just before World War II, that the Great Depression officially came to an end.[4]

During monkey years, individuality and freedom are essential. Many liberties and rights have been recognized, established, and protected during monkey years; however, the opportunity for the establishment of these liberties requires the people to seize the moment and act. In the United States, women gained the right to vote after many decades of effort, lobbying, marches, and protests in the monkey year of 1920. This occurred just as public sentiment began to turn in their favor following the legalization of women's suffrage in New York and the

---

[1] "The History and Development of Batteries," by Jose Alarco and Peter Talbot (2015). www.phys.org/news/2015-04-history-batteries.html
[2] "This Month in Physics History," by Leah Poffenberger (2019). www.aps.org/publications/apsnews/201904/history.cfm
[3] "Fact or Fiction?: Archimedes Coined the Term 'Eureka!'" in the Bath," by David Biello (2006). www.scientificamerican.com/article/fact-or-fiction-archimede/
[4] "Great Depression," by Christina D. Romer (1998). www.britannica.com/event/Great-Depression

public support of President Woodrow Wilson.[5] Similarly, the Civil Rights Act was passed by President Lyndon B. Johnson after many protests and marches took place throughout the United States in 1968.[6]

Monkey years give rise to ambition, risk-taking, and achievement, even if disregarding the rules is necessary for success. This inevitably leads to many competitive situations and conflicts. Monkeys act first, and worry about the consequences afterward. This passionate desire to overcome obstacles, and dissatisfaction with the status quo, often results in major outbursts of energy and on a global scale, including large military offensives. In June of 1944, the largest naval invasion in human history occurred when the allied forces landed on the Normandy coast of France.[7] Monkeys have a heart of courage, a high level of intelligence, and an intuitive ability to know when to act, which allows them to thrive in competitive and combative situations. These same qualities have been sought and cultivated by many leaders throughout history in order to learn how to successfully wield power.

Monkey years also bring about great changes in the world through natural disasters and extreme weather conditions. Many large earthquakes, powerful hurricanes, and even plagues, famines, and droughts have occurred during monkey years. By preparing for the natural disasters in advance, many losses can be avoided or mitigated. As global climate change continues, these types of major natural events occur more regularly, but monkey years are traditionally the times when they are most severe. In 1980, one of the most dramatic natural disasters occurred when the Mount St. Helen's volcano erupted in Washington. This is still considered to be the most disastrous and deadly volcanic eruption in United States history.[8]

Qi

The time of the day related to the monkey is 3 to 5 pm, matching the urinary bladder meridian. This is a time when yin energy begins growing, and issues that require correction begin to appear before projects can be completed. The urinary bladder active at this time detoxifying the kidneys and various tissues. This is also

---

[5] "19th Amendment to the U.S. Constitution: Women's Right To Vote (1920)," by The National Archives and Records Administration (1920). www.archives.gov/milestone-documents/19th-amendment

[6] "Civil Rights Act (1964)," by The National Archives and Records Administration (1964). www.archives.gov/milestone-documents/civil-rights-act

[7] "World War II: D-Day, The Invasion of Normandy," by The Dwight D. Eisenhower Presidential Library, Museum & Boyhood Home (2022). www.eisenhowerlibrary.gov/research/online-documents/world-war-ii-d-day-invasion-normandy

[8] "1980 Cataclysmic Eruption," by U.S. Geological Survey (n.d.). www.usgs.gov/volcanoes/mount-st-helens/1980-cataclysmic-eruption

the time when the lungs are at rest, recovering their strength after stabilizing the abundant yang qi earlier in the day.

The urinary bladder is responsible for collecting and storing the waste liquids from the body before excreting them as urine. In traditional Chinese medicine and Daoist medicine, the urinary bladder is also closely related to the function of the lower burner, or lower *dantian*. The urinary bladder's function produces the "bladder fire" which is responsible for evaporating water, heating the lower burner, and transforming *jing* (essence) into *qi* (energy). The energy that is produced by this process is used to supply the entire meridian system, as well as aid in the process of spiritual transformation. Monkeys behave similar to the way that the bladder *qi* functions in that they are skilled at overcoming difficulties through a fiery process of transformation, that results in spiritual growth and personal development.

The ghost point that is associated with the monkey is known as Ghost's Hall (*guitang*); it matches the point Upper Star— Polaris (*shangxing*, GV-23) of the acupuncture system. It is located on the center-line of the skull between the forehead, and the apex, approximately one inch above the hairline (Johnson 2014, 606). This point is essential because it is largely responsible for our ability to reason and use logic. It is used to treat the sinuses, eye and vision issues, facial swelling, and psychological "wind" conditions, which includes mania, severe depression, bi-polar disorder, and other related mental conditions (Deadman et al. 2007, 556).

Traditionally, the monkey is most commonly associated with the heart. Monkeys have exceptionally strong hearts and great circulation. This is largely due to the significant amount of time that they spend climbing in the tree canopy. By using their arms regularly, monkeys have developed strong hearts and healthy circulation. Also, when primates feel any kind of discomfort or illness in their chest, they rub, scratch, and beat the area to create movement and stimulate healthy *qi* and blood flow. Because of their heavy reliance on the strength of their heart and chest muscles, monkeys rarely suffer from any kind of cardiovascular or respiratory diseases, including heart attacks or asthma.

With strong circulation and frequent climbing, primates develop great physical strength and flexibility. Gorillas are especially known for their incredible strength, and most fully grown adult males can lift objects that weight nearly five thousand pounds. Gorillas, baboons, mandrills and other large primates are fierce fighters, and their cardiovascular strength makes them incredibly resistant to injury. Monkeys and primates do not prefer to fight, but they will not hesitate to do so if necessary. Monkeys follow their heart, and they engage in every activity passionately and whole-heartedly.

In Chinese and Daoist medicine, the heart is responsible for housing the *shen*, or spirit, which is closely related to the individual's thinking ability, wisdom, and willfulness. This includes the prenatal mind, which relates to the individual's personality, intuition, disposition, and goals; as well as their postnatal mind, which includes the learned intelligence, skills, habits, and abilities. Monkeys are renowned for their high level of intelligence, agility, and strength. They are clever, intelligent, and wise, due to their development of healthy, vibrant heart *qi*. When the heart lacks energy, there is depression and lethargy; and when it is overly stressed, restlessness, anxiousness, and anger result. When the heart is healthy, then the individual is able to remain harmonious with others, peaceful, wise, and forgiving.

Special Abilities and Traits

Monkeys can travel through the tree canopy as easily as they can move on the ground. Their opposable thumbs; long, flexible limbs; hand-like feet; and externally situated shoulder and hip joints; allow monkeys and apes to effortlessly climb and swing. Many species also have a long prehensile tail, often referred to as a "fifth limb," that aids in climbing. Some species have a leathery patch near the end of their tail, which provides increased grip, allowing it to support additional weight. Monkeys and cats are the only two animals that can survive a fall from a significant height. For monkeys, this is due to the fact that they are more easily able to orient themselves and gain their bearings while moving through the air. Their ability to understand their orientation helps monkeys to make quick and accurate decisions while they are jumping or falling, and their flexible limbs allow them to act on these decisions.

Monkeys Are Highly Intelligent

Monkeys have a level of intelligence that is comparable to a seventeen-year-old human being. In fact, in the Daoist zodiac system, any monkey that has developed the ability to walk upright is categorized as a human being. Monkeys have developed their own languages, tools, social structures, and positions of leadership within their troops. In *Animal Behavior*, John Paul Scott notes,

> Species with special abilities for grasping and moving objects vastly increase their ability to adapt to their environment, and an animal which has good manipulatory organs tends to be rated as intelligent. . . Grasping and manipulation are often associated with the habit of living in trees. . . Man is unique among the primates in the degree to which the hind limbs are used only for locomotion and the front limbs are used only for grasping and prehension" (1972, 48-50).

With their intense curiosity and intelligence, as well as their dexterous hands, monkeys are skilled thieves, and they can often be observed stealing from human beings, various animals, and each other. These incidents often lead to disputes, fights, and changes in social status within the various groups of monkeys. By recognizing that infighting leads to injury, distrust, and vulnerability to predators, many primate species have developed highly evolved sets of rules within their troops.

Monkeys often live on the grounds of Daoist and Buddhist temples, allowed to roam freely. Many buildings hold sacred statues with altars and offerings, which may include fruits, seeds, and other foods. The monkeys clearly understand that the offerings on the altars are not to be touched. However, occasionally monkeys have tested this and decided to steal a piece of food. When a disciple discovers that a monkey has stolen an offering, they immediately walk over to the group of monkeys to address the issue, yelling loudly at them to signal displeasure. Then the leader of the group quickly emerges and approaches the disciple who leads him to the altar where the food was stolen, and again expresses displeasure. When the monkey leader fully understands the disciple's meaning, they both return to the group and the leader addresses the other monkeys. After grunting, gesturing, and making various noises until the group understands. The monkey troop gathers together and pushes out a single member, the one who stole the offering. The disciple then takes this monkey to the altar to scold him for his actions as well. Stories like this illustrate the level of intelligence and group organization that primates have, and the complexity of their social order.

Monkeys have also developed ways of voting for their leaders. Daoists have spent centuries carefully observing the behaviors of the monkeys that live on temple grounds, and when the time comes for them to install a new leader for the troop, the monkeys gather together to make their decision. They choose a large tree, to be the location for their voting, and begin by gathering together to converse and gesture toward one another. Then, over the next few minutes, all of the monkeys climb up into the tree and bend one of the small, newly formed branches in a specific direction, indicating which "candidate" they feel should be their leader. After every member of the troop has cast their vote, the monkeys then climb into the tree once again, beginning with the leaders, to count the number of bend twigs in the tree, and determine the results.

Monkeys have often been observed using improvised tools to accomplish difficult tasks. Some primates use thin sticks inserted into anthills and termite mounds to extract insects that were previously unreachable. Some monkeys gather fresh fruits and nuts that are too difficult to open into individual piles for ripening. Once the fruit has aged for a week or so, it is more brittle and easier to open. These same monkeys have also been observed using primitive stone hammers and anvils to crack open strong nuts and palm fruits.[9] Some species have even learned to use sticks and stones as weapons in battles with others.

As monkeys have come into greater contact with human beings, they have learned to become even more intelligent. Many species have learned to wash off their fruit and leaves in rivers and pools of water before eating them after observing human beings. Monkeys have been trained to be both guards and

---

[9] "Yellowstone" by BBC Natural History Unit (2009). www.dailymotion.com/video/x6xrez7

soldiers, and they easily understand what is expected of them. Monkeys have been taught how to use guns, swords, staffs, and other weapons with a surprising amount of skill. Due to their extraordinary agility and keen awareness, monkeys can learn to dodge bullets in some cases. The monkey's strong heart gives them great courage, even in the face of difficulties.

Monkeys understand the principles of firearms, and other weapons, and they quickly respond to the subtle body movements and intentions of others. Some monkeys have even begun learning how to use the basic functions of cell phones. After observing humans, certain species of monkey are also beginning to get "married" in rudimentary marriage ceremonies, and demonstrating an understanding of the principles of devotion and monogamy. Needless to say, monkeys are highly intelligent and adaptable creatures, and they are learning faster every day.

Monkeys Are Acutely Sensitive

Primates have acute hearing and eyesight. Monkeys are often seen giving the "thousand-yard stare" which is a sign of intelligence and acute visual perception. Many Daoists would also say that monkeys have "thousand-yard hearing" as well, with their sensitive aural ability. When monkeys are at rest in the tree canopy, they always continue to watch and listen carefully to their surrounding environment.

Most primates have vision that is three times more acute than human beings giving them 20/6.33 vision. Their vision is enhanced because they spend much of their lives exercising their eyes. As monkeys peer through the canopy, they move their eyes within their sockets in every possible direction. This strengthens the muscles that surround the eyes and the optical nerves, bringing more blood flow to these areas. This also means that primates almost never suffer from cataracts or blurred vision. By constantly looking through the tree canopy and focusing their vision on objects at varying distances, monkeys have developed binocular vision that is able to zoom in and quickly refocus. Small, nocturnal prosimians, such as tarsiers and galagoes, have also developed the ability to see with extreme clarity at night, in low-light conditions. Other monkeys have developed eyesight that is able to detect movement and patterns in conditions of low visibility, such as dense fog and smoke.

Monkeys have the second-best hearing ability of all the animals of the zodiac. They are capable of hearing the sounds and calls of other primates originating from over twenty miles away through the jungle and forest canopy. Monkeys accurately pinpoint the direction of origin of the sounds that they hear and determine if it was produced by a friend or a foe. Gorillas create a percussive sound by beating their chest as a warning to rivals, which can be heard for over a mile in the dense jungle. While monkeys and humans hear roughly the same low frequencies, monkeys can hear a full octave of frequencies higher than human beings, meaning that they can perceive the lower ultrasonic tones.[10]

The Doctor of the Jungle

Monkeys are skilled at intuitively understanding medical issues, especially problems related to the bones and musculature. Daoists often say that the personality of the monkey is half prime minister, and half doctor. At many Daoist temples where monkeys are allowed to live on the temple grounds, the monkeys and apes actively observe the disciples as they perform their exercises, like *taiji*, *gongfu*, and *qigong*. If they observe any misalignment or irregular movements in their practice, they immediately approach and begin treating the issue. If the practitioner is suffering from a frozen shoulder, for instance, the arm's range of motion will be limited. The monkey will begin to lift, manipulate, and press on the injured arm to locate the root of the issue. When a painful area has been found, the monkey will actively press and manipulate the area to correct the issue.

This form of treatment is so effective because monkeys are skilled at locating the source of the condition with their sensitive hands; and their exceptional strength and dexterity allows them to manipulate and correct the issues with ease. Monkeys are good at learning the methods of acupressure and acupuncture because they regularly correct their own medical issues in the wild, both through trail-and-error and by observing others. Monkeys can be seen in the wild slapping themselves as an expression of excitement and happiness, to communicate with others, and to treat their own medical issues. Slapping the chest can help to alleviate respiratory issues, while rubbing the chest can help to alleviate cardiovascular issues. Gently slapping the skin and the face can also help to alleviate various skin conditions, including wrinkles, dry skin, and blemishes.

Monkeys can diagnose a patient's illness through visual observation, listening, and smelling. Their high level of intelligence and memory, allow monkeys to identify hundreds of different herbs, and learn their healing properties. There are even certain temples that have specialized animal treatment departments where monkeys treat patients regularly. Even though monkeys may seem primitive and erratic at times, they are righteous at heart and they truly enjoy helping others. Monkeys that have been taught how to cultivate their *qi* and heal themselves can regularly live up to seventy years old.

---

[10]"What Are the Monkey's Strongest Senses?" by Dondi Ratliff (n.d.). www.animals.mom.com/monkeys-strongest-senses-10743.html

Cultural and Spiritual Concepts

The Monkey King

In many eastern countries, like China and India, the monkey king has been a revered spiritual symbol for centuries. The Chinese Classic *Journey to the West* was originally written by a famous Daoist describing the significant events of his life, but was later changed to represent Buddhist ideals rather than Daoist. Nevertheless, many of the characters, and some of their symbolism, remains the same, and the monkey king, Sun Wukong, is one of the story's main characters. The monkey king represents the feelings of the heart, and throughout the story, he learns the proper way to express his passions, and the way toward spiritual advancement.

The term "monkey mind" refers to a mind that is restless, undisciplined, whimsical, confused, indecisive, and unyielding This represents the way that the mind of the heart behaves before it has learned to develop true strength and devotion. Monkeys are always trying to reach for the stars and become masterful, and the way that they go about achieving this greatness demonstrates their level of wisdom and skill. Often young monkeys attempt to achieve greatness by leaping as far as they can, only to fall and embarrass, or injure, themselves. Older wiser monkeys, on the other hand, will swiftly and skillfully move through the canopy; never over-reaching, but executing their movements with precision and grace.

Monkeys can also be seen near bodies of water at night trying to reach and grasp at the reflection of the moon in the water's surface. This illustrates the ambition of the monkey, as well as the gullibility of the untrained heart, that can easily be fooled with misdirection and false promises. In Daoism, the heart is often imagined as a body of water; the calmer it is, the more accurately it reflects one's true feelings, and the easier it is to receive clear answers and visions. The monkey mind, with its restlessness and agitation, becomes distracted by almost everything, preventing the heart-mind from becoming calm and reflecting true, accurate answers. Because of these associations, monkeys represent both foolishness and wisdom. When a person is heart-centered and emotionally sensitive, they can suffer from the symptoms of monkey mind, and yet, at times when they are calm, they can also discover fundamental truths about themselves and the world around them.

The monkey spirit that lives in the heart enjoys gambling, because gambling in moderation, and understood in the proper context, helps develop hope for the future, faith, and a positive outlook. If the only element of success was hard labor and suffering, then nearly everyone in the world would feel discouraged, exhausted, and in despair. Only through the recognition that luck and opportunity play a part in our lives can we have hope for great success, and feel motivated to try our best. The monkey knows the truth behind the phrase "fortune favors the brave," and convinces us that courage in the face of darkness is meaningful because it strengthens our character.

Monkeys are often associated with the symbolism of peaches, because they are the monkey's favorite treat, almost always choosing peaches before other fruits. The peach is the talisman that invites the monkey spirit, demonstrating the strong association between them. Peaches are symbols of fertility, immortality, strength, and gracefulness. In *Journey to the West*, the relationship between the monkey king and the immortal peaches is described:

> The monkey king, Sun Wukong, was becoming more and more mischievous, and his antics soon became a major topic of discussion among the gods. They invited the monkey to join them in heaven, thinking that they could keep a watchful eye on him. The monkey king quickly accepted the invitation, assuming that he would be granted an honorable place as one of the gods. Instead, he was given one of the lowliest of jobs, as a stable boy. When the Queen mother of the West threw her lavish banquet at the Jade Palace, the monkey king wasn't invited, and he became enraged at his perceived mistreatment. Therefore, the monkey king decided to sneak into the palace, and gain immortality by his own hand.
>
> The Jade Palace was surrounded by magical, divine peach trees that belonged to the empress, and the fruit of these special trees took three thousand years to ripen. A single bite granted not only immortality, but also great strength. On the day of the banquet, the monkey king convinced the palace guards to let him into the orchard unattended to take a peaceful nap. However, as soon as the guards had their backs turned, he quickly climbed the largest peach tree, gobbled up the peaches of immortality, and fled.

This story illustrates the willful, devious, and clever nature of the immature heart, and how it can develop great strength and renewed vitality by partaking in heavenly activities. As the story continues, the monkey begins to learn that its own spiritual nature is inescapable, and that even with great power, change and transformation are inevitable. The monkey is the ninth animal of the zodiac, and in Daoism, the number nine represents mastery, great power, and longevity. The fact that the monkey was chosen to be the ninth animal is significant, because it illustrates the numerous similarities between these two concepts. The monkey represents an energy that is constantly active, just like the function of the heart. Both the monkey and rooster represent energies in nature, as well as the heart and mind, that are consistently present. They give us guidance and hope in unpredictable circumstances.

People Who Embody the Monkey

People born in the year of the monkey are lively, imaginative, whimsical and fascinating, as well as determined, powerful, and unyielding. Monkey people are always active and engaged. Whether they are exercising, socializing, working on projects, studying, or just playing and acting goofy, monkeys are never without novelty and imagination. Monkey people have a multitude of talents, and their wide range of skills helps them to accomplish nearly anything that they put their mind to.

Monkeys are quick and agile, physically and mentally. Their highly intellectual nature allows them to combine different disciplines to create new thoughts and ideas. They are resourceful and cunning, and they demonstrate their numerous skills masterfully, and with grace. Monkey people have a way of being able to talk their way into (or out of) nearly any situation, because their words are direct and prudent. Monkey people have a highly acute sense of danger and misfortune, and they quickly make their escape form any dangerous or precarious situations before they become unmanageable. Monkeys are nature's escape artists, and people who embody the spirit of the monkey search for various options in every situation.

The motto of the monkey person is "it is easier to ask for forgiveness, than permission." This means that when faced with a decision, monkey people often act first, and review the implications of their actions later. This allows them to be quite lucky at times, and quite unfortunate at others. Over time, this practice provides the monkey person with a wealth of first-hand knowledge that can lead to great wisdom, and experience generates opportunity.

Due to their willful nature, if a monkey person ever seeks advice, it is best to ask them for their opinion first, and support the first thing that comes to their mind. This allows them to trust their own decision-making skills, and to apply their full energy to their decision because it was their own. Monkeys also have a knack for being rather indirect and testing the limits of others, so by helping them follow their own advice, greater trust is developed. When a monkey person gets an idea and decides to follow it, they will find creative solutions to achieve it.

Monkey people are intelligent, and they practice their analytical skills by reading and studying nearly everything that they come across. Monkey people often study obscure subjects just for the entertainment value. Their wide-range of interests and creativity allow them to apply numerous, often exotic, principles in new ways. Monkey people usually have great memories, and when they learn a subject at great depth, they rarely forget the nuances. Monkeys can easily use their intelligence for both persuasion or argumentation, making them effective communicators.

Monkey people are usually focused on their own goals, and while they usually avoid manipulating others, they are opportunists. They are persuasive and confident, which often convinces others to see things from their perspective. This skill allows them to achieve success, build rapport with others, and escape dangerous situations. Monkeys suffer from the same insecurities and vulnerabilities that most other people face; however, they avoid dwelling on their faults and weaknesses, and focus on what is necessary. This means that many monkey people can suffer from a feeling of loneliness, even when they are surrounded by others, but solitude and focus quickly restores their confidence.

To achieve a more harmonious life, monkey people should do their best to share their honest feelings and vulnerabilities with trusted loved ones. This can help develop emotional depth, and alleviate the loneliness that monkeys often experience. When this process is mastered, they can feel greatly liberated and truly fulfilled. In nature, monkeys are both highly intelligent and highly social, in balanced proportion. In relationships, monkeys are exciting and creative partners. They may require time to learn the details of relationship dynamics, but with practice, they can become masterful and create abundant happiness. When they become parents, they often have great fun with their children and develop close bonds. In family life, the heartfelt energy of monkey people blossoms, and in order to be stronger for their loved ones, the desire to improve themselves increases as well.

Monkey people are so successful, skillful, and confident that they often have a difficult time choosing how and where to apply their efforts. Monkeys can be greatly successful in nearly any field; however, whatever their vocation, monkeys need to learn how to apply their efforts in a disciplined manner. Monkeys have a curious, erratic, and over-excited nature which can sometimes lead to a low attention span and decreased productivity. Therefore, they should choose a career where they can apply their creativity, and they encounter new challenges often. Many monkey people become entertainers, musicians, and movie stars because of the unique challenges that each project brings. They can be wonderful entrepreneurs, researchers, politicians, investors, and salesmen. Monkeys often succeed at anything that makes them feel free, in control, or creative.

Even though people born during monkey years are often fond of gambling, they are usually great with their own finances. Monkey people often see the maintaining a budget and developing wealth as a game that can be won with skill and intelligence. While they entertain high-risk investments, and they like to spend lavishly on themselves and their loved ones, they can quickly develop the discipline necessary for maintaining a healthy finances. Monkey people have two sides; one that is disciplined, and one that likes to take risks, and both of them are courageous. Monkey people are always seeking ways to make their dreams into a reality. Quite often they are successful, and inevitably their endeavors lead to great wisdom.

External Zodiac
Eagles

The eagle is the outer animal of the monkey category, and those born under the sign of the monkey have the inner focus, skill, and killer instinct of the eagle. The eagle category of the zodiac refers to all types of raptors, including hawks, buzzards, vultures, and falcons. Eagles and condors are the high achievers of the animal kingdom, and the excellence that they bring to every task is remarkable. Like monkeys, eagles are talented, highly acute, and extremely intelligent. Eagles are so talented at hunting prey, that they only need to spend a small part of their day hunting and feeding. During the rest of the day, they soar, build nests, migrate, and spend time with their family.

Monkeys and eagles are courageous and fearless creatures that don't hesitate to defend themselves or their loved ones from predators. However, while eagles are swift and decisive, monkeys are often more tentative, and like to test boundaries before they act. While monkeys use their agility and brute strength to battle effectively, eagles rely on swiftness and precision in their attacks to quickly end a fight before it becomes drawn out and costly. Eagles move through the sky with grace and excellence, and their talons are long, sharp, and powerful. Their talons deliver so much power, that they often have a difficult time releasing their prey.

Eagles and monkeys are both regal and noble creatures that recognize the importance of healthy self-esteem and self-reliance; however, while monkeys behave in ways that are similar to rulers or emperors, eagles have more in common with generals or advisers. By taking a high perspective, eagles assess the big picture, and by diving down with determination and courage, they effect the reality on the ground. Both monkeys and eagles demonstrate the importance of being able to travel between heaven and earth, and the effectiveness that the marriage of these two perspectives can bring. Excellence in daily life comes partly as a result of regularly spending time above daily frustrations and societal pressures, in a calm state of reflection.

Monkeys and eagles demonstrate that taking a higher perspective can be freeing and extremely fun, even if it is sometimes lonely. Monkeys have a wonderful time playing in the tree canopy, swinging from branch to branch, and similarly, eagles can be seen playing in air currents, and doing somersaults high in the sky. The mating ritual of the American bald eagle is a fantastic display of arial playfulness. A pair of bald eagles will soar, dive, tumble, and roll together in the sky, even grasping each other's talons to synchronize their movements, before soaring upward to repeat the process. This 'dance' builds trust and intimacy, to develop emotional bonds before mating.

Like monkeys, eagles are often clever and agile enough to steal things from others. Eagles wait in the sky, observing the movements on the ground below, and if they spot another predator making a successful kill, then they often swoop down to snatch it away. Delegating hard work to others is one of many ways that eagles conserve their energy. They are opportunistic and prepared to take action quickly. While eagles are extremely effective and efficient, they are also highly visible, and if a person with an eagle spirit acts in an excessive or selfish way, they can find themselves becoming increasingly isolated.

Qi

Unlike monkeys, eagles are carnivorous and they must rely on their killer instinct to survive. Eagles have a ruthless, no-nonsense attitude when it comes to hunting and gathering resources. Eagles snatch up any form of prey that they can carry, and the larger species can even lift small deer and sheep into the sky. Most eagles prefer to eat live prey, and only eat carrion opportunistically. Some raptor species however, have a diet that consists almost entirely of dead animals. Buzzards and vultures, for instance, have developed the ability to easily locate carcasses in their large habitats. Buzzards, or turkey vultures, have a keen sense of smell, which allows them to locate rotting carcasses in dense forests and jungle. These birds also recognize the signs of weakness in animals, and they begin to gather nearby when they sense that death is near.

Eagles are known for extraordinary eyesight. Depending on the species, they can see between four to eight times better than humans. This is because they have a high concentration of cone cells in the retina, their eyes are quite large, and they move their eyes within their sockets often (Burnie and Wilson 2001, 286). All this allows eagles to not only have keen depth perception but vision that does not lose resolution as the focus moves further away. Daoists emphasize the daily practice of exercising the eyes by rotating them within the orbital sockets, in order to enhance vision like the monkey and the eagle. One eye (left for men, right for women) is rotated fifty times clockwise, then fifty times counter-clockwise; then the next eye is rotated in the same manner. This should be done with both eyes closed until the practice is concluded. Afterwards, the eyesight should be more vibrant, clear, and acute.

Even though eagles do not have external ears, most species have excellent hearing. Raptors that hunt over areas of thick vegetation, such as harriers, are known for their acute aural sense, which allows them to locate prey hiding in the bush (Burnie and Wilson 2001, 286). Most eagles have hearing that is roughly equivalent to human beings, however, their hearing is focused a bit more on higher frequencies rather than lower ones because their vocalizations are high pitched.

Special Abilities and Traits

When bald eagles find their mates, one of the first things that they do is build a large, elaborate nest. Males gather materials for the nest, while the females build it. The nest can be located either in a tree or on the ground, but they are always large, sometimes reaching 13ft (4m) tall (Burnie and Wilson 2001, 291). The largest eagle's nest ever found was 20ft tall and nearly 10ft in diameter.[11] This demonstrates that to achieve greatness it is necessary to have a safe space that is comfortable and peaceful. For this reason, eagles represent the sense of family and belonging, as well as responsibility toward our loved ones. This is the feeling of home and familiarity that is carried in the heart. While hard work, determination, and courage are necessary to achieve success; proper rest, a safe place to recover, and the care of our loved ones is also quite important.

Eagles understand the principles of sacrifice, and the value of the process of rebirth. Eagles begin to show signs of aging at the age of 30, however, they can decide to rejuvenate themselves to achieve greater longevity. The process of achieving rebirth is stressful, painful, and arduous, but it produces significant benefits. When the eagle feels that it is time to begin the process, it will fly off on its own and find a secluded spot in the forest. It begins by pulling out many of its own feathers, as well as pulling and tugging on its talons, sometimes to the point of removing them. It may even break its own beak by smashing it on a rock. Finally, when the bird is exhausted and can no longer continue, it retreats to a safe location, and allows its body to recover. When the healing is complete, the eagle will have produced new plumage, new talons, and a beak; its blood and internal organs will be nourished and strong. If the eagle chooses not to go through this process, its lifespan will be approximately 45 years; however, after completing the rebirth process, they can live nearly 70 years. This is yet another way that the eagle demonstrates the determination, self-assurance, and sacrifice that is necessary to achieve great success.

Cultural and Spiritual Concepts

At the White Cloud Temple, eagles fly above the grounds, keeping a close eye on any intruders that try to enter. They would also follow the great masters as they travelled, guarding them and protecting their spirit. The sound of the eagle's cry serves as both a warning to the righteous, and a deterrent to evil. Even some of the principles of taiji were inspired by observing the battles between eagles and snakes. Both of these animals have unique fighting methods, and they reside in opposite ends of the landscape, one occupying the highest space, and the other occupying the lowest.

---

[11] "An Anecdotal History of Bald Eagle Nests in America," by Jim Wright (2015). www.dukefarms.org/footer/blog/an-anecdotal-history-of-bald-eagle-nests-in-america/

Eagles are so skillful and intelligent that the great Mongol leader Genghis Khan utilized eagles as part of his army. The Mongols and the Tibetans are both known for raising large and powerful hunting eagles. When Genghis Khan began his military campaign into western lands, he appointed a handful of extremely large eagles to guide his forces as generals. These eagles were trained to soar high above the land and give out calls to the military leaders down below, guiding them to the correct paths and warning them of approaching danger.

The famous Daoist master Qiu Chuji gained the trust of Genghis Khan by demonstrating his power over one of these great eagles. He said, "If one of your eagles is placed on my hand, he will not attack, nor will he fly away until I allow him to." Believing this to be nearly impossible, Genghis Khan agreed, and with his powerful *qi*, Qiu Chuji successfully rendered the great eagle helpless without laying a hand on it.

Just like monkeys, eagles represent the spirit that resides in the heart. They teach us that it is necessary to retreat from time to time, and reach for the highest heavenly perspective that we can manage. Self-evaluation and situational awareness can eliminate fear and produce courage in the face of darkness and danger, even when there seems to be no end in sight. When we calm our heart, and rise to a higher perspective, we gain a more complete understanding about our place in the world. By embracing the energy of the eagle, we can become confident that spirit is with us at all times, that we are not alone no matter how things appear. Monkeys and eagles remind us that all of our challenges are meant to bring about changes for the better. By recognizing spirit and living life accordingly, the experience of life begins to improve, and long-lasting benefits begin to emerge. Many people have imagined life to be like a school, and all of our experiences to be lessons in a classroom. The eagle is here to tell us to seize this unique opportunity, and strive to be the best student that we can be.

Quotes from Famous Monkeys

Nothing strengthens authority so much as silence.
- Leonardo Da Vinci

You have to accept whatever comes, and the only important thing is that you meet it with courage, and with the best that you have to give.
- Eleanor Roosevelt

It is the mark of an educated mind to entertain a thought without accepting it.
- Lowell L. Bennion

Give me freedom to know, to utter, and to argue freely according to conscience, above all liberties.
- John Milton

There is no excellent beauty that hath not some strangeness in the proportion.
- Francis Bacon

Destiny is what we are drawn toward, and fate is what we run into.
- Wyatt Earp

The greatness of a man is not in how much wealth he acquires, but in his integrity, and his ability to affect those around him positively.
- Bob Marley

Attempt the impossible to improve your work.
- Bette Davis

You build on failure. You use it as a stepping stone. Close the door on the past. You don't try to forget the mistakes, but you don't dwell on it.
- Johnny Cash

There are no regrets in life, just lessons.
- Jennifer Aniston

A hero is someone who voluntarily walks into the unknown.
- Tom Hanks

To conquer fear is the beginning of wisdom.
- Bertrand Russell

10

Rooster

Water Rooster
26th January 1933 to 13th February 1934

Wood Rooster
13th February 1945 to 1st February 1946

Fire Rooster
31st January 1957 to 17th February 1958

Earth Rooster
17th February 1969 to 5th February 1970

Metal Rooster
5th February 1981 to 24th January 1982

Water Rooster
23rd January 1993 to 9th February 1994

Wood Rooster
9th February 2005 to 28th January 2006

Fire Rooster
28th January 2017 to 15th February 2018

Earth Rooster
13th February 2029 to 1st February 2030

Metal Rooster
1st February 2041 to 22nd January 2042

Water Rooster
19th February 2053 to 8th February 2054

Wood Rooster
5th February 2065 to 26th January 2066

Rooster

The rooster category of the zodiac represents all of the birds in the animal kingdom. Roosters are direct, clear, vigilant, responsible, punctual, reliable, gregarious, chivalrous, elegant, fertile, vibrant, fierce, and effective communicators. Domesticated roosters and chickens are a subspecies of the red jungle-fowl that originated in southeast Asia (Burnie and Wilson 2001, 297). Roosters spend their time eating, crowing, establishing their pecking order, and watching over their hens and chicks. They are communal and family oriented, watching over the other hens and chicks as they casually search the ground for food; and they guard the group against any approaching danger. Roosters also share any food that they find with the other chickens in their brood. Roosters are omnivores that will eat seeds, grains, worms, centipedes, caterpillars, and most other insects. They have even been known to hunt some small animals, like mice, snakes, and lizards.

Roosters live in pastures, fields, jungles, and forests. Domesticated chickens roost together in a hen house, but in the wild, they often make their roosts and nests in the branches of trees. Chickens cannot fly long distances like other birds, but they can fly short distances to reach the low branches of trees, get over low fences, and to defend themselves. Hens lay eggs regardless of whether roosters are present. At their peak, hens can lay nearly an egg per day, but as they get older their egg laying rate diminishes. Hens often continue to lay eggs for the duration of their lives, between five to ten years. When hens have an abundance of food and a low stress environment, the quality and quantity of their eggs improves; but if they are lacking nutrition or continually stressed, their egg production will slow or even cease.

Roosters and hens have a fleshy, vibrant red crest on their head called a comb, and equally vibrant flaps of skin next to their beaks called wattles. The combs and wattles of the males are often larger and more prominent than those of the hens. Often displaying vibrant colors in their feathers, and large prominent tail feathers. In addition to attracting mates, the comb is also used to cool the body by bringing hot blood to the surface of the skin to cool.

Roosters are naturally aggressive toward rival males, and they often fight for breeding privileges with the hens of the brood. Hens are not usually violent, however, within each brood there is a pecking order which establishes a hierarchy among the members. The roosters that are more dominant, and therefore higher on the pecking order, have breeding privileges with the hens, while the hens that are higher on the pecking order, roost in more desirable areas and have priority with food. In a flock with only one male, the rooster is always at the top of the hierarchy; however, he must also be caring, gentle, and protective in order for the group to thrive.

Roosters have four toes on each of their claws, three projecting forward and one projecting backward, and a single large spur, or talon further up the leg. Their sharp claws allow them to dig and scratch at the ground to uncover seeds and small insects, while their opposing claws allow them to grip perches and prey. The spurs of the rooster are hard outgrowths of keratin on the back side of each leg, just above the claws, and they are used only as weapons. Keratin is the same material that forms human fingernails, and the horns of animals like goats, rams, and rhinoceros. Rooster spurs can cause significant damage, making them formidable fighters. They can cause significant wounds, even to large animals and human beings; however, human fatalities from a rooster attack are quite rare. Roosters are courageous protectors, and they will go to great lengths to protect their brood.

Roosters crow regularly, and they have various calls for different purposes. Roosters famously crow at dawn every morning, but they also have a call that they use to attract females and announce their presence to other males; and they have two different calls to alert the flock to danger, one for danger on the ground and another for danger in the sky. Some rooster species, such as the Kosovo, Denizli, and Tomaru Long Crowing roosters, as well as a number of others, have been bred to have uniquely long crows that most other breeds do not. Some birds can continue crowing for close to thirty seconds before running out of breath.

Calendar

The rooster is the tenth animal of the zodiac. It is associated with the eight month of the Chinese lunar calendar that lasts from approximately September 8th to October 8th in the Gregorian calendar, and to the two-hour period between 5 pm and 7 pm. This is the time when the summer season is beginning to wane, and the cool, yin energy of the year is rising. Rooster years are times when the hard work of the past finally comes to fruition. During these years diligence, alertness, and forthright action are emphasized to protect the fruits of our labors, and the motivation to achieve our goals. There are often many enjoyable social gatherings during rooster years, especially with close friends and family. Rooster years can include a bit of conflict because the themes of strength and independence are prevalent, but they are also years of increased closeness, understanding, and appreciation for what we truly love.

Daoists believe roosters are capable of calling down the energy of heaven, to earth. Similarly, during rooster years, idealistic vision and creative innovation are popular, leading to new technologies and revolutionary concepts. Roosters are creatures that are capable of effective planning and creativity, as well as disciplined action. The idea of the nuclear chain reaction was first conceived by Leo Szilard in the rooster year of 1933. Twelve years later, in the rooster year of 1945, the idea was realized, and the first nuclear chain reaction was created at Los Alamos military base in New Mexico, quickly followed by the use of the first atomic bomb in Hiroshima.[1] In the following rooster year, 1969, the United States successfully landed a manned spacecraft on the surface of the moon and Neil Armstrong took the first steps on the lunar surface.[2] Both nuclear power and space travel represent the capacity to envision outcomes and create practical methods of achieving them.

Roosters are protective of their loved ones, and they do all that they can to help their brood prosper. Because this sentiment prospers during rooster years, it leads to policies and habits aimed at supporting and protecting the people, which, over time, leads to increased spending and economic growth. For example, in 1933, just as the great depression was hitting its most dismal point, a new president, Frederic Delano Roosevelt, was elected and immediately implemented numerous new policies and work projects to stabilize the economy and provide employment to millions of United States citizens. This would mark the beginning of the economic recovery for the country, and subsequently, many other countries as well.[3] Twenty-four years later in 1957, the "baby boom" would reach its peak when massive economic growth and affordable housing stimulated the birth rate of many of the allied countries after World War II.[4]

Roosters are strong and independent, which is illustrated by their tall, proud posture and their prominent crowing. Similarly, during the rooster years, numerous modern countries have declared their independence and began self-governance. The American Civil War began in the year of the rooster of 1861 when confederate troops, vying for independence, fired on Fort Sumter in South Carolina's Charleston Harbor.[5]

Even though they are proud and independent creatures, roosters are also capable of great cooperation, as long as that cooperation is of mutual benefit, and scarcity is not a pressing issue. With enough hens, food, and room in a pen, multiple roosters can live together cooperatively. All of the chickens benefit in this scenario because multiple roosters can protect the flock more effectively. This principle was illustrated in 1945 when the United Nations was founded, and again in 1993, when the European Union was officially established, both which were rooster years.[6]

Roosters are associated with the fire element and they can be seen scratching in the dusty ground to uncover seeds during the heat of the day. In rooster

---

[1] "Leo Szilard," by David Wargowski (2019). www.atomicheritage.org/profile/leo-szilard

[2] "Apollo 11," by Sarah Loff (2015). www.nasa.gov/mission_pages/apollo/apollo-11.html

[3] "FDR's First Inaugural Address Declaring 'War' on the Great Depression," by The National Archives and Records Administration (2016). www.archives.gov/education/lessons/fdr-inaugural

[4] "What Caused the Baby Boom?" by Matt Rosenberg (2018). www.thoughtco.com/baby-boom-overview-1435458

[5] "American Civil War," by Jennifer L. Weber (1999). www.britannica.com/event/American-Civil-War

[6] "History of the United Nations," by United Nations (n.d.). www.un.org/en/about-us/history-of-the-un

years, excessive heat, droughts, famine, and soil erosion have been common problems. In 1921, the great Russian famine occurred, leaving millions of people starving. This was due to a number of factors, including economic devastation from WWI, a lack of modern farming equipment, droughts in the Volga region, and numerous Soviet policies, including exporting grain during the famine to support the economy, and the policy of dekulakization which killed many of the country's most productive farmers in the name of communist ideology.[7]

In 1933, the following rooster year, the great Dust Bowl phenomenon began to strike many farming communities in the central United States when vast amounts of topsoil eroded and was carried away by the wind. This phenomenon was caused by severe droughts and over-farming, as well as the implementation of dry-farming methods such as crop rotation, soil conservation, and anti-erosion techniques by inexperienced farmers.[8]

Increased heat and decreased resources mean that tempers flare quickly and easily during rooster years, so extra care should be taken to calm the heart, soothe extreme emotions, and be alert and aware of others. While establishing their pecking order, roosters can sometimes break the skin, and the sight of blood fuels their violent tendencies, often resulting in an all-out battle. This same tendency can be found in human beings as well, on an individual level, as well as group or national levels. One small attack can be a spark that ignites a much larger conflict. Therefore, great diligence and awareness is necessary during these years.

This increased sense of pride, heat, and fiery energy can also provide opportunities for both the rise and fall of dictators throughout the world. Adolf Hitler became the Chairman of the Nazi party in the rooster year of 1921. In the following rooster year of 1933, he was appointed Chancellor of Germany, banned all other political parties, and passed the "Enabling Act" which effectively made him the dictator of Germany. Yet, twelve years later, it was this same sense of pride that brought an end to the reign of Adolf Hitler in 1945.[9] Numerous wars have both begun and ended during rooster years with this increased focus on self-determination and the need to provide for others.

On the other hand, the excess heat and the stress of responsibility that accompanies this year also leads to the desire to relax and express the feelings of the heart. The rooster, with its unique crowing, is the animal of the zodiac that rules over sound and music, and along with plenty of music, there are many celebrations, festivals, and large gatherings that can be enjoyed during these years. Roosters love to sing loudly and show off their brilliant colors, making this a

---

[7] "How Joseph Stalin Starved Millions in the Ukrainian Famine," by Patrick J. Kiger (2019). www.history.com/news/ukrainian-famine-stalin

[8] "Dust Bowl," by History.com Editors (2009). www.history.com/.amp/topics/great-depression/dust-bowl

[9] "Rise to Power of Adolf Hitler," by Alan Bullock and Baron Bullock (1998). www.britannica.com/biography/Adolf-Hitler/Rise-to-power

great time for enjoying, creating, and promoting art of all kinds, especially fashion and home décor items.

Qi

The time of the day that relates to the rooster is between 5 pm and 7 pm; the time of the kidney meridian. This is the time when the yin energy of the day begins to overtake the yang, and everything begins to cool down as nighttime approaches. This is also the height of the harvest season of the day, when the rewards of recent hard work and completed projects are reaped. This is a time when the final bit of effort is necessary to make sure that projects are either completed, or paused in a way that can easily be continued when necessary. Most animals at this time are doing their best to take advantage of the remaining sunlight, and beginning to prepare themselves for the cold of the night.

The hours between 5 pm and 7 pm are also when the kidneys are at their most active, allowing them to metabolize the body's fluids, store nutrients, and utilize vitamins more efficiently; as well as nourish and create bone marrow. This is a time when the body's blood sugar level begins to decrease, and with it, the body's energy. This is the point of the day where the body feels the sensation of pain the least because the yang energy of the kidneys is activated. It is also a vulnerable time for the heart, and therefore, it is not advisable to exercise vigorously or exert significant effort at this time.

Birds do not have urinary bladders in order to reduce their body weight and facilitate flight. Therefore, their urination and defecation functions are connected, and both actions occur simultaneously from the same orifice. In chickens (and all types of birds), the solid waste from the colon, and the liquid waste from the ureter, both enter the cloaca before being excreted. The ureter of the chicken connects directly from the kidney to the cloaca. Birds often excrete waste between twenty and forty times per day again to reduce body weight and facilitate flight.[10] Chickens have two kidneys located on either side of the vertebral column, however, unlike human beings, the kidneys of chickens are three-lobed structures that excrete uric acid rather than urea. Urea is a waste product that is excreted in human beings through both urine and sweat, whereas uric acid is the final product of the urinary system in humans, and is excreted only in the urine. Birds do not produce urea and excrete only uric acid in solid form.[11]

The kidneys are the vital organs that are responsible for metabolizing and processing the liquids of the body, and in Chinese medicine they are also responsible for housing the fire of the *mingmen*, or "life gate." This is the life force energy

---

[10] "Chicken Kidney Anatomy - The Vital Organ of Bird Urinary System," by Anatomy Learner (2021). www.anatomylearner.com/chicken-kidney-anatomy

[11] "Chicken Kidney Anatomy - The Vital Organ of Bird Urinary System," by Anatomy Learner (2021). www.anatomylearner.com/chicken-kidney-anatomy

of the body, and it is responsible for keeping all of the body's tissues and systems vital and healthy. This energy is also responsible for the individual's drive and willpower. When the kidneys are healthy and functioning well, then the individual will exhibit strength, determination, passion, masculinity, wisdom, and courage. The rooster's heavy reliance on their kidneys in daily life strengthens them and develops their sense of courage and resoluteness. The kidneys also store the body's *jing* essence, which is a physical manifestation of the life-force, and contributes to virility, fertility, and a high libido. This is the energy that allows hens to produce so many eggs, and for a single rooster to protect their brood from dangerous predators.

The ghost point that is associated with the rooster is the Ghost's Leg (gui-tui); it matches the point Pool at the Bend (*quchi*, LI-11) in the acupuncture system (Johnson 2014, 606). This point is located on the outside edge of the arm, at the very end of the crease that is formed when the arm is bent at the elbow. It is used to detoxify the lungs, remove excess heat, reduce high fevers, boost immune function, relieves diarrhea, hot flashes, and menstrual issues; and treats various skin conditions, including itchiness, hives, redness, and acne (Deadman et al. 2007, 112).

The rooster is symbolic of fire, and its energy is capable of reducing the effects of heat on the body. In Chinese medicine, when heat *qi* effects the body it can result in a fever, exhaustion, dizziness, nausea, and diarrhea. By treating the rooster point, either with acupuncture, moxibustion, or massage, the immune system function is increased, and the body is able to relax and begin healing. This point is also able to repair the arms, or "wings", of the body and prevent them from developing any stagnation or tension.

Along with the kidneys, the rooster is also associated with the small intestine. The small intestine is responsible for extracting the beneficial nutrients from the food material that has already been processed by the stomach, known as chyme. The intestine has small, thin membranes that allow the nutrients to pass through while keeping the waste material contained within. In traditional Chinese medicine, this is described as the process of separating the clear *qi* from the turbid *qi*. Once extracted, the nutrients are carried to the spleen via the blood stream to be distributed to the areas of the body where they're needed. The waste material continues downward to the excretory system to be removed from the body.

The rooster performs functions in nature that are similar to the functions that the small intestine plays within the body. The rooster is a master of distinguishing evil, negative energy from clear, righteous energy, and the small intestine helps the heart to sort through various choices and determine the best course of action. Roosters spend a great deal of their day observing their surroundings looking for any predators that may be lurking nearby. The energy of the rooster promotes alertness and clear thinking which allow for an enhanced ability to distinguish choices that are good for us, from ones that are detrimental. Roosters always remain clear, courageous, and decisive because they recognize the potential danger in hesitation, when action is required. Similarly, the small intestine is largely responsible for the intuitive "gut feelings" that we receive when we know that crucial moments are approaching.

The rooster's energy can be used to treat and heal many conditions. By consuming chicken, the temperature of the body rises and the immune function is increased. Chicken soup is famous for its healing properties and is often used as a remedy for the common cold. The temperature of the human body is normally between 97.7°F and 98.6°F, however, the body temperature of a rooster is normally 104°F. If a human being's body temperature was measured at 104°F, then they would be said to have a high fever and their thinking process would be affected to the point where confusion and delirium was beginning to set in.

Consuming chicken causes the body temperature to rise, though not excessively, and enhances the immune system. For centuries, Daoist doctors have understood that for every additional degree in body temperature (measured in Celsius), the immune function will increase sixfold. Eating duck, on the other hand, decreases body temperature, thereby reducing fever and calming the nerves. Normally, in spring and summer months, it is more beneficial eat chicken to cultivate yang energy, while in fall and winter, it is better to eat duck to nourish yin.

While chicken soup benefits the body as a whole, broth made from rooster claws is a potent remedy for arthritis. In Daoism, the hands, paws, or claws of all animals are called "heaven eyes" and are known to contain powerful *qi*. The rooster contains some of the best energy for cultivating the healing potential of the hands. Rooster energy is especially suited to reducing pain, and a rooster's blood and liver can be used to effectively treat these conditions. The act of pecking or clawing is also an effective healing technique. Birds naturally peck and groom themselves to maintain their health. They peck to remove damaged or dirty feathers, insects, parasites, and to stimulate their muscles and skin.

Special Abilities and Traits

Roosters Have Excellent Vision

Roosters and birds have vision is incredibly sensitive and acute, and they rely on their visual senses to accurately guide them during flight. "Nocturnal rodents such as mice and rats use the tactile senses a great deal, and this is what gives a mouse its air of constant scurrying activity. By contrast, a bird, which depends on sight, will often limit its investigative behavior to simply turning its head" (Scott 1972, 60). Roosters, and chickens have tetrachromatic vision meaning they have four types of cones in their eyes allowing them to see red, blue, green, and ultraviolet light. Therefore, roosters can see many more colors and shades of light than human beings.

Due to the fact that rooster's eyes are so sensitive, they perceive even subtle fluctuations of light. For instance, fluorescent lights which appears solid, or steady, to human beings, appear like a flashing strobe to roosters who can perceive the individual electrical pulses in the bulb. Therefore, fluorescent lighting causes the roosters to become highly irritable and stressed. In addition to having acute vision, they also are capable of looking across an arc of 300° because their eyes are situated on the sides of their head; and they can direct their eyes independently, in order to look in different directions at once.[12] Finally, the pineal gland within the brain, which can sense the presence or absence of light, is highly developed in birds, allowing them to perceive some aspects of light and their environment without the use of their physical eyes.

Roosters Control Pain

In Daoism, centipedes are symbolic of the spinal column, and of all types of pain conditions. Back pain in particular is thought to be related to the energy of centipedes. In the practice of feng shui, telephone poles are associated with the centipede energy, and if they are located too close to a place of residence, then the people who inhabit that building often suffer from back issues and chronic pain. To treat back pain and pain in general, the energy of the rooster is required. Being the natural enemy of the centipede, the rooster's energy is able to counteract the issues associated with it.

The area between the C7 and T1 vertebra is the location where the wings of birds, and the arms of humans, attach to the spine. By massaging, stretching, and creating space in this area, shoulder pressure and back pain are reduced, and range of motion is increased in the arms. In Chinese medicine, the rooster is often referred to as the "controller of pain", or the "commander of pain", for this reason. By envisioning a centipede at the location of the third eye on the forehead, the rooster energy of the heart is stimulated, and pain will be reduced throughout the body. Also, observing birds fly for five to ten minutes, twice per day, is an ancient and natural way of treating issues in the neck and C7 area as well.

Due to the fact that roosters do not have teeth, they use their gizzards to grind and break down their food. The gizzard is a strong muscular sac that squeezes and break down the previously eaten food. Roosters occasionally swallow small pebbles and stones which are then held in their gizzard increasing the organ's ability to grind and process food material. Due to the fact that chicken gizzards and stomachs are capable of handling and processing stones within the body, consuming these organs helps the human body develop the strength to process both gall-stones and kidney stones. This is because these organs contain energy that tonifies and strengthens the tissues of the inner organs, allowing them to process solid materials more easily.

---

[12] "10 Interesting Facts About Chicken Vision," by VAL-CO Editors (n.d.). www.valco.com/10-interesting-facts-chicken-vision

Cultural and Spiritual Concepts

Birds are a highly intelligent and varied group of animals with numerous unique behaviors and skills. While science describes the evolution of birds and the ability of flight as being developed from certain dinosaur species, especially the Archaeopteryx. Daoism has its own understanding of how the process of evolution unfolded. The scientific and Daoist conceptions of the process of evolution have been at odds many times in the past, however, as discoveries continue to made, the two modalities are increasingly coming into harmony with one another.

Birds share a lot of their DNA with certain dinosaur species, and yet they also have many anatomical features that suggest they could be closely related to fish. The Daoist theory of avian evolution is that fish developed flight, before animals existed on land. Therefore, an ancient form of flying fish is thought to be the ancestor of modern birds, and all creatures that now live on land, including human beings.

Crows have learned to become agile fliers for their size, and their intelligence and maneuverability has allowed them to become skilled hunters, fighters, and thieves. Crows are extremely intelligent and clever creatures that can even outsmart many human beings. Crows have learned how to use simple tools and they have developed a complex language of calls that they use to communicate to and direct one another. They hunt and attack in groups supporting each other as they fight. Crows represent soldiers and protection, but in excess they can be destructive.

Doves and pigeons, along with many other bird species, are extremely skilled navigators, and they can find their way even when they are removed from their natural environment by a great distance. When doves or pigeons circle in the air, often in large groups, they are calibrating their sensitivity to earth's magnetism and honing their ability to navigate. Also, when doves attempt to fly over a large body of water, they are smart enough to carry a small stick with them, so that when they become exhausted, they can drop the stick in the water, and land on it for a temporary rest.

Sooty terns, which are similar in size to doves and pigeons, have developed the ability to sleep for mere seconds before waking up again, so that they can sleep while flying. This allows these birds to remain in flight almost indefinitely. From the moment they learn how to fly, to the time of their first breeding, they remain in flight continuously for roughly four to five years.[13] Its close relative, the arctic tern, makes the longest yearly migration of any bird, traveling roughly 20,000 miles from the arctic to the Antarctic and back again (Burnie and Wilson 2001, 307).

---

[13] "Sooty Tern Migration," by Michael Tennesen (2007). www.nwf.org/Magazines/National-Wildlife/2008/Sooty-Tern-Migration

Eagles are extremely strong, swift birds, and they are some of the most skilled predators in the rooster category. Eagles can fly higher than nearly any bird and descend back down to the earth with control and great speed. Their ability to hunt with such great efficiency allows them to spend a majority of their time creating nests and soaring in the sky. In Tibet and Mongolia, golden eagles have been raised and trained for centuries to be incredible hunters. Genghis Khan was famous for having his large trained eagles lead his troops as they traveled through unknown foreign lands.

Swallows have developed the ability to sense the direction that the wind will blow in advance, to guide them in the design and construction of their nests. Swallows build their nests in the beginning of the year, and they always make sure to orient the opening of their nests away from the yearly general direction of wind to keep warm and prevent debris from being blown in. Swallows are extremely agile fliers and spend much of their time in the sky. They fly so often, that they have evolved to always drink water while in flight, which exemplifies their extremely active lifestyle.

Wood peckers are known as the "tree doctors" by many Daoists because of their ability to determine the health of a tree and locate and remove any parasitic insects that may be burrowing within. Their chiseling behavior also stimulates the trees and improves their health. Trees that are used for storage or feeding by woodpeckers often grow taller and stronger than other, similar trees in the surrounding environment.

Roosters Represent Music

Daoist mythology describes how the rooster's song is so beautiful that it causes the sun to rise in the morning, and this magnificent combination of beauty and skillfulness earned the rooster the title of 'king of the birds.' The rooster's crow is perhaps its most unique quality, and the importance of this sound in nature cannot be over-estimated. Birds have high frequency songs and calls, while other creatures, like wolves, have low frequency howls and calls. The rooster's crow is capable of climbing through a nearly infinite number of tonal degrees from low to high with many overlapping tones, therefore the rooster is said to govern all types of songs, music, and sounds within nature.

Many birds, such as crows and pigeons, only sing one or two notes, while songbirds can sing many. However, only the rooster's crow consists of the five primary notes of the pentatonic scale, which form the foundation of most types of music. In the past, the Daoists that studied music would tune their instruments to the rooster's crow each morning, and they would study the sounds of the rooster each day to learn about music, sound, and tonality.

There is an old poem in China that says that "the rooster *sings* to call forth the day" this is a description of the rooster's musical function in nature. Daoists refer to the rooster as "god equipment" because it functions like an alarm clock for nature, stressing the importance of developing a strong routine and following the cycles of nature. The rooster is a messenger that describes the relationship between the movements of the heavens and the actions of the earth. Even the crown of the rooster is symbolic of the rising sun with its vibrant red color and projecting rays.

The daytime belongs to the human beings, but the nighttime belongs to the animals, and the rooster rules this relationship. Therefore, the rooster teaches us how to unify with nature by acting in accordance with its cycles. The rooster crows at the time when yang energy overtakes the yin (dawn), and when the yin energy overtakes the yang (dusk). It is important to be humble, respectful, and even spiritual during these times. Dawn is a time when there is an opportunity for gathering potent, productive energy that can last throughout the day, and dusk is a time when rest, recovery, and introspection are emphasized. During these two times, stress levels can high, and arguments can easily occur, so patience, tolerance, solitude, and humility can help to mitigate these issues. At the White Cloud Temple, when the rooster crows at sunrise, the monks strike a gong, and when the rooster crows at sunset, trained rodents and monkeys beat a drum. These practices celebrate the sacredness of dawn and dusk, and act as a reminder to practice reverence throughout life.

The rooster's crow calls down heavenly energy to the earth, and it represents the tones of nature. Natural sounds balance out the stress and disharmony that is caused by violent, made-man, or unnatural sounds. Listening to all types of sounds, especially sounds of nature, helps achieve calm and balance in the mind. Living organisms and natural environments heal themselves with the numerous sounds that nature creates. Human beings exist within this natural symphony, and our mental, emotional, and physical health is surprisingly dependent on the healing sounds of the animals and nature. Rabbits and prey animals are encouraged to breed by the howls of the wolves in the night. Even reptiles and fish seem to enjoy the crow of the rooster, and the sound of wind blowing through the trees. By developing the habit of calming the mind and listening to the surrounding environment, enhanced longevity and intelligence can be developed. Some of the most healing natural sounds to listen to are the crow of a rooster at dawn, the calls of songbirds, the sounds of flowing water, and the cries and coos of babies.

The Phoenix

The rooster represents the fiery energy of the heart. Like fire, the human heart cannot rest as long as it exists. It must maintain its function at all times to keep the body alive. The heart is also like a light bulb that can only be turned on and off so many times before it burns out. This is similar to the function of the rooster and the monkey in nature. While some animals have natural functions that only apply at certain times of year, such as bears, both the rooster and the monkey are related to the heart and therefore neither one can cease its natural function.

All of the animals of the zodiac are afraid of fire, even ghosts and spirits. Since roosters represent fiery, solar energy they have the ability to scare away ghosts and shield against evil. When the rooster crows at dawn and calls forth the light of the sun, its vibrant energy scares away all of the evil that lingers during the night. Roosters can help to alleviate nightmares because the passionate energy of the heart balances out the logical energy of the mind, which reduces fear, fright, defeatism, and narrow-mindedness.

In Feng Shui theory, four chickens (one rooster and three hens) form an energetic talisman that will create a shield against evil spirits and people. Today, many people keep dogs to protect their homes from intruders. While dogs alert the home owners when an intruder arrives on the property, the rooster talisman begins thwarting the intruders from the moment that they intend to invade the property. With this form of protection, any person with ill intentions toward the property or its inhabitants run into all kinds of misfortune as they attempt to carry out their plans.

The wild rooster is considered to be the incarnation of the magical, mythological phoenix. As a significant heavenly creature, the qi of the phoenix is extremely powerful and benevolent. In China and Daoism, the phoenix is nature's representation of angels, and all of the blessings and good fortune that they bring. The phoenix has the ability to understand the spiritual level of reality, and knows the fate and destiny of all beings in advance. The phoenix blesses the spirits of the world to help them make the correct decisions and ease their suffering.

In the human realm, the phoenix energy is represented by beautiful women. Roosters are strongly associated with the values of marriage and family life. The color associated with the rooster is a deep red or purple, and like the appearance of beautiful women this color inspires romance, partnership, marriage, and the benefits of family life. The feces of certain birds have also been traditionally used as a form of cosmetic cream and beauty treatment in China and Japan for many centuries. Beautiful women have a powerful, magnetic energy that disarms the masculine and can cause many distractions and disruptions in an environment.

To understand the thinking and perceptive abilities of the heart more fully, studies were conducted in China, where the surgically removed heart of a male human being was kept alive by various machines in a hospital, and exposed to various stimuli while its behavior was observed. When a beautiful woman was brought into the room with the heart, it began beating faster and more vigorously in response, without any additional stimuli. This is a demonstration of the way that the yang energy of the man responds to the potent yin energy of a beautiful woman. This is also a demonstration of the natural relationship between the heart and beauty.

People Who Embody the Rooster

People born in the year of the rooster are generally forthright, enthusiastic, faithful, magnetic, and noble. Roosters are naturally calm and peaceful, but their fiery energy can be ignited at a moment's notice. Roosters exemplify the virtues of integrity and honesty, communicating clearly and directly with their speech and actions. This can greatly reduce irrationality and emotional drama, but it can also lead to friction and conflicts. Rooster people should be careful not to be overly frank with emotionally sensitive people, because their sharp words could lead to emotional wounds and trust issues. That being said, roosters greatly enjoy company and conversation, sharing with others helps calm their nervous system and acts as a healthy outlet for their abundant energy.

Rooster people are colorful, vibrant, and energetic. They are usually quite active and often seek the company of like-minded people by joining athletic/exercise clubs, various special interest groups, and being the life of the party, often by hosting the party themselves. With their magnetic personality, roosters enjoy popularity and fame, and they often find themselves as the center of attention. They naturally become vibrant and spirited when they have the spotlight, and know how to command a room.

Roosters have high expectations of themselves and others, and they often fill their days with numerous tasks and projects. Roosters are exceptionally skilled at developing plans and detailed strategies. They love to be prepared and organized, and they feel comforted by having thought through all possible outcomes of a situation. The sense of security that they derive from systematic planning can cause them to seem aloof at times, but it also allows them to take quick, effective action when necessary. Roosters are analytical and intelligent, but they never let their abundant thoughts allow them to hesitate when decisive action is required.

In their career, roosters make excellent managers and business owners because of their sense of teamwork, their ambition, and their direct, honest nature. Roosters often do quite well in advertising, public relations, politics, corporate environments, real estate, and anything to do with finance or wealth management. Their sense of flair and organizational skills allow them to be great hosts, party planners, museum curators, restaurant managers, and they thrive at nearly everything that has to do with creating a fun, exciting experience. As natural protectors with a keen intellect, roosters make wonderful teachers, school administrators, and mentors. Their incredible courage, honor, and sense of authority also allows people born during rooster years to be skillful police officers, soldiers, sailors, and martial artists.

Roosters are organized and meticulous, which allows them to manage their personal finances scrupulously. They can become quite wealthy if they stick to their natural tendencies, and utilize their ability to envision their finances in detail. However, if roosters do not make a concerted effort to stay disciplined and focused on their priorities, their fortunes can dissipate as quickly as they appeared. Roosters can often be so family oriented and interested in their social life, that saving and investing may take a backseat to being generous and creating memorable moments.

Roosters are passionate, creative lovers, and they have high libidos. While some rooster people can be quite promiscuous, they have an equally intense passion for the simple pleasures of family life, and joy of settling down with a partner. Once they have put down roots and committed themselves to another, roosters are loyal, caring, attentive, devoted partners. As parents, roosters are just as attentive, reliable, and devoted as they are with their partner. They set healthy boundaries and easily join children in their sense of joy and happiness. They also set high expectations for themselves and others, and they encourage their children to achieve their best, but they can sometimes be overly strict and demanding.

External Zodiac
Deer

The deer is the outer animal of the rooster category, and like roosters, deer are family oriented, caring, attentive, and noble creatures. The deer category of the zodiac also includes caribou, elk, and moose. Deer spend most of their time grazing and migrating, sometimes over vast territory. Most species travel in sexually segregated groups throughout most of the year, gathering together only during the mating, or rutting, season. Deer are unique in that they shed their antlers every year, regrowing them again the following spring. They use their antlers as fighting instruments during the rut against rival males, and as a way to attract the attention of females (Burnie and Wilson 2001, 238).

While roosters aggressively attack any perceived threats, deer would always prefer to escape, rather than risk injury. Like hens, female deer, or hinds, are the ones that bear the responsibility of raising the young. The stags remain with their harem for a number of months after breeding to vigilantly scouting for any approaching danger, but then leave to become solitary or to rejoin their group of stags for the warmer months of the year. Some deer species such as the pronghorns of North America gather together in large herds of over a thousand during the winter, and break into smaller, individual groups during the summer months (Burnie and Wilson 2001, 238-41).

Qi

Deer are herbivores, and animals that eat a diet of strictly vegetation often tend to be more peaceful. Deer are survivors that have highly acute senses, coats that both keep them warm and provide camouflage, and the ability to quickly escape most predators. Deer have a deep connection to the land and plant-life, and they are adapted to survive in difficult environmental conditions. Deer have wide hooves that allow them to travel easily over soft terrain such as mud, snow, and river banks. Their hooves allow them to move with speed and agility when chased by predators, and they run at speeds of over 40mph (64kph) and jump vertically nearly eight feet. Some deer species have learned to survive on a diet of grasses and twigs that has little variety, while other species have developed the ability to survive on many different types of plant-life depending on what is available. Moose have developed the skill of being able to submerge themselves in shallow water to graze on the aquatic plants that grow near the bottoms of lakes, swamps, and riverbeds.

Deer have a sense of smell that is at least a thousand times more acute than human beings because they have far more olfactory receptors. Elk and caribou, which often live in colder climates, and survive harsh winters partly because they use their acute sense of smell to locate lichen, grasses, and herbs that are located underneath the snow. Deer can pick up the scent of a human being from over a half mile away if the conditions are correct. They also have the ability to detect and analyze several smells at the same time, because they use their Jacobson's organ in conjunction with their snout, and a large part of their brain is dedicated to processing the signals that are received by their olfactory senses.

Just like roosters and birds, deer have developed their eyesight and hearing abilities to detect approaching predators because they are animals that are preyed upon often. The aural sense of deer is much more acute than human beings, and they can move their funnel-shaped ears to pinpoint the source of sounds far more accurately. Due to the fact that deer spend so much of their time in wild, forested areas, they are easily alerted to foreign sounds that do not normally occur in these natural environments. Deer have eyesight that is designed to detect subtle movement, especially at night. Some studies suggest that they are even able to perceive certain frequencies of ultraviolet light, which would further enhance their night vision. Deer also have eyes on the side of their head which allow them to have a 300° field of vision allowing them to scan a wide area without moving their head.[14]

Special Abilities and Traits

Deer antlers are made from calcium, and are essentially large bones that grow directly out of their skull. Only male deer grow antlers, except for caribou or reindeer, where both genders have antlers. Deer shed their antlers during the final part of winter, after the rutting season has ended, and regrow them again in

---

[14] "10 Things You Must Know About Deer Senses," by Daniel Xu (2015). www.outdoor-hub.com/stories/2015/11/09/10-things-must-know-deer-senses/

spring. When the antlers begin to grow, they are covered in soft skin that is covered in fine hairs called "velvet," but by the time rutting season begins in autumn, the velvet has been removed by the deer by rubbing its antlers against trees throughout the year.

Deer use their antlers to posture and battle with other male stags during the rutting season. Deer begin grunting, posturing, and thrashing their antlers against trees and bushes to display their strength. They then walk near rival males to assess their opponent, and if neither stag has backs down, they begin to lock horns and battle by trying to uproot and topple their opponent. The winner will have priority in choosing a mate, or mates. After the rutting season, once the antlers have been shed, the deer often eat their own antlers to reclaim some of the calcium that they contain, and fuel the regrowth process. Deer are the only creatures in nature that shed and regrow antlers.

Cultural and Spiritual Concepts

Deer have been symbols of love, grace, kindness, marriage, family and good fortune for thousands of years. They are renowned for their gentle, compassionate nature and their willingness to express their kindness toward one another. While deer are cautious creatures, they do not judge others or leap to conclusions by acting rashly, but instead simply watch and listen patiently to other creatures, allowing them to display their own nature. It is this quality of innocence and purity that has earned deer their reputation of being noble and graceful creatures. Deer remind us to stay in touch with our innocence, and to be compassionate and tolerant with those around us. Like roosters, deer embody the values of family life and marriage. They express their love by spending a time with their partner, nuzzling and grooming them, and by freely sharing their food with one another.

The Function of Antlers

The antlers of the deer have been considered sacred objects for thousands of years. Hunters, shamans, and medicine men have greatly valued deer antlers for their powerful healing qualities and divine symbolism. A story in Daoism describes the importance of antlers and the relationship between roosters, centipedes, and deer:

> Originally, the rooster had beautiful antlers that crowned its head. One day, as the deer passed by, it noticed the rooster's magnificent antlers while it was crowing at dawn. The deer approached the rooster, and showered him with compliments about his wonderful antlers, even asking a nearby centipede to corroborate his claims. The centipede quickly agreed that the rooster and his antlers were a brilliant sight to behold. After fully expressing his admiration for the rooster's striking appearance, the deer timidly asked if he could try them

on for himself. The rooster, recognizing the innocence of the deer, reluctantly agreed to let him borrow the antlers for a short period. The deer placed the antlers on his head and immediately pranced around the forest with elation and even began to glow with heavenly energy.

At first, the rooster quietly admired the deer's elation, however, after some time the rooster needed to continue on with his tasks and became impatient. The rooster asked for his antlers back so he could carry on, but the deer refused. After experiencing the joy and happiness that they antlers brought him, the deer could not bring himself to them, and decided to keep them for himself. Stunned and outraged, the rooster called upon the Jade Emperor to complain about the deer's theft. The Jade Emperor asked the rooster, "Do you have any proof that the antlers truly belonged to you, or are there any witnesses to this theft? Otherwise, it is only one person's word against another's." The rooster looked around and quickly spotted the centipede still resting quietly nearby. "There!" cried the rooster. "The centipede has been here the whole time. He can tell you the truth of what happened." But when questioned by the Jade Emperor, the centipede stared blankly ahead and remained silent, not knowing what to do.

Because of the centipede's reluctance to speak, the Jade Emperor could not order the deer to return the antlers, dismissed the rooster's claim, and returned to heaven. From then on, the deer has been in possession of the magnificent antlers, and the rooster has never forgiven the centipede for its betrayal. The rooster has been the centipede's worst enemy ever since, eating them at every opportunity.

The horns and antlers of any creature, whether it is the ox, the dragon, the sheep, or the deer are considered to be instruments that connect that creature to the will of heaven. Horns and antlers that point upward toward the sky act like antennae that interpret the messages of heaven. They also allow the creatures that possess them to have an enhanced ability to rise above frustrations, negative emotions, and criticism. The creatures that have antlers, often know many things in advance, and understand the destiny of other living creatures. Even though the rooster no longer has antlers, it has retained its ability to perceive the will of heaven. The deer has long been regarded as a heavenly creature that is connected with instinct, intuition, the stars of the night sky. Together these two creatures represent hope, faith, the connection between heaven and earth.

Quotes from Famous Roosters

Accept the challenges so that you can feel the exhilaration of victory.
- George Patton

You have to believe it first. Don't wait until you see it, then touch it, then believe it.
- Wallace Black Elk

Dost thou love life? Then do not squander time, for that is the stuff life is made of.
- Benjamin Franklin

Courage is the price that life exacts for granting peace.
- Amelia Earhart

You have power over your mind— not outside events. Realize this, and you will find strength.
- Marcus Aurelius

A man, who as a physical being is always turned toward the outside, thinking that his happiness lies outside him, finally turns inward, and discovers that the source is within him.
- Søren Kierkegaard

Go as far as you can see. When you get there, you'll see further.
- J.P. Morgan

Fight for the things that you care about, but do it in a way that will lead others to join you.
- Ruth Bader Ginsburg

It's your outlook on life that counts. If you take yourself lightly and don't take yourself too seriously, pretty soon you can find the humor in our everyday lives. And sometimes it can be a lifesaver.
- Betty White

Energy begets energy.
- Dolly Parton

Fear connotes something that interferes with what you're doing.
- John Glenn

11

Dog

Wood Dog
14th February 1934 to 3rd February 1935

Fire Dog
2nd February 1946 to 21st January 1947

Earth Dog
18th February 1958 to 7th February 1959

Metal Dog
6th February 1970 to 26th January 1971

Water Dog
25th January 1982 to 12th February 1983

Wood Dog
10th February 1994 to 30th January 1995

Fire Dog
29th January 2006 to 17th February 2007

Earth Dog
16th February 2018 to 4th February 2019

Metal Dog
2nd February 2030 to 22nd January 2031

Water Dog
22nd January 2042 to 10th February 2043

Wood Dog
8th February 2054 to 28th January 2055

Fire Dog
26th January 2066 to 14th February 2067

Dog

The dog category of the zodiac represents wild and domestic dogs, coyotes, wolves, jackals, and foxes. Dogs are loyal, faithful, honest, friendly, cooperative, reliable, integrous, brave, protective, cautious, willful, and determined. Dogs are thought to be one of the first animals to be domesticated at approximately 8000 B.C. Dogs have long been known as "man's best friend" because of their loyal, protective nature, their enhanced senses, and their ability to learn. Dogs have been bred and trained to accomplish an extremely wide variety of tasks. Domesticated dogs have more variation between their breeds than any other domesticated species (Burnie and Wilson 2001, 180).

Dogs have muscular bodies and a deep chest, that lends itself to movement and maneuverability on all fours. Some dogs are capable of great endurance, while others have evolved to be explosive sprinters. Dogs are capable of great strength, and a single dog is capable of bringing down creatures much larger than itself, including human beings. Their hind legs and paws, which have four digits each, are designed for strength and forward movement, whereas their front legs, that have five digits each, are used for stability, pivoting, and maneuverability.

Dogs have extraordinary physical stamina on land, and they are instinctively able to swim shortly after being born. Dogs are naturally forest dwelling creatures, but some species have adapted to other habitats. Today, dogs have adapted to nearly every type of environment on earth. Wild canines are found throughout the world, and are only absent from isolated places, such as Madagascar or New Zealand. Canines have long jaws and strong teeth that are designed for attacking prey and tearing meat. They also have highly acute sense organs, with well-developed olfactory, aural, and visual senses (Burnie and Wilson 2001, 180).

Smaller canines, which usually feed on small animals, rodents, and insects, are much more flexible with their social structures, and usually travel in pairs or remain solitary. Larger canines however, are much more likely to travel in packs of up to thirty individuals, led by a dominant pair. The dominant pair of a pack are the only members that are allowed to reproduce, with the rest of the pack often consisting exclusively of their offspring. Canines give birth in the springtime, to a litter of four to twelve pups on average. Young cubs often remain with their family pack until they are well into adulthood to assist in caring for their siblings. Only when they are ready to form their own pack do they leave and fend for themselves.

The pack performs various bonding rituals to keep members close and loyal to one another. Playing, tail-wagging, licking, nuzzling, and excited whining are all forms of bonding that canines use to build camaraderie. Wolves and other canines howl to announce their presence and declare the boundaries of their territory. A wolf's howl can be heard up to six miles away, and it allows various packs to remain separated to avoid unnecessary confrontation (Burnie and Wilson 2001, 180-87).

Dogs are opportunistic and strategic hunters. The smaller species, which hunt by themselves, often stalk and prowl near their prey until they find an opening they can take advantage of. Similar species can be seen using the unique vertical pounce technique to come down on top of their prey, especially in snowy landscapes. The canine will leap almost straight up into the air before coming down on its prey with its front two paws to pin it to the ground before dispatching it. The larger species that form packs are much more strategic in their attacks. The pack uses their endurance to their advantage by moving as a unit to surround their prey, and if necessary, to separate it from its herd. Wolf packs can take down animals as large as a moose, which is over ten times their size. Canines instinctively attack the neck and throat area of their prey to incapacitate it as quickly as possible, and minimize injuries to other members of the pack (Burnie and Wilson 2001, 187).

Dogs are carnivores and they only rarely eat fruits. Being opportunistic hunters, most dogs consume a wide variety of prey. Larger species focus their efforts on the bigger prey in their territory, only because they require more calories to feed all their members. Smaller species like foxes are much less picky and eat nearly anything from rabbits and birds to insects, carrion, and garbage (Burnie and Wilson 2001, 180).

Calendar

The dog is the eleventh animal of the zodiac. It is associated with the ninth month of the Chinese lunar calendar that lasts from approximately October 8th to November 7th in the Gregorian calendar, and to the two-hour period between 7 pm and 9 pm. This represents the ending of the fall season, just before the onset of winter. During this time, the crops that have recently been reaped during the harvest are being traded and stored in preparation for the winter. This is a time when food stores are abundant and people are beginning to wear heavier clothing to protect themselves from the wind and cold. In dog years, many people are often in a conservative mood, seeking to gather, inventory, and protect their resources. This is a time of gathering information, assessing the current situation of things, and determining what can be done to ensure safety and prosperity in the future.

During the dog years, scientific advancement is often practical and prolific. The energy of the dog lends itself to scientific investigation and coming to practical answers. Tried and true methods, and down to earth explanations are the preferred methods in dog years, rather than abstract, creative experimentation. The Apollo 13 space mission took place in the dog year of 1970. After the success of the Apollo 11 and 12 missions demonstrated NASA's ability to land a human being on the moon and achieve precision landings, Apollo 13 was designed to land in a new area of the lunar surface, Fra Mauro, and gather geological and planetary data. The mission was aborted after a malfunction caused an oxygen tank to explode, damaging the spacecraft. The crew and the NASA team then had to focus on finding a practical way to bring the three-man crew safely back to Earth, which included using anything that was available to repair the module.[1]

Dogs are quite realistic and forward-thinking creatures. Wolves, for instance, assess their environment while simultaneously predicting the actions and behaviors of their prey. This means that dog years also find many technologies being applied in major, widespread ways to lay a foundation for future progress. Long-lasting security is necessary to provide for any large group, or pack. During dog years, the instinct to create a safe and secure environment for future generations, causes many countries enact policies, sign treaties, and begin practices that ensure peace and prosperity. The United Nations held its first meeting in 1946, and UNESCO was founded the same year, both with the purpose of preventing the occurrence of future wars.[2] [3] Also, as a result of the strong focus on security, many totalitarian and dogmatic regimes further solidify their grasp on power by pandering to these sentiments. Both the USSR and the Fascist party of Italy rose to power in the year of the dog 1922, and Adolf Hitler fully cemented his hold on power in Germany in 1934 by declaring himself to be the Fuhrer, or absolute leader, of the country.[4] [5] [6]

Economies and businesses usually grow slowly during dog years, but they also develop stability by maintaining a conservative approach. Businesses that are involved in either physical or financial security, as well as businesses that bring communities together, often do well in these years. The British Broadcasting Company, Fidelity Investments, and Amazon.com were all founded in dog years, and each became highly successful by appealing to their customers and bringing people together. Work is accomplished with diligence and competence in a timely manner during these years by focusing on teamwork, unity, and the spirit of camaraderie.

Dogs are not afraid to engage threats, and similarly, in the year of the dog, many injustices are punished, and many criminals are pursued. The courage, instinct, and acute senses of dogs have been extensively utilized by police forces and hunters for centuries; therefore, dogs are often associated with justice and enforcing the rule of law. The Mexican Revolution began in dog year 1910, as a reaction to the oppressive tactics and policies of President Porfirio Díaz who had

---

[1] "Apollo 13," by Brian Dunbar (2017). www.nasa.gov/mission_pages/apollo/missions/apollo13.html

[2] "The San Francisco Conference," by United Nations Editors (n.d.). www.un.org/en/about-us/history-of-the-un/san-francisco-conference

[3] "History of UNESCO," by UNESCO Editors (n.d.). www.unesco.org/en/history

[4] "Soviet Union," by Martin McCauley (1999). www.britannica.com/place/Soviet-Union

[5] "Emilio De Bono," by The Editors of Encyclopedia Britannica (1998). www.britannica.com/biography/Emilio-De-Bono

[6] "Hitler Becomes Dictator of Germany," by History.com Editors (2010). www.history.com/this-day-in-history/hitler-becomes-fuhrer

been in power for decades.[7] And in 1946, the infamous Nuremberg Trials concluded with the sentencing of twelve Nazi criminals for their actions during World War II. This was the first time that the term 'crimes against humanity' was used to prosecute crimes that had not been thought possible by previous generations.[8]

The art and fashion that is created or released in the year of the dog is often iconic and revolutionary in nature. At this time, art has the power to generate a lot of interest, excitement, and controversy. The bikini swimsuit was first debuted in Paris in 1946 and quickly became one of the most iconic, popular, and controversial pieces of fashion during the 20th century.[9] While dogs are highly focused on strength and guardianship, they also love to play, have fun, and express their feelings. Wolves, for instance, all howl together at the full moon as an expression of their inner emotions; however, this also unnerves many other creatures in the surrounding area. Dog years are known for lavish parties, and playful interactions, but consequently this leads to envy and jealousy in others as well. Vulnerability and protection, loving and fighting; these are major themes in the year of the dog.

Qi

The time of the day that relates to the dog is between 7 pm and 9 pm, the time of the pericardium meridian. This is the when many people are beginning to shed the stress of the day, doing what they can to relax after returning home from work. This is also the time of the day when blood pressure is at its highest, which means that people are also at their moodiest, and arguments are easily ignited. Therefore, it is best to avoid serious discussions at this time if possible, and wait until the day's energy settles down further. This is also when sensory perception and physical sensitivity is at its most acute, which makes accidents less likely, and exacerbates aches and pains. Light reading and self-healing treatments, such as soaking the hands or feet in warm water, and drinking hot tea are beneficial at this time.

The dog category of the zodiac is associated with the pericardium. The pericardium is the triple layered fibroserous sac that surrounds and protects the heart, providing an environment of greatly reduced friction so that the heart can pump with minimal effort. It also protects the heart by intercepting toxic pathogens that are seeking to enter the heart through the blood stream. Known as the

[7] "Mexican Revolution," by The Editors of Encyclopedia Britannica (1998). www.britannica.com/event/Mexican-Revolution

[8] "The Nuremberg Trials" by The National WWII Museum (n.d.). www.nationalww2museum.org/war/topics/nuremberg-trials

[9] "A Scandalous, Two-Piece History of the Bikini," by Steve Hendrix (2018). www.washingtonpost.com/news/retropolis/wp/2018/07/05/a-scandalous-two-piece-history-of-the-bikini

"heart master" in Chinese medicine, the pericardium is energetically responsible for protecting the heart from negative emotions by promoting the formation of healthy personal boundaries, and happy, joyful disposition.

The pericardium is also responsible for housing the mental, emotional, and sexual states of the mind, thereby playing a significant role in the individual's thought and decision-making process (Johnson 2014, 539). Canines are masters of guarding their home and territory to protect their family and their resources. Similar to the way that the pericardium protects the heart from damaging emotions and pathogens, canines actively investigate anything that enters their territory, and immediately alert other members to threats. Dogs are loyal, and devoted to protecting the ones that are closest to their heart.

The ghost point that is associated with the dog is known as Ghost's Store (*guicang*); it matches the point Meeting of the Yin (*huiyin*, CV-1) in the acupuncture system (Johnson 2014, 606). This point is located at the perineum, below the genitals; between the genitals and the anus. This point is mainly used for treating dementia, regressed memory conditions, and various mental conditions; as well as regulating the body's yin energy (Deadman et al. 2007, 497-98). The energy of this acupoint is gender specific, only men can treat this area on a male patient, and only women can treat this area on a female patient. This is necessary culturally/socially because many people would feel uncomfortable with a person of the opposite sex touching such a sensitive area, but it is also necessary energetically, because the *qi* contained in this point is sensitive. The *qi* of the *huiyin* point is different depending upon the gender of the individual, and it responds differently to the gender specific energy of others as well.

In addition to the pericardium and the hui yin point, there are four dog-related points that are located on the front of the neck area. The Heavenly Prominence (*tiantu*, CV-22) point just above the sternum and below the throat, the left and right locations of the Man's Welcome (*renying*, ST-9) point near the carotid artery, and the On the Neck (*shanglian quan*, EX-HN-21) point just below the midpoint of the lower jaw. Dogs can suffer from back issues, especially lower back issues, but they have strong necks and almost never suffer from problems in the cervical spine. These are also points that are vulnerable on a dog, as the carotid artery is quite exposed on the side of the neck. Spiked dog collars were originally designed to keep the vulnerable, neck of dogs safe from predators.

The cervical area of most creatures is an essential area for overall health where issues often occur. The neck is where a large amount of blood, nerves, and important structures have to travel through an area with a small diameter. Therefore, many blockages and a lot of tension can occur at this location, and if severely damaged, then the life of the individual can be in jeopardy. When the neck is healthy, limber, and functioning properly, then the brain functions properly, stress on the heart is reduced, and the immune system is supported.

In general, the energy of dogs is yang in nature, and essential to the overall health, energy, and vitality of the environment. When dogs bark, pounce, and shake off water from their coats they are exhibiting the strength and vibrancy of yang energy. When this energy is in excess in a human, it is called "dog condition", and the individual's behavior is characterized by over-excitement and excessive talking. By combing their hair or coat at least 270 times, the excessive yang energy of a person, or a dog, can be calmed and made smoother. This unblocks and aligns the *qi* meridians, increasing longevity. This also helps dogs by moving healthy *qi* toward the hind legs, where they often develop issues.

Dogs and wolves also have strong energy in their paws, because they walk on their wrists which increases speed and agility. Due to the fact that the legs of canines are located within the body wall of the torso, the muscles of their shoulder joints are strong. The lower parts of the legs mainly develop tendon strength, which increases power without the need for increased blood flow. Therefore, the *qi* of wolf's paws can be used to treat many issues of the hands and wrist, especially arthritis.

Special Abilities and Traits

Intelligent and Perceptive

Dogs have an average level of intelligence that is comparable to that of a seven-year-old human being. They are capable of learning a great deal, and they have a good memory. Dogs have been trained to perform a variety of tasks for thousands of years, from herding sheep to rescuing stranded people. Dogs love to be a part of a team, and they understand the importance of working for the good of the group. Sled dogs are a great example of canines that understand how to work as a team. For centuries, dogs have acted as guardians of family homes, businesses, international borders, military bases, and prisons throughout the world. Though dogs have limited visual acuity and resolution, they perceive a slightly wider range of light frequencies than human beings. At the White Cloud Temple, dogs are trained by using florescent pieces of paper that are placed on the floor.

Dogs have one of the best olfactory senses of the zodiac. A dog's sense of smell is 240 times greater than that of a human being, and they can identify scents individually with great precision. Dogs can analyze scents far better than even the most advanced scientific instruments, and they can pick up scents from over 10 miles away, in the right conditions. A highly developed sense of smell is also directly linked to a highly developed understanding of language and communication.

In the wild, dogs communicate effectively with other members of their pack, and domestic dogs easily understand the intentions of the people they live with. They can literally smell the negative intentions of others, in the same way that they can sniff out clues at a crime scene or track people and animals across long distances. The subtle characteristics of a person's body odor betrays their emotional state and their intentions. This can be seen when dogs bark at criminals and dangerous people, but they do not bark at the elderly or children. Dogs are also able to smell changes in a person's physiology and alert them to potentially dangerous health risks.

Dogs rely heavily on their highly acute aural senses. They can differentiate, identify, and navigate the outside world with precision by using their sensitive ears. Dogs have ears that are directional, repositioning themselves to better receive frequencies. They hear sounds four times further than a human being with an equal amount of clarity. They are also able to perceive frequencies that are far above the maximum range of human beings. Dog whistles produce a sound that is high enough in frequency that human beings cannot perceive it, however, dogs are still able to hear it quite clearly. Dogs are also able to sense earthquakes, and act restless moments before they occur, because of the low frequencies that are produced by the fracturing fault lines.

Emotionally Sensitivity

While some canines prefer to remain solitary, most dogs are comfortable forming close bonds, and they enjoy the company of others. The close bonds that are formed in a pack, or a family, become integral parts of a dog's life and motivates many of their actions. Dogs greet one another enthusiastically and a with genuine curiosity. They immediately sniff the sensitive areas of others upon meeting, which provides them with a wealth of information about their health and temperament. The health, temperament, and strength of individuals in a pack helps to determine the leader of the pack, as well as the times when it is necessary for adolescent canines to leave the pack and begin to form a pack of their own.

Even the strict hierarchy that exists within pack helps the individuals to understand their unique role and to create a sense of stability and harmony. When dogs are displeased, they are quick to express their frustration and figure out the issue. Dogs can wag their tails, bark, stare, and move in an anxious, anticipatory way to express their emotions to others, and they quickly let others know how they feel. Their ability to address their emotions, especially anger and frustration, proportionally builds a sense of trust between the members of the pack, and allows them to rely upon each other in dangerous situations.

The Ferocity of Dogs

Canines, and especially wolves, are courageous, fierce, formidable animals. Dogs have a strong, stocky build that allows them to be powerful without being overly vulnerable. They attack with their long, sharp teeth and powerful jaws, keeping the rest of their body low and protected. Wolf packs are extremely skillful and intelligent hunters. Their expert tactics and utilization of the landscape allow them to capture even the most intelligent prey. In nature, wolves are the part of the animal kingdom that polices human beings. Wolves patrol their vast territories in a manner that is similar to the ways that police patrol their neighborhoods, searching for other large predators that may compete for food.

In Yellowstone national park, the wolves that patrolled that area were wiped out by human beings, mainly ranchers that were having their livestock killed. It was quickly noticed that the absence of the wolves was causing a break down in the harmonious balance of the park's ecosystem. In 1995, wolves were reintroduced to the area to restore balance, and they immediately flourished, almost too much. They have since been radio collared so that their movements can be anticipated and they can be scared away instead of being killed.[10] In the wilderness, wolves often attack human beings that have bad intentions or who act in ways that are not harmonious to nature. On the other hand, wolves simply observe people who act harmoniously and respect the laws of nature, allowing them to remain undisturbed. When a wolf finds a human baby alone in the wilderness, it is often compelled to raise it as one of its own rather than attack it as prey.

For centuries, Tibetans have been known for raising many large, powerful dogs. The Tibetan mastiff is perhaps the most large, powerful, and aggressive breed of dog on earth. They can hear extremely well, and they have a thick coat that keeps them warm in the cold Himalayas and protected during combat. They were originally bred to be sheepdogs, to protect the sheep from wolves and other predators in the mountains. A single Tibetan mastiff can fight off a pack of up to ten wolves when they are trained and raised in the proper manner.

Cultural and Spiritual Concepts

The Spirituality of Dogs

Dogs are loyal and auspicious creatures. Both dogs and cats represent money, but they do so in different ways. Cats represent affluence and luxury and they are easy to maintain as pets. Cats enjoy luxurious living and they are kind to their owners in that they are independent and do not require large amounts of energy and attention. Dogs, on the other hand, represent wealth gained through diligence, cooperation, and partnership, which provides a more solid foundation. However, to achieve this, dogs require attention, communication, loyalty and sincerity. The crucial difference is that if the money and wealth are lost, a dog will not leave your side, but a cat will.

Dogs and wolves worship the moon by howling at it, expressing their feelings to nature when the moon is full. There is a saying in Daoism, that says we should "Look to the heavens and respond to the moon." Dogs represent the messages from heaven because they communicate with the moon and stars regularly. Dogs and wolves are masters of utilizing lunar energy, which has been a

---

[10] "Yellowstone" by BBC Natural History Unit (2009). www.dailymotion.com/video/x6xrez7

major factor in the development of their loyal, caring nature. When a baby needs help, it instinctively knows to cry out for its mother, and when dogs need help, they instinctively know to howl at the moon, the mother of nature.

The moon is the mother of all living beings on earth, and whenever our emotions are troubled or we need divine assistance, pouring our hearts out to the moon will bring the relief and blessings that we need. According to the *Yijing*, the moon is the heavenly mother of all living beings, and dogs are the mother of human beings. If you have a pet dog, then it is likely that this dog's spirit used to be your mother, or a close sibling, in a past life. This explains the loyal, self-sacrificing nature of dogs, especially toward human beings. Dogs really are man's best friend. In Daoism, the dog's level of friendliness and loyalty embodies "full responsibility", whereas the friendliness level of all of the other animals is only equal to "half responsibility."

Changing Fate

Dogs represent fortune and luck. While cats represent money, dogs represent fortune. These two categories are similar, but they are distinct. The energy of fortune that dogs provide means that while individual circumstances may seem to be unpleasant and dire on the surface, the overall direction of events is leading to place where happiness and security are solid and long lasting. There are many wealthy people who care deeply for their dogs, and much less with house cats. The energy of "old money," or stable, durable wealth is the type of *qi* that dogs represent.

According to the *Yijing*, keeping one dog is good, but keeping two dogs can be problematic. Keeping only two dogs may lead to sadness and crying for the people who inhabit that environment. Keeping either three or four dogs provides the best energy. The energy of three or four dogs transforms the pet owner into a highly influential person, and their children will naturally do well in their studies. The dog is a natural leader, and is often considered to be the president of the animal world. Dogs are dominant, responsible and territorial creatures that can delegate tasks to others in their pack, and they have an energy that is conducive to self-healing and developing confidence.

People Who Embody the Dog

Dogs are famously loyal, faithful, reliable, honorable. People born during dog years take their responsibilities seriously. They innately understand the importance of acting appropriately at the right moment, and they dedicate themselves to their tasks to the point of self-sacrifice. Dogs are naturally kind, friendly, and happy to serve others, however, they can also be stubborn and headstrong at times. Dog people often fight to defend the rights of others, and have no problem speaking their mind when they feel it to be necessary. Dogs are masters of rallying people to their cause and handling the dynamics of leading a team. They are natural born leaders and guardians of the people. People born during these years are often strong communicators that articulate their ideals well, however, they sometimes come across as harsh and aggressive.

Dogs are loyal and trustworthy, but they also understand the value and the inherent vulnerability in these qualities. This means that dog people are cautious, territorial, and alert to changing circumstances. Dog people spend much of their time going over the various aspects of their lives, searching for any weaknesses that need to be addressed. Dog people feel the best when they can enjoy the simple pleasures in life with the firm understanding that their home, family, and resources are safe and secure. Reassurance, and simply being able to vent their frustrations with trusted friends and family, can help dog people to calm down and avoid excessive worrying.

Dog people do not enjoy changing their minds once they have decided on a course of action. They are firm believers in following through on every task that is taken on, and they often become experts in their chosen field because they prefer specializing, rather than diversifying. Dogs often rely solely on information that is trustworthy and proven, and they do their best to avoid abstract or experimental methods. Dog people usually become wise, clever, and intuitive in a way that is practical and grounded.

In their career, dogs can be extremely successful, especially when they feel motivated by a sense of purpose and meaning. Canines in the world today perform many tasks, and they fulfill their duties with specialized expertise and passion. Dog people can be great scientists, politicians, educators, social workers, doctors, healers, military leaders, lawyers, or judges. With their great leadership capabilities and their dutiful nature, dogs quickly rise to positions of authority in whichever field they choose. In addition to their sense of honor and reliability, they are also intuitive and nurturing, which allows them to have a great sense of artistic style and an eye for design. Dogs can be wonderful painters, architects, musicians, and designers of all types. Dogs can easily inspire passion, sincerity, and a sense of honor with their words, actions, and anything that they create.

Dogs can be quite good with their personal finances, and over time they can develop significant wealth. With their sense of drive and duty, they quickly become leaders in their field, which is often accompanied by generous compensation. Also, dogs are not overly indulgent, and do not often feel the need to overspend. They like to purchase quality items, often for the home, and provide for their loved ones, and anything that is left over, simply adds to their sense of security. Dogs enjoy the feeling of having money set aside for a rainy day, more than the enjoyment of spending it lavishly.

Dogs love to socialize with others, and they make wonderful hosts. Dogs love to gather people together to build relationships and trust, and during a party they can be found making rounds and catering to the guests. They love to chat, and they get a great sense of fulfillment from a deep, genuine conversation.

People born during dog years light up around others, and enjoy having a partner to help channel their abundant energy.

When it comes to relationships, dogs are passionate and loyal partners. They take their time choosing a partner, and they prefer to get to know a person deeply before letting them into their life. Dogs enjoy socializing and engaging in conversation; however, it takes a great deal of successful, trustworthy interaction to be allowed into their heart. Once a dog person trusts their partner and lets them into their heart, their faithfulness and loyalty will be nearly inexhaustible. When it comes to family in general, dogs are extremely caring, protective, and nurturing, however, sometimes they can be prone to worry and anxiety. Dogs enjoy spending time at home with their loved ones, and they are often caring and attentive with everyone in their family. Dog people have a magnificent ability to make everyone feel loved and cared for in a special way without playing favorites.

External Zodiac
Butterfly

The butterfly is the outer animal of the dog category, and like the dog, the butterfly is gentle, animated, and vibrant. Dogs and butterflies represent an opposite but complimentary pairing of energies. When a dog sees a butterfly floating around, it will often chase it and try to catch it, but it rarely succeeds. Butterflies represent a unique and graceful form of energy that is gentle, profound, and difficult to predict. While dogs are animated and excited, as if they are overflowing with energy, butterflies are active while remaining empty, calm, and peaceful.

Butterflies represent carefree joy and happiness, while the dog represents concern for others and the peace that comes from security. Butterflies exemplify the virtue of calmly enjoying the present moment, and the process of transformation. Some species of butterfly are so short lived, that they do not even possess the anatomy that would allow them to eat; they simply enjoy their existence, search for a mate, and lay their eggs. Even with this short life span, butterflies do not rush; they simply enjoy the journey of life and flutter toward their destination. Dogs spend much of their time worrying about future events and the quality of their home and family life, and yet, when they get in touch with their inner nature, they can appreciate the present moment with the same grace and freedom as a butterfly.

Qi

Butterflies are filled with the energy of trees, flowers, and fresh grass. By touching flowers and coming into contact with the grass, we can greatly benefit our overall health and emotions. Butterflies taste the plants they land on with small sensors that are located on their feet, and for human beings, walking on fresh grass with bare feet is beneficial for health, especially for dog people. Dogs love going to the park to roll around and scrap their paws in the fresh grass, and this is a clear example of methods that Daoists use to gather grass *qi*. By walking barefoot on the grass, even for a few minutes, negative ions are removed from the body, and unhealthy *qi* is channeled into the earth where it can be purified and recycled.

Butterflies are sensitive to scent, and they find both flowers and their mates by following scent trails through the air. Similarly, by taking the time to smell the flowers, we can also gather the *qi* of these beautiful plants and benefit our own health. Smelling flowers helps to fortify health, increase longevity, and develop the sense of intuition. It also helps us to develop strong bonds with nature, as well as the people and ideals that mean the most to us.

Butterflies teach us the proper way of getting in touch with nature and learning from the environment. Butterflies take only what they need and spend the rest of their time actively following their bliss. By getting in touch with nature, we are also able to get in touch with what is truly meaningful and fulfilling in life, allowing us to know what is trustworthy and worth defending.

Special Abilities and Traits

Butterflies are perhaps known best for their ability to completely transform themselves from an earth-bound caterpillar, to an airborne butterfly. The butterfly demonstrates the magnificent results that can be achieved when we are willing to adapt and face our challenges with dispassion, honesty, and resilience. In the insect world, there are three types of growth patterns that are used to reach adulthood.

> Primitive insects, such as silverfish, hatch out as small-scale replicas of their parents. from the time it leaves the egg until death, the insect is practically the same except for the fact that it slowly grows larger as it gets older. The second growth pattern is called incomplete metamorphosis, where a special stage occurs between the emergence from the egg and the formation of the adult. The nymph emerges from the egg as a creature that is similar to the adult, but with certain important differences. In winged insects, for example, the nymphs are wingless. It is only in their final molt that they emerge as fully adult insect. The final form of insect growth pattern is known as complete metamorphosis, and is the pattern used by the butterfly. In complete metamorphosis, the larvae that emerges from the egg is markedly different from the adult, often living in different environments and having different habitats. (Farb 1962, 57)

By having the ability to completely metamorphosize, the butterfly represents the ability to use frustration and difficultly to fuel determination, and transform negative circumstances into beneficial ones. Butterflies have the ability to acutely understand their position in life. They understand that like themselves, life is fragile and it is always important to understand where we are in regards to the processes and stages of our life. By recognizing their situation in life with such clarity, butterflies are able to put their worries aside and enjoy the simple pleasures that life offers.

> Butterflies and other insects that go through complete metamorphosis are unique in that while they are in the egg, they develop two separate types of cells within their body, one type for their larval stage, and one for their adult stage. The larval cells do not reproduce, they only grow larger as the larva, or caterpillar, eats, while the adult cells remain dormant. In the pupa stage, the adult cells become active and consume the dying larval cells as the anatomy is re-formed. All of this is done by the secretion of hormones within the insect's body. (Farb 1962, 58-9)

Butterflies understand their purpose and direction in life with such clarity because they pay close attention to their inner subjective experience. Butterflies accomplish the incredible feat of transformation without the use of an advanced intellect or logic, but simply by following an intuitive subjective experience. Similarly, by listening to our intuition, we can understand the intentions of others and the appropriateness of our own actions more deeply.

Cultural and Spiritual Concepts

Butterflies and caterpillars are active and purposeful, while remaining patient and graceful. Caterpillars begin eating leaves and foliage from the moment that they emerge from the egg., and while they rarely take a break, they never seem to move in a frantic manner or be in a rush. When they understand that it is time to move on from their current stage of life, they immediately find a quiet place to begin their transformation. Once they have completed their metamorphosis they emerge as a beautiful butterfly and carry on with life's next phase.

The butterfly's ability to know itself allows it to take advantage of the opportunities in the present moment without hesitation or guilt, and to let them go just as easily when the proper time comes. By acknowledging our present stage in life and living it to the fullest, we build a solid foundation for our future growth, and a deeper self-knowledge that allows us to transform with grace and dignity. Butterflies know when it is time to seek solitude and work diligently on the self, and when it is time, to share the experience of life with others. This creates a state where every moment can be enjoyed to its fullest without being clouded by memories of the past or visions of the future.

Butterflies can be found in nearly all of the colors of the rainbow. Their wings are wonderful examples of nature's beauty, and their colors are only matched by the flowers that they drink from. Butterflies are active during the daytime, and utilize the healing warmth of the sun to keep their fragile bodies active and limber. They demonstrate the healing power of joy, color, nature, pleasant fragrances, and effortless movement. By following the example of butterflies and enjoying the simple pleasures of nature, especially in our adult years with the wisdom of experience, we can support our health, increase our longevity, and be reminded of the qualities of genuine happiness.

Butterflies are masters of transformation, and they emerge as a completely new being after they have completed their metamorphosis. As human beings, we can go through a similar process if we choose. Butterflies completely reform themselves not by changing from the outside-in, but from the inside-out. By exploring our subjective experience, we can discover the ideas and patterns that have acted as the basis for our behaviors and outlook. These ideas and patterns, once discovered, can be remodeled, healed, and reincorporated into our identity when we are introspective.

Mastering the power of transformation requires effort and handling stress at times, but even a few small successes at this deep level of our being can produce magnificent changes in the everyday experience of life. Success, just like butterflies, cannot be captured by chasing and grasping but by developing magnetism and attraction. Butterflies may seem small and fragile, but they are masters of courage, humility, and patience.

Quotes from Famous Dogs

To improve is to change, to be perfect is to change often.
- Winston Churchill

Peace begins with a smile.
- Mother Teresa

Listen; you'll never learn anything by talking. The measure of an intelligent person is the ability to change his mind.
- Kelly Johnson

Every moment of one's existence, one is growing into more or retreating into less.
- Norman Mailer

When one man, for whatever reason, has the opportunity to lead an extraordinary life, he has no right to keep it to himself.
- Jacques Yves Cousteau

Reason is the natural order of truth, but imagination is the organ of meaning.
- C.S. Lewis

The greatest education in the world is watching the masters at work.
- Michael Jackson

If you accept your limitations, you go beyond them.
- Brendan Behan

If you haven't cried, your eyes can't be beautiful.
- Sophia Loren

All that counts in life is intention.
- Andrea Bocelli

We are what we pretend to be, so we must be careful what we pretend to be.
- Kurt Vonnegut

Desire success, court failure.
- Alan Rickman

12

Pig

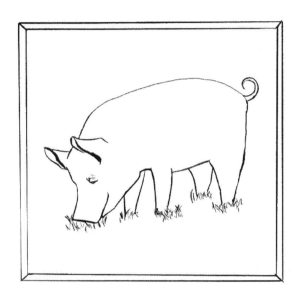

Wood Pig
4th February 1935 to 23rd January 1936

Fire Pig
22nd January 1947 to 9th February 1948

Earth Pig
8th February 1959 to 27th January 1960

Metal Pig
27th January 1971 to 14th February 1972

Water Pig
13th February 1983 to 1st February 1984

Wood Pig
31st January 1995 to 18th February 1996

Fire Pig
18th February 2007 to 6th February 2008

Earth Pig
5th February 2019 to 24th January 2020

Metal Pig
23rd January 2031 to 10 February 2032

Water Pig
10th February 2043 to 30th January 2044

Wood Pig
28th January 2055 to 15th February 2056

Fire Pig
14th February 2067 to 3rd February 2068

Pig

The pig category of the zodiac contains all the members of the suidae family, including hogs, warthogs, boars, babirusas, and also peccaries. Pigs are gregarious, kind, optimistic, easy-going, cheerful, contented, trusting, honest, straightforward, and reliable. They are intelligent and adaptable animals, characterized by a round, barrel-shaped body, slender legs, a thin, curly tail, prominent snout, tusks, a short neck, and a large head. Male pigs are generally solitary for most of the year but will join a family group, called a sounder, that consists of a sow and her piglets during mating season. Peccaries, which are usually a bit smaller than most other pigs, travel in large sounders of up to fifteen members (Burnie and Wilson 2001, 232).

The snout is formed almost entirely from cartilage and is used to dig and push earth while foraging. It is unique to pigs and helps to focus and enhance their olfactory senses. Their tusks are formed from their lower, and sometimes their upper, canine teeth which continue to grow larger until they protrude from the mouth. The tusks are used by the males for defense against predators and also competing with other males for social status and for mating privileges. Female sows have much smaller canines and sometimes lack canines altogether. All pigs have thick skin, but while some species have long, coarse, bristly hair others are almost completely hairless. Pigs also have cloven feet which provide increased balance on uneven terrain and padded "wrists" which they use to kneel down while resting or grazing (Burnie and Wilson 2001, 232).

Pigs mainly inhabit grasslands, marshes, rain forests, savannas, and forested areas and although they are originally from Africa and Eurasia, they have been successfully introduced to many other areas including Australia and the Americas. Pigs usually remain near sources of water mainly because their food sources are located near water and also because they often roll around in water and mud to reduce their body temperature and protect themselves from parasites (Burnie and Wilson 2001, 232).

Pigs are omnivorous and they are not picky eaters. Their diet consists mainly of plant leaves, roots, grasses, fruits, and vegetables, however, they also feed on insects, fungus, rodents, and small reptiles. Pigs have a reputation for gluttony, however, even though they often require a lot of calories to maintain their size and metabolism, they rarely overeat (Burnie and Wilson 2001, 232).

Pigs do not exhibit fear in the face of danger and readily defend themselves against almost any predator. There are two distinct fighting styles that pigs employ; lateral, and head-to head. Pigs with long narrow heads and small tusks such as wild boars fight using the lateral method where they approach each other from the side and slash at their opponent's shoulders and ribs. The head-to-head method is employed by pigs with broad heads and large tusks such as warthogs and involves a face-to-face conflict where the opponents attempt to unbalance one another and knock them to the ground. The lateral fighting method is far more damaging than the head-to-head method because the sides of a pig are far more vulnerable than their heads (Burnie and Wilson 2001, 232).

In nature, male boars remain solitary until mating season begins in November when they join a sow. Males announce their readiness to mate by marking the landscape with urine and saliva which attracts females, and potentially rival males. If a rival male appears, the two will battle for dominance and mating privileges. Domesticated pigs on the other hand often be monogamous and mate for life. After a pregnancy of about 115 days sows give birth to a litter of between approximately ten to twenty piglets. Pigs are the only hoofed mammals that produce litters rather than one or two young (Burnie and Wilson 2001, 232-33). [1]

Calendar

The pig is the twelfth animal of the zodiac. It is associated with the tenth month of the Chinese lunar calendar that lasts from approximately November 7th to December 7th in the Gregorian calendar, and to the two-hour period between 9 pm and 11 pm. This is the beginning of winter; the time of storing and saving resources for when conditions become more favorable and when animals rest. Pigs represent this time of year because they like to sleep a lot and they focus on storing their resources in the form of calories and body weight. It is important to recuperate and protect the body's yin energy at this time of year by consuming nutritious, warm foods and beverages. This is also a time when staying warm an avoiding strenuous exercise is essential to keep the body healthy.

In pig years, most governments are disorganized, vulnerable, and scrambling to establish a predictable, reliable order. On the other hand, most families and romantic partnerships thrive and develop into safe and valuable relationships. Therefore, the year of the pig is a good time for actively developing romance and for alleviating relationship pressures. These are also good years for attracting money in general and for growing a business by developing the company's image and customer relations. The pig's happy-go-lucky nature is inviting to both investors and consumers. Pigs don't mind getting dirty, and during pig years many people will not mind getting their hands dirty and putting in the necessary effort to achieve their goals. This is a year the requires patience and alertness because there are often many ups and downs, as well as periods of rest followed by moments of intense effort and awareness.

Pigs are highly intelligent and intuitive creatures and in the year of the pig many discoveries are made and many technologies are developed. Pig years often see the arrival of breakthrough technologies that allow for rapid development and new applications. In 1923, the development of both the portable radio and the first television components, rapid global mass communication was beginning

---

[1] "Developmental Milestones During Pig Gestation," by Elizabeth Hines (2021). extension. psu.edu/developmental-milestones-during-pig-gestation

to be possible for the first time.[2][3] In 1947, Bell Laboratories developed the first solid state transistor. The transistor was arguably the most important invention of the twentieth century as it replaced the use of vacuum tubes in electronic circuits and allowed for the prolific development of numerous new possibilities with electronic devices.[4]

In pig years, the economy usually does well as many families and individuals are in a lavish spending mood. However, with confusion and delays in both government and many businesses many people also decide to hold their funds or invest in safe options. Pig years are times when many people spend money without thinking while others take advantage of this opportunity to get ahead by becoming more frugal. In 1947, after the great depression gave way to the thriving war-time economy the International Monetary fund began its operations to oversee and manage the interactions between the world's economies.[5]

During pig years people seek out new ways of connecting and communicating with others. When this sentiment combines with a focus on money and luxury, many decide to spend their money on unique and one-of-a-kind items that will allow them to stand out. Major distributing and marketing companies like FedEx and eBay have been founded during these years allowing people to buy and sell items from almost anywhere on the planet quickly and efficiently.

The governmental confusion and general uncertainty of these years often results in the established powers being tested in a number of ways. This could result in coup attempts, civil unrest, and the secession of lands to form independent nations. In 1863, the American Civil War was at its height as the confederate states attempted to secede from the nation resulting in an unforeseeable future for the government. On the first of the year, the emancipation proclamation was issued by president Abraham Lincoln and in the summer, the war's most important battle was fought in the forests and grasslands of Gettysburg, Pennsylvania. This battle marked a turning point of the war and if it had been lost then the American government would have been in great jeopardy.[6]

Years later in 1923, Germany would begin to see the first of many upheavals that would lead to World War II when Adolf Hitler attempted to overthrow the government in the Munich "Beer Hall Putsch."[7] Many countries have also

---

[2] "Edwin Armstrong," by PBS Editors (2004). www.pbs.org/wgbh/theymadeamerica/who made/armstrong_hi.html

[3] "Iconoscope – 1923," by MagLab Editors (2014). www.nationalmaglab.org/education/magnet-academy/history-of-electricity-magnetism/museum/iconoscope

[4] "1947: Invention of the Point-Contact Transistor," by Computer History Museum (n.d.). www.computerhistory.org/siliconengine/invention-of-the-point-contact-transistor

[5] "The IMF in History," by The International Monetary Fund (2021). www.imf.org/external/np/exr/chron/chron.asp

[6] "Gettysburg," by American Battlefield Trust (n.d.). www.battlefields.org/learn/civil-war/battles/gettysburg

[7] "Beer Hall Putsch," by History.com Editors (2009). www.history.com/topics/germany/beer-hall-putsch

achieved their independence amongst the confusion and mismanagement of various governments. India and Pakistan achieved their independence, and the state of Israel was formulated, in the year of the pig, just to name a few, and these achievements all contributed to notable levels of confusion, controversy, and civil unrest.

In the year of the pig, the earth itself is often restless and quite active. These years often produces shorter summers and longer winters. Winter and cold conditions can become particularly severe, problematic, and dangerous. In 1899, an extremely cold winter led to the "Great Blizzard" or "Snow King" event that swept across the continental United States. In that year, temperatures reached below zero as far south as Tallahassee, Florida and ice floes were reported to be moving out of the Mississippi river and into the Gulf of Mexico.[8]

Earthquakes and other geological and environmental phenomenon are also quite common during pig years and this is being exacerbated by global climate change. Needless to say, pig years are times when it is helpful to prepare for emergency situations and events that may affect entire communities. Pig years are also times when many people are hyper-emotional, for better or worse, which contributes to the confusion and makes preparing for these types of events difficult. Pig years are times when a little extra effort, awareness, and caution will go a long way.

While pigs are highly intelligent creatures, they can sometimes be naive as well; overlooking critical details. Pig years are times when distractions are abundant and minor details become crucial to success. These are times when the big picture is the focus and the details of the past twelve years of the zodiac are being scrutinized and reviewed to inform the decisions of the future. This means that in the year of the pig the likelihood of accidents and mistakes is increased. In the pig year of 2019, a large fire began moving through the Notre Dame Cathedral in Paris threatening numerous priceless works of art. Thankfully, the fire was extinguished before the entire building was overtaken by flames and many works of art were removed before they were damaged. It is thought that the cause of the fire was accidental and was possibly linked to the restoration work that was taking place and/or faulty electrical systems.[9]

Pigs are the most happy-go-lucky animal of the zodiac and they do not need a reason to be joyful. Unfortunately, this also means that some people become envious and seek to take advantage of others during pig years, leading to a potential increase in violence and fearfulness. The most notable such event would be the start of the Cold War in 1947 which marked the beginning of decades of

---

[8] "'Snow King' Blizzard, Arctic Outbreak Still Unmatched 123 Years Later," by Brian Lada (2022). www.accuweather.com/en/winter-weather/the-snow-king-blizzard-great-arctic-outbreak-of-1899/1140132

[9] "Notre Dame Fire: New Cause Investigated as 2024 Service Date Confirmed," by Hannah Thompson (2021). www.connexionfrance.com/article/French-news/Notre-Dame-fire-New-cause-investigated-as-2024-service-date-confirmed-on-second-anniversary-of-fire

fear and posturing by the United States and the Soviet Union.[10] Pig years are times when enjoyment and prosperity are abundant, but also when awareness, precaution, and preparedness are required. Pigs are happy-go-lucky partly because they have a 'thick skin', literally and figuratively. During these years we should be courageous and alert, yet this also means that extra effort is required to remain vigilant against becoming too calloused, angry, or naïve by resting and conserving resources.

In entertainment, pig years often see numerous developments in art, film, music, and sports. Pigs are creatures that truly appreciate enjoyment and entertainment, making this an ideal time for both the creation, and appreciation, of all types of artistic endeavors. Anything that catches the eye will be considered valuable and special during pig years. This is a time when standing out from the crowd or going your own way is usually considered to be a good thing. This is also assisted by the prevailing 'thick skin' attitude during pig years which renders nearly all forms of criticism ineffective. This was exemplified in 1947 when Jackie Robinson became the first African American baseball player to compete in the major leagues which had been segregated for more than fifty years.[11] He went on to have a successful career and changed America by focusing on enjoying the game that he loved while remaining unfazed by the criticism of others.

Qi

The time of the day that relates to the pig is 9 pm to 11 pm, matching the triple burner meridian. This is the time when many people are preparing to go to bed and rest. This is also a time when the body's digestive system is at its least active and detoxifying itself, therefore this is not a good time to eat. On the other hand, this is a great time for memory, studying, creativity, and brain function. This is when the spirit becomes highly energized and prominent making it a great time for mental activities and meditation. This is also a time when the body's immune system is producing a higher level of white blood cells while the body's temperature is reduced.

The pig category of the zodiac is associated with the triple burner organ. The triple burner is an organ that is not found in western medicine. Western science has attempted to link the function of the triple burner to the body's metabolic function, however, to this day there is still no direct translation or reference to the triple burner in western medicine. In traditional Chinese medicine, the triple burner is described as a large bowel that contains all of the body's

---

[10] "Cold War," by The Editors of Encyclopedia Britannica (1998). www.britannica.com/event/Cold-War

[11] "Jackie Robinson Becomes First African American Player in Major League Baseball," by (2009). www.history.com/this-day-in-history/jackie-robinson-breaks-color-barrier

internal organs, however, in reality this organ and its three sections exist as an energetic field within the body that surrounds the vital organs.

The triple burner consists of the upper, middle, and lower burners each with its own functions. The upper burner is the area above the diaphragm that contains the lungs and the heart, the middle burner is the area between the diaphragm and the naval that contains the stomach, spleen, and pancreas, and the lower burner is the area below the naval that contains the liver, the kidneys, the urinary bladder, and the intestines. The triple burner uses the body's "true fire" to provide the necessary energy for many of the body's functions. The energy of this organ is used to regulate the water metabolism of the body and assist in the process of digestion by separating the clear *qi* from the turbid *qi*. This is similar to the way that liquids are purified by adding heat to them to separate impurities.

The triple burner's main function is to regulate and process the body's *qi* energy. The lower burner uses the body's "fire" to heat the *jing* (original essence), which is housed in the kidneys, to transform it into *qi* that then rises into the middle burner. The middle burner uses *qi* to nourish the body and simultaneously refines it further into *shen* (spirit) that then rises into the upper burner. The upper burner then disperses the rarefied *shen* energy throughout the body in manner that resembles a vapor or mist.

When the triple burner is functioning optimally it leads to spiritual development. On a mental/emotional level the triple burner helps us to regulate our relationships with others, attracting the relationships that we need into our life and allowing us to let go of the relationships that are no longer serving us. This is because interacting with the outside world in any way is an expression of qi. When the triple burner is functioning optimally and the mind and emotions are calm, the result is a natural state of happiness and peace.

The ghost point that is associated with the pig is known as Ghost's Seal (*guifeng*); it matches the point Sea Spring (*haiquan*, M-HN-37) in the acupuncture system (Johnson 2014, 606). This point is located in the center of the frenulum under the tongue. It is used to treat facial paralysis, lethargy, inflammation, swelling and/or pain in the tongue, as well as mental conditions such as stroke and epilepsy (Deadman et al. 2007, 571). In the year of the pig many people suffer from increased inflammation. Chronic inflammation can lead to numerous health issues such as pain, stiffness, fullness, swelling, fatigue, and cancer. The *haiquan* point is effective at reducing the effects of inflammation by relaxing the blood vessels, regulating the nervous system, and facilitating the connection between the heart and the brain.

Special Abilities and Traits

Happiness and Intelligence

Pigs are extremely intelligent creatures that are capable of learning many of life's greatest lessons and while many other highly intelligent creatures are serious, pigs maintain a strong sense of happiness and well-being. A pig's essence is housed in its head and expressed through its eyes. The fact that such a potent form of energy is located in the head with the brain is a sign of the pig's powerful mental energy. Pigs outperform young children between the ages of three and four years old in various cognition tests. This means that pigs are more intelligent than nearly all domestic animals. This is partly due to the pig's incredible memory capacity. Pigs, like dogs and oxen, have an incredible memory capacity and sense of direction. A number of these animals have been known to have traveled incredible distances on their own to return home after being lost. Pigs are smart enough to use tools and they are able to actively deceive other pigs in order to lead them away from their food stores.

The pig lives a life that is peaceful and calm; it has no natural enemies, and therefore it is not envious of any other animals. While many creatures are startled and uncomfortable around human beings, pigs are relaxed and even excited to be in the presence of humans. Pigs understand the intentions and motivations of human beings to a greater degree than dogs. Pigs instantly become unsettled in the presence of people who are dangerous or have bad intentions.

In Daoism, the fact that pigs are often observed nodding their heads both up and down and left to right directions is seen as a way of attempting to communicate with others. Pigs respond both affirmatively and negatively as needed to try and please everyone. Daoists say that one's personality determines their destiny; and, because pigs have such bright personalities, they also have the ability to mediate and defuse many conflicts. The true intention of any creature can be observed in the quality of their gaze. This is especially true for pigs whose essence resides in the head and eyes, and yet, the eyes of a pig are almost always happy and friendly. Therefore, pigs truly have a generous, friendly, and forthcoming heart.

Out of all of the living creatures, Daoists consider the pig to exhibit perhaps the best lesson of all; allowing yourself to be fooled. While so many human beings strive to understand things, the pig wants to be fooled so that they can appreciate the experience of life. Similarly, the vast audiences spend hours watching their favorite shows hoping to enter a fantasy temporarily for the entertainment, happiness, and inspiration that it provides. Like other highly intelligent animals, such as oxen and sheep, pigs understand the will of heaven which allows them to know many things in advance, including when the end of their life is approaching. Yet even with the knowledge of their impending death, pigs remain calm, happy, and carefree, thinking to themselves "the sooner I die, the sooner that I will be reborn." Throughout their lives, pigs accept their fate with grace and even after their death their eyes still remain friendly.

The Healing Qualities of Pigs

Wild pigs and boars, which have natural *qi* energy, can live long lives and rarely get sick. Pigs eat a wide variety of foods, and therefore, they are naturally attracted to any fruits, plants, or grasses that are thriving and in season. Pigs eat meat when the opportunity presents itself, but due to the fact that they are not naturally predatory animals they only eat meat opportunistically. Since pigs are generally happy most of the time, they rarely develop any conditions that would result from stress, such as hypertension. Finally, while wild pigs are not lazy, they conserve their energy if they can manage it, which preserves their body's function.

In addition to their behavior, the constitution of pigs has contributed greatly to the advancement of modern medicine as well. The tissues and organs of pigs are similar to that of human beings; so much so, that there have been many successful medical transplants of pig tissues into human beings. "Pig skin is able to be grafted onto patients that suffer from severe burns or open wounds producing numerous beneficial results including lower rates of infection, decreased healing time, and more complete healing."[12] There are even numerous cases of pig hearts and other organs being transplanted into human beings without developing subsequent issues or being rejected by the body.

Pigs rarely suffer from inflammation or infection and as a result it is extremely rare for them to develop any type of cancer. Sharks are similar to pigs in that they almost never develop cancer. Eating deep sea fish such as swordfish, tuna, or shark will reduce inflammation and its effects. Proper amounts of exercise and activity also helps to increase circulation and reduce inflammation. Sharks never get cancer because as they swim throughout the water their bodies are in constant motion and they do not stop until they die. This constant motion prevents cancer cells from developing in their tissues. Similarly, the human heart almost never develops cancer because it also continues to function at all times.

Cultural and Spiritual Concepts

Pigs Represent Good Fortune

In China, the pig is a symbol of prosperity and good luck. Pigs remind us that we have all the resources that we need to succeed within ourselves, we simply need to utilize them correctly. Pigs also teach us that we are only as good as the people we surround ourselves with. Pigs are friendly creatures and they represent

---

[12] "Porcine Xenograft Versus Second Intention Healing," by Victoria Sharon (2019). www.clinicaltrials.gov/ct2/show/NCT03931746

the triple burner organ which helps us to manage our personal and social relationships. These relationships provide the energy and opportunities that we need to exercise our power to succeed and prosper. On the other hand, male pigs spend much of their time alone, demonstrating the need for balance between socializing and solitude. By understanding their own needs and wants clearly, pigs demonstrate trust and transparency, which are both fundamental to building lasting relationships.

Pigs even remain calm, yet alert, in the face of disagreements, envy, or aggressive behavior. Therefore, the pig is also symbolic of the importance to maintain a clear view of one's self in the face of the opinions of others. Pigs are often the envy of those around them because of their exuberant satisfaction with the simple pleasures in life and their ability to remain unaffected by critics. However, their genuine warmth and generosity also make it easy for pigs to quickly turn an enemy into a friend.

There is even a famous character/deity in China that is a combination of a man and a pig named Zhu Bajie. This deity is known for his insatiable appetite, both for food and women, and his love of parties and merriment. While he is a powerful, resilient, and capable being, he also gets himself into a lot of trouble by trying to satisfy his desires so often.

> Wu Baolin was once hired to perform a feng shui assessment on a restaurant/bar that was not succeeding. The owners had worked hard to make the business a success and while similar businesses nearby were doing well for themselves, their business was failing and they could not figure out why. When Dr. Wu entered the business, he immediately recognized the issue.
>
> Just inside the entrance was a large statue of Guan Yin Buddha the god of compassion and mercy. This deity was not fond of excessive desires and nearly constant celebration, preferring quiet calm and peacefulness instead. Wu Baolin suggested that the owners remove the statue from the business and replace it with a statue of Zhu Bajie instead to create an environment that was conducive of appetites and celebration. Once the owners did this their business immediately turned around and began to thrive.

The Spirituality of Pigs

Pigs often have a mixed reputation in many cultures around the world. While pigs are seen as creatures of fidelity, fertility, and good fortune, they are also seen as unclean, unscrupulous, gluttonous, cannibalistic, and violent. For instance, Muslims, along with the followers of a number of other religions, are prohibited from eating meat and from engaging with pigs in many ways. There are numerous reasons for this prohibition. The more obvious and practical reasons are that pigs are animals that live in filthy habitats that are often riddled with parasites. Pigs also do not have sweat glands which means that as they consume food without discretion, it is also difficult for them to expel the toxins that their food contains.

This means that pork is often a type of meat that is high in toxins, parasites, and disease. The Spanish influenza epidemic, for example, began when the influenza virus transferred from pigs to human beings.

Some of the more spiritual reasons for the prohibition of pork and contact with pigs relates to various legends and observations. Due to the fact that pigs have only a single tendon on the back of their short neck and their heads are so large compared to the rest of their body, pigs are unable to look upward toward heaven. This is seen in Daoism as a sign that pigs are not a heavenly-oriented creature but an earthly one.

In the *Old Testament*, the fact that pigs have cloven hooves and do not chew cud like ruminant animals means that they are not fit for human consumption. In Islam, there are two legends that describe the reasons that Muslims should not eat pork or handle pigs. The Hui people of China are a group of people who descend mainly from Han Chinese and westerners, often Muslims, who traveled east on the silk road during the Mongolian army's campaign toward Europe. Their culture contains a number of legends and stories that describe various reasons to both respect and avoid pigs. The first legend describes a scene between Allah and his enemy.

> One day Allah was being chased by his enemies when he ran into a pigsty to escape. Once inside, Allah realized that there was no place to hide and decided to hide inside the stomach of one of the pigs. The enemies arrived, they could not find Allah, and quickly gave up their chase. When the episode was over, Allah emerged and in gratitude promised the pig that from that day on, Muslims would not eat pork.

The second legend describes observations of pigs by a village of early Hui people. This legend takes place before the Yuan Dynasty when the Hui still ate pork, which has been a popular type of meat in China for centuries.

> There was once a family of Hui people who owned one sow and three boars. After a happy event, the family decided to host a feast and slaughtered their three boars for the occasion. After the party was over the family began to head home for the evening, but when they arrived, they observed the lonely sow sobbing and kneeling on her front legs three times as a form of worship and prayer before turning around and walking away. The shocked family quickly decided to follow the sow. They tracked her movements all the way up to graves of their ancestors, but when they arrived, there was no sign of the pig and no trace of the pig leaving the area.
>
> The next day, members of the family told their story to the other villagers and the whole group decided to return the tombs of the ancestors to try and find any clues to the pig's whereabouts. When they got to the tombs however, they found no pig, but instead found that the soil around the tomb's entrance had been loosened and scraped away. The people then realized that the sow

must have poured her heart out to the family's ancestors, expressing her sorrow and from that day forward the Hui people and their descendants have refused to eat pork.

Finally, the last story regarding the Hui Muslim's avoidance of pork relates to an event that took place in Xixia (Modern Ningxia province of China) in the early 13th century.

In the early 13th century, a general of the mighty Xixia army was marching his troops near a village when a great flood occurred. The troops who had been marching for a long way without food waited for the flood to subside on high ground. When the flood ended the general sent a few troops into the flooded village to scout for food. When they arrived, they found numerous pigs that had drowned in the flood and the general immediately ordered the men to butcher the animals and begin cooking the pork for the troops.

Unfortunately, as the troops ate the pork, they became ill because the water laden pigs were filled with disease and parasites. The army was stopped in its tracks as the plague swept through the ranks and in a few days the general granted leave to many of his troops to return home and recover from their illness. This had the unintended effect of spreading the plague throughout the empire and soon the disease was taking the lives of many of the Xixia people. The plague and its effects were so widespread the it caused the collapse of the Xixia dynasty and it wasn't long before the land was occupied by nearby countries. This event strongly reinforced the belief of the Hui people who occupied nearby areas that pigs are unclean and unlucky creatures.[13]

While pigs have a mixed reputation among many religious groups, all religions still see pigs as serving a special purpose on the earth, being natural, divinely created creatures. Pigs are considered lucky animals of happiness, abundance, and intelligence by Daoists. The cheerful, carefree nature of pigs is also considered to be one of the best qualities that one can develop.

People Who Embody the Pig

People born in the year of the pig are often cheerful and generous. They work hard to achieve their goals and enjoy the fruits of their labor. Pig people thoroughly understand the hardships and suffering that life entails, as well as the joys of glory and success. This makes it easy for them to relate to others and to help others to achieve an internal balance and carry on through life. The intelligent, relatable, and gregarious nature of Pig types allows them to be very compassionate and provide others with simple, practical solutions.

---

[13] "Why don't Hui people eat Pork: The real reason why Hui people don't eat pork," by One Hundred Thousand Why Editors (2021). www.xuexili.com/why/2542.html

Pigs are wonderful with words. They are articulate, sincere, attentive, gentle, and patient. These qualities allow pigs to put people at ease and to soothe their anxiety and re-frame their negative perceptions. Pig types also prefer to be upfront and frank in difficult situations, rather than dishonest or deceitful. Their honest and caring nature makes pig people trustworthy, loyal, and sincere friends. Wherever pig energy is found it brings about harmony, happiness, and mutual respect.

Pig people love to eat, drink, and be merry and while they rarely seek to harm others intentionally, they can be naive and overlook the consequences of their actions, especially when they are attempting to satisfy their desires. Pigs love to rest and enjoy themselves when the opportunity presents itself, however, when effort is required, pigs are strong and purposeful workers. Pigs often employ the motto "work hard, play hard"; and, they would do well to pay attention to their energy levels so that they don't burnout during these periods.

People born in the year of the pig are often quite successful in their career and work environment. Pigs sharply focus on the task at hand, and once initiated, it is difficult to deter their efforts. Pig people have a reputation for being stubborn and head-strong, however, they are also known to be highly intelligent. While pigs are not easily distracted from their goals, they aren't picky about the ways in which they achieve them. If a pig finds a better way of doing something, it will quickly adopt it.

Pig types are social and they relate well with other people, yet they also enjoy solitude. In their career, Pigs can be productive when working independently and also wonderful at developing business relationships. Pigs would be most successful in a job that would allow them to utilize their industrious, friendly, and forthcoming nature while still allowing them to remain in control of their final goals. Sales, education, culinary arts, psychological therapy, administration, coordination and party planning, performing arts, and writing or journalism are all professional areas where pig people can utilize their natural talents with great success.

Pig people are also extremely intelligent with managing their money and personal finances. The traditional "piggy jar" was shaped like a pig because of its tendency to consume voraciously and not miss a single detail, supporting the idea of saving every penny. Pigs work hard and they quickly master the management of their earnings so that they can enjoy life as much as possible. Pig types are not shy about spending their money, and often buy items on a whim when the mood strikes them. However, their acute intelligence also allows them to perceive the impact that each purchase will have on their overall finances and where their limits lay. Pigs are intelligent investors and they distribute their resources strategically which often earns them a significant amount of wealth. With discipline pig people can quickly create a comfortable nest egg.

Pigs are wonderful socialites and they feel right at home in crowds and parties. Pigs enjoy the pleasures of eating and drinking and they can carry on conversations for long periods of time. Pigs also love hosting parties and catering to their numerous guests. People born in the year of the pig come alive in social settings and genuinely appreciate the opportunity to express themselves with others.

Pig people greatly enjoy relationships and romance and they are sensual and passionate people. In China, the fact that pigs often look behind themselves over their shoulder is symbolic of the pig's attraction to beautiful creatures. Even the pig deity, Zhu Bajie is said to have gotten into trouble for flirting with goddesses and for impregnating a mortal woman. Combined with their cheerful and dedicated nature, the passion of pig people makes them skillful and energetic partners. In family life, pigs seek to provide a comfortable home environment for their loved ones, and they work hard to secure resources for their family's future. Pigs are devoted to their family, and because they are easy-going, they are easy to live with and easy to love.

People born in the year of the pig have a wonderful array of talents and passions they allow them to build happy and fulfilling lives. Their ability to get along with others, their passion for the pleasures of life, and their incredible intelligence and determination allow them to provide for the ones that they love and enjoy the process. While they may be stubborn, and sometimes miss the finer details, they make up for it with their gentle nature and their warm, cheerful personality.

External Zodiac
Spider

Spiders are the outer zodiac animal of the pig category, and while pigs have a manner that is passive, blunt and frank, spiders are active, sensitive and subtle. Spiders are sensitive to the slightest movements and environmental changes. Pigs take a carefree approach to the rhythms and changes of the world relying on their instincts to carry them forward, spiders take a carefully planned approach, selecting the location for their webs with care and managing their food supply. This difference can be attributed to the vastly different anatomies and challenges that these two creatures contend with. While pigs are large, stout, and strong with a thick skin, spiders are delicate, fragile and even brittle. Some larger spiders can even break into pieces if they fall from a significant height.

While spiders and pigs are opposites in many ways, they have a number of similarities as well. Spiders and pigs are both nurturing and caring toward their young for the most part, however, in certain circumstances they quickly turn against their own. In some species of spider, for instance, just after mating, the female will kill and eat the male, and other species specialize in hunting other spiders. Spiders and pigs are caring and generous to their own partners and young, but they both maintain strong boundaries and actively engage threats.

Though they fight in different ways, spiders and pigs can both be ruthlessly aggressive and unforgiving in battle. Pigs also love dirty environments; it often seems that the dirtier pigs get, the happier they become. Similarly, spiders like to build their webs in dark, dirty places where they will not be disturbed by larger creatures and they can go unnoticed by smaller ones. Spiders and pigs are counterparts that help bring about integrity, cheerfulness, and tolerance in the world.

Qi

Spiders are unique creatures that have incredible balance, agility, and coordination. Arachnids have a body that is composed of two segments and four pairs of legs, which is different from insects, that have a body composed of three segments and three pairs of legs. Spiders are also unique in that they spin silk from their abdomens and they have developed numerous ways of utilizing this material to their advantage (Burnie and Wilson 2001, 586). Spiders use their long legs to travel across their webs with grace and accuracy and to orient themselves as they descend from elevated places.

Spiders are cold-blooded creatures that require the heat of the environment to warm their bodies. Different species of spider have adapted to various environmental conditions with some living in humid areas and some living in arid areas. Since they require some heat however, spiders are rarely found in cold climates, such as the arctic. Being cold-blooded, some species of spider have developed the ability to hibernate during the cold months of winter (Burnie and Wilson 2001, 586-89).

Spiders are strictly carnivorous, feeding on other small creatures, mainly insects. Spiders are essential in the ecosystem as they effectively manage the populations of other arachnids and insects. To subdue their prey most spiders have developed venom that can be injected with their fangs. Some larger spiders may catch their prey simply with surprise and physical strength, but most spiders use woven traps to ensnare their prey. Some spiders weave large webs to capture flying prey, others weave spirals and funnels on the ground and in holes to capture prey that walks and crawls. Some species even weave nets that they hold in their legs and cast over their prey as they pass. Like other cold-blooded creatures, spiders have a slow metabolism and can therefore go days and even weeks without eating (Burnie and Wilson 2001, 586-89).

Spiders have fragile bodies composed of a hard exoskeleton on top of their soft tissues. This means that to grow larger a spider must shed its exoskeleton in the molting process. Their hard exoskeleton is susceptible to fracture; therefore, spiders have to be careful to avoid being struck by large objects such as tree branches that are blowing in the wind. Most small spiders can survive falls from high places as they can quickly spin a line of silk to slow their fall, but larger spiders, like tarantulas, rarely survive significant falls.

Just like pigs that also like to inhabit dirty and even filthy environments, spiders often contain numerous parasites, mites, bacteria, viruses, and other diseases. Spiders are often able to continue to function quite well while they are infected with various forms of disease and parasites, but they have little defense against these forms of attack. Ground dwelling spiders are especially prone to infection with parasites, mites, and worms. Still, spiders carry on living their lives as best as possible, making the most of every moment they are afforded.

Special Abilities and Traits

Spider silk is both strong and light, it is stronger than steel, and it has incredible tensile strength. Spider silk is made from proteins that are excreted from the spider's internal glands and connected together into chains in their spinnerets. Spiders can create several different types of silk depending on the purpose that they intend to use it for, some types of silk are dry while others are covered in a sticky substance. Spiders use their silk to weave incredible, intricate webs that serve both offensive and defensive purposes. Spiders use their webs to both catch prey, and as an alert system for approaching predators.

To create a web a spider must lay out a number of structural, guy lines from perched locations such as tree branches or rocks. Once it feels like it has created five to ten adequate support lines in a single plane it will then cut away the additional lines and begin spinning its web within the structure. The spider begins at the center and then moves outward toward the outside edge in a spiral shape attaching silk to each support line as it travels. The support lines of the web are made from silk that is dry and not sticky while the interior web is made from sticky silk (Burnie and Wilson 2001, 586-89).

Many spiders use silk that is not sticky to simply entangle their prey. This has been observed by human beings over millennia and has led to the developments of thread, fishing lines, and rope. Rope traps and harnesses used to capture, and eventually domesticate, animals were developed by human beings after observing the behavior of spiders. The weaving of spider webs then led to the weaving of fishing nets, cloth, and eventually, the invention of the loom. Spider silk, like the flesh of pigs, can be used for numerous purposes in the world. Both of these materials would be specifically useful in the medical field, however, at the present time spider silk cannot be created artificially or organically in great enough quantities for it to be significantly effective. Spider silk could be made into cloth, armor, casts, skin grafts, surgical thread, and many other products with its unique qualities.

Cultural and Spiritual Concepts

The shape of spider webs and nets is reminiscent of eyes, and these things are used to capture. Webs and nets capture prey, while eyes capture images. In China, the spider is often referred to as the "sewing pig" because of the similarities between these two creatures. Just as the essence of a pig is located in its eyes, the essence of a spider is located in its silk webs, which resemble eyes. The power of the gaze is incredibly important and often overlooked. The eyes, like nets, can be used to attract, capture, subdue, and heal others.

Lovers, especially women, use their eyes to capture their intended partners. When two people experience love at first sight, the gaze cannot seem to be broken. The "love at first sight" gaze, seems to say "I see you and you cannot escape." In the animal kingdom, pigs are especially skilled at capturing others with their eyes in this way. Pigs even are able to build relationships with other species because their eyes, and their intentions, are so clear. This technique of capturing is a hallmark of the pig zodiac category and leads to the development of romance and partnership. Webs are light and airy, yet they can still capture prey. Similarly, when a woman's eyes are soft, clear, and bright, they can capture men.

The shape of the web has also been thought to capture thoughts and ideas. This was because over time it was noticed that the presence of a spider web near the place where a person slept often led to a more peaceful and restful sleep. Later it was believed that this occurred because the web could capture the negative thoughts that kept the person awake at night, reducing insomnia. The development of the dream-catcher was based upon the understanding that, like love at first sight, webs and nets can filter our perceptions.

Networking and Communication

The intricacy and unique qualities of spider webs has been fascinating to human beings for thousands of years, and the study of these structures has led to the development of new concepts. Daoists describe the way that language and symbolism was originally developed by human beings after first observing the symbols that were woven into spider webs. The symbols that appeared in webs were interpreted as a form of divination and communication with nature. Similar to dendrochronology, or the study of tree rings, the study of spider webs can lead to an intricate understanding of the subtle patterns that are occurring in nature. The process of representing complex processes and ideas with simple symbols led to the development of language, mathematics, and eventually, to all intellectual disciplines. Even the neurons of the brain are connected to one another in a way that resembles a complex web.

The *Yijing* and the eight trigram symbols, like the early languages of human beings, were derived from the symbols that were observed in the webs of spiders. These symbols were used to understand the nature of all dynamic processes and the wide-ranging effects of subtle of changes. In Daoism, a spider's web, like a tortoise's shell, is said to encompass the whole world. This is known as the "web of heaven" and it forms the network of relationships between all beings and all of nature. In ancient Mediterranean thought, the threads of the spider's web were thought to represent the threads of fate and inevitable destinies that we must face in this life and the next.

Webs and nets represent the networks of relationships that we produce as we carry on through life. In the same way that a spider can feel the subtle vibrations of its web, all living beings can feel the effects of one another's decisions and actions through the web of our relationships and our *qi* energy. The web of heaven covers the entire the entire world; therefore, any event that affects one of us, affects us all in one way or another. Pigs represent the triple burner meridian and this energy is responsible for helping us manage our relationships with others. Together, spiders and pigs represent the importance of our relationships with others as well as to nature itself.

Quotes from Famous Pigs

The greatest strength a man can achieve is gentleness.
- Monty Roberts

Man needs difficulties, they are necessary for health.
- Carl Jung

You cannot do a kindness too soon, for you never know how soon it will be too late.

- Ralph Waldo Emerson

The rivalry is with ourselves. I try to be better than is possible. I fight against myself, not against the other.

- Luciano Pavarotti

Time and money spent in helping men do more for themselves is far better than mere giving.

- Henry Ford

Love yourself first, and everything else falls into place.
- Lucille Ball

I'd rather be optimistic and wrong, than pessimistic and right.
- Elon Musk

To conquer oneself is a greater victory than to conquer thousands in battle.
- Tenzin Gyatso (14th Dalai Llama)

Strength does not come from winning. Your struggles develop your strengths. When you go through hardships and decide not to surrender, that is strength.

- Arnold Schwarzenegger

Death is one moment and life is so many of them.
- Tennessee Williams

Fiction is the truth inside the lie.

- Stephen King

If it's going to come out eventually, better have it come out immediately.
- Henry Kissinger

Bibliography

Aesop. 2003. *Aesop's Fables.* New York: Barnes & Noble Classics.

Allen, David. 2015. *Getting Things Done.* New York: Penguin Publishing Group.

Andrews, Ted. 2007. *Animal Speak: The Spiritual & Magical Powers of Creatures Great and Small.* Woodbury: Llewellyn Publications.

Barash, David P. 1987. *The Hare and the Tortoise: Culture, Biology, and Human Nature.* New York: Penguin Books.

Bear, Sun, et al. 1983. *Sun Bear, The Path of Power.* Spokane: Bear Tribe Publishing.

Bell, F.R. 1959. *The Sense of Taste in Domesticated Animals.* Vet. Rec. 71

Birkhäuser-Oeri, Sibylle. 1988. *The Mother: Archetypal Image in Fairy Tales. Edited by Marie-Louise von Franz. Translated by Michael Mitchell.* Toronto: Inner City Books.

Burnie, David, and Don E. Wilson. 2001. *Animal: Smithsonian Institution.* New York: DK Publishing Inc.

Deadman, Peter, et al. 2007. *A Manual of Acupuncture.* East Sussex: Journal of Chinese Medicine Publications.

Doczi György. 1981. *The Power of Limits: Proportional Harmonies in Nature, Art and Architecture.* Boulder: Shambhala.

Farb, Peter. 1962. *The Insects.* New York: Time-Life Books.

Grunbaum, Mara. 2013. *"Biting Back." Science World Magazine.* Vol. 70 No. 2. pp. 14–17.

Hall, Manly P. 2001. *Secret Teachings of All Ages.* San Bernadino: Pacific Publishing Studio.

Johnson, Jerry Alan. 2014. *The Secret Teachings of Chinese Energetic Medicine.* Vol. 1. Monterey: The International Institute of Medical Qigong Publishing House.

Johnson, Robert A. 2008. *Inner Gold: Understanding Psychological Projection.* Kihei: Koa Books.

Jung, C. G. 2006. *The Undiscovered Self. Translated by R.F.C. Hull.* New York: New American Library.

King, C. M., and Roger A. Powell. 2007. *The Natural History of Weasels and Stoats: Ecology, Behavior, and Management.* New York: Oxford University Press.

Kohn, Livia. 2004. *Cosmos and Community: The Ethical Dimensions of Daoism*. Cambridge: Three Pines Press.

Laozi, et al. 2005. *Tao Te Ching: A New Translation & Commentary*. New York: Barnes & Noble Publishing.

Sams, Jamie, et al. 1999. *Medicine Cards. Revised Expanded ed*. New York: St. Martin's Press.

Scott, John Paul. 1972. *Animal Behavior. 2nd ed*. London: University of Chicago.

Tsu, Lao, and Jacob Needleman. 1972. *Tao Te Ching. Translated by Gia-Fu Feng and Jane English*. 2nd ed. New York: Vintage Books.

Washington, George. 1988. *Rules of Civility & Decent Behaviour in Company and Conversation*. Carlisle: Applewood Books.

Zhuangzi. 1968. *The Complete Works of Chuang Tzu. Translated by Burton Watson*. New York: Columbia University Press.

Quotes from Famous Zodiac Representatives

Rat

"What Alan Turing Means to the US," by The Alan Turing Institute (2019). www.turing.ac.uk/blog/what-alan-turing-means-us

Lawrence, T. E. 1926. *Seven Pillars of Wisdom*. New York: Doubleday Doran.

"13 Quotes from the Most Motivational Man Alive: Dwayne 'The Rock' Johnson," by Isadora Baum (2021). www.menshealth.com/entertainment/a25386775/the-rock-motivational-quotes/

Mozart, Wolfgang A. 2004. *The Letters of Wolfgang Amadeus Mozart, Vol. 1*. Whitefish: Kessinger Publishing.

"The path to success is to take massive, determined action," by Tony Robbins (2015). www.twitter.com/TonyRobbins/status/625921963135864832?lang=en

"Bono U2 Speech: What Is Your Big Idea?" by English Speeches (2020). www.englishspeecheschannel.com/english-speeches/bono-u2-speech/

Parks, Rosa. 1994. *Quiet Strength: The Faith, the Hope, and the Heart of a Woman Who Changed a Nation*. Grand Rapids: Zondervan Publishing House.

Shipman, David. 1974. *Brando*. New York: Double Day Publishers.

Shakespeare, Willi am. 1928. *12th Night*. Boston: Houghton Mifflin.

Gracian, Baltasar. 2008. *The Art of Worldly Wisdom*. New York: Barnes and Noble Inc.

Capote, T. 1968. *Other Voices, Other Rooms*. New York: Penguin.

Ox

Andrews, Robert. 1992. *The Concise Columbia Dictionary of Quotations*. East Sussex: Columbia University Press.

Jacobi, Jolande. 1958. *Paracelsus Selected Writings. Translated by Norbert Guterman*. Princeton: Princeton University Press.

Hill, Napoleon. 2008. *Think and Grow Rich: The Complete Classic Text*. New York: Penguin Publishing.

"Johann Sebastian Bach: A Biography of the Industrious Master," by Vialma Contributors (n.d.). www.vialma.com/en/articles/166/Johann-Sebastian-Bach:-a-biography-of-the-industrious-master

"Walt's Quotes Archives," by Walt Disney Archives Contributors (n.d.). www.d23.com/section/walt-disney-archives/walts-quotes/

"'The Fishermen Know that the Sea Is Dangerous and the Storm Terrible, but They Have Never Found These Dangers Sufficient Reason for Remaining Ashore.'." by Van Gogh Quotes Contributors (2017). www.vangogh-quotes.com/portfolio/the-fishermen-know-that-the-sea-is-dangerous-and-the-storm-terrible-but-they-have-never-found-these-dangers-sufficient-reason-for-remaining-ashore/

Hall, Manly P. 1984. *Lectures on Ancient Philosophy: An Introduction to Practical Ideals*. New York: Philosophical Research Society.

"Malala's Inspiring Mission in Nigeria," by Marie Claire Contributors (2014). www.marieclaire.com/culture/news/a4773/malala-nigeria-bring-back-girls-boko-haram

"Quotes," by JesseOwens.com Contributors (n.d.). www.jesseowens.com/quotes/

"4 Michael Phelps Quotes to Keep You Motivated," by Nicole Farina (2020). www.swimmingworldmagazine.com/news/4-michael-phelps-quotes-to-keep-you-motivated/

Camus, Albert. 1963. *Resistance, Rebellion, and Death*. New York: Modern Library.

"Colin Powell: 'Get Mad, and Then Get Over It,' and 12 Other Rules He Lived and Worked By," by Jade Scipioni (2021). www.cnbc.com/2021/10/18/black-american-trailblazer-colin-powells-13-rules-for-life-and-work.html

Tiger

"What Would Beethoven Think of You?" by Carlos Castillo (2013). www.medium.com/inspiring-people/what-would-beethoven-think-of-you-a1a6bc1552d6

Hegel, Friedrich. 2013. *Lectures on the History of Philosophy 1825-6. Translated by Robert F. Brown.* New York: Clarendon Press.

"27 Of Marilyn Monroe's Most Beautiful Quotes on Love, Life, and Stardom," by Sam Escobar (2022). www.goodhousekeeping.com/beauty/g3603/best-marilyn-monroe-quotes/

"The 22 Best Stevie Wonder Quotes," by Jacob Uitti (2022). www.americansong-writer.com/the-22-best-stevie-wonder-quotes/

"'A Person Always Doing His or Her Best Becomes a Natural Leader Just by . . .," by Greg Lucas (n.d.). www.cal170.library.ca.gov/californias-yankee-clipper-is-born/

"Qualities of Good Leadership for Effective Organisation," by Hiregoudar, Seema, and Dr. G Vani (2018). www.doi.org/10.51244/ijrsi

Steinbeck, John. 2007. *The Short Reign of Pippin IV: A Fabrication.* New York: Penguin Books.

"Cultivating Freedom," by Thich Nhat Hanh (2019). www.thichnhathanhfounda-tion.org/blog/2018/7/6/cultivating-freedom

"The World According to Bill Murray," by Jacob (2018). www.esquire.com/uk/cul-ture/film/news/a8862/bill-murray-quotes/

Branson, Richard. "You Learn by Doing and By Falling Over," by Richard Branson (2014). www.virgin.com/branson-family/richard-branson-blog/you-learn-by-doing-and-by-falling-over

Peterson, Jordan B. 2018. *12 Rules for Life: An Antidote to Chaos.* Toronto: Random House Canada.

Rabbit

"Thoughts & Quotes from Sir David R. Hawkins, M.D., Ph.D. & Susan Hawkins," by Dr. David R. Hawkins (2022). www.veritaspub.com/cate-gory/thoughts-n-quotes-dr-david-r-hawkins/page/9/

Einstein, Albert. 2011. *The Ultimate Quotable Einstien.* Princeton: Princeton University Press.

Orwell, George. 2009. *All Art Is Propaganda.* Boston: Mariner Books.

"Education of the Heart: Cesar Chavez in His Own Words," by Cesar Chavez (n.d.). www.ufw.org/research/history/education-heart-cesar-chavez-words/

"'Let Us Put Our Minds Together and See What Life We Can Make for Our Children'," by Cassandra Clifford (2011). www.foreignpolicy-blogs.com/2008/01/04/%E2%80%9Clet-us-put-our-minds-together-and-see-what-life-we-can-make-for-our-children%E2%80%9D-sitting-bull/

Wilson, David. 2009. *The Weight Loss Illusion.* Lincolnshire: ShieldCrest.

"Robin Williams: On Anniversary of Death, His Advice Still Matters," by Dorrine Mendoza (2019). www.cnn.com/2019/08/11/entertainment/robin-williams-advice/index.html

"Gaye Family's Open Letter about 'Blurred Lines' Verdict," by Susan Whitall (2015). www.detroitnews.com/story/entertainment/2015/03/18/gaye-familys-open-letter-blurred-lines-verdict/24988823/

"The Top 78 Jeff Bezos Quotes on Business, Innovation, Life and More," by Tricia McKinnon (2022). www.indigo9digital.com/blog//-jeff-bezos-quotes

"Interview - Jet Li," by Alliance Magazine Contributors (2014). www.alliancemagazine.org/interview/interview-jet-li/

"A Soul on the Washing Line," by The Economist Contributors (2013). www.economist.com/prospero/2013/09/05/a-soul-on-the-washing-line

Dragon

"5 Unknown Facts and 10 Brilliant Sayings by the Great General, Julius Caesar," by Shkruar Nga Redaksia (2022). www.voxnews.al/english/histori/5-fakte-te-panjohura-dhe-10-thenie-brilante-nga-gjenerali-i-madh-jul-cez-i12301

"Nikola Tesla," by Jonathan Newell (2015). ffden-2.phys.uaf.edu/webproj/212_spring_2015/Jonathan_Newell/index.htm

"Apocryphal Freud: Sigmund Freud' most famous "quotations" and their actual sources," by Alan Elms (2005). www.researchgate.net/publication/7722494_Apocryphal_Freud_Sigmund_Freud'_most_famous_quotations_and_their_actual_sources

Plutarch, and Gregory Zorzos. 2009. *The Life of Alexander. Translated by John Dryden.* CreateSpace Independent Publishing Platform.

"J. R Oppenheimer: 'Prospects in the Arts and Sciences'," by Geraldine Cox (2018). www.findingpatterns.info/scrapbook/prospects-in-the-arts-and-sciences-j-r-oppenheimer.html#:~:text=Both%20the%20man%20of%20science,make%20partial%20order%20in%20total

"At This Time of Challenge and Controversy, We Need Solidarity," by Tefere Gebre (2016). www.aflcio.org/2017/1/16/time-challenge-and-controversy-we-need-solidarity#:~:text=%E2%80%9CThe%20ultimate%20measure%20of%20a,Martin%20Luther%20King%20Jr

"Linear Model of Communication," by Libretexts Editors (2021). www.socialsci.libretexts.org/Under_Construction/Purgatory/Survey_of_Human_Communication/11%3A_Introduction_to_Public_Speaking/11.3%3A_Model_of_Communication

Campbell, Joseph. 2014. *The Hero's Journey: Joseph Campbell on His Life and Work.* Novato: New World Library.

"Salvador Dalí Quotes," by Dali Universe Contributors (n.d.). www.thedaliuniverse.com/en/salvador-dali/quotes

Kant, Immanuel. 2013. *Critique of Practical Reason.* New York: Start Publishing LLC.

"An Interview with Maya Angelou," by Marianne Schnall (2009). www.psychologytoday.com/us/blog/the-guest-room/200902/interview-maya-angelou

Snake

King, Martin Luther. 1963. *Strength to Love.* New York: Harper & Rowe.

Frankl, Viktor Emil, and Hse Lasch. 1962. *Man's Search for Meaning: An Introduction to Logotheraphy.* London: Hodder and Stoughton.

Poe, Edgar Allan. 1981. *Marginalia.* Charlottesville: University Press of Virginia.

"Venetian Years: Childhood And Adolescence: The Memoirs Of Jacques Casanova De Seingalt 1725-1798," by Jacques Casanova de Seingalt (2006). www.gutenberg.org/files/2951/2951.txt

"Muhammad Ali: 6 Best Quotes to Remember the Boxer," by Katie Reilly (2016). www.time.com/4357493/muhammad-ali-dead-best-quotes/#:~:text=%E2%80%9CFloat%20like%20a%20butterfly%2C%20sting,a%20news%20conference%20on%20Oct

Dostoyevsky, Fyodor, and K. A. Lantz. 2009. *A Writer's Diary.* Evanston: Northwestern University Press.

"With 'Fix My Life,' Iyanla Van Zant Opens Next Chapter by Helping Others," by Allison Samuels (2017). www.thedailybeast.com/with-fix-my-life-iyanla-vanzant-opens-next-chapter-by-helping-others

"Roger Bannister: The Journey of a Legendary Runner," by Shelly Westwood (2022). www.runnersgoal.com/roger-bannister/

"Copernicus on True Knowledge," by Big Think Editors (2021). www.bigthink.com/words-of-wisdom/copernicus-on-true-knowledge/

"Festina Lente: Words in Gold," by Capture It in Words Contributors (2016). www.rasmusen.org/special/ameliajane/archives/1287

Chang, Larry. 2006. *Wisdom for the Soul: Five Millennia of Prescriptions for Spiritual Healing.* Washington DC: Gnosophia Publishers.

Horse

"9 Lessons on Power and Leadership from Genghis Khan," by Ryan Holiday (2012). www.forbes.com/sites/ryanholiday/2012/05/07/9-lessons-on-leadership-from-genghis-khan-yes-genghis-khan/?sh=edc476c6996f

Ventura, Steve. 2009. *Work Right: Straight-Talk Strategies for Personal and Profession al Success.* Youngsville: Walk the Talk Co.

"In The Words of Nelson Mandela, 'To Be Free Is Not Merely to Cast Off One's Chains.'," by Stephanie (2019). sites.bu.edu/socialim-pactblog/2019/04/01/in-the-words-of-nelson-mandela-to-be-free-is-not-merely-to-cast-off-ones-chains/

Ehrenkreutz, Andrew S. 1972. *Saladin 1971: A Critical Reinterpretation of the Life and Career of Salah Al-Din.* Albany: State University of New York Press.

Lebesque, Morvan. 1953. *Miracles.* London: Burns & Oates.

Solženicyn Aleksandr, and Thomas P. Whitney. 1974. *The Gulag Archipelago.* New York: Harper & Rowe.

"Warren Buffett's Top 5 Money Tips: Bayntree Wealth Advisors," by Bayntree Wealth Advisors (2021). www.bayntree.com/financial-advice/best-5-pieces-of-money-advice-from-billionaire-warren-buf-fett/#:~:text=As%20he%20said%20%E2%80%9CWithout%20pas-sion,and%20will%20do%20it%20forever

"The Real Value in Setting Goals," by Jim Rohn (2019). www.jimrohn.com/get-in-spired-by-your-goals/

"The Vision of Inayat Khan," by David Marshak (1997). Journal Storage, vol. 48, pp. 153–186.

"Inside Sean Connery's Marriage of 45 Years," by Jennifer Leonard (2021). www.thelist.com/271041/inside-sean-connerys-marriage-of-45-years/

"Forgiveness," by Grace Hunt (2013). www.hac.bard.edu/amor-mundi/for-giveness-2013-03-25

"The Real Story of Davy Crockett," by Jessica James (2023). www.pastlanetravels.com/davy-crockett-homespun-wit-wisdom/

Sheep

Asimov, Isaac. 1951. *Foundation.* New York: HarperCollins Publications.

Davidson, Thomas, and Charles Montague Bakewell. 1904. *The Education of the Wage-Earners: A Contribution Toward the Solution of the Educational Problem of Democracy.* Boston: Ginn & Co.

Dickens, Charles. 1854. *Hard Times.* London: Bradbury and Evans.

"12 Brilliant Quotes from the Genius Mind of Sir Isaac Newton," by Justin Bariso (2016). www.inc.com/justin-bariso/12-brilliant-quotes-from-the-genius-mind-of-sir-isaac-newton.html

"'You've Got to Find What You Love,' Jobs Says," *by* Stanford University (2022). news.stanford.edu/2005/06/12/youve-got-find-love-jobs-says/

Emoto, Masaru. *The Secret Life of Water.* Beyond Words Publishing, 2005.

Schindler, James H. 2015. *Followership: What It Takes to Lead*. New York: Business Expert Press.

Doyle, A. Conan. 1895. *The Mystery of Cloomber*. New York: R.F. Feno and Co.

"50 Bill Gates Quotes," by Investing Answers Expert (2021). www.investinganswers.com/articles/50-quotes-wealthiest-man-america

"Everything You Need to Know About Sir Edmund Hillary," by Jack Clayton (2019). www.mpora.com/mountaineering-expeditions/edmund-hillary/

Monkey

"6 Ways Leaders Use Silence to Increase Their Power," by Avery Blank (2022). www.forbes.com/sites/averyblank/2017/06/20/6-ways-leaders-use-silence-to-increase-their-power-that-you-can-do-too/?sh=a5cd40b27c8d

"Thoughts on the Business Of Life," by Forbes Contributors (2015). www.forbes.com/quotes/2612/

Bennion, Lowell L. *Religion and the Pursuit of Truth*. Deseret Book Co., 1959.

Sullivan, Daniel F. *Milton's Areopagitica & Freedom of Speech on Campus*. St. Lawrence University, 2006.

"Thoughts on the Business Of Life," by Forbes Contributors (2015). www.forbes.com/quotes/2894/

"The Wild West Lives, Quick-Draw," by Jeffrey Lindblom (2021). www.blackhillsfox.com/2021/05/29/the-wild-west-lives-quick-draw/

"Bob Marley on Greatness," by Big Think Editors (2021). www.bigthink.com/words-of-wisdom/bob-marley-on/#:~:text=%E2%80%9CThe%20greatness%20of%20a%20man,affect%20those%20around%20him%20positively.%E2%80%9D&text=Bob%20Marley%20(1945%2D1981),Rastafarian%2C%20and%20Pan%2DAfricanist

"13 Bette Davis Quotes that Will Liberate You as a Woman," by Lea Rose Emery (2017). www.women.com/learoseemery/lists/number-bette-davis-quotes-that-will-liberate-you-as-a-woman

"The Best 20 Johnny Cash Quotes," by Jacob Uitti (2022). www.americansongwriter.com/the-best-20-johnny-cash-quotes/

"12 Tom Hanks quotes that will brighten your day," by Erin McDowell (2020). https://www.businessinsider.com/tom-hanks-inspirational-quotes-2020-4

Marshall, Penny (Director). 1992. *A League of Their Own*. Culver City: Tristar Studios.

Russell, Bertrand. 1927. *Why I Am Not a Christian . . . a Lecture Delivered in London, March 6, 1927*. New York: American Association for the Advancement of Atheism.

Rooster

"General George Patton Jr. Quotes," by Military Connection Contributors (2020). www.militaryconnection.com/military-quotes/george-patton/

H., Black Elk Wallace, and William S. Lyon. 1990. *Black Elk: The Sacred Ways of a Lakota*. New York: Harper and Row.

"Aphorisms & Quotes," by F. W. Elwell (n.d.). www.faculty.rsu.edu/users/f/fel-well/www/HomePage/aphorisms.htm

"Amelia Earhart Quotes," Historical Snapshots Contributors (2022). www.historicalsnaps.com/2022/12/25/amelia-earhart-quotes

Antoninus, Marcus Aurelius. 1964. *Meditations: Marcus Aurelius*. New York: Penguin Books.

"Philosophical Roots of Education Existentialism," by University of Philippines Authors (n.d.). vle.u pm.edu.ph/pluginfile.php/141934/mod_folder/content/0/7.%20Philosophical%20Roots%20of%20Education%20Existentialism.pdf

"J.P. Morgan," by The Editors of Encyclopedia Britannica (2023). www.britannica.com/biography/J-P-Morgan

"Ruth Bader Ginsburg Tells Young Women: 'Fight for the Things You Care About'," by Alanna Vagianos (2015). www.radcliffe.harvard.edu/news-and-ideas/ruth-bader-ginsburg-tells-young-women-fight-for-the-things-you-care-about

"Betty White's 98th Birthday: 10 Quotes from the Legendary Actress," by James Crowley (2020). www.newsweek.com/betty-white-98-birthday-quotes-1482724

"Dolly Parton Says She Feels 'Energized' by 'Fans that Care About Me'," by Benjamin VanHoose (2020). www.people.com/country/dolly-parton-energized-by-working-more-marie-claire-interview/

"Bear Grylls, James Cameron, John Glenn, Chuck Yeager, and Others on Facing Fear," by Jim Clash (2015). www.forbes.com/sites/jimclash/2015/12/20/bear-grylls-james-cameron-john-glenn-chuck-yeager-others-on-facing-fear/?sh=7632f9072762

Dog

"50 Sir Winston Churchill Quotes to Live By," by BBC America Editors (2015). www.bbcamerica.com/blogs/50-churchill-quotes--1015192

"'Peace Begins with a Smile' Mother Teresa," by Kathleen Hogan (n.d.). www.stmarys.academy/d/~board/regina/post/peace-begins-with-a-smile-mother-teresa

Johnson, Clarence L., and Maggie Smith. 1985. *Kelly: More Than My Share of It All.* Washington DC: Smithsonian Institution Press.

"Thoughts on the Business of Life," by Forbes Contributors (2015). www.forbes.com/quotes/11335/

Cousteau, Jacques, and Diolé Philippe. 1979. *Diving for Sunken Treasure.* New York: A & W Visual Library.

Ward, Dr. Michael. 2015. *C.S. Lewis on Imagination and Reason.* Oxford: Oxford University.

"Michael Jackson - In His Own Words," by Benaissa Ghrib (2014). www.ebony.com/michaeljackson/

Behan, Brendan. *The Quare Fellow.* 19 Nov. 1954, Dublin, Pike Theatre.

"'If You Haven't Cried, Your Eyes Can't Be Beautiful," by Cinespia Contributors (2020). www.cinespia.org/if-you-havent-cried-your-eyes-cant-be-beautiful-sophia-loren-cinespia/

"Andrea Bocelli," by Daniel Ross (2013). www.classicfm.com/discover-music/latest/quotes-classical-musicians/andrea-bocelli/

Vonnegut, Kurt. 1962. *Mother Night.* Robbinsdale: Fawcett Publications.

"The Wit and Wisdom of Alan Rickman," by Esquire Contributors (2016). www.esquire.com/uk/culture/film/news/a9364/alan-rickman-best-quotes/

Pig

"Horses Teach Us How to Connect on a Human Level," by Scarlett Lewis (2021). www.pacesconnection.com/g/practicing-resilience/blog/horses-teach-us-how-to-connect-on-a-human-level

"Carl Gustav Jung," by Susan Ratcliffe (2016). www.oxfordreference.com/display/10.1093/acref/9780191826719.001.0001/q-oro-ed4-00006107

"150 Thought-Provoking Ralph Waldo Emerson Quotes," by Stephanie Osmanski (2023). www.parade.com/1079155/stephanieosmanski/ralph-waldo-emerson-quotes/

"Notable Quotes by Luciano Pavarotti for a Perfect Musical Beginning," by Famous People Contributors (n.d.). www.quotes.thefamouspeople.com/luciano-pavarotti-3443.php

"Thoughts on the Business of Life," by Forbes Contributors (2015). www.forbes.com/quotes/4087/

"9 Things Lucille Ball Taught Us About Life," by Megan Angelo (2013). www.glamour.com/story/lucille-ball

"Inside the Music that Inspires Richard Branson, Mark Zuckerberg, and . . .," by Julie Anne Exter (2016). www.inc.com/julie-anne-exter/inside-the-music-that-inspires-richard-branson-mark-zuckerberg-and-elon-musk.html

"Words of Wisdom: Most Inspiring Quotes from 81 Years of Dalai Lama's Life," by Kamalika Mukherjee (2016). www.indianexpress.com/article/life-style/life-style/words-of-wisdom-most-inspiring-quotes-from-81-years-birthday-of-dalai-lama-life-2897920/

"100 Quotes on Strength and Resilience to Help Get Us Through Tough Times," by Kelsey Pelzer (2023). www.parade.com/1012592/kelseypelzer/quotes-for-tough-times/

Williams, Tennessee. 1963. *The Milk Train Doesn't Stop Here Anymore*. New York: Morosco Theatre.

"The Truth Inside the Lie," by Kelley Eskridge (2008). www.kelleyeskridge.com/the-truth-inside-the-lie/

Kissinger, Henry. 2022. *Leadership: Six Studies in World Strategy*. New York: Penguin Press.

Appendix

#	Name	Term	Lifespan	Party Affiliation	Date of Birth, Place of Birth	Zodiac Year	Yin or Yang	Five Phases
1	George Washington	April 30th 1789 to March 4th	1732-1799	Unaffiliated	February 22nd 1732, Popes Creek, VA	Rat	Yang	Water
2	John Adams	March 4th 1797 to March 4th	1735-1826	Federalist	October 30th 1735, Braintree, MA	Rabbit	Yin	Wood
3	Thomas Jefferson	March 4th 1801 to March 4th	1743-1846	Democratic-Republican	April 13th 1743, Shadwell, VA	Pig	Yin	Water
4	James Madison	March 4th 1809 to March 4th	1751-1836	Democratic-Republican	March 16th 1751, Port Conway, VA	Sheep	Yin	Metal
5	James Monroe	March 4th 1817 to March 4th	1758-1831	Democratic-Republican	April 28th 1758, Monroe Hall, VA	Tiger	Yang	Earth
6	John Quincy Adams	March 4th 1825 to March 4th	1767-1848	Democratic-Republican	July 11th 1767, Braintree, MA	Pig	Yin	Fire
7	Andrew Jackson	March 4th 1829 to March 4th	1767-1845	Democratic	March 15th 1767, Waxhaws, SC	Pig	Yin	Fire
8	Martin Van Buren	March 4th 1837 to March 4th	1782-1862	Democratic	December 5th 1782, Kinderhook, NY	Tiger	Yang	Water
9	William Henry Harrison	March 4th 1841 to April 4th 1841	1773-1841	Whig	February 9th 1773, Charles City County, VA	Snake	Yin	Water
10	John Tyler	April 4th 1841 to March 4th 1845	1790-1862	Whig	March 29th 1790, Charles City County, VA	Dog	Yang	Metal

#	Name	Term	Lifespan	Party Affiliation	Date of Birth, Place of Birth	Zodiac Year	Yin or Yang	Five Phases
11	James K Polk	March 4th 1845 to March 4th 1849	1795-1849	Democratic	November 2nd 1795, Pineville, NC	Rabbit	Yin	Wood
12	Zachary Taylor	March 4th 1849 to July 9th 1850	1784-1850	Whig	November 24th 1784, Orange County, VA	Dragon	Yang	Wood
13	Millard Fillmore	July 9th 1850 to March 4th 1853	1800-1874	Whig	January 7th 1800, Moravia, NY	Sheep	Yin	Earth
14	Franklin Pierce	March 4th 1853 to March 4th 1857	1804-1869	Democratic	November 23rd 1804, Hillsborough, NH	Rat	Yang	Wood
15	James Buchanan	March 4th 1857 to March 4th 1861	1791-1868	Democratic	April 23rd 1791, Cove Gap, PA	Pig	Yin	Metal
16	Abraham Lincoln	March 4th 1861 to April 15th 1865	1809-1865	Republican/ National Union	February 12th 1809, Hodgenville, KY	Dragon	Yang	Earth
17	Andrew Johnson	April 15th 1865 to March 4th 1869	1808-1875	National Union/ Democratic	December 29th 1808, Raleigh, NC	Dragon	Yang	Earth
18	Ulysses S Grant	March 4th 1869 to March 4th 1877	1822-1885	Republican	April 27th 1822, Point Pleasant, NC	Horse	Yang	Water
19	Rutherford B Hayes	March 4th 1877 to March 4th 1881	1822-1893	Republican	October 4th 1822, Delaware, OH	Horse	Yang	Water
20	James Garfield	March 4th 1881 to September 19th 1881	1831-1881	Republican	November 19th 1831, Moreland Hills, OH	Rabbit	Yin	Metal

#	Name	Term	Lifespan	Party Affiliation	Date of Birth, Place of Birth	Zodiac Year	Yin or Yang	Five Phases
21	Chester Arthur	September 19th 1881 to March 4th 1885	1829-1886	Republican	October 5th 1829, Fairfield, VT	Ox	Yin	Earth
22	Grover Cleveland	March 4th 1885 to March 4th 1889	1837-1908	Democratic	March 18th 1837, Caldwell, NJ	Rooster	Yin	Fire
23	Benjamin Harrison	March 4th 1889 to March 4th 1893	1833-1901	Republican	August 20th 1833, North Bend, OH	Snake	Yin	Water
24	Grover Cleveland	March 4th 1893 to March 4th 1897	1837-1908	Democratic	March 18th 1837, Caldwell, NJ	Rooster	Yin	Fire
25	William McKinley	March 4th 1897 to September 14th 1901	1843-1901	Republican	January 29th 1843, Niles, OH	Tiger	Yang	Water
26	Theodore Roosevelt	September 14th 1901 to March 4th 1909	1858-1919	Republican	October 27th 1858, New York City, NY	Horse	Yang	Earth
27	William H Taft	March 4th 1909 to March 4th 1913	1857-1930	Republican	September 15th 1857, Cincinnati, OH	Snake	Yin	Fire
28	Woodrow Wilson	March 4th 1913 to March 4th 1921	1856-1924	Democratic	December 28th 1856, Staunton, VA	Dragon	Yang	Fire
29	Warren Harding	March 4th 1921 to August 2nd 1923	1865-1923	Republican	November 2nd 1865, Blooming Grove, OH	Ox	Yin	Wood
30	Calvin Coolidge	August 2nd 1923 to March 4th 1929	1872-1933	Republican	July 4th 1872, Plymouth Notch, VT	Monkey	Yang	Water

#	Name	Term	Lifespan	Party Affiliation	Date of Birth, Place of Birth	Zodiac Year	Yin or Yang	Five Phases
31	Herbert Hoover	March 4th 1929 to March 4th 1933	1874-1964	Republican	August 10th 1874, West Branch, IA	Dog	Yang	Wood
32	Franklin D Roosevelt	March 4th 1933 to April 12th 1945	1882-1945	Democratic	January 30th 1882, Hyde Park, NY	Snake	Yin	Metal
33	Harry S Truman	April 12th 1945 to January 20th 1953	1884-1974	Democratic	May 8th 1884, Lamar, MO	Monkey	Yang	Wood
34	Dwight D Eisenhower	January 20th 1953 to January 20th 1961	1890-1969	Republican	October 14th 1890, Denison, TX	Tiger	Yang	Metal
35	John F Kennedy	January 20th 1961 to November 22nd 1963	1917-1963	Democratic	May 29th 1917, Brookline, MA	Snake	Yin	Fire
36	Lyndon B Johnson	November 22nd 1963 to January 20th 1969	1908-1973	Democratic	August 27th 1908, Stonewall, TX	Monkey	Yang	Earth
37	Richard Nixon	January 20th 1969 to August 9th 1974	1913-1994	Republican	January 9th 1913, Yorba Linda, CA	Rat	Yang	Water
38	Gerald Ford	August 9th 1974 to January 20th 1977	1913-2006	Republican	July 14th 1913, Omaha, NE	Ox	Yin	Water
39	Jimmy Carter	January 20th 1977 to January 20th 1981	1924-	Democratic	October 1st 1924, Plains, GA	Rat	Yang	Wood
40	Ronald Reagan	January 20th 1981 to January 20th 1989	1911-2004	Republican	February 6th 1911, Tampico, IL	Pig	Yin	Metal

#	Name	Term	Lifespan	Party Affiliation	Date of Birth, Place of Birth	Zodiac Year	Yin or Yang	Five Phases
41	George H W Bush	January 20th 1989 to January 20th 1993	1924-2018	Republican	June 12th 1924, Milton, MA	Rat	Yang	Wood
42	Bill Clinton	January 20th 1993 to January 20th 2001	1946-	Democratic	August 19th 1946, Hope, AR	Dog	Yang	Fire
43	George W Bush	January 20th 2001 to January 20th 2009	1946-	Republican	July 6th 1946, New Haven, CT	Dog	Yang	Fire
44	Barack Obama	January 20th 2009 to January 20th 2017	1961-	Democratic	August 4th 1961, Honolulu, HI	Ox	Yin	Metal
45	Donald Trump	January 20th 2017 to January 20th 2021	1946-	Republican	June 14th 1946, New York City, NY	Dog	Yang	Fire
46	Joseph Biden	January 20th 2021 to Present	1942-	Democratic	November 20th 1942, Scranton, PA	Horse	Yang	Water